Women and Leadership

Warren Bennis

A WARREN BENNIS BOOK

This collection of books is devoted exclusively to new and exemplary contributions to management thought and practice. The books in this series are addressed to thoughtful leaders, executives, and managers of all organizations who are struggling with and committed to responsible change. My hope and goal is to spark new intellectual capital by sharing ideas positioned at an angle to conventional thought—in short, to publish books that disturb the present in the service of a better future.

Books in the Warren Bennis Signature Series

JB JOSSEY-BASS

Women and Leadership

The State of Play and Strategies for Change

Barbara Kellerman

Deborah L. Rhode

Editors

Foreword by

Justice Sandra Day O'Connor (Ret.)

BICENTENNIAL
1807
WILEY
2007
BICENTENNIAL

Published by Jossey-Bass
A Wiley Imprint
989 Market Street, San Francisco, CA 94103-1741   www.josseybass.com

Wiley Bicentennial logo: Richard J. Pacifico

Jossey-Bass books and products are available through most bookstores. To contact Jossey-Bass
directly call our Customer Care Department within the U.S. at 800-956-7739, outside the
U.S. at 317-572-3986, or fax 317-572-4002.

Jossey-Bass also publishes its books in a variety of electronic formats. Some content that
appears in print may not be available in electronic books.

Library of Congress Cataloging-in-Publication Data

Women and leadership : the state of play and strategies for change / Barbara Kellerman,
Deborah L. Rhode, editors ; foreword by Justice Sandra Day O'Connor (Ret.).
    p. cm.—(Warren Bennis signature series)
Includes bibliographical references and index.
ISBN 978-0-7879-8833-3 (cloth)
    1. Leadership in women. 2. Sex discrimination against women. 3. Women in the
professions. 4. Women in public life. I. Kellerman, Barbara. II. Rhode, Deborah L.
III. O'Connor, Sandra Day, 1930–
HQ1233.W5846 2007
305.42—dc22   2007013593

Printed in the United States of America
FIRST EDITION
HB Printing   10 9 8 7 6 5 4 3 2

For Elizabeth Cavanagh and Ellen Kellerman

CONTENTS

PART FOUR. REDEFINING THE PROBLEM, RECASTING THE SOLUTIONS

Foreword

Over the last century, the world of women and the landscape of leadership have been fundamentally transformed. In the United States, where it was once considered unseemly for women to vote, or even to assert their right to vote, women now constitute over half of the electorate and occupy many of the nation's highest elective offices. When I graduated from law school a half century ago, women accounted for less than 3 percent of the legal profession. Although I was in the top of my class, the only job offer that I received from a law firm was for that of legal secretary. Three decades later, I became the first woman to sit on the U.S. Supreme Court. Today, women constitute about half of all law students, and they occupy positions of influence in all areas of legal practice.

Yet as this book's research makes all too clear, women's leadership opportunities are still not equal. The statistics are sobering. Women account for less than a fifth of law firm partners, federal judges, college presidents, and congressional representatives; they are only 2 percent of Fortune 500 CEOs and hold only 8 percent of corporate leadership positions. Globally, the situation is no better. Despite striking gains over the last quarter century, including the election of female leaders in some of the world's most powerful nations, only about 6 percent of heads of state are women.

This book provides the most comprehensive account to date of women's persistent underrepresentation in leadership roles, why it matters, and what can be done to change it. Experts from a wide range of disciplines document the traditional stereotypes, exclusion from support networks, and work-family conflicts that restrict women's access to positions of greatest influence.

My own profession illustrates the obstacles. The traditional assumption was that the law was unfit for women and women were unfit for the law. Their "nature" was to nurture, and they were unsuited to "all the nastiness of the world which finds its way into courts of justice."[1] Clarence Darrow was convinced that women could not be "shining lights" at the bar "because you are too kind. You can never be corporate lawyers because you are not cold blooded. You have not a high grade of intellect. I doubt you can ever make a living."[2] Part of what hindered women in proving that wrong was exclusion from informal networks of support and influence that advantaged men.

A fundamental barrier has been women's disproportionate responsibilities in the home, which have often limited their opportunities in the world outside. I gave up my law firm practice for five years until my children were in school. It never occurred to my husband or to me that he should assume a major child-rearing role. Of course, as my husband was also fond of pointing out, things did turn out all right for me in the end. And assumptions about the appropriate gender division of family responsibilities are gradually changing. As the research in this volume demonstrates, however, the home is still not and perhaps will never be an equal opportunity employer.

Women still face barriers on the path to leadership. And just as clearly, this matters for the society we want to create. We will all be better off if women's life experiences, needs, and values are fully reflected in decision-making positions. The presence of women in those positions is also essential to encourage aspirations among the next generation, and to counter reservations about women's capacity for leadership roles. In an increasingly competitive global environment, no society can afford to hobble half its talent pool.

This is not to suggest that women have some distinctively feminine style of leadership. I have often been asked whether women have a unique judicial style. My answer, which is consistent with the research in this volume, is that individuals bring to decision-making roles the totality of their life experiences, not simply gender. As my colleague Justice Ruth Bader Ginsburg put it, "I have detected no reliable indicator of distinctively male or surely female thinking, or even penmanship."[3] We should be wary of invoking a "woman's point of view" that rests on traditional gender stereotypes, for these distort as well as confine human experience. At the end of the day, as former Oklahoma Supreme Court Justice Jeanne Coyne noted, "A wise old man and a wise old woman reach the same conclusion."[4]

It is, however, also the case that gender is part of what informs female leaders' values and priorities. In my own career, I have often felt a special responsibility to represent concerns that would otherwise have gone unaddressed in decision-making bodies dominated primarily by men. For example, as a state legislator, I worked to change family and protective labor laws that drew sex-based distinctions. And as a Justice, I helped to ensure that the Federal Rules of Civil and Criminal Procedure dropped gender-based language, and that the Supreme Court altered its practice of listing female attorneys who argued cases as Miss or Mrs., and male attorneys simply by name. The National Association of Women Judges, of which I am a member, has also played a major role in combating gender bias in the legal system.

The chapters in this pathbreaking volume include countless examples of how women's different backgrounds and commitments have made a fundamental difference in leadership positions. The issues women have championed are not simply women's issues; they implicate fundamental questions of justice and welfare in which both sexes have a stake. Our society has made enormous progress over the past few decades in expanding opportunities for women's leadership. But considerable progress remains to be made. This book is an invaluable resource in that effort. It charts paths yet to be traveled and makes clear why the journey is so important.

—Justice Sandra Day O'Connor (Ret.)

Endnotes

1. *Bradwell v. Illinois* 83 U.S. 130 (1872) (Bradley, J. concurring); In re *Goodell*, 39 Wis. 232 (1875).
2. Karen Berger Morrello, "Bar Admission Was Rough for Nineteenth Century Women," *New York Law Journal* 189 (May 13, 1983): 19.
3. Ruth Bader Ginsburg, Remarks to California Women Lawyers, *Pepperdine Law Review* 22 (1994): 4–5.
4. David Margolick, "Women's Milestone Majority on the Minnesota Supreme Court," *New York Times*, February 22, 1991, B16.

Women and Leadership

Women and Leadership

The State of Play

Deborah L. Rhode, Barbara Kellerman

Some four decades ago, Betty Friedan helped launch the contemporary women's movement with her publication of *The Feminine Mystique*. The book famously identified a "problem that has no name": American women's confinement to a separate and unequal domestic sphere. One factor contributing to women's unequal status was their absence from leadership positions. Another aspect of the problem was the lack of cultural consensus that this absence was itself part of the problem and a matter of social concern.

Over the last several decades, we have named that leadership problem and created a cottage industry to address it. Women's underrepresentation in positions of power generates an increasing array of committees, commissions, consultants, centers, conferences, and commentary such as the chapters that follow. Yet while we have made considerable progress in understanding the problem, we remain a dispiriting distance from solving it.

The Underrepresentation of Women in Leadership Roles

The facts are frustratingly familiar. Despite almost a half century of equal opportunity legislation, women's opportunities for leadership are anything but equal. To be sure, the situation has improved significantly over this period, particularly if leadership is broadly defined to include informal as well as formal exercises of authority.[1]

1

By that definition, the percentage of women in leadership roles is substantial and is increasing dramatically. That is particularly true in management and the professions, where women now occupy roughly half of all jobs.[2] Women also hold positions of power in a wide range of government, nonprofit, and religious contexts.[3] But they are still grossly underrepresented at the top and overrepresented at the bottom of the most influential leadership hierarchies.

In the United States, women are a majority of the electorate but hold only a quarter of upper-level state government positions and 16 percent of congressional seats.[4] Over half of college graduates but less than a quarter of full professors and a fifth of college presidents are female.[5] In management, women account for about a third of MBA classes, but only 2 percent of Fortune 500 CEOs, 6 percent of top earners, 8 percent of top leadership positions, and 16 percent of board directors and corporate officers.[6] In law, women constitute about half of new entrants to the profession but less than a fifth of law firm partners, federal judges, law school deans, and Fortune 500 general counsels.[7] Half the students in divinity school are women, but women are only 3 percent of the pastors of large congregations in protestant churches that have been ordaining women for decades.[8] The gap widens for women of color, who account for only about 4 percent of congressional legislators, 3 percent of full professors, and 1–2 percent of corporate officers, top earners, law firm partners, and general counsels.[9]

From an international perspective, the United States is by no means atypical. However, as subsequent discussion makes clear, neither is it a world leader, at least in the number of women political leaders. At this writing, the United States ranks sixty-ninth in female legislative representation, behind Cape Verde, Singapore, Turkmenistan, Zimbabwe, and the Philippines.[10] Overall, the percentage of women in elective office has grown substantially over the last quarter century, but as several commentators in Part Two of this volume note, progress remains sluggish. Women hold about 16 percent of the seats in parliamentary bodies and about 11 percent of the presiding officer positions. At current rates of change, it would take about a century for women to reach equal representation in legislative offices.[11] A similar pattern is apparent with heads of state. About 6 percent of the world's top political leaders are female, up from less than 1 percent in 1950. Since the 1990s, only about thirty women have served as heads of state, although an increasing number have done so in powerful nations such as the United Kingdom, India, Germany, and Chile.[12]

Comprehensive international data is unavailable for women's representation in leadership roles in business and the professions, but the limited information that has been compiled suggests ample room for progress. For example, across Europe, women make up only about a third of high-level decision makers, including legislators, senior government officials, and business managers. Only 8 percent of directors and 5 percent of top executives in the two hundred largest companies are female.[13]

In some of the most powerful nations, including Germany, Japan, and Great Britain, the figures are still worse.[14] Not a single woman figured in a recent *Fortune* magazine survey of the twenty-five highest-paid CEOs in Europe, and in some countries, no woman has ever headed a large global corporation.[15] In many nations in Asia, Africa, and the Mideast, women have difficulty walking unescorted or working in any setting outside their homes or fields, let alone ascending a leadership ladder.[16] Despite significant national variations, the global workforce is highly gender-segregated and gender-stratified, and progress toward equity at the highest levels has been slow and uneven.[17]

This introduction explores the reasons for these persistent and pervasive inequalities. Although the explanations vary somewhat across national, cultural, and occupational contexts, common obstacles to women's leadership emerge. The following discussion focuses on the United States, which has the most well-developed research on the issue. However, analysis is informed by the international data available, particularly on topics such as political representation and work-family policies on which the United State lags behind other nations.

An initial issue for consideration involves the role of women's own choices in explaining women's underrepresentation in leadership positions. Although these choices play an important part, they cannot be understood in isolation from broader cultural constraints. These include gender biases in leadership opportunities, gender roles in families, inflexibility in workplace structures, and inadequacies in social policies.

Women's Choices

The most common—and for many constituencies, most convenient—explanation for women's underrepresentation in leadership positions is women's choices. Prominent news publications, television talk shows, and employee chitchat all offer variations on a long-standing theme: women who opt out of full-time professional work to keep the home fires burning.[18] In the 1960s, Friedan's *Feminine Mystique* prompted similar explanations for women's absence at leadership levels. "To paraphrase the famous line," wrote the *New York Times* reviewer, "the fault, dear Mrs. Friedan, is not in culture but in ourselves."[19] Four decades later, Lisa Belkin's cover story in the *New York Times Magazine* laid blame in similar places. In her account of the "opt-out revolution," women are underrepresented in leadership positions less because "the workplace has failed women" than because "women are rejecting the workplace." "Why don't women run the world?" asks Belkin. "Maybe it's because they don't want to."[20]

Such explanations capture a partial truth. Women, including those with leadership credentials, do on average make different choices from men; more opt out for at least some period and more who stay in remain childless. In a study by the Center for Work-Life Policy of some three thousand high-achieving American women and men (defined as those with graduate or professional degrees or high honors undergraduate degrees), nearly four in ten women reported leaving the workforce voluntarily at some point over their careers. The same proportion reported sometimes choosing a job with lesser compensation and fewer responsibilities than they were qualified to assume so they could accommodate family responsibilities. By contrast, only one in ten men left the workforce primarily for family-related reasons.[21] Although other surveys find some variation in the number of women who opt out to accommodate domestic obligations, all these studies report substantial gender differences.[22] Almost 20 percent of women with graduate or professional degrees are not in the labor force, compared with only 5 percent of similarly credentialed men. One in three women with MBAs are not working full time, compared with one in twenty men.[23] The overwhelming majority of these women do, however, want to return to work, and most do so, although generally not without significant career costs and difficulties.[24] The same is true in other advanced industrial nations for which data is available.[25]

Findings on career aspirations and expectations are also mixed, but gender differences typically emerge. A survey of some twelve hundred executives in various regions of the world found that substantially more women than men reported reducing career aspirations to accommodate personal and family concerns.[26] In one recent U.S. poll, a third of women (compared to only a fifth of men) reported significant work-family conflicts and a need to make sacrifices involving hours, travel, and stress in order to advance professionally.[27] In most, although not all, studies, fewer highly qualified women than men described themselves as very ambitious, or interested in a CEO position or elective political office.[28] As subsequent discussion indicates, these women are also less likely than their similarly qualified male colleagues to negotiate for professional opportunities.[29]

Gender differences in reproductive choices are also apparent. Much higher percentages of highly credentialed women than men perceive serious problems in reconciling work and family obligations, and much higher percentages of women remain childless. In the international survey noted earlier, female executives were more than twice as likely as their male counterparts to delay marriage or child rearing to establish a career, and 12 percent of women, compared with only 1 percent of men, decided not to have children.[30] Surveys of American senior executives found that 27 percent of the women, compared with 3 percent of the men, had no children, and only 46 percent were married, compared with over 94 percent of male executives.[31] Other elite professions reveal similar patterns. For example, in a study of tenured U.S. academics, half of the women but only a quarter of the men were childless.[32] In short, women who do not opt out of demanding professional positions are more likely to opt out of demanding family obligations.

Yet what is too often missed or marginalized in discussions of women's "different choices" is the extent to which the choices are socially constructed and constrained. What drops out of the opt-out narrative are the complex forces that drive women's decisions. Equally noticeable for their absence are the choices that men make, as spouses, policy leaders, and employers that limit the choices available to women. As subsequent discussion makes clear, explanations focusing solely on women's preferences understate the subtle, often unconscious, biases that both shape the priorities of those who opt out and limit the opportunities for those who opt in. Over the last quarter century, a growing number of women have aspired to leadership on the same terms as men; they have made the same choices as their male counterparts but confront an additional set of obstacles. These barriers deserve greater public attention and policy initiatives.

Gender Bias in Leadership Opportunities

Obstacles in women's path to leadership take several forms. Careers are waylaid by gender stereotypes, gender bias in evaluation and mentoring, gender differences in family responsibilities, and inadequate workplace structures and public policies.

Gender Stereotypes

One of the most intractable obstacles for women seeking positions of influence is the mismatch between the qualities traditionally associated with women and those traditionally associated with leadership. The "great man" model of leadership is still with us—and the term is seldom used generically. Most characteristics associated with leaders are masculine: dominance, authority, assertiveness, and so forth.[33] In recent years, this disjuncture between femininity and leadership has lessened somewhat. Women are becoming more like men in their career aspirations and achievements, and they are more willing to see themselves as having qualities associated with authority.[34] More women now occupy highly visible leadership roles, and recent theories of leadership have stressed the importance of interpersonal qualities commonly attributed to women, such as cooperation and collaboration.[35]

Yet despite these trends, traditional gender stereotypes still leave women with a double standard and a double bind. Men continue to be rated higher than women on most of the qualities associated with leadership.[36] People more readily credit men with leadership ability and more readily accept men as leaders.[37] What is assertive in a man can appear abrasive in a woman, and female leaders risk appearing too feminine or not feminine enough. On one hand, they may appear too "soft"—unable or unwilling to make the tough calls required in positions of greatest influence. On the other hand, those who mimic the "male model" are often viewed as strident and overly aggressive or ambitious. "Attila the Hen" and "the Dragon Lady" have difficulty enlisting respect, support, and cooperation from coworkers.[38] Indeed, some executive coaches have developed a market niche in rehabilitating "bully broads," female managers who come across as insufficiently feminine.[39] An overview of more than a hundred studies confirms that women are rated lower as leaders when they adopt authoritative and seemingly masculine styles, particularly when the evaluators are men, or when the role is one typically occupied by men.[40] Yet other research finds that individuals with masculine styles are more likely to emerge as leaders than those with feminine styles. In effect, women face trade-offs that men do not. Aspiring female leaders risk being liked but not respected, or respected but not liked, in settings that may require individuals to be both in order to succeed.

Other gender-related stereotypes are inconsistent with leadership roles. Having children makes women, but not men, appear less competent and less available to meet workplace responsibilities.[41] The term "working father" is rarely used and carries none of the adverse connotations of "working mother." Attitudes toward self-promotion reflect a related mismatch between stereotypes associated with leadership and with femininity—women are expected to be nurturing, not self-serving, and entrepreneurial behaviors viewed as appropriate in men are often viewed as distasteful in women.[42]

Because such stereotypes operate at unconscious levels and selections for leadership positions involve subjective and confidential judgments, the extent of bias is hard to assess. It is, however, instructive that in experimental settings, résumés are rated more favorably when they carry male rather than female names.[43] And in large-scale surveys of senior executive women, the most frequently cited obstacle to advancement is "male stereotyping and preconceptions."[44] Politicians cite similar barriers and a substantial segment of the public agrees. Although recent polls find that 97 percent of Americans say that they would vote for a qualified woman for president, only about half think the country is ready for a female leader, and even fewer believe that their neighbors are.[45] Although the extent of bias varies somewhat by country, cross-cultural data leaves no doubt about the pervasiveness of traditional gender stereotypes.[46]

Many women also internalize these stereotypes, which creates a psychological glass ceiling. On average, women appear less willing to engage in self-promoting or assertive behaviors, or to take the risks that may be necessary for leadership roles.[47] So too, as one comprehensive overview of gender in negotiations puts it, "Women don't ask." An unwillingness to seem too pushy or difficult and an undervaluation of their own worth often deter women from negotiating effectively for what they want or need.[48] In workplace settings, the result is that female employees may be less likely than their male colleagues to gain the assignments, positions, and support necessary for leadership roles.

Other cognitive biases compound the force of these traditional stereotypes. People are more likely to notice and recall information that confirms their prior assumptions than information that contradicts those assumptions; the dissonant data is filtered out. For example, when employers assume that a working mother is unlikely to be fully committed to her career, they more easily remember the times when she left early than the times when she stayed late. So too, attorneys who assume that women of color are beneficiaries of preferential treatment, not merit-based selection, will recall their errors more readily than their insights. A related problem is that people share what psychologists label a "just world" bias.[49] They want to believe that, in the absence of special treatment, individuals generally get what they deserve and deserve what they get. Perceptions of performance frequently are adjusted to match observed outcomes. If women, particularly women of color, are underrepresented in positions of greatest prominence, the most psychologically convenient explanation is that they lack the necessary qualifications or commitment.

These perceptions can, in turn, prevent women from getting assignments that would demonstrate their capabilities, and a cycle of self-fulfilling predictions is established.[50] In managerial contexts, decision makers generally see women as more suited for jobs involving human relations than those involving line responsibility for profits and losses. The absence of such line experience is the major reason given by CEOs in the United States and abroad for women's underrepresentation in leadership positions.[51] Gender stereotypes also help explain why women are less likely to be viewed as leaders than similarly situated men. For example, in studies where people see a man seated at the head of a table for a meeting, they typically assume that he is the leader. They do not make the same assumption when the person in that seat is a woman.[52]

In-Group Favoritism: Gender Bias in Evaluations and Mentoring Networks

A related problem involves in-group favoritism. Extensive research documents the preferences that individuals feel for members of their own groups. Loyalty, cooperation, favorable evaluations, and the allocation of rewards and opportunities all increase in likeli-hood for in-group members.[53] A key example is the presumption of competence that dominant groups accord to their members but not to outsiders. Members of in-groups tend to attribute accomplish-ments of fellow members to intrinsic characteristics, such as intel-ligence, drive, and commitment. By contrast, the achievements of out-group members are often ascribed to luck or special treatment.[54] Even in experimental situations where male and female perfor-mance is objectively equal, women are held to higher standards, and their competence is rated lower.[55] Moreover, for women, effec-tive performance does not necessarily suggest leadership potential. In one recent study of twenty-eight hundred managers, supervisors who rated female subordinates somewhat higher than men in cur-rent competence rated the women lower in long-term leadership potential.[56]

Again, women often internalize these stereotypes; they gener-ally see themselves as less deserving than men for rewards for the same performance and less qualified for key leadership positions.[57] In male-dominated settings, aspiring female leaders are also sub-ject to special scrutiny and polarized assessments. Gender stereo-types are particularly strong when women's representation does not exceed token levels, and too few counterexamples are present to challenge conventional assumptions.[58] A small number of superstars will attract special notice and receive higher evaluations than their male counterparts, but women who are just below that level tend to get disproportionately lower evaluations.[59] At the same time, the presence of a few highly regarded women at the top creates the illu-sion that the glass ceiling has been shattered for everyone else. And when superstars fail or opt out, their departures attract particular notice and reinforce stereotypes about women's lesser capabilities and commitment.[60]

In-group favoritism is also apparent in the informal networks of mentoring, contacts, and support that are critical for advancement. People generally feel most comfortable with those who are like them in important respects, including gender. Women in traditionally male-dominated settings often remain out of the loop of advice and professional development opportunities.[61] Women of color also experience particular difficulties of isolation and exclusion.[62] Surveys of upper-level U.S. managers find that almost half of women of color and close to a third of white women cite a lack of influential mentors as a major barrier to advancement.[63] In law, 62 percent of women of color and 60 percent of white women, but only 4 percent of white men, feel excluded from formal and informal networking opportunities. Similarly, 44 percent of women of color, compared with 39 percent of white women and only 2 percent of white men, report being passed over for desirable work assignments.[64]

A similar problem confronts potential leaders in other professional and political settings in the United States and abroad.[65] The relatively small number of women who are in positions of power often lack the time or the leverage, or in some cases the inclination, to assist all who may hope to join them. Differences across race, ethnicity, and culture compound the problem. White men who would like to fill the gaps in mentoring often lack the capacity to do so or are worried about the appearance of forming close relationships with women, particularly women of color.[66] Although a growing number of organizations are attempting to respond by establishing formal mentoring programs and women's networks, the playing field is still far from level.

Gender Roles in Family Settings

Ironically, the home is no more an equal opportunity employer than the workplace: only in domestic matters the presumptions of competence are reversed, which creates unequal family burdens. Women are, and are expected to be, the primary caregivers, especially of the very young and the very old. In principle most men support gender equality—but in practice they fail to structure their lives to promote it. Despite a significant increase in men's domestic work over the last two decades, women continue to shoulder the major burden.[67] In one representative survey of high-achieving women, four of ten felt that their husbands created more domestic work than they contributed.[68] In another survey of well-educated professional women who had left the paid workforce, two-thirds cited their husbands' influence on the decision, including their lack of support in child care and other domestic tasks, and their expectation that wives should be the ones to cut back on employment.[69] Most male leaders in business and professional positions have spouses who are full-time homemakers, or who are working part time. The same is not true of female leaders, who, with few exceptions, are either single or have partners with full-time jobs.[70] Few of these husbands are willing to subordinate their own careers to assist their wives.[71] Far more mothers than fathers are single parents, and that is particularly true of women of color, who often assume additional caretaking obligations for their extended family.[72]

Double standards in domestic roles are deeply rooted in cultural attitudes and workplace practices. Working mothers are held to higher standards than working fathers and are often criticized for being insufficiently committed, either as parents or professionals. Those who seem willing to sacrifice family needs to workplace demands appear lacking as mothers. Those who take extended leave or reduced schedules appear lacking as leaders. These mixed messages leave many women with the uncomfortable sense that whatever they are doing, they should be doing something else.[73]

Neither public attitudes nor workplace practices support reversals of the traditional allocation of domestic roles. Fewer than 15 percent of U.S. Fortune 100 companies offer the same paid parental leave to fathers as to mothers, and an even smaller percentage of men take any extended period of time away from their jobs for family reasons.[74] Similar patterns prevail internationally except in the relatively few countries that mandate "use it or lose it" paid leave for men.[75] Employers that only grudgingly accommodate mothers can be even more resistant to fathers. Daddy tracks are noticeable for their absence. Yet workplace policies that disadvantage men also disadvantage women. By discouraging husbands from assuming an equal division of household responsibilities, prevailing parental leave structures reinforce gender roles that are separate and by no means equal. As long as work-family issues are seen as problems primarily for women, potential solutions are likely to receive inadequate attention in leadership circles still dominated by men.

The gender imbalance in family roles reinforces gender inequalities in career development. Women with demanding work and family commitments often lack time for the networking and mentoring activities necessary for advancement. As former Catalyst president Sheila Wellington notes, at the end of the day, "Men head for drinks. Women for the dry cleaners." Men pick up tips; women pick up kids, laundry, dinner, and the house.[76] Although women on leadership tracks can often afford to buy their way out of domestic drudgery, not all family obligations can be readily outsourced. When asked how women can solve the work-family conflict, Gloria Steinem aptly answered: "Women can't, until men are asking that question too." If women are choosing not to run the world, it's partly because men are choosing not to run the washer and dryer.

Inflexible Workplace Structures and Inadequate Public Policies

All these problems are compounded by inadequacies in the workplace and the public policies that address them. Gender inequalities in family roles pose particular challenges for women in leadership positions, which typically require highly demanding schedules. Hourly requirements in most professions have increased dramatically over the last two decades, and what has not changed is the number of hours in the day.[77] For leaders in business, politics, and the professions, all work and no play is fast becoming the norm rather than the exception; sixty-hour workweeks are typical.[78] Technological innovations have created as many problems as they have solved. Although they make it increasingly possible for women to work at home, they also make it increasingly impossible not to. Many high-achieving women remain tethered to their office through their e-mail, fax, beeper, and BlackBerry. Unsurprisingly, most women in upper-level professional and business positions report that they do not have sufficient time for themselves or their families.[79] Some feel they cannot manage a goldfish, much less a child.[80] Many aspiring leaders, particularly women of color, express frustration with workplace demands that compete with commitments to community, religious, and other voluntary organizations that are important in their lives.[81]

Part of the problem is the wide gap between formal policies and actual practices concerning work-family conflicts. Although most women in top managerial and professional positions have access to reduced or flexible schedules, few of these women feel able to take advantage of such options. For example, over 90 percent of U.S. law firms report policies permitting part-time work, yet only about 4 percent of lawyers actually use them.[82] Most women believe, with good reason, that any reduction in hours or availability would jeopardize their career prospects. A wide variety of research finds that even short-term adjustments in working schedules such as leaves or part-time status for less than a year result in long-term reductions in earnings and advancement.[83]

Workplace inflexibility and unmanageable time demands play a major role in women's decisions to step off the leadership track both in the United States and abroad.[84] Although many of these women return to high-powered careers, others find reentry blocked, or less appealing than volunteer work or starting a small-scale business in which they can control their own hours.[85] Some of these alternatives present leadership opportunities of another sort, but far too much talent falls by the wayside.

The fact that caretaking is still considered primarily an individual rather than a social responsibility adds to women's work in the home and limits their opportunities in the world outside it. The United States is almost alone among industrialized nations in failing to guarantee paid parental leave, and only about a tenth of those eligible for the largely unpaid options currently available take advantage of them.[86] Quality, affordable child care and elder care are also unavailable for many women attempting to work their way up the leadership ladder. While these are not simply women's issues, women have paid the highest price for our failure to address them.

Equal opportunity laws have also proven inadequate to ensure equality in leadership positions. Legal remedies for gender bias generally require either proof of intentional discrimination or a pattern and practice that has broad discriminatory impact and is not justified by business necessity.[87] Neither remedy is well suited for those in upper-level professional and management positions. The difficulties of proof and the costs of legal proceedings prevent most women who experience gender bias from seeking legal remedies.[88] These remedies are even less accessible outside the United States, because most nations lack anti-discrimination enforcement structures and class-action procedures that permit cost-effective responses for routine grievances.[89] Even in countries like the United States, which have relatively well-developed legal protections, few individuals want to incur the risks of retaliation or the reputational injuries that accompany formal complaints. Unless liability is clear and damages are substantial, discrimination claims are simply too expensive to litigate. Yet liability is seldom clear for women on leadership tracks, where the criteria for advancement are subjective, and the pool of similar employees is too small to permit meaningful statistical comparisons.

Winning such cases frequently demands fairly explicit evidence of bias, but those who harbor intentional prejudice generally have the sense not to express it publicly.[90] To be sure, a few high-profile cases involving egregious facts continue to arise, and their large damage awards have prompted much-needed changes, particularly in fields such as financial services.[91] But for the vast majority of women who are stymied by subtle bias and inflexible schedules, lawsuits make no sense. "Career suicide" is a common description.[92]

In short, our progress remains partial. We have had only limited success in moving women into leadership roles traditionally occupied by men, and even less in moving men into domestic roles traditionally occupied by women. And we have not yet obtained workplace and social policies that accommodate the needs of both sexes on family-related issues.

The Social Costs of Gender Inequalities

Women's unequal representation in leadership positions poses multiple concerns. Most obviously, the barriers to women's advancement compromise fundamental principles of equal opportunity and social justice. These barriers impose organizational costs as well. Researchers consistently find a positive correlation between the representation of women in leadership positions and business performance measures such as market share and return on investment.[93] Although correlation does not always imply causation, there are strong reasons to believe that diversity in leadership has tangible payoffs.

The most obvious reason is demographic. Women are now a majority of college graduates and a growing share of the talent available for leadership. Organizations that create a culture of equal opportunity are better able to attract, retain, and motivate the most qualified individuals.[94] Reducing the obstacles to women's success also reduces the costs of attrition. It increases employees' morale, commitment, and retention, and decreases the expenses associated with recruiting, training, and mentoring replacements.[95]

A second rationale for ensuring equal access to leadership positions is that women have distinct perspectives to contribute. To perform effectively in an increasingly competitive and multicultural environment, workplaces need individuals with diverse backgrounds, experiences, and styles of leadership.[96] The point is not that there is some single "woman's point of view" or woman's leadership style, but rather that gender differences do make some difference that needs to be registered in positions of power.

Women's Leadership Styles and Priorities

Assumptions about gender differences in leadership styles and effectiveness are widespread, although the evidence for such assumptions is weaker than commonly supposed both in the United States and abroad.[97] The conventional wisdom is that female leaders are more participatory and interpersonally oriented than male leaders and are more likely to adopt empathetic, supportive, and collaborative approaches.[98] This view is consistent with women's self-reports and some small-scale laboratory studies.[99] However, most research reveals no gender differences, particularly when it involves evaluations of leaders by supervisors, subordinates, and peers in real-world settings.[100] Nor do most surveys reveal significant gender differences in the effectiveness of leaders. Indeed, contrary to popular assumptions, large-scale research generally finds that women slightly outperform men on all but a few measures.[101]

What accounts for the inconsistency in findings and the disconnect between conventional wisdom and recent data? Gender socialization and stereotypes play an obvious role; they push women to behave, and to describe their behavior, in ways that are consistent with traditional notions of femininity. Yet the force of these cultural norms is constrained in organizations where advancement requires conformity to accepted images of leadership. It is not surprising that women's styles are similar to those of male counterparts, particularly since recent trends in leadership education have encouraged both sexes to adopt more collaborative, interpersonally sensitive approaches.[102] Nor is it surprising that some studies find superior performance by women leaders, given the hurdles that they have had to surmount to reach upper-level positions and the pressures that they have faced to consistently exceed expectations.[103] Whatever else can be inferred from this research, it is clear that a society can ill afford to lose so many talented women from its leadership pool. To the extent that female leaders gravitate toward a collaborative, interpersonally sensitive approach, it will prove an asset in many leadership settings.

Similar points are applicable to gender differences in leadership priorities. The most systematic research involves commitment to women's issues, and here again, the findings are mixed. For example, most, although not all, evidence indicates that female judges are more supportive than their male colleagues on gender-related issues.[104] And many women judges, both through individual rulings and collective efforts in women's judicial organizations, have spearheaded responses to women's concerns in areas such as domestic violence, child support, and gender bias training.[105] The same is true of women in management and public office, who have often championed causes of particular concern to women. Companies headed by women have significantly higher percentages of female board members than their male-led counterparts in the Fortune 1000.[106] Most research on female politicians both in the United States and abroad finds that they are more likely than their male colleagues to support and sponsor legislation dealing with the interests of women and families, and to rank such legislation among their highest priorities.[107] Women heads of state are also particularly willing to consider gender in political appointments. A prominent case in point is Chile's president, Michelle Bachelet, who kept a campaign promise to fill half of her cabinet seats with qualified women.[108]

Yet not all female leaders share such commitments. Examples such as Margaret Thatcher remind us that electing women is not always the best way to advance women's concerns. Extensive research on U.S. legislatures finds that party affiliation is more important than gender in predicting votes on women's issues, and that ideology is more important in predicting sponsorship of legislation on these issues.[109] Some of the worst congressional voting records on women's rights belong to women, and relatively few female state legislators make women's concerns a top priority.[110] Some women in the United States and abroad still run campaigns with the strategy that California Senator Barbara Boxer wryly described as the traditional wisdom for female candidates: "You never mentioned being a woman . . . you hoped nobody noticed."[111]

The same point could be made about professional and managerial contexts. Many women leaders have made a crucial difference in promoting women's issues and in creating institutional structures that will do the same. For example, female university presidents and managing partners of law firms have been at the forefront of efforts to promote gender equity through fairer evaluation processes, improved work-family policies, and related initiatives.[112] Yet surveys also find large numbers of women leaders who do not actively advocate women's interests.[113] Underlying these different priorities are differences in personal experiences, risks, and influence.

For some female leaders, their own experiences of discrimination, marginalization, or work-family conflicts leave them with a desire to make life better for their successors.[114] Because these women have bumped up against conventional assumptions and workplace structures, they can more readily question roles that men take for granted.[115] Other women end up as advocates partly by default. They may be asked to represent the "woman's view" or be enlisted by colleagues to serve that role.[116]

But not all female leaders are willing to accept that responsibility. They have internalized the values of the culture in which they have succeeded and have little interest in promoting opportunities that they never had. They have "gotten there the hard way," and they have "given up a lot"; if they managed, so can anyone else.[117]

Women's willingness to raise women's issues may also depend on the likely consequences. It matters whether leaders feel secure in their positions and safe in raising gender-related concerns, and whether they expect to benefit directly from the changes in policy or climate that may result.[118] All too often, the risks outweigh the rewards. Surveys of professionals, politicians, and corporate executives reflect common concerns about being branded as a feminist or what is viewed as the functional equivalent: "extremist," "militant," "strident," "oversensitive," "abrasive," "disruptive," or "difficult to work with."[119] Even if they express gender-related concerns in gentle, nonconfrontational terms, women often worry that they will be viewed as "self-serving" "whiners" who are unable to compete without special treatment.[120] These risks may not seem worth taking if women lack confidence that their efforts will do much good. For women of color, who are often especially isolated in upper-level positions, the pressures to avoid divisive issues can be intense.[121]

In short, the difference that gender difference makes depends on context. Putting women in positions of power is not the same as empowering women. But the influence of women holding leadership positions can make a crucial difference in promoting gender equality and improving organizational performance. The challenge remaining is to identify strategies that will assist and encourage women to play that role.

Strategies for Change

To reach greater gender equality in leadership will require expanding opportunities for talented women and enabling them to perform effectively in positions of power. As is obvious from the preceding discussion, such a reform agenda will require strategies on the individual, institutional, and societal levels. This would not, however, be obvious from "leadership lite" publications targeting a popular audience. They focus almost exclusively on personal strategies; the need for structural change receives at best glancing attention. From a marketing standpoint, this makes obvious sense. The target audience, aspiring women leaders, is generally interested in personal solutions; not systemic problems and collective responses. But the effectiveness of individual strategies often depends on institutional reform. For example, women receive endless advice to find the right mentors and maintain a healthy work-life balance, but their chances of doing so may depend partly on organizational culture. Moreover, the jazzed-up, dumbed-down approach of many how-to publications may lead individuals to focus too much attention on fixing themselves and too little on fixing the institutional and societal structures that are at the root of the problem.

Individual Strategies

Both self-help publications and scholarly research underscore certain basic strategies for women who seek a leadership position. They need to understand their own objectives and capabilities, to develop leadership qualities, to obtain mentors, and to balance personal and professional needs.

Self-Awareness. A necessary first step on the path to leadership involves self-reflection. Women need to be clear about their goals and values: What do they want, why do they want it, and what are they prepared to sacrifice to get it?[122] Clarifying those priorities can then help women identify where they want to be in the short and long term and what it will take to get there. Individuals also need to consider their managerial strengths and weaknesses and to obtain adequate feedback from others about necessary improvements.

Leadership Styles and Capabilities. To reach their desired goals, women must demonstrate leadership abilities. To that end, they should seek challenging assignments, acquire appropriate job experience, develop informal relationships with influential colleagues and clients, and cultivate a reputation for effectiveness that exceeds expectations.[123] They also need an authentic leadership style that fits their organization.[124] According to a survey of women managers and professional consultants, that includes finding a "style that men are comfortable with."[125] In many contexts, projecting a decisive and forceful manner without seeming arrogant or abrasive is an essential skill. But as most experts emphasize, women also need a style with which they are comfortable. If the style they can employ most effectively does not mesh with their workplace culture, it may be prudent to find a different workplace.[126]

Formal leadership training and coaching can sometimes help in developing interpersonal styles and capabilities such as risk taking, conflict resolution, and strategic vision.[127] Newly emerging executive education programs for women can also target challenges that upper-level female managers confront.[128] Such assistance can often help with self-promotion. This poses a particular concern for women, who are typically socialized to view self-aggrandizing behaviors as unfeminine and unattractive.[129] Yet aspiring female leaders need to be sure that their contributions achieve adequate visibility and recognition, and they need to ask for support and rewards commensurate with performance. Women who wait passively for their work to be valued may benefit from expert advice on how to highlight their abilities or how to find others who can do it for them.

Models, Mentors, and Networks. Guidance can come from both role models and mentors. These can but need not be the same individuals. Aspiring leaders need multiple sources of support, contacts, and career development opportunities from both men and women and from both inside and outside their organizations.[130] Leaders themselves can also benefit from mentoring relationships. Quite apart from the satisfaction that comes from assisting those most in need of assistance, upper-level professionals may receive more tangible payoffs from fresh insights and from the loyalty and influence that their efforts secure. Talented junior colleagues generally want to work for effective mentors and to support them in leadership roles. Women who don't socialize or "do lunch" in order to get work done need a broader definition of work. Results matter—but relationships are part of what is necessary to achieve them.[131]

The most effective mentoring relationships typically arise naturally among individuals who share important similarities, such as sex, race, ethnicity, background, and interests. This presents problems in organizations that have too few women in leadership positions to aid all those seeking assistance and too few powerful men who are comfortable filling the gaps. The problems are compounded when senior women are already overextended with work and family responsibilities, and are worried about the appearance of favoritism if they direct all their mentoring to junior women. The result is often a form of "managerial cloning," in which a largely white male leadership unreflectively replicates itself.[132]

Some organizations have responded to these challenges with women's networks and with formal mentoring programs that match employees or allow individuals to select their own pairings. Other employers have diversity officers who help groom talented women for advancement. Such initiatives serve a variety of useful functions, but they are no substitute for the mentoring that occurs more naturally during collaborative projects and shared activities.[133] Nor are superficial contacts at women's networking events a replacement for deeper relationships with men as well as women who can open doors at senior leadership levels.[134] For women juggling competing commitments, the key is to be strategic in their efforts, and to recognize that those from whom they seek assistance are under similar pressures. The best mentoring generally goes to the best mentees, who are reasonable and focused in their needs and who make sure the relationship is mutually beneficial.

Time Management and Work-Family Choices. Setting priorities and managing time effectively are also critical leadership skills. Setting boundaries, delegating domestic tasks, and developing effective reduced hour, flextime, or telecommuting arrangements are obvious strategies. Women who temporarily opt out of the workforce need to stay involved in their fields. They can assist the transition back to paid employment through participation in professional associations and development of expertise through continuing education courses, volunteer activities, and reentry programs specially targeted to their needs.[135]

In trade publications, success stories abound. Female leaders frequently manage to have it all, though not always at the same time. But missing from the analysis are the unhappy endings: those women whose efforts to have a life take them off the leadership track and leave no time for collective efforts that might make better choices available. That gap points up a broader weakness in the how-to literature; its focus on individuals limits its effectiveness in solving the challenges it identifies.

Leadership Lite: The Contributions and Limits of Self-Help. As self-help literature goes, most publications on women's leadership seem better than average. They generally offer useful common sense in accessible prose, with enough personal anecdotes and real-world examples to make the strategies concrete. The best of the literature draws on relevant research and pinpoints recurrent mistakes by aspiring leaders.

There are, however, serious limitations in these publications. One stems from their stunningly generalized approach to complex issues. Most trade books offer all-purpose prescriptions on the apparent assumption that all leadership contexts are basically the same. Some publications are explicit on the point. Linda Clark's *Leadership Essentials for Women*, a guide targeted to leaders of Christian organizations, begins: "Through thirty years as a women's leader working with women in local churches . . . I have come to realize that women everywhere have the same basic needs. . . . It doesn't matter whether you are leading a school project, heading a team for a publicity presentation at your firm, or teaching a women's Bible group. The same leadership skills apply to any leadership role."[136] Our own experience of almost thirty years and review of leadership research suggest just the opposite. To the extent that any useful generalization can be drawn, it is that context matters. Leaders must respond to the culture and expectations of followers.

A related problem involves the superficial categorizations and simplistic sound bites that may sell books but are unlikely to solve real leadership challenges. For example, one publication divides leaders into thinkers and feelers who fit four color-coded personality types and use eight leadership styles.[137] Another guide offers "Seven Secrets of Successful Women" and packages everything aspiring leaders need to know into four "p" principles: performance, perseverance, practice, and patience.[138] Journalist Gail Evans compiles half a dozen examples of what "men can do at work that women can't" (cry, fidget, yell, be ugly, have sex, or show bad manners).[139] Other authors dwell on advice that seems painfully obvious: do not sleep with the boss, do not dress provocatively, do not advertise mistakes or uncertainty. Although a central theme in the self-help literature involves balancing work, family, and personal needs, discussion rarely strays beyond well-worn homilies: women need to learn to say no, buy domestic help, accept imperfection, and make time for relationships, both personal and professional.[140] They also must learn when to say yes to events that on the surface seem unnecessary but that are in fact important opportunities to "see and be seen," "meet and greet," and "show and tell."[141]

It is hard to imagine that advice of this sort will be enough to propel women into leadership positions. The same is true of commercial leadership development conferences that lure participants not with knowledgeable experts but with media celebrities like Brooke Shields or recreational add-ons like tai chi and mountain climbing.[142]

On the difficult challenges, such as what to do when confronting evidence of discrimination, how-to publications and workshops are generally silent or evasive. For example, none of the "Seven Secrets" broach this topic. The best the book can muster is to note that "there are certainly several approaches to the problem," and to list the most obvious: "ignore it, fight it, work around it."[143] No guidance is offered on choosing among them; rather readers are simply advised to "work harder than their male counterparts," learn to "move in a man's world," "have the right networks," and be "top performers by anyone's standards."[144] The women who can manage all that probably aren't the ones buying this book.

A further problem with these pop publications is their unquestioned acceptance of prevailing definitions of success. The assumption is that women value, or should value, the same things as men. Gail Evans's best-selling *Play Like a Man* puts the point directly. "To a guy, everything counts. The size of his office, the size of his staff, the size of his salary, the size of anything that can be measured. And they're always keeping score." If women don't do the same, they will be "perceived as losers." Anyone willing to settle for a "cramped office and dumpy furniture" doesn't "know the score" and won't be taken seriously.[145] Lois Frankel, in *Nice Girls Don't Get the Corner Office*, makes a similar claim: "Money is power." And girls who don't fight for salaries are not only underpaid but undervalued.[146] Almost never do these publications acknowledge the possibility that women could, or should, have a different set of priorities than pay and perks: more humane hours, better work-family and child care policies, greater support for community service, and so forth. Rather, the emphasis is on enabling women to score higher under rules not of their own making.

Women's capacity to change the rules through collective action gets at best glancing attention in these publications. Their relentless focus on individual advancement diverts attention from institutional reform. The leadership lite objective is getting more women into positions of power. What they do when they get there is a matter of little apparent concern. Yet as the following discussion suggests, it is women's leadership on women's issues that is often critical in opening the opportunities that pop publications exalt.

Women's Leadership on Women's Issues. Women on the leadership track have unique opportunities and corresponding obligations to promote changes that will make leadership accessible to others. As citizens, women can support policies, politicians, and practices that will advance gender equity. As professionals and community activists, women can make equalizing leadership opportunities a priority. And as parents, women can model effective leadership and challenge the child-rearing patterns that work against it.

As leadership experts note, the culture generally and parents inadvertently often reinforce behaviors that perpetuate traditional gender roles and gender inequalities. Giving sophisticated military games to boys and dolls to girls is a case in point. Over a billion Barbies have been sold in 150 countries, and the most popular accessories include jewelry, recipe boxes, and vacuum cleaners.[147] A parody by *Onion* magazine of a fictional CEO Barbie speaks volumes about the messages being sent. The magazine describes a mock protest against Mattel for bringing out a doll that fosters "ridiculously unattainable images." The company's mock response is a statement by its all-male leadership claiming that the CEO doll represents a positive image and demonstrates that "young girls can be anything they want. There is nothing standing in their way."[148] The challenge for parents is to reinforce their daughters' aspirations while also preparing them for the obstacles that still, in fact, stand in the way.

Organizational Strategies

The most important factor in ensuring equal access to leadership opportunities is a commitment to that objective, which is reflected in workplace priorities, policies, and reward structures.[149] That, in turn, requires accountability for results and strategies that will assess progress on gender issues.

Commitment and Accountability. A necessary first step is commitment from the top. An organization's leadership team needs to acknowledge the importance of diversity and equity, to assess its progress in achieving them, and to hold individuals at every level of the organization accountable for improvement.[150] The most systematic evidence available to date suggests that having a diversity plan and the staff and structures to implement it is the most effective strategy in increasing women's access to managerial positions.[151] Part of that plan should include making performance on gender-related issues part of evaluation and compensation systems. Experts put it bluntly: "Hit [supervisors] in their W-2s, and their hearts and minds will follow."[152] This is not to suggest that simply tying salaries to the number of women in leadership positions is the best strategy. For example, one company that attempted to provide financial incentives for employing women at senior levels found that male employees' resentment made the "grab a girly" approach counterproductive.[153] But a more comprehensive approach, which holds upper-level personnel responsible for a range of efforts and results, is essential to align diversity principles with organizational practices. Decision makers need to be held accountable in recruitment, retention, and promotion, as well as practices that influence those processes, such as evaluation, assignments, mentoring, and work-family accommodation.

Measuring and Monitoring Results. To make such progress, employers need concrete assessments of results. On this point, conventional wisdom is right: organizations get what they measure. And too few organizations adequately measure gender equity.[154]

Employers should compile information on recruitment, hiring, promotion, and retention, broken down by sex as well as by race and ethnicity. Surveys of current and former employees can also provide valuable information on equity and quality-of-life issues. Decision makers need to know whether men and women are advancing in equal numbers and whether they feel equally well supported in career development.[155] Where possible, employers should assess their own progress in comparison with similar organizations and the best practices identified by experts.[156] In some contexts, experienced diversity consultants can help identify barriers to equal opportunity and design appropriate responses.[157]

Organizations also need to monitor the effects of gender equity initiatives on women's leadership. Many organizations invest substantial time and money in diversity training programs that have no measurable impact on outcomes. Although some small-scale studies find that such programs may improve awareness and attitudes, others find risks of backlash from white male participants.[158] And virtually no evidence documents improvements in the representation of women in upper-level positions as a result of such training.[159]

Other practices that may affect leadership opportunities should also be subject to scrutiny. One practice involves the process by which individuals are evaluated for promotion and selected for leadership positions. Decision makers should screen written evaluations for stereotypical characterizations; develop objective, outcome-related criteria to supplement subjective assessments; review assignments to ensure equal opportunities for career development, and educate individuals about how to give and receive effective performance evaluations.[160]

Quality of Life and Work-Family Initiatives. Any serious commitment to expand women's leadership opportunities requires a similarly serious commitment to address work-family conflicts that stand in the way of advancement. Best practices and model programs are readily available on matters such as flexible and reduced schedules, telecommuting, leave policies, and child care assistance.[161] Such options are critical in retaining potential leaders. In surveys of high-achieving women, between two-thirds and four-fifths identify work-family issues as a major part of the problem and the solution for women's advancement.[162] Most of these women rate schedule flexibility as more important than compensation.[163] Although the details of effective policies vary across organizations, two important factors are mutual commitment and flexibility. Technologies that blur the boundaries between home and work can help, but not if individuals remain constantly on call, hostage to schedules not of their own making.

Organizations also need to ensure that women who seek temporary accommodations do not pay a permanent price. Stepping out should not mean stepping down: individuals on reduced or flexible schedules should not lose opportunities for challenging assignments or eventual promotion. Nor should women who temporarily opt out lose all contact with the workplace. Part-time consulting arrangements and employer-supported career development opportunities can build loyalty and assist the transition back.[164]

Finally, and most important, family and quality of life concerns need to be seen not just as women's issues but also as organizational priorities. Options like parental leave and flexible schedules should be gender neutral in fact as well as in form, and men should be encouraged to take advantage of them. Time should be available for both sexes to acquire the broad experience that comes from family and civic pursuits. Policies need to be monitored to ensure that options are available in practice as well as in principle, and that individuals at the highest leadership level feel able to use them.[165] In short, if employers want the most able and diverse leadership candidates possible, the working environment needs to do more to attract and retain them.

Mentoring Programs and Women's Networks. The importance of mentors has long been recognized, but, as noted earlier, the institutionalization of mentoring has lagged behind. Formal programs can help fill the gap. Of course, relationships that are assigned are seldom as effective as those that are chosen.[166] But some access to advice and support may be better than none. At the very least, structured programs can keep talented but unassertive women from falling through the cracks, and they can also remove concerns about appearances of favoritism or sexual impropriety that sometimes inhibit mentoring relationships. Well-designed initiatives that evaluate and reward mentoring activities can improve participants' skills, satisfaction, and retention rates.[167] The only systematic large-scale study to date has found that mentoring programs are correlated with modest gains in female representation in managerial positions, and that women of color benefit most.[168]

A related strategy involves support for women's networks in workplaces, professional associations, and minority organizations.[169] These networks sponsor a variety of activities, such as workshops, seminars, speaker series, and informal social events. Common goals include linking professionals with potential clients and customers, developing career advancement skills, and representing women's shared concerns in their professions or workplaces. Affinity groups for women of color are especially critical in reducing participants' sense of isolation.[170] By bringing potential leaders together around common interests, these networks can encourage mentoring, enhance reputations, and forge coalitions on gender-related issues. Participants often gain not only skills but motivation to use them on behalf of other women. The only large-scale survey of the effectiveness of such networks found that they had a modest correlation with women's advancement in management.[171] Small-scale program evaluations have also demonstrated payoffs in client development, promotion, job satisfaction, and workplace reforms.[172] The "small wins" that collective efforts can secure often lay the foundations for fundamental change.[173]

Societal Strategies

Women's access to leadership is influenced by a broad range of public and private sector initiatives. Regulatory agencies, stakeholder organizations, and professional associations should hold employers more accountable for performance on gender equity issues. Public policy should do more to reduce work-family conflicts. Professional associations should take additional steps to identify and reward best practices, support members' career development, and press for societal and workplace reforms. Universities should improve coverage of diversity-related topics in their curricula and model best practices in their own leadership.

Government Regulation and Public Policy. One obvious way to increase women's representation in leadership positions is to strengthen equal opportunity requirements and expand resources for enforcement. As earlier discussion noted, a central limitation of current oversight structures is the absence of systematic, public information about gender equity and the related difficulty of proving gender bias.[174] Ironically enough, current liability rules deter some organizations from compiling data that might lay foundations for sex discrimination lawsuits. To neutralize this deterrent and enhance accountability, leading experts have recommended requiring employers over a certain size to disclose data concerning recruitment, retention, and promotion.[175] Other countries have imposed effective requirements along these lines.[176] The availability of such information for U.S. employers would make it easier for them to benchmark their performance relative to other similarly situated organizations and for stakeholders to hold poor performers responsible.

Another crucial strategy is to increase antidiscrimination enforcement resources. In the United States, neither of the primary oversight bodies, the Equal Employment Opportunity Commission or the Department of Labor's review office for federal contractors, has adequate capacity to monitor compliance with gender equity requirements. The same is generally true of state commissions. Yet when such agencies do intervene, the result is typically a significant improvement in women's representation in upper-level positions.[177] To increase the frequency of enforcement efforts, U.S. agencies will need additional financial support and other countries will need to strengthen their remedial structures.[178] Those reforms are most likely to occur only if advocates of women's rights exert greater political pressure.

Increased pressure is also necessary concerning child care, elder care, parental leave, and related policies. Such initiatives are critical in addressing the work-family conflicts that often derail women on leadership tracks. For example, experience in European countries suggests that offering men paid parental leave can increase their child-rearing involvement and that access to quality, affordable child care can increase women's labor force participation.[179] However, these policies are not in themselves sufficient to secure gender equality in family obligations and leadership opportunities. Comprehensive reforms are essential to reduce work-family conflicts and to encourage greater numbers of men to assume substantial caregiving responsibilities.[180]

Proportional Representation.   One reform that would make others more likely is to ensure women's greater political representation. To that end, a growing minority of countries employ voluntary or legally mandated quotas for women in public office.[181] Such preferential policies take a variety of forms. The most widespread but typically least effective strategies are voluntary quotas or targets established by political parties to specify the number of candidates that should be female. The most effective but least common approach is to set aside a certain number of positions for women through constitutional or statutory requirements. An intermediate approach is to mandate that a certain proportion of candidates be women. Mandatory strategies obviously work best in electoral systems that employ proportional representation; quotas for elected officials are not easily implemented in countries that, like the United States, rely on single-member districts. Chapters Six and Seven in this volume discuss other aspects of the issue.

The wisdom of such preferential treatment is subject to considerable controversy. Opponents claim that quotas violate meritocratic principles and stigmatize female representatives as less qualified than their male counterparts. Problems are compounded where the pool of women with adequate credentials is insufficient, and those selected are relegated to positions of least influence. Further difficulties arise when male party leaders select women who are not advocates on women's issues. In both cases, the result may be a system in which women's increased presence makes more of a symbolic than substantive difference.

Yet in many nations, some form of preferential treatment is preferable to the alternative, at least in the short term. In countries where women make up at least half of the electorate, they deserve more than the token representation that traditional electoral processes have produced. If quotas appear inconsistent with meritocratic principles, so too does the old-boy network that they replace. Preferential treatment is a fact of life in politics as we know it; the only issue is which groups are being preferred and how openly. At the very least, efforts to increase the representation of women enhance the legitimacy of democratic institutions as well as diversify the pool from which leaders are chosen. If that pool includes too few qualified women, the best response is to improve the recruitment, mentoring, and training processes. To be sure, mandatory quotas are not the answer for every political system, but finding ways to increase gender balance should be a priority.

Similar points could be made about proportional representation in other contexts. As noted in Chapter Seven, considerable attention has focused on Norway's requirement that women constitute 40 percent of the boards of directors of publicly owned or publicly traded companies. Such requirements are implausible in nations like the United States, where a majority of the electorate is opposed to quotas in most business settings.[182] But even in these countries, there is often sufficient support for gender equity to make some form of voluntary preferential treatment acceptable.

Professional, Stakeholder, and Public Interest Organizations. Professional and public interest organizations can pursue various options to promote and prepare women for leadership and to encourage other groups to do the same. National, state, and local entities can follow the lead of organizations such as Catalyst and the American Bar Association Commission on Women in the Profession that have showcased model policies and best practice standards. Professional and stakeholder organizations can also monitor employers' progress and enlist their commitment to specific gender-equity goals and timetables.[183] Together with professional schools and women's organizations, these professional associations can also provide more training, mentoring, and educational programs on diversity-related issues and can lobby for public policy reforms.

In addition, organizations that publish indexes for socially responsible investing and corporate social responsibility should include measures of gender equity. Only a few publications now include information along these lines, despite evidence that women are interested in receiving it.[184] An Ethical Investment Research Service survey found that a majority of women want their pension funds to favor companies with good records on equal opportunity.[185] To make that possible, better information needs to be available. More organizations should follow the lead of the Calvert Women's Principles, the first global corporate code of conduct focusing on gender equity. Companies that accept these principles agree to implement and report on proactive policies designed to eliminate sex-based discrimination and to recruit women for upper-level managerial positions.[186] The key reporting requirements specified in these principles should become part of the standard criteria for measuring corporate social responsibility. In turn, this information would enable investors, consumers, and public-interest organizations to pressure businesses to assist more women in moving to leadership positions.

Educational Institutions. Universities in general, and business, professional, and public policy schools in particular, could do more to convey the importance of diversity and to model the strategies necessary to achieve it. At a minimum, that will require greater integration of diversity-related issues in core curricula and greater efforts to address the underrepresentation of women in leadership roles.[187] Professional and MBA programs could also increase research support for scholars, as well as continuing education for practition-ers, on gender equity issues. Decision makers need to know much more about what works in the world, and educational institutions have a unique opportunity and corresponding responsibility to help fill the gap.

Conclusion

> It has long since come to my attention that people
> of accomplishment rarely . . . [stayed] back and let
> things happen to them. They went out and
> happened to things.[188]
>
> —*Elinor Smith*

It has come to our attention in preparing this overview that more and more women share Smith's conclusion. Fewer women are con-tent to stay back, and those who advance are changing the land-scape of leadership. The chapters that follow are intended to assist that struggle. The challenges are substantial, but so too are the tal-ents of women leaders and the men who support them.

Endnotes

1. Howard Gardner, *Leading Minds* (New York: HarperCollins, 1995), 6; Sue J. M. Freeman and Susan C. Bourque, "Leader-ship and Power: New Conceptions," in Sue J. M. Freeman, Susan C. Bourque, and Christine M. Shelton, eds., *Women on Power: Leadership Redefined* (Boston: Northeastern University Press, 2001), 3, 14. For the diversity in definitions, see Nancy J. Adler, "Global Leaders: Women of Influence," in Gary N. Powell, *Handbook of Gender and Work* (Thousand Oaks, CA: Sage, 1995), 233, 241.
2. Pamela Kephart and Lillian Schumacher, "Has the 'Glass Ceil-ing' Cracked? An Exploration of Women Entrepreneurship," *Journal of Leadership and Organizational Studies 12* (2005): 2.

3. For example, it is estimated that women account for about half of the board members and organizers of interfaith community groups. Amy Caiazza, "Six Strategies That Encourage Women's Political Activism," *Research-in-Brief*, Newsletter of the Institute for Women's Policy Research (Washington, DC), April 2006, 1.

4. Center for Women in Government and Civil Society, *Women in State Policy Leadership, 1998–2005* (Albany: Center for Women in Government and Civil Society, State University of New York, 2006), 1; Center for American Women in Politics, *Election Results Show Advances for Women* (Rutgers, NJ: CAWP, Eagleton Institute of Politics, November 8, 2006), 1.

5. U.S. Department of Education, "National Center for Education Statistics, 1993–1994 Through 2003–2004: Integrated Postsecondary Education Data System Fall Staff Survey," Table 243 (March 2005); "The Chronicle Survey of Presidents of 4-Year Colleges," *Chronicle of Higher Education*, November 4, 2005, 38.

6. Catalyst, "2005 Census of Women Corporate Officers and Top Earners of the Fortune 500," 2005, available online: www.catalystwomen.org, access date: December 10, 2006; U.S. Equal Employment Opportunity Commission, *Glass Ceilings: The Status of Women as Officials and Managers in the Private Sector* (Washington, DC: Equal Opportunity Employment Commission, 2004); Alliance for Board Diversity, "Women and Minorities on Fortune 100 Boards," available online: http://216.15.177.66/ABDReport.pdf.

7. Paula Patton, "Women Lawyers: Their Status, Influence, and Retention in the Legal Profession," *William and Mary Journal of Women and the Law 11* (2004): 173, 174; American Bar Association Commission on Women in the Profession, *Current Glance of Women and the Law* (Chicago: ABA Commission on Women in the Profession, 2003), 1; Association of American Law Schools, "Statistical Report on Law School Faculty and Candidates for Law Faculty Positions (2004–2005)," prepared

by Richard A. White, available online: www.aals.org/statistics/ 0405/html/0405_T4B_tit.html, access date: December 10, 2006.

8. Neela Banerjee, "Clergywomen Find Hard Path to Bigger Pulpit," *New York Times*, August 26, 2006, A1.

9. For Congress, see Center for American Women in Politics [CAWP], "Women of Color in Elective Office 2006: Fact Sheet" (Rutgers, NJ: CAWP, Eagleton Institute of Politics, 2006). For professors, see U.S. Department of Education, "Postsecondary Integrated Data System," Table 228. For corporate officers, see Lisa Takeuchi Cullen, "Pathways to Power: Race, Gender, and Work," *Time*, Inside Business, December 2005, A3. For lawyers, see Elizabeth Chambliss, *Miles to Go: Progress of Minorities in the Legal Profession* (Chicago: ABA Commission on Racial and Ethnic Diversity in the Legal Profession, 2005); National Association of Law Placement (NALP), *Women and Attorneys of Color at Law Firms* (Washington, DC: NALP, 2004).

10. Inter-Parliamentary Union Web site, Women in National Parliaments, available online: www.ipu.org/wmn-e/classif.htm (providing data on female representation in national legislatures), access date: December 10, 2006. For discussion, see Anne E. Kornblut, "Ascent of a Woman," *New York Times*, June 11, 2006, A6; Marie Wilson, "Closing the Leadership Gap," *Ms.*, Summer 2004, 14.

11. Pippa Norris, *Electoral Engineering* (Cambridge, United Kingdom: Cambridge University Press, 2004), 180.

12. See Yvonne Galligan and Manon Tremblay, eds., *Sharing Power: Women, Parliament, Democracy* (London: Ashgate, 2005); "Women in Politics: Beyond Numbers," available online: http://archive.idea.int/women/parl/ch4c.htm, access date: December 10, 2006; Augusto Lopez-Claros and Saadia Zahidi, *Women's Empowerment: Measuring the Global Gender Gap* (Geneva, Switzerland: World Economic Forum, 2005).

13. International Labor Organization, *Breaking Through the Glass Ceiling: Women in Management* (Geneva, Switzerland: International Labor Organization, 2004); Rana Foroohar, "Myth

and Reality: Forget All the Talk of Equal Opportunity. European Women Can Have a Job—But Not a Career," *Newsweek International*, February 27, 2006.

14. "A Woman's Place . . . More Female Managers Should Have Seats on the Board," *Financial Times*, October 17, 2005, 20; "The Conundrum of the Glass Ceiling," *Economist*, July 23, 2005, 63. For data on executives in eight countries in North America, Europe, and Asia, see Accenture, *The Anatomy of the Glass Ceiling: Barriers to Women's Professional Advancement* (New York: Accenture, 2006).

15. "The Conundrum of the Glass Ceiling," 63.

16. Sue Hayward, *Women Leading* (Houndmills, UK: Palgrave Macmillan, 2005), 151.

17. International Labor Organization, *Breaking Through the Glass Ceiling*, 20; Gary N. Powell and Laura M. Graves, *Women and Men in Management* (Thousand Oaks, CA: Sage, 2003), 3, 25.

18. Lisa Belkin, "The Opt Out Revolution," *New York Times Magazine*, October 26, 2003, 42.

19. Lucy Freeman, "The Feminine Mystique," *New York Times*, April 7, 1963, 46.

20. Belkin, "The Opt Out Revolution," 42.

21. Sylvia Ann Hewlett and Carolyn Buck Luce, "Off-Ramps and On-Ramps: Keeping Talented Women on the Road to Success," *Harvard Business Review*, March 2005, 43–45.

22. Findings range from 12 to 75 percent. Compare Nachum Sicherman, "Gender Differences in Departures from a Large Firm," *Industrial and Labor Relations Review* 49 (1996): 493, with Monica McGrath, Marla Driscoll, and Mary Gross, *Back in the Game: Returning to Business After a Hiatus: Experience and Recommendations for Women, Employers, and Universities* (Philadelphia: Wharton Center for Leadership and Change and the Forte Foundation, 2005), 7. However, a consistent finding is that far fewer men report this concern.

23. Claudia Wallis, "The Case for Staying Home," *Time*, March 22, 2004, 51, 53.

24. Hewlett and Luce, "Off-Ramps and On-Ramps," 45–47.

25. International Labor Organization, *Breaking Through the Glass Ceiling*; Foroohar, "Myth and Reality."

26. International Labor Organization, *Breaking Through the Glass Ceiling*, 47.

27. Celinda Lake and Kellyanne Conway with Catherine Whitney, *What Women Really Want* (New York: Free Press, 2005), 87.

28. In the study by the Center for Work-Life Policy, only a third of women, compared with over half of men, described themselves as "extremely" or "very" ambitious. Sylvia Ann Hewlett, Carolyn Buck Luce, Peggy Shiller, and Sandra Southwell, *The Hidden Brain Drain: Off-Ramps and On-Ramps* (New York: Center for Work-Life Policy, 2005), 4. In a survey of senior executives in multilateral corporations, 19 percent of men, compared with 9 percent of women, wanted the CEO position: "Helping Women Get to the Top," *Economist*, July 23, 2004, 11. See also Patricia Sellers, "Power: Do Women Really Want It?" *Fortune*, October 13, 2003, reporting a finding that women had lower career aspirations than similarly situated men. By contrast, a Catalyst study found no such differences in the desire for the chief executive slot. Joan S. Lublen, "Women Aspire to be Chief as Much as Men," *Wall Street Journal*, June 23, 2004, D2; Catalyst, *Women and Men in United States Corporations: Same Workforce, Different Realities* (New York: Catalyst, 2004). Richard Fox takes up the issue of women's lesser political ambitions in Chapter Eight of this volume, but for a study finding that women elected to state legislative office have ambitions similar to those of their male colleagues, see Center for American Women and Politics, *Women in State Legislatures: Past, Present, Future* (Rutgers, NJ: Center for American Women and Politics; Eagleton Institute of Politics, 2001), 1–2.

29. Linda Babcock and Sara Laschever, *Women Don't Ask: Negotiation and the Gender Divide* (Princeton, NJ: Princeton University Press, 2003), 1–11.

30. International Labor Organization, *Breaking Through the Glass Ceiling*, 47.
31. Catalyst, *Women and Men in United States Corporations*, 3; "Empowering Women in Business," n.d., Feminist Majority Foundation, available online: www.feminist.org/research/business/ewb_myths.html, access date: December 10, 2006.
32. The study involved academics twelve years after receipt of their Ph.D.'s. Mary Ann Mason and Marc Goulden, "Marriage and Baby Blues: Redefining Gender Equity in the Academy," *Annals of the American Academy* 596 (2004): 86, 92.
33. Peter Glick and Susan Fisk, et al., "Ambivalent Sexism," in Mark P. Zanna, ed., *Advances in Experimental Social Psychology*, 33 (Thousand Oaks, CA: Academic Press, 1999), 115–118.
34. Michael Robert Dennis and Adrianne Dennis Kunkel, "Perceptions of Men, Women, and CEOs: The Effects of Gender Identity," *Social Behavior and Personality* 32 (2004): 155, 166–168; Alice H. Eagly, "Achieving Relational Authenticity in Leadership: Does Gender Matter?" *Leadership Quarterly* 16 (2005): 459, 469. See also Sabine C. Koch, Rebecca Luft, and Lenelis Kruse, "Women and Leadership—20 Years Later: A Semantic Connotation Study," *Social Science Information* 44 (2005): 9, finding decline in association between men and leadership.
35. Eagly, "Achieving Relational Authenticity in Leadership," 469; Alice H. Eagly, Mary C. Johannesen-Schmidt, and Marloes van Engen, "Transformational, Transactional, and Laissez-Faire Leadership Styles: A Meta-analysis Comparing Women and Men," *Psychological Bulletin* 129 (2003): 569; John David Yoder, "Making Leadership Work More Effectively for Women," *Journal of Social Issues* 57 (2001): 815; Cristina Trinidad and Anthony H. Normore, "Leadership and Gender: A Dangerous Liaison?" *Leadership and Organization Development Journal* 26 (2005): 574, 583. This point is frequently made in trade publications; see Esther Wachs Book, *Why the Best Man for the Job Is a Woman: The Unique Female Qualities of Leadership* (New York: Harper Business, 2000).

36. Catalyst, *Women Take Care, Men Take Charge: Stereotyping of Business Leaders* (New York: Catalyst, 2005).
37. Laurie A. Rudman and Stephen E. Kilianski, "Implicit and Explicit Attitudes Toward Female Authority," *Personality and Social Psychology Bulletin 26* (2000): 1315.
38. Alice Eagly and Steven Karau, "Role Congruity Theory of Prejudice Toward Female Leaders," *Psychology Review 109* (2002): 574; Dawn L. Brooks and Lynn M. Brooks, *Seven Secrets of Successful Women* (New York: McGraw-Hill, 1997), 195; Eagly, "Achieving Relational Authenticity in Leadership," 470; Babcock and Laschever, *Women Don't Ask*, 87–88.
39. Neela Banerjee, "The Media Business: Some 'Bullies' Seek Ways to Soften Up: Toughness Has Risks for Women Executives," *New York Times*, August 10, 2001, C1.
40. Anthony Butterfield and James P. Grinnell, "Reviewing Gender Leadership and Managerial Behavior: Do the Decades of Research Tell Us Anything?" in Powell, *Handbook of Gender and Work*, 223, 235; Alice H. Eagly, Mona G. Makhijani, and Bruce G. Klonsky, "Gender and the Evaluation of Leaders," *Psychological Bulletin 111* (1992): 17; Jeanette N. Cleveland, Margaret Stockdale, and Kevin R. Murphy, *Women and Men in Organizations: Sex and Gender Issues at Work* (Mawah, NJ: Erlbaum, 2000), 106, 107; Rochelle Sharpe, "As Leaders, Women Rule: New Studies Find That Female Managers Outshine Their Male Counterparts in Almost Every Measure," *BusinessWeek Online*, November 20, 2000, available online: www.businessweek.com, access date: December 10, 2006.
41. Amy J. C. Cuddy, Susan T. Fiske, and Peter Glick, "When Professionals Become Mothers, Warmth Doesn't Cut the Ice," *Journal of Social Issues 60* (2004): 701, 709; Kathleen Fuegen, Monica Biernat, Elizabeth Haines, and Kay Deaux, "Mothers and Fathers in the Workplace: How Gender and Parental Status Influence Judgments of Job-Related Competence," *Journal of Social Issues 60* (2004): 737, 745; Claire Etaugh and Denise Folger, "Perceptions of Parents Whose Work and Parenting

Behaviors Deviate from Role Expectations," *Sex Roles* 39 (1998): 215.

42. Eagly and Karau, "Role Congruity Theory of Prejudice Toward Female Leaders," 111.

43. Babcock and Laschever, *Women Don't Ask*, 94; Rhea Steinpreis, Kathleen Sanders, and D. Ritzke, "The Impact of Gender on the Review of the Curriculum Vitae of Job Applicants and Tenure Candidates: A National Empirical Study," *Sex Roles* 4 (1999): 509.

44. Catalyst, *Women in Corporate Leadership: Progress and Prospects* (New York: Catalyst, 1996), 37. See also International Labor Organization, *Breaking Through the Glass Ceiling*, at 4 (discussing role of stereotypes).

45. "A Woman for President," CBS *New York Times* Poll, February 5, 2006. For obstacles to women in politics, see Ruth Mandel and Kim Fridkin Kahn, *The Political Consequences of Being a Woman* (New York: Columbia University Press, 1996); and Susan J. Carroll, ed., *Women and American Politics: New Questions, New Directions* (New York: Oxford University Press, 2003).

46. See International Labor Organization, *Breaking Through the Glass Ceiling*, 2, 24, 58–59; Hayward, *Women Leading*, 152–158.

47. Babcock and Laschever, *Women Don't Ask*, 88; Carol Hymowitz, "Through the Glass Ceiling," *Wall Street Journal*, November 8, 2004, R1. That point is widely acknowledged in trade publications featuring advice for aspiring women leaders. See Donna L. Brooks and Lynn M. Brooks, *Seven Secrets of Successful Women* (New York: McGraw-Hill, 1997), 63–65, 147–153; Gail Evans, *Play Like a Man, Win Like a Woman: What Men Know About Success That Women Need to Learn* (New York: Broadway, 2000), 68–87.

48. Babcock and Laschever, *Women Don't Ask*, 1–11, 41–44.

49. Melvin J. Lerner, *The Belief in a Just World* (New York: Plenum Press, 1980), vii–viii; Virginia Valian, "The Cognitive Basis of Gender Bias," *Brooklyn Law Review* 65 (1999): 1059.

50. Deborah L. Rhode, *Balanced Lives: Changing the Culture of Legal Workplaces* (Chicago: American Bar Association Commission on Women in the Profession, 2002), 16; Linda Krieger, "The Content of Our Categories: A Cognitive Bias Approach to Discrimination and Equal Employment Opportunity," *Stanford Law Review* 47 (1995): 34.

51. Sheila Wellington, Marcia Brumit Kropf, and Paulette Gerkovich, "What's Holding Women Back," *Harvard Business Review*, June 2003, 18; International Labor Organization, *Breaking Through the Glass Ceiling*, 57.

52. Valian, "The Cognitive Basis of Gender Bias," 1048–1049.

53. Marilyn B. Brewer and Rupert J. Brown, "Intergroup Relations," in Daniel T. Gilbert, Susan T. Fiske, and Gardner Lindzey, eds., *The Handbook of Social Psychology* (New York: McGraw-Hill, 1998), 554–594; Susan T. Fiske, "Stereotyping, Prejudice and Discrimination," in Gilbert et al., eds., *Handbook of Social Psychology*, 357–414; Barbara Reskin, "Rethinking Employment Discrimination and Its Remedies," in Mauro Guillen et al., eds., *The New Economic Sociology: Developments in an Emerging Field* (New York: Russell Sage, 2000), 218–244; Laura M. Graves, "Gender Bias in Interviewers' Evaluations of Applicants," in Powell, *Gender and Work*, 145, 154–155.

54. Jennifer Crocker, Brenda Major, and Claude Steel, "Social Stigma," in Gilbert et al., eds., *Handbook of Social Psychology*, 504–553; John F. Dovidio and Samuel L. Gaertner, "Stereotypes and Evaluative Intergroup Bias," in Diane M. Mackie and David L. Hamilton, eds., *Affect, Cognition, and Stereotyping* (San Diego: Academic Press, 1993), 167–193; Martha Foschi, "Double Standards for Competence: Theory and Research," *Annual Review of Sociology* 26 (2000): 21–42; Krieger, "The Content of Our Categories," 1161–1248; Cecilia L. Ridgeway, "Interaction and the Conservation of Gender Inequality: Considering Employment," *Contemporary Sociology* 62 (1997): 218.

55. Martha Foschi, "Double Standards in the Evaluation of Men and Women," *Social Psychology* 59 (1996): 237; Jacqueline Landau, "The Relationship of Race and Gender to Managers' Rating of Promotion Potential," *Journal Organizational Behavior* 16 (1995): 391.

56. Lin Coughlin, "The Time Is Now: A Leaders' Personal Journey," in Lin Coughlin, ed., *Enlightened Power: How Women Are Transforming the Practice of Leadership* (San Francisco: Jossey-Bass, 2005), 1, 8.

57. Valian, "The Cognitive Basis of Gender Bias," 1050; Deborah L. Rhode, "The Difference 'Difference' Makes," in *The Difference "Difference" Makes: Women and Leadership* (Stanford, CA: Stanford University Press, 2003), 9.

58. Virginia Valian, *Why So Slow? The Advancement of Women* (Cambridge: MIT Press, 1999), 39–40; Galen V. Bodenhausen, C. Neil Macrae, and Jennifer Garst, "Stereotypes in Thought and Deed: Social Cognitive Origins of Intergroup Discrimination," in Constantine Sedikides, J. Schopler, and C. A. Insko, eds., *Intergroup Cognition and Intergroup Behavior* (Mahwah, NJ: Erlbaum, 1998); Robin Ely, "The Power in Demography: Women's Social Construction of Gender Identity at Work," *Academy of Management Journal* 38 (1995): 589–634.

59. Monica Biernat and Diane Kobrynowicz, "Gender and Race-Based Standards of Competence: Lower Minimum Standards but Higher Ability Standards for Devalued Groups," *Journal of Personality and Social Psychology* 72 (1997): 555; Madeline Heilman, "Description and Prescription: How Gender Stereotypes Prevent Women's Ascent Up the Organizational Ladder," *Journal of Social Issues* 57 (2001): 666; Madeline Heilman et al., "The Vagaries of Sex Bias," *Organizational Behavior and Human Decision Processes* 41 (1998): 98–99.

60. Alessandra Stanley, "For Women, to Soar Is Rare: To Fail Is Human," *New York Times,* July 13, 2004, E1; David Carr, "To Reach the Heights, First Be Male," *New York Times,* January 9,

2005, C1; Kephart and Schumacher, "Has the 'Glass Ceiling' Cracked?" 9.

61. Rhode, "The Difference 'Difference' Makes," 12. Ida O. Abbott, *The Lawyers' Guide to Mentoring* (Washington, DC: NALP, 2000); Belle Rose Ragins, "Gender and Mentoring Relationships: A Review and Research Agenda for the Next Decade," in Powell, *Handbook of Gender and Work*, 347, 350–362; Catalyst, *Women in Corporate Leadership*; Timothy O'Brien, "Up the Down Staircase," *New York Times*, March 19, 2006, A4.

62. Ella L. J. Edmondson Bell and Stella M. Nkomo, *Our Separate Ways: Black Women and the Struggle for Professional Identity* (Boston: Harvard Business School Press, 2001), 123–132; Bernardo M. Feldman, "The Color and Culture of Gender in Organizations: Attending to Race and Ethnicity," in Powell, *Handbook of Gender and Work*, 17, 18–26; Catalyst, *Women of Color in Corporate Management: Dynamics of Career Advancement* (New York: Catalyst, 1999), 15; David Wilkins and G. Mitu Gulati, "Why Are There So Few Black Law Firms: An Institutional Analysis," *University of California Law Review* 84 (1996): 493; Deborah L. Rhode, *The Unfinished Agenda: Women and the Legal Profession* (Chicago: ABA Commission on Women and the Profession, 2001), 16.

63. Catalyst, *Women of Color* (New York: Catalyst, 2000), 13; Catalyst, *Women in Corporate Leadership*, 37.

64. American Bar Association Commission on Women in the Profession, *Visible Invisibility: Women of Color in Law Firms* (Chicago: ABA Commission on Women and the Profession, 2006).

65. For the United States, see O'Brien, "Up the Down Staircase," A4; Abbott, *The Lawyers' Guide to Mentoring*; Catalyst, *Women in Law* (New York: Catalyst, 2001); National Association for Law Placement, *The Lateral Lawyer: Why They Leave and What Makes Them Stay* (Washington, DC: NALP, 2000), 4. For international data, see International Labor Organization, *Breaking*

Through the Glass Ceiling, 20–28, and Accenture, *The Anatomy of the Glass Ceiling.*

66. Ragins, "Gender and Mentoring Relationships," 361–363.

67. Bureau of Labor Statistics, *American Time Use Survey* (Washington, DC: Bureau of Labor Statistics 2004), n.p.; Donald G. McNeil, "Real Men Don't Clean Bathrooms," *New York Times,* September 19, 2004, E3.

68. Sylvia Ann Hewlett, *High-Achieving Women* (New York: Center for Work-Life Policy, 2001); Sylvia Hewlett, *Creating a Life: Professional Women and the Quest for Children* (New York: Talk Miramax Books, 2002), 143.

69. Pamela Stone and Meg Lovejoy, "Fast-Track Women and the 'Choice' to Stay Home," *Annals of the American Academy of Political and Social Science* 596 (2004): 62, 66.

70. Joan Williams, *Unbending Gender: Why Family and Work Conflict and What to Do About It* (New York: Oxford University Press, 2000), 71.

71. Mark Williams, "So Where Are the Corporate Husbands?" *New York Times,* June 24, 2001.

72. Sylvia Ann Hewlett, Carolyn Buck Luce, and Cornell West, "Leadership in Your Midst: Tapping the Hidden Strength of Minority Executives," *Harvard Business Review,* November 2005, 74, 79.

73. Cameron Stracher, "All Aboard the Mommy Track," *American Lawyer,* March 1999, 126; Meredith K. Wadman, "Family and Work," *Washington Lawyer,* November/December 1998, 33; Abbie F. Willard and Paula A. Patton, *Perceptions of Partnership: The Allure and Accessibility of the Brass Ring* (Washington, DC: NALP, 1999); Cynthia Fuchs Epstein, Robert Saute, Bonnie Oglensky, and Martha Gever, "Glass Ceilings and Open Doors: Women's Advancement in the Legal Profession," *Fordham Legal Review* 64, no. 2 (1995): 306, 391–399.

74. Rhode, "The Difference 'Difference' Makes," 15; Martha Burke, *Cult of Power* (New York: Scribner, 2005), 271.

75. See Foroohar, "Myth and Reality." For discussion of Scandinavian leave policies, see Susan Mayne, *Employment Law in Europe* (Oxford, UK: Butterworth-Heinemann 2001); Mark Landler, "Quoth the Raven: I Bake Cookies, Too," *New York Times*, April 23, 2005, E5; Elina Pylkkanen and Nina Smith, *Career Interruptions Due to Parental Leave: A Comparative Study of Denmark and Sweden* (Paris, France: OECD, March 2003).

76. Sheila Wellington and Catalyst, *Be Your Own Mentor* (New York: Random House, 2001), 110.

77. Juliet B. Schor, *The Overworked American: The Unexpected Decline of Leisure* (New York: Basic Books, 1992), 1–5, 79–82.

78. Wallis, "The Case for Staying Home," 52; Williams, *Unbending Gender*, 71; Arlie Russell Hochschild, *The Time Bind: When Work Becomes Home and Home Becomes Work* (New York: Henry Holt, 1997), 70.

79. Wallis, "The Case for Staying Home," 52; Williams, *Unbending Gender*, 71; Hochschild, *The Time Bind*, 70; Patricia Sellers, "It's Good to Be the Boss," *Fortune*, October 16, 2006, 137 (quoting CEO Indra Nooyi, "balance . . . is for the birds").

80. Patrick McGeehan, "Wall Street High Flier to Outcast: A Woman's Story," *New York Times*, February 10, 2002, 1 (quoting Allison Schieffelin). See John Birger, "The Outsider," *Fortune*, October 16, 2006, 170 (quoting CEO Patricia Woertz, who was once advised by a supervisor not to have children: "Get yourself fixed and expense it").

81. Hewlett, Luce, and West, "Leadership in Your Midst," 77.

82. Patton, "Women Lawyers," 173, 189.

83. Ann Crittenden, *The Price of Motherhood: Why the Most Important Job in the World Is Still the Least Valued* (New York: Metropolitan/Owl Books, 2001), 96; see also Cynthia Fuchs Epstein, Carroll Seron, Bonnie Oglenski, and Robert Saute, *Part-Time Paradox* (New York: Routledge, 1999).

84. For the United States, see Hewlett and Luce, "Off-Ramps and On-Ramps," 45; Kephart and Schumacher, "Has the 'Glass

Ceiling' Cracked?" 10; Jenny Anderson, "The Fork in the Road: Can Women and Wall Street Work Together?" *New York Times*, August 6, 2006, Section 3, 1. For international patterns see Foroohar, "Myth and Reality."

85. Hewlett and Luce, "Off-Ramps and On-Ramps," 45; Kephart and Schumacher, "Has the 'Glass Ceiling' Cracked?" 10.

86. Marc Mory and Lia Pistilli, "The Failure of the Family and Medical Leave Act: Alternative Proposals for Contemporary American Families," *Hofstra Labor and Employment Law Journal 18* (2001): 689.

87. Title VII of the Civil Rights Act of 1964, 42 U.S.C. §§ 2002–2.

88. Deborah L. Rhode and Joan Williams, "Legal Perspectives on Employment Discrimination," in Faye J. Crosby, Margaret S. Stockdale, and Ann S. Rupp, eds. *Sex Discrimination in the Workplace: An Interdisciplinary Approach* (London: Blackwell, 2007); Brenda Major and Cheryl Kaiser, "Perceiving and Claiming Discrimination," in Laura Nielsen and Robert Nelson, eds., *The Handbook on Employment Discrimination Research: Rights and Realities* (The Netherlands: Springer, 2005); K. A. Dixon, Duke Storen, and Carl E. Van Horn, *A Workplace Divided: How Americans View Discrimination and Race on the Job* (New Jersey: John J. Heldrich Center for Workplace Development, Rutgers University, 2002), 15.

89. Foroohar, "Myth and Reality"; International Labor Organization, *Breaking Through the Glass Ceiling*.

90. *Riordan v. Kaminers*, 831 F. 2d 690, 697 (7th Cir. 1987); Rhode and Williams, "Legal Perspectives on Employment Discrimination."

91. Patrick McGeehan, "Discrimination on Wall Street? Run the Numbers and Weep," *New York Times*, July 14, 2004, C1; Patrick McGeehan, "Morgan Stanley Settles Bias Suit with $54 Million," *New York Times*, July 13, 2004, A1.

92. McGeehan, "Wall Street High Flier to Outcast," C1; Reed Abelson, "If Wall Street Is Dead End, Do Women Stay to Fight or Go Quietly?" *New York Times*, August 3, 1999, C1.

93. Catalyst, *The Bottom Line: Connecting Corporate Performance and Gender Diversity* (New York: Catalyst, 2004); "The Special Report: Women in Business," *Economist*, July 23, 2005, 64; Cleveland, Stockdale, and Murphy, *Women and Men in Organizations*, 363; Business and Professional Women's Foundation and American Management Association, "Compensation and Benefits: A Focus on Gender" (New York: American Management Association, 1999); Susan Stites-Doe and James J. Cordiro, "The Impact of Women Managers on Firm Performance: Evidence from Large U.S. Firms," *International Review of Women and Leadership*, July 1997.

94. Hewlett and Luce, "Off-Ramps and On-Ramps," 54; Catalyst, *Women in Corporate Leadership*, 70 (reporting survey in which 98 percent of senior executive women cited demographic reasons to support initiatives aimed at women's advancement). Catalyst, *Women in Corporate Management*; Robin Ely and David Thomas, "Making Differences Matter: A New Paradigm for Managing Diversity," *Harvard Business Review*, September-October 1996, 79.

95. Williams, *Unbending Gender*, 71–73; Boston Bar Association, "Facing the Grail: Confronting the Cost of Work-Family Imbalance," 1999, 39, available online: www.bostonbar.org/prs/workfamilychallenges.htm, access date: December 10, 2006; Catalyst, *A New Approach to Flexibility: Managing the Work-Time Equation* (New York: Catalyst, 1997), 20–21.

96. Alliance for Board Diversity, *Women and Minorities on Fortune 500 Boards* (New York: Alliance for Board Diversity, 2005); Catalyst, *Women in Corporate Management*; Ely and Thomas, "Making Differences Matter," 79.

97. For the United States, see Alice H. Eagly and Wendy Wood, "Explaining Sex Differences in Social Behavior: A Meta-Analytic Perspective," *Personality and Social Psychology Bulletin* 17 (1991): 306; Alice H. Eagly and Blair T. Johnson, "Gender and Leadership Style: A Meta-Analysis," *Psychology Bulletin* 108 (1990): 233; Eagly, Makhijani, and Klonsky, "Gender and

the Evaluation of Leaders"; Alice H. Eagly, Steven J. Karau, and Mona G. Makhijani, "Gender and the Effectiveness of Leaders: A Meta-Analysis," *Psychological Bulletin 117* (1995): 125–145. For international contexts, see Nancy J. Adler, "Global Leaders: Women of Influence," in Powell, *Handbook of Gender and Work*, 239, 253.

98. Betsy Wangensteen, "Managing Style: What's Gender Got to Do With It?" *Crain's New York Business*, September 29, 1997, 23; Terry Carter, "Paths Need Paving," *American Bar Association Journal*, September 2004, 34; see also Jean Lipman-Blumen, "Connective Leadership: Female Leadership Styles in the 21st Century Workplace," *Social Perspectives 35* (1992): 183, 200–201; Judy Wajcman, *Managing Like a Man: Women and Men in Corporate Management* (University Park: Pennsylvania State University Press, 1998), 66.

99. Cleveland, Stockdale, and Murphy, "Gender and Leadership," in Jeanette N. Cleveland, Margaret Stockdale, Babara A. Gutek, and Kevin R. Murphy, *Women and Men in Organizations: Sex and Gender Issues at Work* (Mahwah, NJ: Erlbaum, 2000), 307; Eagly and Johnson, "Gender and Leadership Style," 233–256; Eagly, Karau, and Makhijani, "Gender and the Effectiveness of Leaders," 125–145; Robert I. Kabacoff, "Gender Differences in Organizational Leadership: A Large Sample Study," paper presented at the American Psychological Association Convention, San Francisco, 1998.

100. Gary N. Powell, *Women and Men in Management* (New York: Sage, 1988), 45–49, 105–109; Karin Klenke, *Women and Leadership: A Contextual Perspective* (New York: Springer, 1996), 160; Kabacoff, "Gender Differences in Organizational Leadership" (finding no difference in task orientation); Gary N. Powell, "One More Time: Do Female and Male Managers Differ?" *Academy of Management Executive 4* (1990): 68; Eagly and Johnson, "Gender and Leadership Style," 246–247; Cheryl Simrell King, "Sex Role Identity and Decision Styles: How Gender Helps Explain the Paucity of Women at the

Top," in Georgia Duerst-Lahti and Rita Mae Kelly, eds., *Gender Power, Leadership, and Governance* (Ann Arbor: University of Michigan Press, 1995), 67–92. See Mats Alvesson and Yvonne D. Billing, *Understanding Gender in Organizations* (New York: Sage, 1998), 146, 151; Linda Molm and Mark Hedley, "Gender, Power and Social Exchange," in Cecilia L. Ridgeway, ed., *Gender, Interaction and Inequality* (New York: Springer, 1992), 8; Marilyn J. Davidson and Ronald J. Burke, eds., *Women in Management Current Research Issues* (Vol. 2), (London: Sage 2000); Tiffany Manual, Susan Shefte, and Deborah J. Swiss, *Suiting Themselves: Women's Leadership Styles in Today's Workplace* (Cambridge, MA: Radcliffe Public Policy Institute and The Boston Club, 1999).

101. Brian S. Moskal, "Women Make Better Managers," *Industry Week*, February 3, 1997, 17; Sharpe, "As Leaders, Women Rule."

102. Cleveland, Stockdale, and Murphy, *Women and Men in Organizations*, 293–299; Barbara Kellerman, *Reinventing Leadership: Making the Connection Between Politics and Business* (Albany: State University of New York Press, 1999), 149. See also Lipman-Blumen, "Connective Leadership," 183–201.

103. Catalyst, *Women in Corporate Leadership*.

104. Theresa M. Beiner, "What Will Diversity on the Bench Mean for Justice?" *Michigan Journal of Gender and Law* 6 (1999): 113 (suggesting some differences on civil rights suits); Sue Davis, Susan Haire, and Donald R. Songer, "Voting Behavior and Gender on the U.S. Court of Appeals," *Judicature* 77 (1993): 129 (finding some differences in employment discrimination and search and seizure cases but not obscenity cases); Jennifer L. Peresie, "Female Judges Matter: Gender and Collegial Decisionmaking in the Federal Appellate Courts," *Yale Law Journal* 114 (2005): 1759, 1776, 1778 (finding female appellate judges more willing to rule for plaintiffs in sex harassment and sex discrimination cases after controlling for factors such as ideology, race, and prior employment); Elaine Martin and

Barry Pyle, "State High Courts and Divorce: The Impact of Judicial Gender," *University of Toledo Law Review* 36 (2005): 923 (finding that women judges were more supportive of women in divorce cases after controlling for party affiliations); Jennifer A. Segal, "Representative Decision Making on the Federal Bench, Clinton's District Court Appointees," *Policy Research Quarterly* 53 (2000): 137, 142–146 (finding few gender differences but noting that male judges were somewhat more supportive of women's issues than female judges); Donald Songer et al., "A Reappraisal of Diversification in Federal Courts: Gender Effects in the Court of Appeal," *Journal of Politics* 56 (1994): 425 (finding some gender differences in sex discrimination cases but concluding that most studies find few if any differences in appellate rulings). For overviews of such studies, see Theresa Beiner, "Female Judging," *University of Toledo Law Review* 36 (2005): 821–829; Fred O. Smith Jr., "Gendered Justice: Do Male and Female Judges Rule Differently on Questions of Gay Rights?" *Stanford Law Review* 57 (2005): 2087, 2089–2091 (finding difference on gay rights issues).

105. Rhode, "The Difference 'Difference' Makes."

106. Martha Burk, "The 40 Percent Rule," *Ms.*, Summer (2006), 57 (25 percent for the Fortune 500 and 33 percent for the 500–1000).

107. Karen L. Tamerius, "Sex, Gender, and Leadership in the Representation of Women," in Georgia Duerst-Lahti and Rita Mae Kelly, eds., *Gender Power, Leadership, and Governance* (Ann Arbor: University of Michigan Press, 1996), 93, 108; Sue Thomas, *How Women Legislate* (New York: Oxford University Press, 1994), 92; Michele Swers and Amy Caizza, "Transforming the Political Agenda? Gender Differences in Bill Sponsorship on Women's Issues," reprinted in Institute for Women's Policy Research, *Research-in-Brief* (October 2000): 1; Julie Dolan, "Support for Women's Interests in the 103rd Congress: The Distinct Impact of Congressional Women,"

Women and Politics 18 (1997): 81; Susan J. Carroll, "The Politics of Difference: Women Public Officials as Agents of Change," *Stanford Law and Policy Review* 5 (1994): 11; Ruth B. Mandel and Debra L. Dodson, "Do Women Officeholders Make a Difference?" in Paula Ries and Ann J. Stone, eds., *The American Women 1992–1993: A Status Report* (New York: Norton, 1992); Sue Thomas, "Women in State Legislatures: One Step at a Time" in Elizabeth Adell Cook, Sue Thomas, and Clyde Wilcox, eds., *The Year of the Woman: Myths and Realities* (Boulder, CO: Westview Press, 1996), 141–60; Susan J. Carroll, ed., *The Impact of Women in Public Office: An Overview* (Indianapolis: Indiana University Press, 2001), 5.

108. Tyler Bridges, "In Americas, Women Rising to the Top Jobs," *Miami Herald*, March 3, 2006, A1.

109. Dolan, "Support for Women's Interests in the 103rd Congress," 86–89; Swers and Caizza, "Transforming the Political Agenda?" 4; Susan Gluck Mezey, "Increasing the Numbers of Women in Office: Does It Matter?" in Cook, Thomas, and Wilcox, *The Year of the Woman*, 255–270; Tamerius, "Sex, Gender, and Leadership," 107.

110. Tamerius, "Sex, Gender, and Leadership," 107; Center for American Women in Politics, "The Impact of Women in Public Office," 14.

111. Barbara Mikulski, Barbara Boxer, Susan Collins, et al., *Nine and Counting: The Women of the Senate* (New York: Perennial, 2001), 102 (quoting Boxer). A recent case in point involves Angela Merkel, who avoided women's issues for much of her campaign to become Germany's first woman chancellor. See Shada Islam, "They Are Women, Hear Them Roar," *Business Times* (Singapore), October 19, 2005, Views and Opinions, 1.

112. For academia, see Nannerl Keohane's "Women's Initiative" at Duke, which brought substantial improvements for faculty, staff, and students, as did Shirley Tilghman's work-family policies initiatives at Princeton. Jane Stancill, "Keohane's Last Goal Unsettled: Women's Initiative Facing New Leaders,"

News & Observer (Raleigh, North Carolina), June 27, 2004, A1; John Hechinger, "The Tiger Roars: Under Tilghman, Princeton Adds Students, Battles Suit, Takes on Eating Clubs," *Wall Street Journal,* July 17, 2006, B1; Patricia Valdata, "The Ticking of the Biological and Tenure Clocks: Princeton University Institutes New Policy, Placing the School at the Forefront of Family Friendly Workplaces," *Diverse Issues in Higher Education 44* (November 17, 2005): 34. For gender initiatives in law firms, see Katherine Bartlett and Deborah L. Rhode, *Gender and Law: Theory, Doctrine, and Commentary* (Boston: Aspen Press, 2006).

113. Susan Nossel and Elizabeth Westfall, *Presumed Equal: What America's Top Women Lawyers Really Think About Their Firms,* 2nd ed. (Franklin Lakes, NJ: Career Press, 1998), 30, 187, 261, 266–67, 349, 365; Joanne Martin and Debra Meyerson, "Women and Power: Conformity, Resistance, and Disorganized Co-action," in Roderick Kramer and Margaret Neale, eds., *Power and Influence in Organizations* (New York: Sage, 1998), 340; Susan J. Ashford, "Championing Charged Issues: The Case of Gender Equity Within Organizations," in Kramer and Neale, eds., *Power and Influence in Organizations,* 349, 375–376.

114. Eagly and Wood, "Explaining Sex Differences in Social Behavior," 306; Eagly and Johnson, "Gender and Leadership Style," 233; Eagly, Makhijani, and Klonsky, "Gender and the Evaluation of Leaders"; Eagly, Karau, and Makhijani, "Gender and the Effectiveness of Leaders."

115. Constance H. Buchanon, *Choosing to Lead* (Boston: Beacon Press, 1996), 213.

116. Wangensteen, "Managing Style," 23; Carter, "Paths Need Paving," 34. See also Lipman-Blumen, "Connective Leadership"; Wajcman, *Managing Like a Man,* 66.

117. Nossel and Westfall, *Presumed Equal,* 126, 261, 277.

118. Ashford, "Championing Charged Issues," 365–366; Rhode, "The Difference 'Difference' Makes," 24.

119. Ashford, "Championing Charged Issues," 369–370, 375. See also Nossel and Westfall, *Presumed Equal*, at 105, 108; Amy H. Handlin, *Whatever Happened to the Year of the Woman: Why Women Still Aren't Making It to the Top* (Denver: Arden Press, 1998), 52.

120. Ashford, "Championing Charged Issues," 370, 375; see also Jennifer L. Pierce, *Gender Trials: Emotional Lives in Contemporary Law Firms* (Berkeley: University of California Press, 1995), 176–177; Nossel and Westfall, *Presumed Equal*, 50, 59, 105; Peter Glick and Susan T. Fiske, "Hostile and Benevolent Sexism," *Psychology of Women 21* (1997): 119, 129.

121. Mitu Gulati and Devon Carbado, "Race to the Top of the Corporate Ladder: What Minorities Do When They Get There," *Washington and Lee Law Review* 61 (2004): 1645, 1685.

122. Carol Gallagher, with Susan Gallant, *Going to the Top* (New York: Penguin, 2000), 9, 35–36; Margaret N. Ruderman and Patricia J. Ohlott, *Standing at the Crossroads: Next Steps for High-Achieving Women* (San Francisco: Jossey-Bass, 2002), 24–25.

123. Catalyst, *Women in Corporate Leadership*, 15; Rhode, "The Difference 'Difference' Makes," 33; Katherine Giscombe, *Making Change: Creating a Business Case for Diversity* (New York: Catalyst, 2002); Freeman, Bourque, and Shelton, *Leadership and Power*, 48.

124. Ruderman and Ohlott, *Standing at the Crossroads*, 23–24; Gallagher, *Going to the Top*, 153–155.

125. Catalyst, *Women and Men in United States Corporations*; Catalyst, *Women in Corporate Leadership*, 15, 21; Eleanor Clift and Tom Brazaitis, *Madame President* (New York: Routledge, 2003), 321, 324.

126. Rhode, "The Difference 'Difference' Makes," 34; Gallagher, *Going to the Top*, 153–154.

127. Klenke, *Women and Leadership*, 242–249; see Kellerman, *Reinventing Leadership*, 175–178; Minority Corporate Counsel

Association 2000 Survey of Fortune 500 Women General Counsel (Washington, DC: Minority Corporate Counsel Association, 2000).

128. Erin White, "Female Training Classes Flourish," *Wall Street Journal*, September 25, 2006, B3.

129. Peggy Klaus, "Good Girls Don't Brag, Do They?" in Coughlin, ed., *Enlightened Power*, 331; Evans, *Play Like a Man, Win Like a Woman*, 75; Carol Hymowitz, "Women Put Noses to the Grindstone, and Miss Opportunities," *Wall Street Journal*, February 3, 2004, B1. See generally Pat Heim, *Hardball for Women: Winning at the Game of Business* (New York: Penguin, 1992).

130. Abbott, *The Lawyers' Guide to Mentoring*; Rhode, "The Difference 'Difference' Makes," 29–30; Gallagher, *Going to the Top*, 164–175; Ruderman and Ohlott, *Standing at the Crossroads*, 59–68.

131. Gallagher, *Going to the Top*, 51.

132. Brooks and Brooks, *Seven Secrets of Successful Women*, 29. For discussion of men's comfort level, see Rosabeth Moss Kanter, *Men and Women of the Corporation* (New York: Basic Books, 1993), 41–42.

133. Dana Mattioli, "Programs to Promote Female Managers Win Citations," *Wall Street Journal*, January 30, 2007, B7; Gallagher, *Going to the Top*, 167; Cleveland, Stockdale, and Murphy, *Women and Men in Organizations*, 374; Catalyst, *Women in Corporate Leadership*, 29.

134. Gallagher, *Going to the Top*, 179.

135. Mattioli, "Programs to Promote Female Managers Win Citation," B7; Hewlett and Luce, "Off-Ramps and On-Ramps," 52–54; Ann Marie Chaker, "Business Schools Target At-Home Moms," *Wall Street Journal*, May 10, 2006, D1; Daniel McGinn, "Getting Back on Track," *Newsweek*, September 25, 2006, 62.

136. Linda Clark, *Leadership Essentials for Women* (Birmingham, AL: New Hope, 2004), 10.

137. Shoya Zichy, *Women and the Leadership Q* (New York: McGraw-Hill, 2001), xix, 9–10, 15, 28–29.

138. Brooks and Brooks, *Seven Secrets of Successful Women*, 7, 10.

139. Evans, *Play Like a Man, Win Like a Woman*, 121–132.

140. Brooks and Brooks, *Seven Secrets of Successful Women*, 137–147; Gallagher, *Going to the Top*, 187–195.

141. Lois P. Frankel, *Nice Girls Don't Get the Corner Office* (New York: Warner Business, 2004), 104.

142. Linkage, Incorporated's "Women in Leadership" Summit, November 6–9, 2005, in San Francisco featured film star Brooke Shields, journalist Charlayne Hunter-Gault, and Liz Murray, the subject of a television movie chronicling her transition from homelessness to Harvard. For tai chi weekends, see Sheryl Nance-Nash, "To Gain Ground, Female Execs Beat Retreats," Women's eNews, May 17, 2005, Available online: www.womensenews.org (by subscription).

143. Brooks and Brooks, *Seven Secrets of Successful Women*, 172.

144. Brooks and Brooks, *Seven Secrets of Successful Women*, 171–172.

145. Evans, *Play Like a Man, Win Like a Woman*, 56, 58, 59.

146. Frankel, *Nice Girls Don't Get the Corner Office*, 72.

147. Powell and Graves, *Women and Men in Management*, 39.

148. "CEO Barbie Criticized for Promoting Unrealistic Career Images," *Onion*, September 7, 2005.

149. Klenke, *Women and Leadership*, 173; Catalyst, "2005 Census," 34; Catalyst, *Advancing Women in Business* (New York: Wiley, 1998), 6, 12–13; Catalyst, *Women of Color in Corporate Management*, at 69; Mary C. Mattis, "Organizational Initiatives in the USA for Advancing Managerial Women," in Davidson and Burke, *Women in Management*, at 275.

150. Rhode, "The Difference 'Difference' Makes," 26–27, Barbara Reinhold, "Smashing Glass Ceilings: Why Women Still Find It Tough to Advance to the Executive Suite," *Journal of Organizational Excellence 24*, no. 3 (2005): 43–55, see 46–50; Sheila Wellington, Marcia Brumet Kropf, and Paulette R. Gerkovitch,

"What's Holding Women Back?" *Harvard Business Review*, June 2003, 18; Catalyst, *Advancing Women in Business*, 5–6, 11–12; Catalyst, *Women of Color in Corporate Management*, at 69–74; Cecilia L. Ridgeway and Shelley J. Correll, "Limiting Inequality Through Interaction: The End(s) of Gender," *Contemporary Sociology* 29 (2000): 118; Gary N. Powell, "Reflections on the Glass Ceiling: Recent Trends and Future Prospects," in Powell, *Handbook of Gender and Work*, 343.

151. Alexandra Kalev, Frank Dobbin, and Erin Kelly, "Best Practices or Best Guesses? Diversity Management and Remediation of Inequality" (unpublished paper, 2006), available online: http://rwj.berkeley.edu/akalev/papers/AAPractices041006.pdf, access date: March 6, 2007.

152. Thomas Adcock, "Persistent Problem: Women Lawyers Still Lag Far Behind Their Peers in Other Professions When It Comes to Making Partner, Report Finds," *New York Law Journal*, February 10, 1005, A1 (quoting Wellington); see also Hewlett, Luce, and West, "Leadership in Your Midst," 80.

153. Wajcman, *Managing Like a Man*, at 99.

154. Wellington, Kropf, and Gerkovich, "What's Holding Women Back?"; Reinhold, "Smashing Glass Ceilings," 46; Sandra Guy, "Most Corporations Don't Tell Diversity Data," December 30, 2005, available online: www.womensenews.org (by subscription).

155. Catalyst, *Advancing Women in Business*, at 6–7; International Labor Organization, *Breaking Through the Glass Ceiling*, 2, 6.

156. Catalyst, *Women of Color in Corporate Management*, at 32–33, 66; Mattis, "Organizational Initiatives," 275.

157. Ely and Thomas, "Making Differences Matter."

158. For positive effects on attitudes, see Kimberly D. Krawiec, "Cosmetic Compliance and the Failure of Negotiated Governance," *Washington University Law Quarterly* 81 (2003): 487. For backlash, see Mark Bendick Jr., Mary-Lou Egan, and Suzanne M. Lofthejelm, *The Documentation and Evaluation of*

Anti-Discrimination Training in the United States (Washington, DC: Bendick and Egan Economic Consultants, 1998); Thomas E. Nelson, Michele Acker, and Manis Melvin, "Irrepressible Stereotypes," *Journal of Experimental Social Psychology 32* (1996): 13; Kalev, Dobbin, and Kelly, "Best Practices or Best Guesses?" For outcomes, see Kalev, Dobbin, and Kelly, "Best Practices or Best Guesses?"

159. Kalev, Dobbin, and Kelly, "Best Practices or Best Guesses?"; Krawiec, "Cosmetic Compliance." See also Bar Association of San Francisco 1999 Interim Report: Goals and Timetables for Minority Hiring and Advancement (March 2000), 34–37; Ridgeway and Correll, "Limiting Inequality Through Interaction," at 118.

160. American Bar Association, Commission on Women in the Profession, *Fair Measure: Toward Effective Attorney Evaluations* (Chicago: Commission on Women in the Profession, American Bar Association, 1997), 9–24; Laura Graves, "Gender Bias in Interviewers' Evaluations of Applicants: When and How Does It Occur? in Powell, *Handbook of Gender and Work*, 145–155.

161. American Bar Association, Commission on Women in the Profession, *Lawyers and Balanced Lives: A Guide to Drafting and Implementing Workplace Policies for Lawyers* (Chicago: Commission on Women in the Profession, American Bar Association, 1990), 25; Catalyst, *A New Approach to Flexibility*; Boston Bar Association Task Force, "Facing the Grail."

162. Hewlett and Luce, "Off-Ramps and On-Ramps," 50–51; Wellington, Kropf, and Gerkovich, "What's Holding Women Back?" 18.

163. Hewlett and Luce, "Off-Ramps and On-Ramps," 51.

164. McGinn, "Getting Back on Track," 62–64; Mattioli, "Programs to Promote Female Managers," B7

165. Rhode, *Balanced Lives*, 15–16; 23–24; Powell, "Reflections on the Glass Ceiling," 341.

166. Cleveland, Stockdale, and Murphy, *Women and Men in Organizations*, at 374; Catalyst, *Women in Corporate Leadership*, at 29.
167. Catalyst, *Women in Corporate Leadership*, at 29; Abbott, *The Lawyers' Guide to Mentoring*, at 25, 32–33.
168. Kalev, Dobbin, and Kelly, "Best Practices or Best Guesses?"
169. Hewlett and Luce, "Off-Ramps and On-Ramps," 54; Catalyst, *Creating Women's Networks: A How-To Guide for Women and Companies* (New York: Catalyst, 1999), 5.
170. Gallagher, *Going to the Top*, 243–244; Hewlett, Luce, and West, "Leadership in Your Midst," 79, 81.
171. Kalev, Dobbin, and Kelly, "Best Practices or Best Guesses?"
172. Catalyst, *Creating Women's Networks*; Terry, "Marketing Groups Shape New Rainmakers," *Perspectives*, Fall 2000, 8; Hewlett, Luce, and West, "Leadership in Your Midst," 81; Sheryl Nance-Nash, "Wall Street Women: Forming Their Own Inside Circle," April 10, 2006, available online: www.womenesenews.org (by subscription); Mattioli, "Programs to Promote Female Managers," B7.
173. For discussion of small wins, see Debra E. Meyerson, "A Modest Manifesto for Shattering the Glass Ceiling," *Harvard Business Review*, January 1, 2000, 1.
174. Guy, "Most Corporations Don't Tell Diversity Data."
175. William T. Bielby, "Minimizing Workplace Gender and Racial Bias," *Contemporary Sociology* 29 (2000): 120; Susan Sturm, "Second Generation Employment Discrimination: A Structural Approach," *Columbia Law Review* 101 (2002): 458; Rhode and Williams, "Legal Perspectives on Employment Discrimination."
176. For discussion of the Australian legislation, see Kate Grosser and Jeremy Moon, "Gender Mainstreaming and Corporate Social Responsibility: Reporting Workplace Issues," *Journal of Business Ethics* 62 (2005): 327, 330.
177. See Kalev, Dobbin, and Kelly, "Best Practices or Best Guesses?" For the value of external oversight in ensuring internal com-

pliance structures, see Sturm, "Second Generation Employment Discrimination," 458. On successful EEOC interventions, see Nancy Kreiter, "Equal Employment Opportunity: EEOC and OFCCP," in Dianne M. Piché, William L. Taylor, and Robin A. Reed, eds., *Rights at Risk: Equality in an Age of Terrorism* (Washington, DC: Citizens' Commission on Civil Rights, 2002), 153–159, available online: www.cccr.org/Chapter12.pdf, access date: December 11, 2006.

178. International Labor Organization, *Breaking Through the Glass Ceiling*, 3; Foroohar, "Myth and Reality."

179. See E.U. Council Directive 96/34/EC, June 3, 1996 (on the framework agreement on parental leave); see also Crittenden, *The Price of Motherhood*. NGOs have emerged to support "use-it-or-lose-it" paternal leave for men. See, for example, "Modern Men in Enlarged Europe," http://www.dadcomehome.org/en/, access date: February 7, 2007.

180. For overviews, see International Labor Organization, *Breaking Through the Glass Ceiling*, 2–4; Foroohar, "Myth and Reality"; Landler, "Quoth the Raven," E5.

181. International Labor Organization, *Breaking Through the Glass Ceiling*, 25–26 (noting that 75 countries had such quotas).

182. For polling data, see Bartlett and Rhode, *Gender and Law*.

183. For an example, see the San Francisco Bar Association's "Glass Ceiling Initiative," described in Jane Di Renzo and Sharon Jones, *Walking the Talk: Creating a Law Firm Culture Where Women Succeed* (Chicago: American Bar Association, Commission on Women in the Profession, 2004).

184. Grosser and Moon, "Gender Mainstreaming and Corporate Social Responsibility," 333–335.

185. Grosser and Moon, "Gender Mainstreaming and Corporate Social Responsibility," 335.

186. *The Calvert Women's Principles: A Global Code of Conduct for Corporations* (Bethesda, Maryland: The Calvert Group, 2004).

187. For example, women account for about half of entering law school classes, but only 25.3 percent of full professors and 19 percent (34 of 179) of law school deans. See Association of American Law Schools, "Statistical Report on Law School Faculty and Candidates for Law Faculty Positions (2004–2005)."

188. Elinor Smith, quoted in Evans, *Play Like a Man, Win Like a Woman*, 35.

Part One

Gender Differences and Gender Stereotypes

1

CROSSING THE BRIDGE

Reflections on Women and Leadership

Nannerl O. Keohane

At the reunion of the class of 1961 at Wellesley last June, I took advantage of the presence of dozens of talented women who had experienced the world before Betty Friedan's book, reached maturity during second-wave feminism in the 1970s, and lived through several decades of women's liberation and post-feminism. These women have been engaged in life as writers and artists, scientists and heads of foundations, volunteers in their communities, mothers and grandmothers, citizens and observers of the world around them.

Around the breakfast table in the dormitory, standing in the line for the clambake and the annual parade, I asked my classmates a simple question: "Do women lead differently from men?" Every single one of them said yes. When I probed to ask what they meant, the answers centered on more collaborative behavior, concern for colleagues and subordinates, less competition for status. Four dozen members of the Wellesley Class of 1961 are hardly a representative sample of anything. But I found this experience thought provoking. Since I am agnostic on this question and would be hard-pressed to

For comments that proved helpful in revising this chapter, I am grateful to participants in the conference on Women and Leadership at Harvard, and especially to Barbara Kellerman and Deborah Rhode. A second version was presented to one of the luncheon seminars of the Center for Human Values at Princeton, and I thank those colleagues for their thoughtful questions and suggestions. I am grateful also to Robert O. Keohane for his comments on the final drafts.

give a simple answer, I was struck by the immediacy as well as the unanimity of the response.

In this chapter, with substantial help from Virginia Woolf, I explore some of the grounds for this widely held belief that women lead differently from men and its implications for women who hold power. Woolf's stimulating essays deserve to be more widely known. Her writings are delightful to read and ponder; it is a pleasure to learn from her and quote her insights. And although she seldom touched directly on women and leadership, her discussion of the transition women were making into the professions in her own time provides a fresh and subtle way to think about the topic.

In the pages that follow, I pose the puzzle that animates this chapter and identify some places where we might look for answers. Then I turn to Woolf for her insights and suggest ways we might build on those insights for a more nuanced understanding of women as leaders.

I first consider the contexts in which women have provided leadership across the centuries, and ask what is new today. I comment on the similarities between the belief that women have a different style of leadership and the obstacles that have kept women out of positions of authority in the past. Next, I provide a brief overview of some social science theories that provide grounds for assuming that women will lead differently, findings that would justify holding such an assumption, paying special attention to the concept of "feminist epistemology." Against that background, I turn to two works of social analysis by Virginia Woolf that I have found particularly thought provoking. At one level Woolf might be said to offer a "feminist epistemology" in her account of why women approach life differently from men; but she is skeptical about claims that women are different from men in fundamental dimensions of our personalities that will survive changes in our situation. As the age-old condition of "separate spheres" gives way to more common experiences for women and for men, Woolf shows why it makes sense to assume that we will behave in more similar and converging ways.

Finally, I ask what this all means for answering the question that poses the puzzle for this chapter: why might it be reasonable to assume that women will lead differently from men?

What Does It Mean to Say That Women Lead Differently?

Throughout human history and across many cultures, leadership has been closely associated with masculinity: the king, the father, the boss, the lord are stereotypical images of leadership. This association of leadership and masculinity encourages the expectation that women will behave differently from men when we do exercise authority: that we will lead in what are thought of as "typically female" ways. This expectation is held both by those who believe that because of our femaleness women are not really capable of using power effectively, and by those who believe that because we are women, we are thereby superbly equipped to use power more sensitively than men and help solve the problems of the world. Old-fashioned male chauvinists and successful women executives alike tell us that women do indeed lead differently.[1] Thus either "I told you so" or "Hallelujah!" may be held to be the appropriate response to this claim.

What might it mean to say that females have a distinctive style of leadership? This question should be distinguished from four others, all closely related. The first is whether women in power set different goals from men—whether we are more likely to advance policies that deal with family life or the specific needs of women in employment. The second has to do with the types of positions women leaders are more likely to occupy; it could be that the positions themselves (human resources or staff jobs) differ in ways that explain any disparities one might find. The third is a question about obstacles: perhaps the ways in which women lead differently arise because subordinates who are uncomfortable with a woman boss resist behavior that would be thought perfectly appropriate for a man. And the fourth question is a normative variant: *should* women lead differently? That is, would the world be better off if women used some of our putatively womanly skills to wield power in non-traditional ways?

The answers to these questions no doubt have some bearing on the answer to the first, but they are not the same question. The point is this: when a woman occupies a post that has always been held by a man and is charged with broad responsibility for an orga-nization with multiple goals and interests, will her style of leader-ship differ in predictable ways from that of a man in the same job just because she is a woman?

Careful reflection on how women actually behave when we hold power makes clear that individual women display different styles of leadership, just as men in such positions have always done.[2] It is clearly not true that all women in all positions of leadership behave in ways that are "typically womanly," whatever definition one might use. Leadership is such a multifaceted, complex phe-nomenon that a generalization about all leaders or all women lead-ers cannot survive scrutiny.

Yet many people—not just my Wellesley classmates—would grant that this is true and nonetheless assert that the fact of being a person of one sex or the other has observable and durable implica-tions for how one might use power. One might put this in terms of probabilities: the typical female leader differs from the typical male leader, so the chances that a woman will lead in a way we might characterize as notably feminine are greater than the probability that a male leader will behave in such a way. This would be analo-gous to saying that females as females have a distinctive style of writing novels or throwing a ball, making friends or expressing our emotions, even though some women write hard-boiled crime nov-els or throw overhand, and some men write romance novels or eas-ily talk about their sentiments. Alternatively, one might say that although a particular woman leader may behave most of the time in ways that cannot be distinguished from what a man would do in the same circumstances, there will be other occasions when her femaleness makes a difference.

What arguments might be used to support such a contention about women as leaders?

What Does the Record of Women in Power Show?

Women across history have been leaders in certain contexts. These include all-female settings such as convents or women's colleges and occasions when blood or dynasty trump gender, so that a Hatshepsut or Elizabeth I can be a ruling monarch. When men are temporarily absent—Quaker Nantucket, when most of the men were out at sea whaling for long periods, or in wartime contexts—women have had opportunities to lead. Women are often leaders in social movements where women's interests are held to be especially involved, such as woman's suffrage, the prohibition movement, or the settlement house and social work campaigns of the late nineteenth century.

Women have provided leadership in many more informal contexts—the heads of European salons, wise-women healers, or market women in Africa or the French Revolution. They have in many societies had authority over servants, slaves, or serfs, but one would be hard-pressed to call this leadership. Women have also had the ability to shape matters to their own purposes in many contexts where they would certainly not be called leaders. The familiar image of the power behind the throne, the dowager empress, or the powerful mistress (what one might call the *éminence rose*) makes clear that women have often had ample power in the sense of influence rather than authority. But as Deborah Rhode sums it up: "For most of recorded history, women were largely excluded from formal leadership positions."[3]

What is new these days is that significant numbers of women are exercising authority in institutionalized settings over men and women of comparable social and economic status. Today there are women senators, governors, corporate CEOs, university presidents, rabbis, generals, Anglican priests, and Supreme Court justices. It is no longer plausible to contend that all women are incapable of leadership in all kinds of positions of authority. This was indeed the position taken, usually with more heat than light, by quite a few political philosophers—and innumerable ordinary folk—for many centuries.[4] In more recent years, there is evidence that the concept of women as leaders is becoming more familiar and more comfortable to many people, at least in parts of Europe and North America.

Then why is the number of women in visible, demanding leadership positions still so small? Relying on the report of the Federal Glass Ceiling Commission, Rhode reported that in the mid-1990s, "more than 95 percent of corporate executives and 85 percent of elected officeholders" were male.[5] The "pipeline theory" is no longer convincing; the line has proved to be filled with obstacles and prone to leakage. Many factors contribute to this outcome, including the difficulty of juggling career and marriage and the "second shift" that women are still expected to work.[6] Popular culture, a formidable force in shaping expectations for young people in our society, rarely suggests full-scale ambition as an appropriate lifestyle for a person of the female sex.

The obstacles women continue to face even in organizations that provide opportunities for leadership rest on heavily gendered conceptions of human life, including leadership. Such conceptions demonstrate the residual power of assumptions that kept women out of power in the past, the belief in separate spheres and different capacities possessed by human beings according to their sex. These assumptions support a worldview in which wielding power is a man's job and women do their part through caring, supporting, mothering, and providing services to men. The same assumptions are associated with the belief that when we women do in fact exercise power, we will use it in certain typically female ways.

Thus the assumption that women will lead differently has some troubling implications that proponents of this belief may not have considered fully. It is often taken for granted that women will be more nurturing, caring leaders than men. Yet nurturing leaders are vulnerable to the charge of "not being tough enough," not being comfortable with power. And women who defy the stereotype and behave too aggressively are often condemned as bitchy and unwomanly. As a number of chapters in this book make clear, this is a classic Catch-22 situation.

Several successful women leaders, including Margaret Thatcher, Indira Gandhi, and Golda Meir, have been "the best men in their cabinets" by all reports, including their own. They rejected the nurturing and caring model and adopted stereotypically masculine behavior in order to succeed at their jobs and be accepted as "real leaders." Other women have used their femaleness to gain an apparent advantage over male colleagues through seduction or playing what we might call the "helpless card" to evoke chivalric support. Still others have behaved like mothers or sisters, looking after others in the workplace as women have done in the home over the centuries.

Thus if we look around us and across history, we find a range of behaviors and approaches. Many women have either used or actively denied their femaleness in ways that suggest that being female is indeed relevant to holding power. Is this apparent use or denial of femininity simply a residue of all those centuries in which most of the power was held by men, so that a woman in power looks different or exotic no matter what she does? Or are women in fact "leading differently"? Since so many observers expect that we will behave differently, behavior may be coded in this way regardless of our intentions or our accomplishments. What can we learn from the experts?

What Does Contemporary Social Science Tell Us About Women as Leaders?

There have been quite a few psychological experiments in which volunteers are put in situations where leadership is called for, and any difference between males and females in taking the role of leader is duly noted. "Leadership" in these settings is usually defined as guiding deliberations, organizing a project, or providing initiative. A familiar distinction between "task leadership" and "expressive leadership" is often used in these experiments, with the former being more intellectual and initiative-oriented, whereas the latter involves support for members of the group, making it easier for the group to cohere and get its work done.

Such experiments sometimes find slight statistical differences between the sexes, especially when women are in a small minority or when some members of the group are regarded as task leaders and others provide the more supportive type of leadership. But the differences are rarely large, and are even smaller in situations where social status, expertise, and other resources are involved—not to mention same-sex situations. Moreover, these experiments hardly simulate the conditions of people in positions of authority or long-term power holding. The participants do not know each other, have no lasting ability to help or harm each other, and are entirely removed from the institutional contexts in which leadership usually occurs. Thus it is unlikely that they will tell us much about how actual leaders in top positions in corporate or government life behave.

Alice H. Eagly and Blair T. Johnson, in their overview of such experiments on leadership, note that "ingrained sex differences in traits and behavioral tendencies, a spillover of gender roles onto organizational roles, and subtle differences in the structural position of women and men could cause leadership behavior to be somewhat sex-differentiated even when occupants of the same organizational role are compared. Therefore, some evidence of sex differences in leadership style in organizational studies would not be surprising." However, they follow Rosabeth Moss Kanter and others in hypothesizing that "organizational roles are more important than gender roles," so that "differences between men and women occupying the same leadership role in organizations would be smaller than differences between men and women observed in other types of leadership research, namely laboratory experiments and assessment studies."[7]

In fact, their careful meta-analysis produces a somewhat more complex picture. Most differences are indeed seen in informal settings, the prime locations for the "spillover of gender roles." The authors argue that the criteria organizations use for selecting managers "and the forces they maintain for socializing managers into their roles minimize tendencies for the sexes to lead or manage in a stereotypic manner" in more institutional contexts. Yet even in organizational settings they found some evidence that "women's leadership styles were more democratic than men's."[8]

The influential line of argument stemming from Carol Gilligan's *In a Different Voice* holds that women are more likely than men to make moral judgments based on caring or personalistic views, rather than on the grounds of abstract justice. A number of scholars have followed this lead; several have developed theories of caring as a distinctively female trait (including Joan Tronto and Nel Nodding).[9] Sara Ruddick has developed the implications of mothering as the source of female morality, and linked it with the emphasis on caring. Such theories would indeed support the assumption that women will approach power differently from men.

Eleanor Maccoby points out that girls and boys behave differently even when forward-thinking parents attempt to raise them without gender stereotyping—in choices of companions, play habits, and other social interactions. She ascribes these differences to "genetic predispositions" as well as to cognitive factors: the greater language facility of girls and the tendency of boys to indulge in rough-and-tumble play. Patterns developed through sex self-segregation as early as the third year of life persist through adulthood, she argues, and have significant consequences not only in intimate relations between the sexes but also in the workplace and many other areas.[10]

Another area for exploring this question that has recently opened up is brain imaging. Tania Singer and her colleagues have found that women react more empathetically than men in situations involving pain inflicted on another human being who is perceived as having acted unfairly, or in the exaction of revenge. As the authors put it in concluding their report: "Further experiments are needed to confirm the gender specificity of the effect. It is possible that our experimental design favoured men because the modality of punishment was related to physical threat, as opposed to psychological or financial threat. Alternatively, these findings could indicate a predominant role for males in the maintenance of justice and punishment of norm violation in human societies."[11] Alternatively, of course, they could also indicate that women in our society have been differentially socialized to feel concern about harm to others.

What Can We Learn from the Experience of Girls and Women?

Almost all cultures promote particular forms of education and experience for young girls, designed to make them sexually appealing to men and to prepare them for the women's work of caring for others and providing support for the men in their lives. It is reasonable to expect this preparation to have a distinct influence on how one behaves as an adult, including how one uses power, which should be true even across other significant social differences, such as age, culture, race, and social class. Thus black women in the United States may have more in common with black men than with white women on many measures, but as women, they experience life in ways that differ systematically from their brothers and these experiences have recognizable features in common with those of white women.

"Feminist epistemology" or "standpoint theory" provides one avenue for understanding assertions such as this in a more systematic fashion.[12] Standpoint theory's most distinctive contributions rest on the argument that oppressed groups have a privileged vantage point on the world, and for at least some theorists, this perspective is gained collectively through struggle. Almost all observers have noted that women do not conceive of themselves as a class and do not organize to pursue shared goals except in particular situations of active feminism or social revolution. Whatever it is that women share, it cannot be said to come from collective struggle. The disinclination of women to engage in anything like class struggle is even clearer today than it was during the robust women's movement in the 1970s and 1980s, when Nancy Hartsock and other second-wave feminists developed standpoint theory.

But the notion that our take on the world is dependent on some basic factors in our lives is worth preserving. As Alison Wylie puts it: "The point of departure for standpoint analysis is commitment to some form of a situated knowledge thesis: social location systematically shapes and limits what we know."[13] Thus, just as it makes sense to claim that workers in a capitalist society look at the world differently from their bosses and that feudal peasants did not see the world exactly as their lords did, so it makes sense to expect that women may look at the world differently from men.

The fundamental argument here is that we need to understand knowledge as socially situated, not some sort of freestanding or abstractly objective "view from nowhere."[14] As the most obvious of the many differences among human beings, sex would seem to be an excellent candidate for grounding a distinctive epistemology. Living in the world as a girl and then a woman provides access to some experiences that are not available to boys and men and denies the possibility of others. Given that this is true, it might seem perfectly reasonable to expect that people with these different experiences will act differently in power, as in many other settings.

How do we get a handle on such rich and complex phenomena? It is in this context that I suggest turning to the works of Virginia Woolf.

A Room of One's Own: Virginia Woolf on Women Throughout History

Although Virginia Woolf is known primarily for her novels, she was also a prolific author of essays, including two books of social analysis with a strongly feminist bent: *A Room of One's Own* and *Three Guineas*. In these works Woolf focuses on the sources, implications, and durability of differences between the sexes. The two books offer closely reasoned accounts of the situation of women in society across the centuries and the obstacles to the development of women as free, creative, truthful human beings. They distill a life-time of social observation, reading, and conversation, and a novelist's sense of how human beings move through the world. This background makes her work especially relevant to understanding claims about experience and socialization in a deep and resilient fashion.

Woolf's essays also have special resonance in an era of post-modernism and skepticism about magisterial philosophy. The arguments of the social theorist are here transmuted by the rich use of irony, fictional history, quotation, and literary criticism. Woolf draws on "all the liberties and licences of a novelist" to make her arguments. She cautions her audience: "When a subject is highly controversial—and any question about sex is that—one cannot hope to tell the truth. One can only show how one came to hold whatever opinion one does hold. One can only give one's audience the chance of drawing their own conclusions as they observe the limitations, the prejudices, the idiosyncrasies of the speaker. Fiction here is likely to contain more truth than fact."[15]

In *A Room of One's Own* Woolf's major concern is with women's writing; but her account of the obstacles to women's cre-ativity and freedom is clearly relevant to determining why women have so seldom been leaders in the past and might now approach power somewhat differently from men. She provides numerous examples of ways in which almost all women throughout history have lived lives different from their menfolk of the same family or social class.

Woolf notes that most women throughout the ages have been financially dependent upon their husbands and their fathers. She shows how this has been a major impediment to women's creativ-ity and sense of self. It has been in women's interest to flatter and defer to men in order to get on in the world, and men have proved eminently susceptible to such flattery and deference. Women have "served all these centuries as looking-glasses possessing the magic and delicious power of reflecting the figure of man at twice its natural size." To walk into a room regularly and believe oneself the superior of half the people there does marvelous things for self-confidence.[16] And, "creatures of illusion as we are," any accomplishment depends greatly on confidence in oneself. Lacking such dependable measures to enhance their own self-confidence, women have found it much harder to push forward in the world. And accustomed as they are to basking in such superiority, men are understandably reluctant to relinquish it.

The financial dependence of women upon men, according to Woolf, has made it impossible for most women to think boldly, act independently, live as free, creative human beings. The deference and flattery that inflates male egos through an unquestioned sense of sex superiority has invidious effects on the way both men and women think about the female sex. Certainly beings so constituted seem ill prepared to exercise authority over men. And when they do, as in the case of Elizabeth I or Mary Queen of Scots, someone is sure to echo in some form John Knox's complaint about "the monstrous regiment of women."[17]

Based on this analysis, Woolf's prescription is straightforward: "A woman must have money and a room of her own if she is to write fiction." (Or, one might add, be elected to office or chosen to head a corporation.) And Woolf insists that this is not merely a symbolic insight. "Intellectual freedom depends upon material things. . . . That is why I have laid so much stress on money and *a room of one's own*."[18]

Virginia Woolf presents the two sexes as fundamentally asymmetrical. The constricted situations and lack of economic power that have characterized women have led not only to the good qualities of nurturing and sensitivity to others but also to less desirable qualities: the rust and corrosion of unused talents brings fear and bitterness, anger, sour frustration, and laxity of mind. Woolf refuses to idealize her sex, but her portrait is deeply sympathetic. She imagines what life is like for the millions of women who have cooked all those dinners, washed all the plates and cups, and sent the children off to school, so that the years slip by and "nothing remains of it at all."[19]

She is considerably harsher in her account of the effects of power and dominance on men. "True, they had money and power, but only at the cost of harbouring in their breasts an eagle, a vulture forever tearing the liver out and plucking at the lungs—an instinct for possession, the rage for acquisition which drives them to desire other people's fields and goods perpetually; to make frontiers and flags, battleships and poison gas; to offer up their own lives and their children's lives."[20] She comments on the dominance of the egotistical "I," the obsessive virility that makes the reader feel as though she "had been caught eavesdropping at some purely masculine orgy," and the incessant male tendency to rank and compare and categorize.

In analyzing the work of brilliant eccentric writers such as Margaret of Newcastle, who had plenty of time, money, and solitude, Woolf finds that the impediments to women's accomplishments also include the lack of being taken seriously, of an interested audience to praise and criticize with care rather than either to scorn or flatter. "For masterpieces are not single and solitary births; they are the outcome of many years of thinking in common." Here, with the imagery of birth and motherhood, Woolf offers one of her most telling convictions: that women's creativity, women's accomplishment, depends on having precursors, companions who are women, to make up a tradition and a sisterhood that allows us to believe in our own gifts. "For we think back through our mothers if we are women."[21]

The same lack of precursors and companions—what we now call role models—has also meant that few women have thought about leadership as an appropriate woman's role. If a young woman has never known a female leader, it will be difficult for her to imagine herself becoming a leader, or to know how she should behave once she does have power.

In the concluding chapter of A Room of One's Own, Woolf holds forth the ideal of an androgynous mind that combines the best capacities of man and woman and avoids the deficiencies of each. Following the lead of Coleridge, Woolf develops the idea of the brain that includes two powers, male and female, with the former predominant in men and the latter in women, yet with the two parts living in harmony. She asserts that creative work can be done only if a "marriage" of these opposites is consummated in the mind; poetry "ought to have a mother and a father."[22] The images of creativity are physical and quite specifically heterosexual, strongly reinforcing the idea of a necessary fusion between the male and the female in any good productive enterprise.

One of the charges often lodged against the notion of androgyny is that it preserves the imputed differences between the sexes in the very effort to transcend them. If certain traits or ways of thought remain "womanly" and others "manly," familiar stereotypes about the differences between the sexes are perpetuated. For Woolf, the apparent flaw in the androgyny argument is part of its attraction: she does not wish to do away with all the differences between the sexes; she prefers to preserve those that lend diversity and variety to life while avoiding the defects that attend artificial differences. This would be a world in which women and men continue to differ in appearance and in some fundamental traits and values, but the exaggerated differences between us, and the special disabilities imposed on women, are avoided. Such a vision appears to promise everything.

Yet Woolf consistently takes the view that these attributes thought of as womanly are not immutably rooted in biology; they are the product of the situation of women during those "centuries of hard discipline." She avoids essentialist explanations in her work, asserting that the distinctive womanly traits are acquired through what anthropologist Michelle Rosaldo later called "concrete social interactions," produced by "the relationships that women forge, the social contexts they (along with men) create—and within which they are defined."[23] How can these traits be retained without the isolation and subordination that helped create them? And how can they be present in the minds of men who have not shared such experiences?

Three Guineas: Crossing the Bridge from Private to Public Life

The predominant thrust of *A Room of One's Own* is the desirability of women moving from our position outside the establishment to become insiders in our own right, joining androgynously with sympathetic men in the work of the world. *Three Guineas* is the argument of an outsider who firmly resists inclusion and charts out a path of her own. *A Room of One's Own* retains something of the veiled quality that Woolf attributes to many great women writers of the past. In *Three Guineas* Woolf asserts that it is time to lay aside the delicacy and silence that have muted women's writing over all these centuries and "attempt, face to face, a rough and clumsy analysis" of male fear and anger.[24]

In *Three Guineas*, written in 1938, Woolf's vision of an androgynous harmony that includes a flowering of female creative genius was replaced by an ominous future that can be forestalled, if at all, only by women collectively preserving the virtues instilled by the deprivations and disadvantages that attended the lives of women in the past. Yet at the same time women must somehow gain enough power and financial independence to provide a counterweight to patriarchy.[25]

Three major areas of difference between members of the two sexes are identified here. In the first place, women and men have had very different educations, in the largest sense of experience of the world as well as the more narrow sense of academic learning. Second, there is a fundamental difference in instinct between the two sexes where violence is concerned. This is the only instance where Woolf attributes a sex difference to instinct rather than experience and situation. Finally, men and women differ markedly in their control of wealth and other resources.

For all these reasons of disparate experience, education, instinct, and control of wealth, "it would seem to follow then as an indisputable fact that 'we'—meaning by 'we' a whole made up of body, brain and spirit, influenced by memory and tradition—must still differ in some essential respects from 'you.' . . . Though we see the same world, we see it through different eyes."[26] Passages such as these provide a subtle and thought-provoking account of a distinctive woman's perspective on the world.

But according to Woolf, her own time was a crucial "moment of transition." For the first time, education and the professions were open to women, yet they had not enjoyed these advantages long enough to be changed and shaped by them. To make this point she often relied on the image of women on a bridge between the private houses of the West End and the bustling busyness of the Houses of Parliament and the City of London. And she uses the fresh perspective provided by this bridge between two worlds to offer an extensive critique of the public world as men have created it.

From that particular vantage point on the world, a vantage point unavailable both to women immured in domestic concerns and to male social theorists conditioned by life in the public world, Woolf wants us to see clearly aspects of human life that have before been difficult to discern. On one hand, there are the consequences for female activity and character—both positive and negative—of the demands of the private house on women's lives, especially the duties of looking after children and aged parents, which women do far more frequently than men. On the other, there are the consequences for the male character of the demands of the public world with its competition, multiple loyalties, and incentives to ambition and greed. And the two different worlds are so firmly sex-typed that men find it very difficult to adjust to the idea of a woman in the public world.

Thus, notes Woolf, "The peculiar odor of 'Miss' " on an application form carries a disturbing and inappropriate connotation; it transmits a particular vibration: that of sex, which carries with it "the swish of petticoats, the savour of scent," or some other odor obnoxious in the examination room or boardroom. "What charms and consoles in the private house may distract and exacerbate in the public office." And "as for 'Mrs.,' it is a contaminated word, an obscene word," carrying as it does the continual reminder of sex and marriage, alien to the public world.[27] No wonder women leaders these days are more and more insisting on the title Ms.

For Woolf, the profound differences between the experiences of the private house and public life explain not only why women might find it difficult to cross the bridge but why men find it hard to imagine women on the other side, and why women who do achieve some measure of power face such daunting obstacles in the attempt to be treated with some measure of equality. In the same passage, she summarizes these differences of experience and expectation with the term "atmosphere," which she says is "plainly a very mighty power. Atmosphere not only changes the sizes and the shapes of things; it affects solid bodies, like salaries, which might have been thought impervious to atmosphere. An epic poem might be written about atmosphere, or a novel in ten or fifteen volumes."

Woolf's account also demonstrates why women might well be expected to approach power differently from men, once we have access to it. Coming from the private house, with experiences primarily drawn from serving others, flattering or cajoling men, and taking care of children or older people, women's attitudes toward power and ways of using it must differ from those of the men who have spent their lives in the public realm, subject to the various motivations and ambitions Woolf describes.

One might then expect to count Woolf firmly among those who assume that women will hold power and provide leadership differently from men. But to do so would overlook one of the most subtle aspects of her theory: the traits or attributes ascribed to women on the basis of their experience in the private house are linked precisely to that experience, and thus are neither innate nor durable. Once women enter public life, there is no reason to believe that we will retain the distinctive features of the private house, either positive or negative—the nurturing or the pettiness, the deep caring or the hypocrisy. Once women are educated like men and enter the same professions, Woolf expects that women will be likely to take on the characteristics of the public realm and behave "just like men." Once we cross the bridge, our standpoint begins to change in subtle ways.

Thus one of the main purposes of *Three Guineas* is to explore ways in which women might retain the distinctive virtues acquired through the centuries spent in the private house, without also retaining the characteristic private-house vices of pettiness, hypocrisy, ignorance, and sexual manipulation.[28] She surely does not want women to remain immured in private life; she wants us to have opportunities to develop other talents and pursue other dreams as full and free human beings, including leadership in public life. But simply to have women in public life take on the same characteristics that men have so often displayed would be, in her view, to miss a historic opportunity. The virtues women have brought to their traditional tasks—qualities of self-sacrifice, care for others, a sense of proportion, and lack of arrogance or pomposity— would surely contribute significantly to the solution of the huge public dilemmas of her time and help ward off the dangers of an ominous future, if they could be sustained in public life.

The transitional moment offers a precious opportunity to change the world for the better, as women begin to participate in public life. But Woolf has no illusions about the ease with which this change might take place. To make it possible for women to enter public life without copying men in all respects and falling prey to the same vices of egoism, arrogance, and aggressive competition, Woolf names three requirements.

Her first requirement is straightforward and not overly demanding: "any woman who enters any profession shall in no way hinder any other human being, whether man or woman, white or black, provided that he or she is qualified to enter that profession, from entering it; but shall do all in her power to help them."[29] Support others as they begin their journey up the ladder, rather than paying attention solely to your own progress to the top. And beware of the assumption that only certain kinds of people are fit to do your work. That is exactly the assumption that kept women out of the professions, and without authority, for so long.

Woolf next counsels that women remain faithful to the teachers that led to their distinctive virtues in the past. And these teachers are "poverty, chastity, derision, and freedom from unreal loyalties." In this context, *poverty* means earning "enough money to live upon," enough "to be independent of any other human being and to buy that modicum of health, leisure, knowledge and so on that is needed for the full development of body and mind. But no more. Not a penny more." *Chastity* means refusing to sell your mind, by analogy with women refusing to sell their bodies in the past. *Derision* means refusing honors and marks of success, avoiding "all methods of advertising merit," believing that "ridicule, obscurity and censure are preferable, for psychological reasons, to fame and praise." And *freedom from unreal loyalties* teaches us to rid ourselves of the pride of nationality, our religion, college, family, or sex.[30]

As if this were not enough, the third condition is equally harsh: that we refuse to join the societies of insiders that flow from those "unreal loyalties" and catch us up in just those behaviors she wants us to avoid. Instead, she proposes a "Society of Outsiders," composed of women in professional capacities who bond together secretly and informally, "without so much as a form to be filled up."[31]

Virginia Woolf's stark challenges lead us to think about how power is used and the impact it can have on the persons who exercise it. Some of her counsels, thoughtfully applied, could no doubt improve the tenor of public life and leadership without undermining a leader's effectiveness. But more fundamentally, Woolf's suggestions demonstrate little understanding of how complex institutions work. Her proposal bears more than a passing resemblance to the approach to power exemplified by the second-wave feminism of the 1970s. Following her suggestions to the letter was not, I assume, what Woolf intended anyone to do, given her penchant for irony and fictional flights of fancy; but if one tried, such a course of action would no doubt offer the same kinds of rewards in solidarity and sisterhood as those experienced by that generation of feminists—and fall victim to the same pitfalls of ineffectiveness and isolation from the centers of power.

If one insists on being an outsider, one can remain so—but one cannot hope to provide leadership within an institution. A woman who decides to enter public life will need to recognize that even the best-constituted organizations have significantly different demands and opportunities from those of the private house. This is due not to some deficiency in human nature or the male variant thereof but to the way complex human institutions work. And women leaders who wish to provide attractive examples for young women must be willing to accept honors and recognition—with appropriate grace and modesty—rather than insisting on invisibility.

Thus if we want to cross the bridge into public life, yet not lose touch with virtues women have traditionally displayed in the private house, we must figure out how we can profit from Woolf's counsel without denying ourselves the focus and resilience that make it possible to flourish on the other side.

Thinking About the Future: Where Do We Go from Here?

So where does this leave us in answering the question: On what grounds would it be reasonable to assume that women will lead differently from men? There appear to be ample grounds for this assumption, given the different experiences that girls and boys, men and women, have in almost every culture known to us. Whatever may or may not be true about the configuration of our genes or the impact of our hormones, this seems to be sufficient reason to assume that when we do hold power, women will use it differently.

As Virginia Woolf reminds us, however, experiences and expectations change over time, and human beings are subject to the rules in place in whatever activity we engage, whatever organizations we decide to join. As women cross the bridge from the private house to public life, it is equally reasonable to assume that on the other side of the bridge we will adopt the forms of behavior that have generally led to success in this world in the past. In Woolf's view, if female leaders are more likely to be nurturing and male leaders more aggressive, this says more about our past experiences than about our instincts; the differences will not long survive the crossing of the bridge. But is that the end of the story?

Not long after publishing *Three Guineas*, Virginia Woolf, despairing of the darkening atmosphere of Europe on the eve of war and haunted by her personal demons of depression, put stones in her jacket pocket and walked into the River Ouse. If Woolf had lived longer and had the opportunity to observe and spend time with women who became leaders, she might well have recognized that many of the pressures on leaders are not associated with male arrogance; some come from the context and the situation of holding power itself. She might have written about women in power who found ways to retain qualities she thought essential to human flourishing without refusing to do the things leaders must do: make hard decisions, compete effectively for resources, stand up for what you believe should be done in the interests of the institution you lead. With her novelist's gifts, she might have shed light on how a conscientious woman could confront the problem we call "dirty hands," the complex moral dilemmas leaders inevitably face, with clarity, sensitivity, and integrity. And she would surely have noted the importance of examples of women leaders in inspiring others to want to emulate them, just as women authors have done.

For men as well as women who hold power, Woolf would have pressed the importance of sustaining some detachment from the post one occupies, a sense of proportion and honesty with oneself, rather than allowing oneself to believe all the good things flatterers offer leaders. She pointed out the dangers that lurk in the path of those who accept the familiar trappings and temptations of power unthinkingly. And she counseled against becoming so completely caught up in any position of authority that one loses touch with the natural world, with music and poetry and conversation, becoming nothing more than "a cripple in a cave."[32] She would, above all, remind us to ask ourselves occasionally the questions she held out to us as a mantra: "What is this 'civilization' in which we find ourselves? What are these ceremonies and why should we take part in them? What are these processions, and why should we make money out of them? Where in short is it leading us, the procession of the sons of educated men?"[33]

Organizations impose their own requirements for success; they can also evolve over time. Insofar as women have had experiences that lead us to understand the value of sensitivity to other human beings, we should try to retain this insight when we cross the bridge, rather than jettisoning it as wholly inappropriate to the public world. But we must also recognize that leadership in complex institutions requires a degree of dispassionate competitiveness and single-mindedness that would be out of place on the domestic side of the bridge. I remain convinced that careful observation of successful women leaders will reveal that we do indeed display toughness, institutional focus, and cool judgment. We often follow the same strategies for achieving the institution's goals that a man in the same position would employ. We are willing to make hard decisions about other people's lives and contributions when the decisions are essential to the success of the institutions, as they often are, even though they lead to hurt feelings or career losses for those other people, as they often do.

Like many successful male leaders, we also try to be sensitive to the talents and feelings of those who work with us and for us. Women who do this should not be regarded as behaving in some narrowly female way, even if they may be drawing on their experience as mothers or caretakers. But courage, steeliness, and a willingness to accept some degree of the loneliness that comes with authority are also essential to success. No one is well served when women leaders who display these features are condemned because they depart from some stereotypic conception of femininity.

In the end, there must be a balance in leadership between nurturing and toughness, just as there is, for instance, in good mothering. Yet the balance is different on the two sides of the bridge, because the relationships, goals, and activities are not the same. In this context, the familiar liberal distinction between public and private life serves us well, and we should resist efforts to deny or dissolve this distinction. It may be true that in many respects "the personal is political," as the feminist mantra has it; but there are meaningful differences between the obligations, duties, and opportunities available to human beings on the two sides of this bridge that Woolf described so well. Women and men in power both need to recognize the distinctive requirements of public life, including both the demands of holding power and our responsibilities to those we lead.

Is androgyny, then, the answer? I am not sure what that would mean; but I do think that all of us would be well served by an awareness that strengths often ascribed to the other sex can be valuable to both men and women in complex human activities like holding power. Most important, however, we should remember that each of us leads, as we love and befriend, in a distinctive and individual fashion. We should recognize this as a source of strength in the leadership of any organization or society. And we should avoid imposing gender stereotypes that would make it harder for any of us to explore the path of leadership that is most promising to us as individuals. Our world, like Virginia Woolf's, clearly needs good leaders wherever we can find them.

Endnotes

1. For an instance of the latter, see Marie C. Wilson, *Closing the Leadership Gap: Why Women Can and Must Help Run the World* (New York: Viking Penguin, 2004).
2. In their thought-provoking book *Same Difference: How Gender Myths Are Hurting Our Relationships, Our Children, and Our Jobs* (New York: Basic Books, 2004), Rosalind Barnett and Caryl Rivers demonstrate some of the difficulties with generalizations in matters such as these.
3. Deborah L. Rhode, *The Difference "Difference" Makes* (Stanford, CA: Stanford University Press, 2003), 3.
4. Susan Moller Okin, *Women in Western Political Thought* (Princeton, NJ: Princeton University Press, 1979).
5. Deborah L. Rhode, *Speaking of Sex: The Denial of Gender Inequality* (Cambridge, MA: Harvard University Press, 1997), 2, 253.

In making generalizations such as these, I focus on the United States, the country I know best; some of my comments would be equally pertinent to other countries, but some of them would not. We should not assume either that the United States is representative of other countries or on the leading edge of change. In some ways we are, but in many ways we are not.

6. Arlie Hochschild and Anne Machung, *The Second Shift* (New York: Avon Books, 1990).

7. Alice H. Eagly and Blair T. Johnson, "Gender and Leadership Style: a Meta-Analysis," *Psychological Bulletin 108*, no. 2 (1990): 236, 246, 249. Rosabeth Moss Kanter's views are summarized in *Men and Women of the Corporation* (New York: Basic Books, 1977).

8. Sumru Erkut, *Inside Women's Power: Learning from Leaders*, CRW Special Report #28 (Wellesley, MA: Wellesley Centers for Women, 2001) analyzes the different styles of women as leaders in several complex organizations.

9. Virginia Held, ed., *Justice and Care: Essential Readings in Feminist Ethics* (Boulder, CO: Westview Press, 1995).

10. Eleanor Maccoby, *The Two Sexes* (Cambridge, MA: Harvard University Press, 1998), 287, 292–293.

11. Tania Singer et al., "Empathic Neural Responses Are Modulated by the Perceived Fairness of Others," *Nature* advance online publication (18 January 2006), 1–4.

12. Sandra Harding, ed., *The Feminist Standpoint Theory Reader* (London: Routledge, 2004), and Nancy Hartsock, *The Feminist Viewpoint Revisited and Other Essays* (Boulder, CO: Westview Press, 1998).

13. "Why Standpoint Matters," in Harding, *The Feminist Standpoint Theory Reader*, 339–351.

14. *The View from Nowhere* is the title of Thomas Nagel's book (Oxford: Oxford University Press, 1986).

15. Virginia Woolf, *A Room of One's Own* (New York: Harcourt, Brace, Jovanovich, 1929), 4.

16. Woolf, A *Room of One's Own*, 35–36. Simone de Beauvoir makes a similar observation: "The most mediocre of males feels himself a demigod compared with women. . . . Here is miraculous balm for those afflicted with an inferiority complex, and indeed no one is more arrogant toward women, more aggressive or scornful, than the man who is anxious about his virility." *The Second Sex*, trans. H. M. Parshley (New York: Random House, 1974 [1949]), xxviii–xix.

17. As John Knox puts it in the opening paragraph of *The First Blast of the Trumpet Against the Monstrous Regiment of Women* (1558): "To promote a woman to beare rule, superioritie, domination, or empire above any realme, nation or citie, is repugnant to nature, contumelie to God, a thing most contrarious to his revealed will and approved ordinance, and finallie it is the subversion of good order, of all equitie and justice."

18. Woolf, A *Room of One's Own*, 110–112.

19. Woolf, A *Room of One's Own*, 93.

20. Woolf, A *Room of One's Own*, 38–39.

21. Woolf, A *Room of One's Own*, 79.

22. Woolf, A *Room of One's Own*, 100–101.

23. Michelle Rosaldo, "The Use and Abuse of Anthropology: Reflections on Feminism and Cross-Cultural Understanding," *Signs* 3 (1980): 400.

24. Virginia Woolf, *Three Guineas* (London: Harcourt Brace, 1938), 128. The book takes its name from the fictional experience that provides its framework: a woman at her writing desk considering three requests for money for charitable purposes.

25. Woolf uses "patriarchy" very much as later feminists have employed it, to describe the entire structure of male-dominated society. She moves from the struggle with one's own father to "the struggle with fathers in general, with the patriarchy itself." *Three Guineas*, 65.

26. Woolf, *Three Guineas*, 18.

27. Woolf, *Three Guineas*, 52.

28. Woolf firmly rejects one familiar feminine strategy: using sexual attraction through the "looking glass relationship" to persuade men to do what women want. She contends that this form of influence is "either beyond our reach, for many of us are plain, poor or old; or beneath our contempt, for many of us would prefer to call ourselves prostitutes simply and to take our stand openly under the lamps of Piccadilly Circus rather than use it." *Three Guineas*, 15.

29. Woolf, *Three Guineas*, 66.

30. Woolf, *Three Guineas*, 80.

31. Woolf, *Three Guineas*, 115.

32. Woolf, *Three Guineas*, 72, where she warns that "people who are successful in their professions" because they devote all their time to their work and have no time to appreciate beautiful things or engage in conversation gradually lose their senses and even their humanity.

33. Woolf, *Three Guineas*, 63.

2

THE GREAT WOMEN THEORY OF LEADERSHIP?

Perils of Positive Stereotypes and Precarious Pedestals

Todd L. Pittinsky, Laura M. Bacon, Brian Welle

Increasingly, motherhood is being recognized as an excellent school for managers, demanding many of the same skills. . . .

What business [leadership] needs now is exactly what women are able to provide, and at the very time when women are surging into the work force.[1]

—*Sally Helgesen*

These quotations from Sally Helgesen's popular book on women and leadership, *The Female Advantage: Women's Ways of Leadership*, illustrate an increasingly common discourse on leadership that

The authors would like to extend their gratitude to Ruth Wageman, who generously offered her time and ideas, greatly assisting the early formation of this chapter. Jenny McFlint provided very insightful comments on a draft, for which we are grateful. Scott Webster, Sara Singer, and members of the Allophilia Lab at the John F. Kennedy School of Government were also extremely helpful with their tips and brainstorming. We appreciate the guidance and support of the editors of this volume, Barbara Kellerman and Deborah Rhode. Finally, we thank the Center for Public Leadership for supporting our research work.

posits some interesting points: current leadership is lacking a sincere, nurturing, relational, communal, collaborative component; women have certain traits and styles (for example, sincerity, collaboration, inclusiveness); and these uniquely and solely prepare women—the missing ingredient—for effective leadership.

We refer, in a shorthand way, to these arguments as an emerging "great women theory of leadership"; that is, arguments that women are, for example, caring, nurturing, collaborative, and inclusive, thereby predisposing them to be effective leaders. We use the plural *women* rather than *woman*, to express the tendency of the approach to clump women together using group-based stereotypes. No one person or group has been advocating this as a theory in so many words, but this chapter highlights a general trend—marked by a stereotyping of women's leadership—that has gained momentum in the last ten to fifteen years, especially in nonacademic leadership literature. A look at the titles of recent books reveals this phenomenon: *The Woman's Advantage: 20 Women Entrepreneurs Show You What It Takes to Grow Your Business*; *Why the Best Man for the Job Is a Woman: The Unique Female Qualities of Leadership*; and *Enlightened Power: How Women Are Transforming the Practice of Leadership*. By placing women on a pedestal, albeit a precarious one, advocates of this great women approach to leadership use positive stereotypes about women's traits to argue in support of why women are uniquely effective, why they are desperately needed as leaders, and why organizations should pay attention.

We first argue that, via positive stereotypes, a fundamental principle of the great man (or trait) theory of leadership is being applied to women's leadership, but at the group rather than the individual level. Next, drawing from the social psychology research literature, we identify and discuss four ways in which this approach can be perilous for women, men, and effective leadership in general. In conclusion, solutions are offered for the degendering of leadership, including a discussion of functional leadership.

The Great Women Approach to Leadership

Gandhi, Mandela, Churchill, Eisenhower, Napoleon, Caesar: These were great men who arose in times of need and displayed brilliant leadership. The key assertion of the "great man" approach, which gained popularity in the early twentieth century, is that these great men boasted qualities many said to be intrinsic, which made them fit to be great, mythic, heroic leaders, filling a leadership gap.[2]

Today, the great man theory is considered by many to be an outdated and sexist trait theory. It is ironic, then, that we find ourselves barraged by a female version. Today we hear—from the media and even from scholarly sources—the belief and expectation that women possess certain traits that are specific to being female, and that it is, in fact, these particular feminine traits that allow women to lead more effectively than men. Thus, women and the traits they hold, in the great women approach, are considered to be what leadership now needs most.

For years, this binary and discrete categorization of masculine and feminine traits, and their link to leadership, has been a focus of research. As early as fifty years ago, researchers enumerated stereotypes commonly applied to men (independent, objective, assertive, unemotional, and active) and women (dependent, subjective, passive, and emotional).[3] Schein demonstrated in 1973 and 1975 that the stereotype of an effective manager had much more in common with stereotypes of men than those of women, considering attributes such as leadership ability, self-confidence, assertiveness, aggressiveness, forcefulness, and logic.[4] One and a half decades later, Heilman, Block, Martell, and Simon found that men, more than women, were still described as more similar to successful managers.[5] And in this volume, Kellerman and Rhode write that notions of leadership are still wrapped up in the idea of masculinity, where dominance, authority, and ambition are valued over interpersonal qualities often considered more feminine, such as cooperation and collaboration.[6] They suggest that the dearth of women in leadership positions represents a mismatch of characteristics. Indeed, traditional great man leadership traits (agentic, competent, powerful, masterful, assertive, independent) seem incongruous and at odds with women's presumed qualities (expressive, collaborative, gentle, friendly, pleasant, socially sensitive).[7]

However, during this time, a new pattern began to emerge, and it has gained momentum of late. While clinging to this idea of "women's natural traits," many began to argue for a type of leadership exercised by women. This style—which supposedly features women's unique ability to collaborate, transform, and nurture, as well as their relational, charismatic, nonbureaucratic, nonhierarchical manner—is attributed with filling a gap in the leadership world that men were heretofore unable to fill. The great women theory of leadership prioritizes and necessarily attributes stereotypically feminine traits to women—and calls them "great" for it.

Consider, as an example of the great women approach, Judy Rosener's provocative and very influential *Harvard Business Review* article, "Ways Women Lead," which describes this new kind of female leader: "Women leaders don't covet formal authority. They have learned to lead without it."[8] A very interesting claim from this article, which was based on a 1989 study at the International Women's Forum, is that these women picked up this distinctive leadership style from their "shared experience as women."[9] Due to their prominence in roles that differed because of gender (wives, mothers, community volunteers, teachers, nurses), women were allowed and indeed encouraged to be cooperative, supportive, understanding, gentle, emotional, and vulnerable. When they more recently moved into leadership positions, the article reports, women succeeded because of—not in spite of—these female characteristics. Rosener writes: "While men have had to appear to be competitive, strong, tough, decisive, and in control, women have been allowed to be cooperative, emotional, supportive, and vulnerable. This may explain why women today are more likely than men to be interactive leaders."[10]

By now, the great women theory has gained prominence in leadership training programs, the political arena, the media, and the vernacular. Consider the words of former Archbishop of Cape Town Desmond Tutu: "Some of the best initiatives are those that occur because women are involved. . . . It is almost a tacit acknowledgement of the crucial role that women play in nurturing, nurturing life."[11] Tutu speaks of a revolution in which women were not afraid to be feminine: "This revolution . . . is the last, best chance for making this globe hospitable to peace, to make this globe hospitable to compassion, hospitable to generosity and caring." In another example, a *Newsweek* feature on women and leadership, Oprah Winfrey states during an interview: "All the women leaders I have met led with a greater sense of intuition than men."[12] The same feature spotlights Xerox, in which women hold almost a third of top management jobs. There, the prominence of women is said to have changed the culture to "a kinder culture"; the article notes that "instead of shaking hands, executives sometimes greet with hugs."[13]

Does a gendered perspective advance our understanding of leadership? Does it hold promise for closing the leadership gender gap? Are there unintended results of gendering leadership in this way? As this new type of "female leadership" is being theorized and celebrated for its collaborative, inclusive, charismatic nature, women have been pegged as necessarily and disproportionately possessing these traits. In an attempt to glorify women and highlight their value in the leadership market, stereotypical claims about the "ways women lead" and "how women are" have been made that may be more damaging than helpful in the long run. The functions of leaders—the things leaders do to get the job done effectively—have been endangered, forgotten, and lost amid discussions of gender and style. As a result, the benefits of these group-based notions of women's leadership, although framed in a positive light, may be precarious, with a perhaps surprisingly negative impact on the interests of women, of men, and of good leadership more generally.

Positive Stereotypes: Precarious Pedestals

Negative stereotypes are often applied to women, a practice that can lead to discriminatory policies, devaluation of their work, and even— through self-fulfilling prophecies—diminished performance. Mark Agars, in a literature review, concludes that stereotyping is "a certain and meaningful contributor to the limited presence of women in high-level positions."[14] Clearly, such negative stereotypes are a problem. But can the same be said for positive stereotypes about women? We argue that putting women on a pedestal the way great women approaches do is perilous for four reasons. By characterizing and stereotyping leadership traits as gendered, we ultimately exclude, misrepresent, mold, and polarize the sexes, and leadership in general.

Some might argue that having a gendered concept of leadership may be beneficial to women, especially as it extols the benefits of a female leadership style. This perspective is supported by some of the literature on positive stereotypes. Positive stereotypes can enhance performance and even others' recall of performance. In one illustrative study by Pittinsky, Shih, and Ambadi, participants for whom positive stereotypes were made salient performed better.[15] Another study by the same researchers found that participants' recall of others' performance was also enhanced by positive stereotypes.[16] And research by Levy, Slade, Kunkel, and Kasl shows that positive self-perceptions of aging have even been found to add approximately seven and a half years to longevity.[17] Positive stereotypes, indeed, can be adaptive or helpful.

We do not argue that positive stereotypes about women will hurt each individual woman in every case; in fact, notions of a warmer, gentler leadership style may sometimes benefit women. However, a rigid adherence to gender demarcation can be inaccurate and counterproductive, helping women advance into leadership positions in one instance (in stereotypically feminine tasks, for example), but hurting them in others (in stereotypically masculine tasks). Indeed, the positive traits glorified by the great women theory of leadership at times come at a cost and could exacerbate, rather than ameliorate, current divisive gender issues in leadership. Furthermore, we suggest as a viable alternative the degendering of leadership—the disassociation of gender from leadership traits and characteristics—which may provide a more accurate, and more equalizing, playing field for both genders.

By arguing against positive generalizations about women, we do not dismiss women's contributions to leadership situations. As Hunt highlights, in reference to the nature of women's leadership (especially in regard to peacemaking), women have long been community leaders, often without formal authority, so they have learned to work around rigid structures. They are often the caretakers in and after wars and thus have a lot invested in peace, and they often have more credibility, having not participated in the failed or violent leadership structures of the past.[18] We agree that women have strength of leadership and should therefore be equally represented, adding variance and broadening the range of possible leadership styles. We do not, however, argue that women are a monolithic group, possessing a set of specific traits and styles exclusive to women that qualify them as better leaders.

We also do not go so far as to deny that differences between women and men exist. In the ongoing debate, which has been under way for years, about sex differences in organizational leadership, participants are roughly split into two camps: "gender stereotypical" and "no differences."[19] We will examine arguments from both camps but join neither. Rather, we posit that the best research evidence suggests that differences, if and when they exist, are minimal; effect sizes for findings of difference between women's and men's leadership are modest. In other words, empirical research on gender differences often reveals very small actual differences between men and women's leadership styles, but these differences are often exaggerated or overemphasized either by the researchers or by those interpreting the data. We argue that this categorization (and consequential polarization) of masculine-versus-feminine leadership becomes a cyclical chicken-and-egg scenario: The more differences are discussed, the more they are perpetuated.

This chapter should not be misconstrued as arguing that the positive traits and styles discussed cannot apply to women. Rather, we argue that building a case for the inclusion of women in leadership based on stereotypes and overgeneralization is the wrong means to an important end: equal representation of women in leadership roles. Groupwide trait-based flattering (or unflattering) stereotypes—our minds' way of categorizing people into simple packages without acknowledging the fuller story—can be perilous. Very perilous, indeed.

Peril #1: Excluding

The most substantial way in which the great women approach endangers women (and men and leadership in general) is that an adherence to certain positive stereotypes creates fertile ground for exclusion. First, if stereotypes encourage inclusion of women for certain types of jobs because of their particular styles, these same stereotypes exclude women from certain types of jobs for which they may not be considered fit. Specifically, when supposed feminine traits such as communality, cooperation, warmth, nurturing, and gentility are touted as specific and unique to women, jobs or tasks that require opposing or different traits may not seem appropriate for women. Second, the great women approach will lead to exclusion (via prescription and dislike) of women whose competency and agency render them unlikable and less influential, since they do not display the traits this approach advocates. Then, victimized by the double bind created by these two exclusionary tactics, women who are especially competent at jobs that are considered masculine will be exceptionally penalized. Finally, some interesting research suggests that the stereotypes advocated by the great women approach may have hidden negative stereotypes that accompany the so-called positive ones, which will eventually subtly mark women for exclusion.

First, let us consider how the great women approach hinders women's recruitment or leadership emergence. What roles and positions exist today that might seem inappropriate for women, especially if their advantage as women sees them as caring, nurturing helping?[20] Crisis situations? War? Decisive roles requiring autonomy? Role-congruity theory predicts that, when expectations for the leader role are incongruent with female stereotypes, women will be less likely than men to emerge as leaders.[21] Eagly and Karau found that role incongruity led to prejudice against female leaders in two ways: Women were perceived less favorably than men as potential leaders, and leadership behaviors of women were evaluated less favorably than those of men.[22] Normative stereotypes about women's ways of leading, then, are likely to influence perceptions of their competence, especially for masculine-typed jobs. Indeed, in Gorman's research on hiring in large U.S. law firms, she showed that when stereotypically masculine characteristics comprised a large part of the selection criteria, women were hired less often.[23] When the selection criteria included more stereotypically "feminine" traits, women were better represented among new hires. The great women approach provides support, if unintentionally, to claims that women—given their underlying strength at the notion of feminine leadership—may not meet the criteria for positions that require directive or hierarchical mind-sets. We also see this play out in Ritter and Yoder's study of leadership-emergence tasks, wherein even women who usually tended to emerge as leaders retreated and let men dominate during what they regarded as masculine tasks.[24] The great women approach reinforces perceived incongruence between masculinized task demands and women's leadership.

Next, stereotypes—even seemingly positive ones like niceness—add a normative slant to leadership, advocating that women should lead in a certain way.[25] Great women approaches set up the belief that women not only do act in certain ways, but should do so, as well. Heilman's research demonstrates that gendered stereotypes about what women are like (descriptive) and their subsequent expectations about how they should act (prescriptive) can lead to a devaluation of their performance, denial of credit for their success, and even penalization for being competent.[26] Furthermore, as stereotypes set expectations of warmth, interpersonal focus, and soft leadership, women who tend to lead in an agentic or directive way suffer.

Rudman and Glick report a "backlash effect," in which the feminization of middle-management job descriptions may, rather than work to the advantage of women, "reinforce discrimination against the most competent and ambitious among them."[27] In their research of the costs of "kinder, gentler" images of middle managers, they expose the double standard that applies to women during the hiring process: Female applicants considered to be agentic were rated less socially skilled than agentic male applicants, resulting in discriminatory hiring for the feminized jobs. And communal applicants, of both sexes, received low hiring ratings across the board. This situation occurs outside the laboratory, as well. Consider the case of *Price Waterhouse v. Hopkins,* in which the U.S. Supreme Court determined a woman had been discriminated against on the basis of her sex.[28] She was considered by other partners as "an outstanding professional" and by a member of the state department as "extremely competent, intelligent," "strong and forthright, very productive, energetic and creative." However, other partners described her as "macho"; another suggested that she "overcompensated for being a woman"; a third advised her to take "a course at charm school." Her evaluator told her (the only woman of the eighty-eight proposed for partnership) that she could improve her chances for partnership if she would "walk more femininely, talk more femininely, dress more femininely, wear make-up, have her hair styled, and wear jewelry." These are clear examples of the kinds of situations great women approaches may exacerbate, by setting expectations of women's style of leadership and endangering those women who do not meet those expectations.

Thus we have seen the threat of exclusion of women from certain types of jobs and the exclusion of certain types of women from jobs. Empirical research also supports the claim that the great women approach is precarious for those women who combine success with male gender-typed tasks; they will be further penalized through dislike and lack of follower support. Thus, there is a double bind: Women must be assertive and dominant to be viewed as competent, but exhibiting that assertion and dominance causes them to be liked less and be less influential.[29] In three studies, Heilman, Wallen, Fuchs, and Tamkins investigated reactions to women's success in a typically masculine job.[30] When women were reported as successful (in the top 5 percent of their field), participants liked them significantly less, and personally derogated them more than equivalently successful men. Being disliked also revealed vast career implications, including lower overall evaluations and less reward allocation. These negative reactions occurred only when the women's success was in what is considered to be a male arena. The work of Heilman and Okimoto confirmed these data, again showing that successful women in male gender-typed jobs were rated as interpersonally unpleasant.[31] Their research indicates that women *can* be perceived as both likable and competent, but they still have to prove that they fit into the stereotypes that prescribe them; only when they were *explicitly* described as communal or warm did the evaluators rate them as likable.

Finally, Eagly, Makhijani, and Klonsky's meta-analysis (that is, an integrative statistical synthesis of past research) of women's leadership highlights the peril of labeling leadership as particularly feminine.[32] There was an overall tendency (although small) of participants to rate women less favorably. Although this tendency was common among male evaluators, it was particularly common when leadership was carried out in stereotypically masculine styles, which is to say autocratic or directive, and when the female leaders occupied typically male-dominated roles. The great women approach, then, increases the likelihood that women who lead in autocratic ways will be penalized for straying from the new, glorified feminine style of leadership.

Finally, positive stereotypes about women may also be associated with accompanying negative stereotypes. Viewing women's leadership as desirably feminine overlooks more complicated, associated sexist stereotypes and inadvertently encourages them. Fletcher describes this concept: "Although new models implicitly acknowledge that relational wisdom is critical to business success, they do not take into account that acting on this wisdom requires displaying characteristics that subtly mark us as 'feminine' and 'powerless.'"[33] Researchers such as Glick and Fiske have found a similar phenomenon in ambivalent sexism (or benevolent and hostile sexism), in which feelings are not completely negative, but rather positive characterizations are intertwined with negative stereotypes.[34] Women, the researchers find, tend to be relegated to one of two buckets, termed either "cold and competent" (generally reserved for female leaders in the workplace) or "friendly but futile" (women who are personally ambitious, leading a family). Perceptions of men's competence, on the other hand, do not seem to be mutually exclusive with perceptions of warmth. For instance, when women become mothers, they trade their perceived competence for warmth. Interestingly, men do not lose points in competence ratings when they become fathers but instead simply gain perceived warmth.[35] To the extent that great women approaches are providing support to the societal view that women are warm and arguing that this very warmth makes them competent, they may be subtly reinforcing the view that women are incompetent.

From all of this research, we see how exclusive notions of great women's leadership can be. First, positive stereotypes about women disproportionately hurt those women who do not possess or publicly express those characteristic traits and styles. Second, women will likely be overlooked for leadership situations that call upon traits and styles with which women are not typically associated. And when women particularly excel at leadership not considered to be feminine, they are penalized. Finally, the emphasis of the great women approach on positive female traits and styles could be reinforcing a set of characteristics that may in the long run expose women in leadership positions as less desirable, given the negative stereotypes that often accompany such attributes.

Peril #2: Misrepresenting

Are women different from men? And, if they are different, are the differences the result of gender socialization, ongoing gender stratification, or both? One women's leadership-development program is advertised in these terms: "Women are not the same as men. And you should be thrilled!"[36] And in a recent panel on diversity and leadership, Swanee Hunt, former U.S. ambassador and current chair of Women Waging Peace at Harvard's Kennedy School of Government, hypothesized that more female leaders would make the world a more peaceful place; for instance, she proposed that, had there been a larger representation of women in the U.S. Congress, the country might not have gone to war in Iraq. Ayaan Hirsi Ali, a former member of the Dutch Parliament also serving on the panel, fervently disagreed that women would be any less likely to go to war than men.[37] Even female world leaders possess starkly contrasting beliefs about whether women as a group are substantially different from (and in this case, more peaceful than) men.

Answering questions on the degree of sex differences goes far beyond the bounds of this chapter, but one thing is clear and relevant to the current discussion: Advocates of a great women approach would like to think great gender differences exist, despite research to the contrary. In fact, as Eagly and Johnson have observed, differences between men's leadership and women's leadership tend to be less pronounced in actual leadership situations than in more decontextualized laboratory situations.[38] Leadership differences based on stereotypes of women are often exaggerated, misidentified, or overstated by the great women approach.

Effect sizes of leadership differences between men and women are often very small; differences between men and women are often exaggerated and socially polarized, rather than statistically confirmed. Reviews by Bartol and Kanter, for instance, indicate that empirical studies rarely reveal the stark gender differences of leaders that one might expect, given the existing gendered stereotypes.[39]

Indeed, according to most research, it is more myth than reality that women and men lead differently. Thus, the great women approach truly does misrepresent leadership by women by portraying it as starkly different from men's.

In a meta-analysis of women's leadership evaluations, Eagly and Johnson found that, in actual organizations, female and male leaders did not differ in interpersonally oriented versus task-oriented styles.[40] Women were expected to exhibit more of the former, but no significant differences emerged. These studies are the most ecologically valid, as field studies (rather than those simulated in the laboratory) are the closest to what plays out in the real world. Similarly, Rice, Instone, and Adams studied the effects of sex-based differences in two six-week programs at the U.S. Military Academy in basic and field training; they failed to detect significant differences between the sexes in terms of leadership process and the relationship between leadership success and process.[41] This study at West Point, the researchers note, is consistent with the literature's lack of findings on sex differences in a military setting. It is principally research in small-group laboratory studies or decontextualized attitude surveys where such sex-difference effects emerge. Rice, Instone, and Adams point to Butterfield and Powell's summary of this trend: "It is now commonly believed that actual (leader sex) differences in the behavior of real leaders are virtually nonexistent."[42] Bass drew the same conclusion: "The preponderance of available evidence is that no consistently clear pattern of differences can be discerned in the supervisory style of female as compared to male leaders."[43] Thus any statement or belief that presents all female leaders as starkly different from their male counterparts misrepresents reality.

Sometimes actual differences do emerge, and in many more instances, differences are believed to emerge between female and male leaders, whether or not bona fide differences exist. For instance, Eagly and Johnson found that across all kinds of studies (within the organization, the laboratory, and assessment studies) women tended to lead in a more democratic or participatory style, whereas men adopted an autocratic or directive style. In addition, we often hear that women in public office will spend more money on health care, environmental issues, and education. And female political candidates are sometimes perceived by the public to be more capable of handling what are thought of as domestic issues, education, the environment, and health care, whereas male candidates are seen as having strength in national security, taxes, and homeland security.[44] There is evidence for this: Burrell found that women's voting records in the U.S. House of Representatives indicate that women were more likely than men to support "women's issues" such as gender equity, day care, flextime, and reproductive health.[45] And Chattopadhyay and Duflo, in a study of women's leadership in India, found that women were more likely to invest in the projects and programs more relevant to women's concerns.[46] However, Schwindt-Bayer and Corbetta found evidence to the contrary: With controls for party and constituency influences, no actual differences in women's and men's voting records were found.[47] And in the Introduction to this book, Kellerman and Rhode write that although women are better advocates for women's concerns in general, party affiliation is a better predictor of voting records than is sex. They also point out that some women have notoriously poor voting records in regard to these concerns and do nothing to further women's issues. So the jury is out. It is difficult to say whether men and women act differently when in leadership positions, especially considering that women represent such a small proportion of political and organizational leadership.

While strong conclusions about differences or lack thereof between women and men are difficult if not impossible to make, given the current state of the science, it is very clear that the nature of the arguments made in great women approaches are reductionist and misrepresent claims from available research. This is particularly true when they move beyond actual behaviors to stereotypes. In doing so, they overlook similarities between men and women. While the magnitude of the differences is unclear, it is fair to say that exaggerated claims about differences can misrepresent and ultimately undermine women as leaders.

Peril #3: Molding

People have strong expectations for women's leadership style that are particularly reinforced by the great women approach, which essentially encourages and celebrates a female way of leading. In some instances, men and women might lead in the same ways, but observers perceive them differently, blinded by expectations. In other cases, men and women might lead in a similar fashion, but the leaders themselves perceive their own styles differently, swayed by others' expectations. Finally, men and women actually might begin to lead in different ways, in response to gender-based expectations of leadership set forth in the great women approach. Beliefs and expectations can all too easily become self-fulfilling prophecies; women's leadership is thus molded as others' expectations influence women's own behaviors.[48]

How do expectations shape behavior? First, people have expectations of others. For example, there is an interculturally shared view of female-specific leadership competence, according to which women possess a higher interpersonal orientation than men. A cross-cultural study of Australians, Germans, and Indians, conducted by Sczesny, Bosak, Neff, and Schyns, confirmed this view.[49] It could be that such beliefs actually have observers' seeing the same behavior differently.

Next, people start perceiving their own leadership in gendered terms. Actual differences do not emerge nearly as much as stereotypes would have us think, but we certainly describe leadership as though they do—this is part of the molding process. After conducting research on hundreds of businesses, Cliff, Langton, and Aldrich report that a business owner's sex has no effect on the extent of the firm's bureaucracy or the femininity of its employment relationships; both male and female owners manage their firms with a mix of masculine and feminine approaches, according to the researchers.[50] What is most notable, however, is that the business owners often described their own leadership—how they organize and manage the firms—in different, gender-stereotypic ways, even when in practice such differences do not exist.

It is suggested by Cliff, Langton, and Aldrich that a misattribution could be occurring: Observers tend to attribute less bureaucracy to female owners, but it could be organization size that mediates this effect. As in Rosener's study, most of the organizations studied were small, with fewer than a hundred employees. And, consider, in Rosener's influential study, that the frame of reference was the women's perspectives on themselves; these were self-reports about the participants' own leadership qualities, rather than reports from people in the organization who evaluated them. This notion—that the leaders themselves are perpetuating gendered stereotypes—shows us how the great women approach may powerfully influence men's and women's views of others and themselves, to the point where they are acting similarly but describing themselves in polarized ways.

Finally, women and men actually begin acting the way followers expect them to act because of their gender; their leadership is molded by the stereotypes until they match. Women start to describe their own leadership in a certain way—and act that way—given the expectations and beliefs of others. Subordinates, for example, may respond more positively to female leaders who exhibit expected styles, in effect rewarding these behaviors.

Thus, the great women approach socializes a certain kind of leadership. It characterizes women and men with certain styles and subtly (and sometimes not so subtly) may cause the female leaders themselves, along with the rest of us, to expect certain styles from women and different styles from men. Because of expectations of their leadership, women are often molded into certain ways of leading. One female professor we interviewed said, "I'm always expected to smile when I teach, because women smile more. I know my students like that. But I can't always smile, especially when the class is unmotivated or underprepared."[51] Often there are connotations of a mother role, which women are molded into playing. Fletcher writes: "Women are often expected to nurture selflessly, to enable others while expecting nothing in return, to work mutually in non-mutual situations, and to practice less hierarchical forms of interacting even in hierarchical contexts. Thus, many women experience the so-called female advantage as a form of exploitation, where their behavior benefits the bottom line but does not mark them as leadership potential."[52] Because of the emphasis on a nurturing, mothering approach, female colleagues are often expected to embrace and care for their coworkers (and listen to how they had a bad weekend) in ways that their male counterparts are never expected to.[53]

Is it possible that molding and socialization explain the gender differences that emerge in some studies? For instance, in the meta-analysis by Eagly and Johnson, women displayed a more interpersonally oriented leadership in laboratory experiments and assessment studies.[54] In addition, women led in a more participatory, democratic way than men, and men adopted a more autocratic and directive approach. Second, in terms of different styles of leadership, Eagly, Johannesen-Schmidt, and van Engen found that female leaders were more transformational than their male counterparts and also engaged in more contingent reward behaviors (usually associated with transactional leadership).[55] Men were more likely to display transactional and laissez-faire leadership.[56] Social learning theories can account for these findings. Observers view leadership through a certain lens and expect to see a particular kind of leadership, given the sex of the individual in charge. People adopt these styles of leadership over time because it is expected of them. Eagly and colleagues hypothesize that gender roles and gender-specific norms may have an influence on leadership by way of "spillover and internalization."[57] They agree that molding may have an effect: "This likely consistency of at least some aspects of transformational leadership with the female gender role would allow these behaviors to be fostered in women by the spillover of its norms onto organizational behavior and many women's personal acceptance of these norms as standards for their own behavior."[58]

Because of such pervasive stereotypes about women's leadership— the very ones advocated by a great women approach—it is difficult to separate how women think they are supposed to act, how people expect women to act, and how women begin to act. This is the very molding we underscore as one of the perils of great women approaches. The harm of molding, in the end, is twofold. First, under this approach, we see the stifling of full leadership potential, as a vast array of possibilities and styles gives way to the narrow, molded, conventional forms of leading. Second, as Fletcher notes, exploitative, submissive strains of leadership are exposed when what is labeled feminine leadership turns into selflessness.

Peril #4: Polarizing

Delineating leadership into so-called masculine and feminine styles is a very black-and-white way of viewing the field: two styles divided, in a reductionist manner, along gender lines. Consider the comment of Anita Roddick, the founder of The Body Shop, quoted in the book *The Female Advantage*: [gesturing to the New York skyline] "Buildings like this are so ridiculous! If women ran the world, we wouldn't have all these ugly phallic towers!"[59] Stereotypes are used to simplify the complexities of individuals and leadership and are prescribed indiscriminately, with little if any consideration to deviations. The great women approach advocates this polarization. Like all stereotypes—both positive and negative—notions of feminine and masculine leadership categorize and polarize styles that should (or could) be used by all leaders, regardless of sex. In so doing, the stereotyping limits the scope of techniques available to both groups. Finally, the polarizing effect of the great women approach may have deleterious effects on men, as well, as their inclinations to engage in certain forms of leadership may be stymied or misconstrued as a result of being labeled feminine.

As Heilman points out, characterizing men as "aggressive, forceful, independent, and decisive" and women as "kind, helpful, sympathetic, and concerned about others" polarizes masculinity and femininity; these conceptions are oppositional, with the understanding that one group is missing what is given to be prevalent in the other.[60] The logic behind certain stereotypes being mutually exclusive is the phenomenon of "separate spheres," articulated by Fletcher.[61] The world tends to become categorized in a bipolar fashion: public world ("produce things") and private world ("grow people"). As Fletcher describes them, these two spheres are considered separate, unequally valued, and, most important for this chapter, sex-linked. Fletcher submits that this framework explains why we so easily label characteristics as feminine and masculine, tags that are accompanied by implicit associations about their respective effectiveness. The world at large is predisposed to such categorical thinking, and the great woman approach only encourages it.

The second issue pertains to the consistent and persistent labeling of traits and their associations with a specific gender, and the perpetuation of such polarization therein. For an example of the persistence of the gender associations used to frame leadership, consider the analysis of U.S. Senate and gubernatorial debates conducted by Banwart and McKinney.[62] These scholars argued that men and women are using both masculine and feminine communication styles, not relying on the one typically represented by their gender. For example, men are seen to employ feminine leadership styles by speaking collectively and relating to issues in a personal way, and women appropriate masculine styles by being decisive, aggressive, and launching personal attacks. Why subscribe to these categories, thereby promulgating them, when an alternate explanation could be that men and women simply tend to exhibit a wide range of leadership behaviors, and that there is not necessarily one masculine and one feminine style?[63] The leadership enterprise has become contaminated with these polarizing perceptions of women's leadership traits, to the point where they are now quite pervasive. Once adopted as a lens for understanding leadership, gendered views have proven extremely resistant to change.

As we have seen, positive stereotypes place women on a very precarious pedestal, one that may not be adaptive to women's longer-term integration into leadership roles. The polarization of feminine and masculine traits and styles pulls women to one extreme, pushes men to another, and leaves little room for variance, individualism, and diversity: the remainder of the leadership continuum. This polarizing approach may have deleterious effects for male leaders, as well. While books like *The Best Man for the Job Is a Woman* celebrate the great women approach, is it accurate or productive to say that one gender alone has what it takes to save the world of leadership? Do stereotypes about women diminish our expectation that men will also engage in collaboration, cooperation, personal contacts, encouragement, and participation? Will men be limited or chastised when they enact styles more commonly displayed by women? Data suggest that communal, rather than agentic, job applicants of both genders are seen as less competent.[64] Thus, a leader who exhibits warmth may be penalized, regardless of the individual's gender. However, given the approach that advocates women's interactive, transformational approach as more effective (and men's transactional or laissez-faire approach as less effective),[65] it would be interesting and worthwhile for research to test directly whether the masculine stereotypes of agency, dominance, and hierarchy (which are also polarized) may sometimes be considered a deficit, and whether these stereotypes are exacerbated by emerging beliefs about women's superior leadership styles.[66]

As a final aspect of polarizing leadership, consider the great women approach and how the media and women themselves invoke such a bipolar situation. In Peru's 2006 presidential race, one could observe the great women approach in action.[67] Referring to the presidential candidacy of former congresswoman Lourdes Flores, one individual interviewed on the campaign trail said, "All our lives, men have governed. But the time for a woman has arrived!" Another supporter, through a translator, claimed, "I like her because she is a woman, and she's going to fight for all things that men have not done up until now. She has promised a lot, but I think she'll deliver because she speaks with sincerity." And coverage from National Public Radio certainly enjoys the salience of her gender, this polarization of male versus female: "There is no doubt that this is a woman who wants to become Peru's next President. . . . Here at a rally in support of Lourdes Flores, the theme of female power is everywhere. The emcee for the evening is a man, in drag. Many of the performers are women, and instead of banners with slogans, people are waving color-coordinated balloons."[68] When did masculinity come to equal "banners with slogans" and femininity "color-coordinated balloons"? Here the media conflates the concept of female power with balloons and men in drag. Flores also invoked her own gender, frequently ending speeches with the phrase: "You have my word as a woman." We are far from equality, and this approach only leads us astray.

At best, under this polarized approach, women are considered charismatic, inclusive, collaborative, transformative, and extremely competent. Need gender be cited as the reason for such accolades? The United States has witnessed women's suffrage, the women's rights movement, and an increase, albeit modest, in the percentage of women in leadership positions in the last century. However, these recent claims about women's leadership may threaten our increasing notion of equality. How did it come to be that many of the constituencies that at one time were arguing for a lack of attention to gender difference are now often basking in these differences?

Degendering Leadership

For sure, one of the most interesting things about the great women approach is that women—as scholars, practitioners, and as consumers of leadership development materials—are its most ardent supporters. Women seem to be just as likely, if not more so, to believe in and advocate for stereotypes about women and leadership. All the books mentioned early in this chapter were written by women. As is the case with negative stereotypes of women, both women and men hold gender-stereotypic beliefs.[69]

Recognizing the limitations of an approach that replaces a history of glorifying individual male leaders with the glorification of female leaders collectively, how best to take women off the precarious pedestal? What lies beyond a great women approach? Most important, we believe, scholars and practitioners must think in terms of the functions of leadership, think about what leaders need to accomplish. The great women approach—with its group-based notions of gendered leadership—considers traits and styles rather than functions, and as a result is limiting as a framework. Leadership involves executing a certain number of functions—functions such as putting in place an enabling structure, setting a compelling direction, envisioning a desired end state and communicating this to others, thinking of nonobvious ways to accomplishing goals, securing resources or assistance needed to support group efforts, coaching, forecasting future conditions, and gathering information about goals and task requirements.[70] All these functions can be fulfilled in various ways, and can lead to achieving a leadership goal. The critical piece, for theory and practice, is that the function, rather than the behavior or style (gendered or not), is the unit of analysis.[71]

Although it is sometimes provocative to ponder the differences between women and men, the sexiness should be taken out of the female-male divide. Recognition should be made that similarities between the sexes are far more prevalent than differences, and instead of analyzing the suitability of an entire gender in a leadership context, attention should be paid to the functions of effective leadership necessitated by a given situation. A great women approach is dangerous in that it polarizes leadership. Functional approaches more accurately focus attention on the antecedents of effective leadership. These can be accomplished by both genders and through a number of different styles. Functional leadership, the lens for analyzing leadership that we advocate, considers actions leaders take to motivate, enable, and direct, rather than obsesses over particular styles or traits.

Viewing leadership through this lens serves to degender it, as it deemphasizes the traits and styles held up by other theories, which tend to have affiliated gender stereotypes, and at the same time highlights the various functions that leaders must execute—none of which are exclusive to a particular gender. Functional leadership allows us to focus on a level of abstraction where commonality across gendered styles—if gendered styles do in fact exist—can be seen. For instance, there are many ways of building rapport that men and women may enact (similarly or differently) to get a job done well. Similarly, there are a great number of ways to enact leadership, and gendering only serves to further exclude, misrepresent, mold, and polarize.

Conclusion

There is, through the great women approach to leadership, much attention paid to women's supposed warmer leadership traits and styles—such as collaboration, cooperation, personal contacts, encouragement, participation, interaction, sensitivity, communality— which uniquely prepare them to lead in the aforementioned way. However warm and positive they may seem, however, such stereotypes can be precarious to women and indeed to all those individuals interested in the study and practice of effective leadership. The use of generalizations based on gendered traits and styles is a perilous strategy to achieve an important end—more women in power—and is a precarious pedestal indeed.

Endnotes

1. Sally Helgesen, *The Female Advantage: Women's Ways of Leadership* (New York: Dell, 1990), 31, 39.
2. Certainly, these were great leaders, but one of the major problems that arose with the great man theory is the recognition that certain traits are successful only in certain situations with certain followers. In addition, historical, economic, cultural, and political context—as well as followership—are now considered crucial to the study of leadership, no less important than the acts of a given individual; Barbara Kellerman, *Bad Leadership* (Boston: Harvard Business School Press, 2004). This theory also tends to exclude other historical manifesta-

tions of leadership involving teams of leaders, ethnic and racial minorities, and, of course, women.

3. Inge K. Broverman, "Sex Role Stereotypes: A Current Appraisal," *Journal of Social Issues* 28, no. 2 (1972): 59–78; John P. Sherriffs and Alex C. McKee, "The Differential Evaluation of Males and Females," *Journal of Personality* 25 (1957): 256–271; both cited in Robert W. Rice, Debra Instone, and Jerome Adams, "Leader Sex, Leader Success, and Leadership Process: Two Field Studies," *Journal of Applied Psychology* 69, no. 1 (1984): 12–31.

4. Virginia E. Schein, "The Relationship Between Sex Role Stereotypes and Requisite Management Characteristics," *Journal of Applied Psychology* 57 (1973): 95–100; and Virginia E. Schein, "Relationship Between Sex-Role Stereotypes and Requisite Management Characteristics Among Female Managers," *Journal of Applied Psychology* 60 (1975): 340–344.

5. Madeline Heilman, Caryn J. Block, Richard F. Martell, and Michael Simon, "Has Anything Changed? Current Characterizations of Men, Women, and Managers," *Journal of Applied Psychology* 74, no. 6 (1989): 935–942.

6. Barbara Kellerman and Deborah Rhode, "Viable Options: Rethinking Women and Leadership," *Compass* 2, no. 1 (2004): 14–17, 37.

7. Kellerman and Rhode, "Viable Options"; Alice Eagly and Steven J. Karau, "Role Congruity Theory of Prejudice Toward Female Leaders," *Psychological Review* 109 (2002): 573–598; Amanda Diekman and Alice Eagly, "Stereotypes as Dynamic Constructs: Women and Men of the Past, Present, and Future," *Personality and Social Psychology Bulletin* 26, no. 10 (2000): 1171–1188; John E. Williams and Deborah L. Best, *Measuring Sex Stereotypes: A Multination Study* (rev. ed.) (Thousand Oaks, CA: Sage, 1990); Laurie A. Rudman and Peter Glick, "Feminized Management and Backlash Toward Agentic Women: The Hidden Costs to Women of a Kinder,

Gentler Image of Middle Managers," *Journal of Personality and Social Psychology 77*, no. 5 (1999): 1004–1010; Alice Eagly, *Sex Differences in Social Behavior: A Social-Role Interpretation*, (Hillsdale, NJ: Erlbaum, 1987), xii; Judy B. Rosener, "Ways Women Lead," *Harvard Business Review*, November-December 1990, 119–125.

8. Rosener, "Ways Women Lead," 123.

9. Rosener, "Ways Women Lead," 119.

10. Rosener, "Ways Women Lead," 124.

11. "Women Should Rule—Tutu," *News 24*, October 8, 2004. Report of speech in News 24. Retrieved from www.news24.com/News24/South_Africa/News/0,,2-7-1442_1570773,00.html on January 16, 2007.

12. Barbara Kantrowitz, Holly Peterson, and Pat Wingert, "How I Got There." Interview with Oprah Winfrey on Women and Leadership. *Newsweek*, October 24, 2005. Retrieved from www.msnbc.msn.com/id/9712069/site/newsweek on October 26, 2006.

13. Daniel McGinn, "In Good Company," *Newsweek*, October 24, 2005. Retrieved from www.msnbc.msn.com/id/9709961/site/newsweek on October 24, 2006.

14. Mark D. Agars, "Reconsidering the Impact of Gender Stereotypes on the Advancement of Women in Organizations," *Psychology of Women Quarterly 28*, no. 2 (2004): 103–111; see p. 103.

15. Todd L. Pittinsky, Margaret Shih, and Nalani Ambady, "Will a Category Cue Affect You? Category Cues, Positive Stereotypes and Reviewer Recall for Applicants," *Social Psychology of Education 4* (2000): 53–65.

16. Margaret Shih, Todd L. Pittinsky, and Nalani Ambady, "Stereotype Susceptibility: Identity Salience and Shifts in Quantitative Performance," *Psychological Science 10*, no. 1 (1999): 80–83.

17. Becca R. Levy, Martin D. Slade, Suzanne R. Kunkel, and Stanislav V. Kasl, "Longevity Increased by Positive Self-

Perceptions of Aging," *Journal of Personality and Social Psychology 83*, no. 2 (2002): 261–270.

18. Swanee Hunt, "G8: The Good News and Bad News." *Leadership*, 2001. (Publication of the Center for Public Leadership, Kennedy School of Government, Harvard University.)

19. Please see Jennifer E. Cliff, Nancy Langton, and Howard E. Aldrich, "Walking the Talk? Gendered Rhetoric vs. Action in Small Firms," *Organization Studies 26*, no. 1 (2005): 63–91.

20. Helgesen, *The Female Advantage*, 21.

21. Barbara A. Ritter and Janice D. Yoder, "Gender Differences in Leader Emergence Persist Even for Dominant Women: An Updated Confirmation of Role Congruity Theory," *Psychology of Women Quarterly 28*, no. 3 (2004): 187–193; Eagly and Karau, "Role Congruity Theory."

22. Eagly and Karau, "Role Congruity Theory."

23. Elizabeth H. Gorman, "Gender Stereotypes, Same-Gender Preferences, and Organizational Variation in the Hiring of Women: Evidence from Law Firms," *American Sociological Review 70*, no. 4 (2005): 702–728.

24. Ritter and Yoder, "Gender Differences in Leader Emergence Persist."

25. Diana Burgess and Eugene Borgida, "Who Women Are, Who Women Should Be: Descriptive and Prescriptive Gender Stereotyping in Sex Discrimination," *Psychology, Public Policy, and Law 5*, no. 3 (1999): 665–692; Eagly, *Sex Differences in Social Behavior*, xii; James R. Terborg, "Women in Management: A Research Review," *Journal of Applied Psychology 62* (1977): 647–664.

26. Madeline E. Heilman, "Description and Prescription: How Gender Stereotypes Prevent Women's Ascent Up the Organizational Ladder," *Journal of Social Issues 57*, no. 4 (2001): 657–674.

27. Rudman and Glick, "Feminized Management and Backlash Toward Agentic Women," 1009.

28. *Price Waterhouse v. Hopkins*, U.S. Supreme Court, 490 US 228, 1989. Retrieved from http://caselaw.lp.findlaw.com/

cgibin/getcase.pl?navby=case&court=US&vol=490&invol=
228 on August 16, 2006.

29. Brian Welle and Madeline E. Heilman, "The Exclusion of
Women from Full Engagement in the Workplace: The Role
of Gender Stereotypes," in D. Steiner, S. Gilliland, and D. Skar-
licki, eds., *Research in Social Issues in Management* (vol. 5)
(Charlotte, NC: Information Age Publishing, in press).

30. Madeline E. Heilman, Aaron S. Wallen, Daniella Fuchs, and
Melinda M. Tamkins, "Penalties for Success: Reactions to
Women Who Succeed at Male Gender-Typed Tasks," *Journal
of Applied Psychology* 89, no. 3 (2004): 416–427.

31. Madeline E. Heilman and Tyler G. Okimoto, "Averting
Penalties for Women's Success: Rectifying the Perceived
Communality Deficiency," *Journal of Applied Psychology* 92,
no. 1 (2007): 81–92.

32. Alice H. Eagly, Mona G. Makhijani, and Bruce G. Klonsky,
"Gender and the Evaluation of Leaders: A Meta-Analysis,"
Psychological Bulletin 111, no. 1 (1992): 3–22.

33. Joyce K. Fletcher, "The Greatly Exaggerated Demise of Heroic
Leadership: Gender, Power, and the Myth of the Female
Advantage," *Insights 13* (2002): 1–4; see p. 3.

34. Peter Glick and Susan T. Fiske, "The Ambivalent Sexism
Inventory: Differentiating Hostile and Benevolent Sexism,"
Journal of Personality and Social Psychology 70 (1996): 491–512.

35. Amy J. C. Cuddy, Susan T. Fiske, and Peter Glick, "When
Professionals Become Mothers, Warmth Doesn't Cut the Ice,"
Journal of Social Issues 60, no. 4 (2004): 701–718; Susan T.
Fiske, Amy J. C. Cuddy, Peter Glick, and Jun Xu, "A Model
of (Often Mixed) Stereotype Content: Competence and
Warmth Respectively Follow from Perceived Status and
Competition," *Journal of Personality and Social Psychology 82*,
no. 6 (2002): 878–902.

36. Melinda Taylor, CorporateHOPE and EVEolve Web site.
Retrieved from www.corporatehope.com/why_invest.htm on
June 13, 2006.

37. Swanee Hunt and Ayaan Hirsi Ali, "Realizing the Open Society: A Discussion on Islam, Gender and Free Speech," panel at Center for Government and International Studies, May 9, 2006, Harvard University.

38. Alice H. Eagly and Blair T. Johnson, "Gender and Leadership Style: A Meta-Analysis," *Psychological Bulletin* 108, no. 2 (1990): 233–256.

39. Kathryn M. Bartol, "The Sex Structuring of Organizations: A Search for Possible Causes," *Academy of Management Review* 3 (1978): 805–815; Rosabeth M. Kanter, *Men and Women of the Corporation* (New York: Basic Books, 1977).

40. Eagly and Johnson, "Gender and Leadership Style."

41. This included (1) downward communication content, (2) downward communication quality, (3) upward communication, (4) valence, (5) bases of power, (6) influence tactics, (7) contingencies, (8) attributions. Rice, Instone, and Adams, "Leader Sex, Leader Success, and Leadership Process."

42. D. Anthony Butterfield and Gary N. Powell, "Effect of Group Performance, Leader Sex, and Rater Sex on Ratings of Leader Behavior," *Organizational Behavior and Human Performance* 28 (1981): 129–141; see p. 130. (Cited in Rice, Instone, and Adams, "Leader Sex, Leader Success, and Leadership Process," p. 27.)

43. Bernard M. Bass, *Stogdill's Handbook of Leadership: A Survey of Theory and Research* (rev. ed.) (New York: Free Press, 1980), 499.

44. Mary C. Banwart and Mitchell S. McKinney, "A Gendered Influence in Campaign Debates? Analysis of Mixed-Gender United States Senate and Gubernatorial Debates," *Communication Studies* 56, no. 4 (2005): 353–374.

45. Cited in Jennifer L. Lawless and Richard L. Fox, *It Takes a Candidate: Why Women Don't Run for Office* (Cambridge, England: Cambridge University Press, 2005).

46. These researchers looked specifically at Village Councils in West Bengal and Rajasthan, at Council head positions reserved

for women. Raghabendra Chattopadhyay and Esther Duflo, "Women as Policy Makers: Evidence from a Randomized Policy Experiment in India," *Econometrica 72*, no. 5 (2004): 1409–1443.

47. Leslie A. Schwindt-Bayer and Renato Corbetta, "Gender Turnover and Roll Call Voting in the U.S. House of Representatives," *Legislative Studies Quarterly 29*, no. 2 (2004): 215–229. Cited in Lawless and Fox, *It Takes a Candidate*.

48. For more on this topic, please see Robert K. Merton, "The Self-Fulfilling Prophecy," *Antioch Review 8* (1948): 193–210; Robert K. Merton, "The Self-Fulfilling Prophecy," in *Social Theory and Social Structure* (New York: Free Press, 1957), 421–436.

49. Sabine Sczesny, Janine Bosak, Daniel Neff, and Birgit Schyns, "Gender Stereotypes and the Attribution of Leadership Traits: A Cross-Cultural Comparison," *Sex Roles 51*, no. 11–12 (2004): 631–645.

50. Cliff, Langton, and Aldrich, "Walking the Talk?"

51. Ruth Wageman, personal interview, Center for Public Leadership, Harvard University, May 23, 2006.

52. Fletcher, "The Greatly Exaggerated Demise of Heroic Leadership," 3.

53. Ruth Wageman, personal interview, May 23, 2006.

54. As was noted earlier, the meta-analysis by the same researchers on organizational studies yielded no leadership differences. Eagly and Johnson, "Gender and Leadership Style."

55. Alice H. Eagly, Marcy C. Johannesen-Schmidt, and Marloes L. van Engen, "Transformational, Transactional, and Laissez-Faire Leadership Styles: A Meta-Analysis Comparing Women and Men," *Psychological Bulletin 129*, no. 4 (2003): 569–591.

56. *Transformational* leadership, originally attributed to Burns, involves effective leaders who, by inspiring their followers, nurture their ability to contribute to the organization. James MacGregor Burns, *Leadership* (New York: HarperCollins,

1978). Transformational leadership is contrasted with *trans-actional* leadership, which involves establishing an exchange relationship with subordinates. Finally, *laissez-faire* leadership is a style marked by a failure to take on management responsibility. (From Eagly, Johannesen-Schmidt, and van Engen, "Transformational, Transactional, and Laissez-Faire Leadership Styles").

57. It should be noted that, in many of these cases, the types of leadership women display are considered to be better or more effective. Transformational leadership, for instance, Eagly, Johannesen-Schmidt, and van Engen write, shares a lot in common with "leaders' feminine personality attributes" and is more often displayed by women than by men, who tend to engage more in transactional and laissez-faire styles of leadership. It is also considered to be more effective in general. Yet Eagly and Johnson write that they are unwilling to infer that this means women possess a definitive leadership advantage: "Because experts on leader effectiveness ordinarily maintain that the effectiveness of leadership styles is contingent on features of the group or organizational environment . . . we are unwilling to argue that women's relatively democratic and participative style is either an advantage or disadvantage" (Eagly and Johnson, "Gender and Leadership Style," 249).

58. Eagly, Johannesen-Schmidt, and van Engen, "Transformational, Transactional, and Laissez-Faire Leadership Styles," 573.

59. Anita Roddick, cited in Helgesen, *The Female Advantage*, 6.

60. Heilman, "Description and Prescription," 659.

61. Fletcher, "The Greatly Exaggerated Demise of Heroic Leadership."

62. Banwart and McKinney, "A Gendered Influence in Campaign Debates?"

63. Interestingly, in Rosener's study, as well, the women describe themselves as having an equal mix of traits considered

"feminine" (excitable, gentle, emotional, submissive, sentimental, understanding, compassionate, sensitive, dependent), "masculine" (dominant, aggressive, tough, assertive, autocratic, analytical, competitive, independent), and "gender-neutral" (adaptive, tactful, sincere, conscientious, conventional, reliable, predictable, systematic, efficient) ("Ways Women Lead," 121). If women hold masculine and gender-neutral traits just as often as feminine ones, could it be that these categories should be abandoned?

64. Rudman and Glick, "Feminized Management and Backlash Toward Agentic Women."

65. Eagly, Johannesen-Schmidt, and van Engen, "Transformational, Transactional, and Laissez-Faire Leadership Styles."

66. See Eagly, Johannesen-Schmidt, and van Engen, "Transformational, Transactional, and Laissez-Faire Leadership Styles," especially the work on transactional and transformational leadership and their relative effectiveness.

67. Lourdes Garcia-Navarro, "Flores Vies to Become Peru's First Female President," National Public Radio *Morning Edition*, April 7, 2006; Monte Hayes, "Woman Joins Presidential Race in Peru," Associated Press, May 31, 2006. Retrieved from wtop.com/index.php?nid=389&pid=0&sid=742073&page=1 on June 19, 2006.

68. Garcia-Navarro, "Flores Vies to Become Peru's First Female President."

69. Rhea E. Steinpreis, Katie A. Anders, and Dawn Ritzke, "The Impact of Gender on the Review of the Curricula Vitae of Job Applicants and Tenure Candidates: A National Empirical Study," *Sex Roles 41*, no. 7–8 (1999): 509–528; Heilman, Wallen, Fuchs, and Tamkins, "Penalties for Success."

70. For more on functional leadership, please see Ruth Wageman, "How Leaders Foster Self-Managing Team Effectiveness: Design Choices Versus Hands-On Coaching," *Organization Science 12*, no. 5 (2001): 559–577; J. Richard Hackman, *Lead-*

ing Teams: Setting the Stage for Great Performances (Boston: Harvard Business School Press, 2002); J. Richard Hackman and Richard E. Walton, "Groups Under Contrasting Management Strategies," in P. S. Goodman, ed., *Designing Effective Work Groups* (San Francisco: Jossey-Bass, 1986), 141–159; J. Richard Hackman and Ruth Wageman, "A Theory of Team Coaching," *Academy of Management Review 30*, no. 2 (2005): 269–287.

71. Leslie A. DeChurch and Michelle A. Marks, "Leadership in Multiteam Systems," *Journal of Applied Psychology 91*, no. 2 (2006): 311–329.

3

OVERCOMING RESISTANCE TO WOMEN LEADERS

The Importance of Leadership Style

Linda L. Carli, Alice H. Eagly

Women have more access to leadership in organizations than ever before. In the United States about one-quarter of all chief executive positions are held by women. And women have at least half ownership of nearly 50 percent of all privately held U.S. firms.[1] Nevertheless, women continue to be rare at the top of the largest corporations. Indeed, in the Fortune 500, women hold less than 2 percent of the CEO positions and are 16 percent of corporate officer positions.[2] Impediments to women's leadership still exist and slow women's advancement to positions at the highest levels of power and authority. Women who advance must work harder and negotiate a more challenging path to leadership than men do.

Stereotypes About Women, Men, and Leaders

The unique pressures placed on female leaders derive in part from the relation between stereotypes about leaders and stereotypes about women and men. National and cross-national surveys reveal consensus about people's gender stereotypes. People consider men to be agentic, possessing traits such as ambition, confidence, self-sufficiency, dominance, and assertiveness, whereas they consider women to be communal, possessing traits such as kindness, helpfulness, concern for others, warmth, and gentleness.[3]

And how are leaders perceived? In general, because men are the more common occupants of most leadership roles, leaders are thought to have more agentic than communal qualities.[4] As a result, stereotypes about leaders match quite well with stereotypes about men. Because of this similarity between people's mental associations about men and leaders, men can seem usual or natural in most leadership roles. Therefore, they do not need to be concerned about tailoring their leadership style to be accepted as legitimate. Men usually do not need to worry as much about appearing to be too masculine or too feminine and are freer than women to execute leadership as they see fit.

In contrast, women leaders are at a disadvantage because associations about women are typically inconsistent with those about leaders. Although this incongruity appears to be decreasing over time, it has not disappeared. Thus people more easily credit men with leadership ability and more readily accept men as leaders.[5]

The challenge for female leaders is further complicated by the fact that gender stereotypes are not merely descriptive but prescriptive as well.[6] Consequently, people not only expect women to be warm, kind, and sensitive, they prefer women to behave in such communal ways. Women who fail to show a warm, sensitive side may be seen as difficult and unlikable.

Because of these stereotypes, female leaders face a double bind.[7] To fulfill the requirements of the female gender role, they are expected to be especially communal, and to fulfill the requirements of the leader role, they are expected to be especially agentic. But many agentic behaviors can be seen as incompatible with being communal. As a result, women leaders are vulnerable to becoming targets of prejudice. Often people consider women unqualified because they lack the stereotypical directive and assertive qualities of good leaders. But people also frequently dislike women who possess and display those very abilities because highly directive and assertive behavior can be incompatible with the communal stereotype of the female gender role. Because of the prescription for female communion, people expect women to avoid behavior that is too threatening or directive, or that seems to overtly seek leadership, influence, or status.[8] People therefore often resist leadership by women.

Resistance to Female Leaders

Evidence of the rejection of female leadership comes from studies of people's reactions to women who are highly agentic. For example, in one experiment involving interactions between pairs of college students, one member of each pair was a male or female actor trained to communicate in either a communal style by agreeing with the other person or in a more dominant, status-asserting style by overtly disagreeing. People disliked the dominant woman and responded to her dominance with anger, irritation, and hostility, whereas they did not express hostility toward a man who was equally dominant. In addition, the female actors exerted more influence concerning the topic when communal than when dominant, but male actors were equally influential in these two conditions.[9]

Other research confirms that women using a self-asserting or threatening style have less influence than men using the same style, or than women using a communal, supportive style.[10] Such agentic behavior is more acceptable in men than in women because agency is associated with the male gender role.

Resistance to female agency is especially evident in people's perceptions of highly successful female leaders. In experiments where people were presented with descriptions of successful female or male managers, the women were seen as more pushy, selfish, abrasive, and manipulative compared to their male counterparts. Likewise, women who succeed in male-dominated professions frequently elicit hostile responses. In an experiment illustrating this phenomenon, women described as succeeding in the masculine careers of electrical engineer or electrician were perceived as less likable, attractive, happy, and socially desirable than women described as succeeding in the feminine careers of day-care provider or nurse.[11]

Just as people tolerate assertiveness and dominance in men more than in women, they are also more tolerant of self-promotion in men. People consider women who describe their achievements in a self-promoting manner as less deserving of recognition or support than less self-promoting women, whereas men are not penalized for self-promotion. Women who self-promote generally exert less influence than more modest women and are less well liked even though people who self-promote are considered more competent than their more modest counterparts. Why? Boastfulness and self-promotion are incompatible with the selflessness and other-directedness inherent in the female gender role.[12]

Because men possess higher status than women, when women attempt to wield influence and leadership they compete with men for power and authority. This competition is particularly acute in male-dominated and higher-level leadership positions, where men have more to lose from women's advancement. As a result, men disapprove of high levels of competence and authority in women more than in men.[13]

Men particularly resist the influence of agentically competent women. In an experiment examining the effectiveness of assertive versus tentative speech, tentative speech was marked by verbal disclaimers such as "I may be wrong" or "I'm no expert" and hedges such as "sort of" or "kind of," and assertive speech was marked by the absence of such disclaimers and hedges.[14] Men were equally influential in these two speech conditions. When speaking competently, women were perceived to be more competent and exerted greater influence over a female audience as a result, but were less able to influence the opinions of a male audience than when speaking tentatively. In essence, men were more influenced by a woman they perceived to be low rather than high in competence, rating the competent woman as less trustworthy and less likable than her less competent counterpart. Other studies have confirmed this finding that women can increase their influence with men by communicating in ways that both men and women consider less competent than regular speech.[15]

Because of the demand for female communion, women who are too assertive can undermine their chances of getting a job or advancing in their careers. In one study in a large financial institution, the more the male subordinates displayed direct and assertive influence tactics, the more they received favorable performance reviews and mentoring from their supervisors. But supervisors gave more mentoring to female subordinates who used weak and indirect influence tactics. In another study, corporate executives were presented with a description of a job applicant's answers to interview questions and asked to indicate how likely they would be to hire that applicant. The executives expressed more interest in hiring the male job applicants who were most assertive, but were least likely to hire the most assertive women. Similarly, an experiment demonstrated that managers and other adults considered a woman to be too demanding and insufficiently nice when she asserted herself by asking for a bigger salary while applying for promotion. As a result, they considered a woman making such a request to be less desirable to hire than a woman who accepted the salary she was offered.[16]

Clearly, people expect women to be more communal than men and penalize women who don't seem communal enough. This is one half of the double bind that women face when attempting to exert influence, authority, and leadership. The other half derives from people's doubts about women's agency. Because people automatically assume that men possess considerable agency, men receive the benefit of the doubt as leaders. But because women are thought to possess less agentic competence, people hold women to a higher standard of performance. In fact, experiments show that people must be given very clear and unambiguous evidence of a woman's substantial superiority before judging the woman to be better than a man at typical group tasks.[17]

Because people generally are more influential when they are considered to be competent, the perception that women are less agentically competent than men makes it difficult for women to exert influence. When women make important contributions to discussions, for example, they are likely to be ignored or discounted. In one group experiment, when information was contributed by an individual man, group members were over five times more likely to use it than when the identical information was contributed by an individual woman. In another experiment, groups were better able to recognize the person who was their most expert member when that member was a man than when it was a woman. In fact, the expertise of the female experts—but not the male experts—was discounted and rated by group members as below average for their group.[18]

A double standard requires female leaders to work harder to receive comparable evaluations to men. In experiments, when people evaluate male and female leaders depicted as leading in the same ways, the men are perceived to be more competent leaders than the women. People especially favor men over women in masculine settings, where women might be expected to be less expert, but men are favored even in gender-neutral settings. Only in decidedly feminine contexts are women seen to be equal to men. As a result, people devalue female leaders more in male-dominated than female-dominated leadership roles and prefer to hire men over women for masculine and gender-neutral jobs, and women over men only for feminine jobs.[19] Of course, positions involving authority and leadership are perceived as masculine, so female leaders have to perform exceptionally well to be accepted as competent leaders.

The double bind thus places two unique demands on women leaders: to display superior ability to overcome doubts about their competence as leaders and to temper their competence with communion to fulfill the demands of the female gender role. In fact, this competent, warm style can undermine resistance to women's influence and leadership. Delivering this style requires an artful balancing act on the part of female leaders. In an experiment illustrating the advantages of this balance, participants listened to a woman or man who spoke in either a highly competent style, using relatively rapid, articulate speech, or a highly competent and warm style, using rapid, articulate speech as well as friendly nodding and smiling.[20] The male speaker was equally well liked and influential, no matter how he spoke. And women responded equally favorably to the female speaker, regardless of her style. But men found the woman to be less likable and more threatening when she was merely competent, and they were less influenced by her as a result. Only when the woman combined competence and warmth was she successful in influencing men.

Leadership Styles of Women and Men

So how do women leaders cope with the double bind, which creates resistance and uneasiness about their leadership style? It would be surprising if women's leadership styles were exactly the same as men's. In fact, on the average, women do lead somewhat differently, but these differences are more subtle than claimed by the authors of popular books about women's leadership styles.[21] Also, as research has established, the challenges that women often face as leaders have not channeled them into inferior leadership styles. In fact, the leadership styles more typical of women than men resemble those recommended by most experts on leadership.

First let us consider what leadership style is. Styles are relatively consistent patterns of interaction that typify leaders as individuals. These styles do not consist of a particular set of fixed behaviors but instead encompass a range of behaviors that have a consistent meaning or function. Leaders of course vary their behaviors within the confines of their style, depending on the situation and audience. For example, a leader with a typically democratic style might display the collaborative behaviors of consulting, discussing, or negotiating, depending on the circumstance. Moreover, leaders with typical styles may nevertheless abandon their characteristic styles in certain situations. In a crisis, for example, a leader whose typical mode is democratic might become highly directive because an emergency situation demands quick, decisive action.

One of the arguments against the idea that women and men have different leadership styles is that roles demand particular styles so that men and women in the same role would behave essentially the same.[22] Although managerial roles do shape styles in particular directions, managers also have some freedom to vary the way in which they carry out their jobs. For example, research on *organizational citizenship behavior* shows that many people go beyond the requirements of their organizational roles.[23] Examples of such behavior include helping others with their work and volunteering for work that is not part of one's job. More generally, leadership roles allow their occupants considerable discretion to be friendly or more remote, to provide extensive or limited mentoring of subordinates, and so forth. These discretionary aspects of leadership are most likely to differ between women and men because they are not closely regulated by leader roles.

Why might female leaders' styles differ from those of men? As we have argued, women are faced with accommodating the conflicting demands of their roles as women and as leaders. Because of the tension between the communal qualities that people prefer women to have and the predominantly agentic qualities expected in leaders, female leaders are buffeted by cross-pressures. Their leadership can be constrained by negative reactions to their more masculine behaviors, such as asserting clear-cut authority over others. However, a style that colleagues regard as soft, indirect, or indecisive can derail female executives because it may be regarded as "not tough enough" for wielding authority. Given such cross-pressures, finding an appropriate and effective leadership style is not an easy task for women. Female managers recognize this challenge. Catalyst's study of Fortune 1000 female executives thus found that 96 percent rated as *critical* or *fairly important* "developing a style with which male managers are comfortable."[24]

How do women proceed? In one way or another, women generally split the difference between the masculine and feminine demands that they face. Successful female leaders generally find a middle way that is neither unacceptably masculine nor unacceptably feminine. But is there evidence that men and women really differ in how they lead? The answer is yes: Empirical research is extensive and does demonstrate small but important differences in the leadership styles of women and men.

Most research on leadership style conducted prior to 1990 distinguished between *task-oriented style*, defined as leader behaviors that accomplish assigned tasks, and *interpersonally oriented* style, defined as leader behaviors that foster good interpersonal relationships. Robert Bales introduced this distinction in 1950, and many other researchers developed it. Another important distinction was between leaders who behave democratically and allow subordinates to participate in decision making, or who behave autocratically and discourage subordinates from participation. This distinction, labeled *democratic* versus *autocratic* leadership or *participative* versus *directive* leadership, was developed by a number of researchers. To assess sex differences and similarities in these styles, Alice Eagly and Blair Johnson reviewed 162 studies that provided quantitative comparisons of women and men on relevant measures.[25]

This meta-analysis of studies from 1961 through 1987 found that leadership styles were somewhat gender-stereotypical in studies with student participants and other participants not selected for occupancy of leadership roles, such as general samples of employees. In these studies, women more than men manifested relatively interpersonally oriented and democratic styles, and men more than women manifested relatively task-oriented and autocratic styles. In contrast, sex differences were more limited in organizational studies that assessed managers' styles. The only consistent difference obtained between female and male managers was that women adopted a more democratic (or participative) style and a less autocratic (or directive) style than men did. Although this average sex difference was relatively small, 92 percent of the available comparisons went in the direction of a more democratic or participative style among women. A subsequent meta-analysis that surveyed studies published between 1987 and 2000 produced similar findings.[26]

In the 1980s and 1990s, new distinctions about leadership styles emerged among leadership researchers working to identify the types of leadership that are attuned to the conditions of contemporary organizations. These conditions include accelerated technological growth and increased complexity of organizations' missions. Accompanying these changes are increasing workforce diversity, intense competitive pressures, and the globalization of many organizations.

In this environment, the traditional ways of managing have lost much of their force, and more complex relationships of interdependency have emerged.[27]

Leadership scholars responded to these challenges by studying leadership that is future oriented rather than present oriented and that strengthens organizations by inspiring followers' commitment and enhancing their ability to contribute creatively to organizations. An approach of this type initially emerged in a book by political scientist James MacGregor Burns, who delineated a type of leadership that he labeled *transformational*. As subsequently elaborated by other leadership scholars, transformational leadership involves establishing oneself as a role model by gaining followers' trust and confidence. Such leaders delineate future goals, develop plans to achieve those goals, and innovate even when their organization is already successful. By mentoring and empowering their subordinates, such leaders encourage them to develop their potential and thus to contribute more effectively to their organization. Related traditions incorporated many of these same qualities (for example, *charismatic leadership*).[28]

Leadership researchers contrasted transformational leaders with *transactional* leaders, who appeal to subordinates' self-interest by establishing exchange relationships with them. This type of leadership involves clarifying subordinates' responsibilities, rewarding them for meeting objectives, and correcting them for failing to meet objectives. In addition to these two styles, researchers distinguished a *laissez-faire* style that is marked by an overall failure to take responsibility for managing. Transformational, transactional, and laissez-faire leadership are most commonly assessed by the Multifactor Leadership Questionnaire, known as the MLQ.[29] As shown in Table 3.1, this instrument represents transformational leadership by five subscales, transactional leadership by three subscales, and laissez-faire leadership by one scale.

Is transformational leadership generally effective? To find out, management scholars Timothy Judge and Ronald Piccolo meta-analyzed eighty-seven studies, testing the relationships between these

Table 3.1   Definitions of Transformational, Transactional, and Laissez-Faire Leadership Styles in the Multifactor Leadership (MLQ) Questionnaire and Mean Effect Sizes Comparing Men and Women

MLQ Scale and Subscale	Description of Leadership Style	Effect Size
Transformational		–0.10
Idealized influence (attribute)	Demonstrates qualities that motivate respect and pride from association with the leader	–0.09
Idealized influence (behavior)	Communicates values, purpose, and importance of organization's mission	–0.12
Inspirational motivation	Exhibits optimism and excitement about goals and future states	–0.02
Intellectual stimulation	Examines new perspectives for solving problems and completing tasks	–0.05
Individualized consideration	Focuses on development and mentoring of followers and attends to their individual needs	–0.19
Transactional		
Contingent reward	Provides rewards for satisfactory performance by followers	–0.13
Active management-by-exception	Attends to followers' mistakes and failures to meet standards	0.12
Passive management-by-exception	Waits until problems become severe before attending to them and intervening	0.27
Laissez-faire	Exhibits frequent absence and lack of involvement during critical junctures	0.16

Note: Table is from Eagly, Johannesen-Schmidt, and van Engen, 2003, Tables 1 and 3. Effect sizes are means of all available studies, with more reliable values weighted more heavily. Positive effect sizes for a given leadership style indicate that men had higher scores than women, and negative effect sizes indicate that women had higher scores than men. No effect size appears for overall transactional leadership because its component subscales did not manifest a consistent direction.

styles and leaders' effectiveness. Transformational leadership did prove to be effective overall.[30] As for transactional leadership, leaders' effectiveness related positively to its "contingent reward" component, which features rewarding subordinates for appropriate behavior. This aspect of transactional leadership was almost as effective as transformational leadership and especially predicted followers' satisfaction with their leaders. Also, effectiveness showed only a weak positive relationship to leaders' pointing out flaws to subordinates and otherwise using punishment to shape their behavior (the style aspect known as "active management-by-exception"). As expected, intervening only when situations become extreme (the passive aspect of management-by-exception), was ineffective, as was laissez-faire leadership.

When sufficient research comparing men and women on these styles had accumulated, Alice Eagly, Mary Johannesen-Schmidt, and Marloes van Engen carried out a meta-analysis of forty-five such studies. Although many types of managers were represented, the majority were from either business or educational organizations. The measures of leadership style were completed by the leaders themselves or by their subordinates, peers, or superiors.[31]

As displayed in Table 3.1, this meta-analysis revealed that female leaders were more transformational than male leaders and also engaged in more of the contingent reward behaviors that are one component of transactional leadership. Among the five subscales of transformational leadership, women most exceeded men on the individualized consideration subscale that identifies supportive, encouraging treatment of subordinates. Also, male leaders were more likely to manifest two other aspects of transactional leadership (active and passive management-by-exception) and laissez faire leadership, although fewer studies had assessed these aspects of style. All of these differences between male and female leaders were small, consistent with large individual differences within each sex.

In summary, women, more than men, manifest leadership styles that relate positively to effectiveness, and men, more than women, manifest styles that relate only weakly to effectiveness or that hinder effectiveness. Corroborating these results, an excellent large-scale study primarily of business managers, which was not available when the meta-analysis was conducted, has yielded very similar findings.[32]

Overall, women's leadership styles surely provide no basis for denying them access to leadership roles. On the contrary, women lead in a style that appears to recommend them for leadership. For many years, leadership researchers have called for transformational and collaborative styles to manage the complexities of contemporary organizations.[33] Specifically, as we have indicated, women's styles tend to be more democratic and participative, compared with men's more autocratic and directive styles. Also, female managers tend to adopt a transformational style and use more rewards to encourage appropriate subordinate behavior. In contrast, men, more than women, attend to subordinates' failures to meet standards and display the more problematic styles that involve avoiding solving problems until they become acute and being absent or uninvolved at critical times.

What accounts for this particular pattern of findings? Causes may derive from several factors:

- The ability of the transformational repertoire (and contingent reward behaviors) to resolve some of the typical incongruity between leadership roles and the female gender role because these styles are not distinctively masculine
- Gender roles' influence on women's leadership by means of the spillover of gender-specific norms, which would facilitate the more feminine aspects of transformational leadership, especially individualized consideration
- Double standards by which women have to be more highly competent than men as leaders to obtain leadership roles in the first place[34]

Although blending agency and warmth is generally a useful and effective strategy for female leaders, it can be less effective in very masculine domains and in leadership positions that are most heavily male dominated. In such highly masculine environments, there may be little or no precedent for more feminine and interpersonally oriented leadership styles and little tolerance for female leaders. In such environments, obviously sexist or hostile behavior can also pose difficulties for women. In fact, resistance to women in the form of sexual harassment occurs most frequently in settings with a high percentage of men, such as the military. To address strong male resistance, women leaders in very masculine environments may see no alternative but to emulate the leadership style used by the male leaders who predominate in these settings. Indeed, women's greater democratic style disappears in more masculine domains.[35]

Conclusion

Women leaders experience challenges not faced by their male counterparts. They confront doubts about their competence as leaders, but at the same time may be criticized for displaying too much agency and not enough communion. This double bind undermines women's influence and creates resistance to women's leadership. Women leaders face these competing demands of their roles as women and as leaders, which may contribute to their manifesting leadership styles that are competent and agentic, yet simultaneously warm and communal. Women's somewhat greater use of transformational leadership and the rewarding aspect of transactional leadership encompasses this integrated balance of agency and communion.

Although people's masculine perceptions of leadership have placed women leaders at a disadvantage, these perceptions are changing in ways that increasingly favor women. Global competition, technological growth, increased workforce and customer diversity, and accelerated social change have all placed increasing pressure on organizations to find new and creative approaches to leadership and management. Traditional models of management are being rejected in favor of more democratic, participatory, and team-based approaches.[36]

In addition, the increasing numbers of women in leadership positions are beginning to transform cultural stereotypes about leaders. For example, people's associations of masculinity with management are weakening. Although men are still favored, there is now greater acceptance than in the past of women as bosses and political leaders.[37] These changes in stereotypes and attitudes are likely to continue as more women gain entry to positions of authority and rise to higher levels of leadership in business, politics, and other fields. As a result, resistance to women leaders is likely to lessen, making it easier for women to become leaders and for their leadership to be accepted.

Endnotes

1. For chief executives, see U.S. Bureau of Labor Statistics, "News: Employment Characteristics of Families in 2005," April 2006, available online: www.bls.gov/news.release/pdf/famee.pdf, access date: June 5, 2006. For business ownership, see Center for Women's Business Research, "Women-Owned Businesses in the United States 2006: Fact sheet," 2006, available online: www.cfwbr.org/assets/344_2006nationalfactsheet.pdf, access date: December 13, 2006.

2. Catalyst, "2005 Catalyst Census of Women Corporate Officers and Top Earners of the Fortune 500," 2006, available online, http://catalyst.org/files/full/2005%20COTE.pdf, access date: August 10, 2006.

3. Frank Newport, "Americans See Women as Emotional and Affectionate, Men as More Aggressive: Gender Specific Stereotypes Persist in Recent Gallup Poll" (February 21, 2001), available online: http://brain.gallup.com, access date: January 25, 2004; John E. Williams and Deborah L. Best, *Measuring Sex Stereotypes: A Multination Study* (Thousand Oaks, CA: Sage, 1990).

4. Virginia E. Schein, "A Global Look at Psychological Barriers to Women's Progress in Management," *Journal of Social Issues* 57 (2001): 675–688.

5. For evidence of incongruity in associations between women and leaders, see Alice H. Eagly and Steven J. Karau, "Role Congruity Theory of Prejudice Toward Female Leaders," *Psychological Review* 109 (2002): 573–598; Schein, "A Global Look." For changes in these associations over time, see Emily E. Duehr and Joyce E. Bono, "Men, Women, and Managers: Are Stereotypes Finally Changing?" *Personnel Psychology* 59 (2006): 815–846; Sabine Sczesny, Janine Bosak, Daniel Neff, and Birgit Schyns, "Gender Stereotypes and the Attribution of Leadership Traits: A Cross-Cultural Comparison," *Sex Roles* 51 (2004): 631–645.

6. Eagly and Karau, "Role Congruity Theory."

7. Alice H. Eagly and Linda L. Carli, "Women and Men as Leaders," in John Antonakis, Anna T. Cianciolo, and Robert J. Sternberg, eds., *The Nature of Leadership* (Thousand Oaks, CA: Sage, 2004), 279–301.

8. Linda L. Carli, "Gender, Interpersonal Power, and Social Influence," Journal of Social Issues 55 (1999): 81–99.

9. Linda L. Carli, "Gender and Social Influence: Women Confront the Double Bind" (paper presented at the 26th International Congress of Applied Psychology, Athens, Greece, July 16–21, 2006).

10. Michael Burgoon, Thomas S. Birk, and John R. Hall, "Compliance and Satisfaction with Physician-Patient Communication: An Expectancy Theory Interpretation of Gender Differences," *Human Communication Research* 18 (1991): 177–208; Steve L. Ellyson, John F. Dovidio, and Clifford E. Brown, "The Look of Power: Gender Differences in Visual Dominance Behavior," in Cecilia L. Ridgeway, ed., *Gender, Interaction, and Inequality* (New York: Springer-Verlag, 1992), 50–80; Susan Shackelford, Wendy Wood, and Stephen Worchel, "Behavioral Styles and the Influence of Women in Mixed-Sex Groups," *Social Psychology Quarterly* 59 (1996): 284–293.

11. For perceptions of female and male managers, see Madeline E. Heilman, Aaron S. Wallen, Daniella Fuchs, and Melinda M. Tamkins, "Penalties for Success: Reactions to Women Who Succeed in Male Gender-Typed Tasks," *Journal of Applied Psychology* 89 (2004): 416–427; Madeline E. Heilman, Caryn J. Block, and Richard F. Martell, "Sex Stereotypes: Do They Influence Perceptions of Managers?" *Journal of Social Behavior and Personality* 10 (1995): 237–252. For hostile responses to women in male-dominated professions, see Janice D. Yoder and Thomas L. Schleicher, "Undergraduates Regard Deviation from Occupational Gender Stereotypes as Costly for Women," *Sex Roles* 34 (1996): 171–188.

12. For perceptions of how deserving self-promoting women are, see Robert A. Giacalone and Catherine A. Riordan, "Effect of Self-Presentation on Perceptions and Recognition in an Organization," *Journal of Psychology* 124 (1990): 25–38; Wilhelmina Wosinska, Amy J. Dabul, Robin Whetstone-Dion, and Robert Cialdini, "Self-Presentational Responses to Success in the Organization: The Costs and Benefits of Modesty," *Basic and Applied Social Psychology* 18 (1996): 229–242. For influence and liking, see Carli, *Gender and Social Influence;* Laurie A. Rudman, "Self-Promotion as a Risk Factor for Women: The Costs and Benefits of Counterstereotypical Impression Management," *Journal of Personality and Social Psychology* 74 (1998): 629–645.

13. Linda L. Carli, "Gender Effects on Persuasiveness and Compliance Gaining: A Review," in John S. Seiter and Robert H. Gass, eds., *Perspectives on Persuasion, Social Influence, and Compliance Gaining* (Needham Heights, MA: Allyn & Bacon, 2004), 133–148.

14. Linda L. Carli, "Gender, Language, and Influence," *Journal of Personality and Social Psychology* 59 (1990): 941–951.

15. See, for example, Melannie Matschiner and Sarah K. Murnen, "Hyperfemininity and Influence," *Psychology of Women*

Quarterly 23 (1999): 631–642; Gabriel Weimann, "Sex Differences in Dealing with Bureaucracy," *Sex Roles* 12 (1985): 777–790.

16. For mentoring, see Bennett J. Tepper, Sheryl J. Brown, and Marilyn D. Hunt, "Strength of Subordinates' Upward Influence Tactics and Gender Congruency Effects," *Journal of Applied Social Psychology* 23 (1993): 1903–1919. For the hiring study, see E. Holly Buttner and Martha McEnally, "The Interactive Effect of Influence Tactic, Applicant Gender, and Type of Job on Hiring Recommendations," *Sex Roles* 34 (1996): 581–591. For salary negotiations, see Hannah Bowles, Linda Babcock, and Lei Lai, "It Depends Who Is Asking and Whom You Ask: Social Incentives for Sex Differences in the Propensity to Initiate Negotiation" (unpublished manuscript, Harvard University, 2006).

17. For evidence of a higher standard for women, see Monica Biernat and Diane Kobrynowicz, "Gender- and Race-Based Standards of Competence: Lower Minimum Standards but Higher Ability Standards for Devalued Groups," *Journal of Personality and Social Psychology* 72 (1997): 544–557; Madeline E. Heilman, "Description and Prescription: How Gender Stereotypes Prevent Women's Ascent Up the Organizational Ladder," *Journal of Social Issues* 57 (2001): 657–674. For evidence that women must outperform men to be seen as equal, see Madeline E. Heilman and Michelle C. Haynes, "No Credit Where Credit Is Due: Attributional Rationalization of Women's Success in Male-Female Teams," *Journal of Applied Psychology* 90 (2005): 905–916; Shackelford, Wood, and Worchel, "Behavioral Styles and the Influence of Women."

18. For greater use of information contributed by men, see Kathleen M. Propp, "An Experimental Examination of Biological Sex as a Status Cue in Decision-Making Groups and Its Influence on Information Use," *Small Group Research* 26 (1995): 451–474. For greater recognition of male than female experts, see Melissa C. Thomas-Hunt and Katherine W. Phillips,

"When What You Know Is Not Enough: Expertise and Gender Dynamics in Task Groups," *Personality and Social Psychology Bulletin 30* (2004): 1585–1598.

19. For research on leaders, see Alice H. Eagly, Mona G. Makhijani, and Bruce G. Klonsky, "Gender and the Evaluation of Leaders: A Meta-Analysis," *Psychological Bulletin 111* (1992): 3–22. For research on hiring, see Heather K. Davison and Michael J. Burke, "Sex Discrimination in Simulated Employment Contexts: A Meta-Analytic Investigation," *Journal of Vocational Behavior 56* (2000): 225–248. The preference for men in gender-neutral jobs comes from an unpublished analysis by Heather Davison, 2005.

20. Linda L. Carli, Suzanne J. LaFleur, and Christopher C. Loeber, "Nonverbal Behavior, Gender, and Influence," *Journal of Personality and Social Psychology 68* (1995): 1030–1041.

21. For example, Judy B. Rosener, *America's Competitive Secret: Utilizing Women as Management Strategy* (New York: Oxford University Press, 1995).

22. Rosabeth Moss Kanter, *Men and Women of the Corporation* (New York: Basic Books, 1977); Marloes L. van Engen, Rien van der Leeden, and Tineke M. Willemsen, "Gender, Context and Leadership Styles: A Field Study," *Journal of Occupational and Organizational Psychology 74* (2001): 581–598.

23. Walter C. Borman, "The Concept of Organizational Citizenship," *Current Directions in Psychological Science 13* (2004): 238–241; Philip M. Podsakoff, Scott B. MacKenzie, Julie B. Paine, and Daniel G. Bachrach, "Organizational Citizenship Behaviors: A Critical Review of the Theoretical and Empirical Literature and Suggestions for Future Research," *Journal of Management 26* (2000): 513–563.

24. Catalyst, *Women in Corporate Leadership: Comparisons Among the US, the UK, and Canada* (New York: Catalyst, 2001). http://www.catalyst.org/files/fact/US,%20UK,%20Canada%20WICL%20Comparisons.pdf, access date: February 17, 2007.

25. Robert F. Bales, *Interaction Process Analysis: A Method for the Study of Small Groups* (Reading, MA: Addison-Wesley, 1950); Alice H. Eagly and Blair T. Johnson, "Gender and Leadership Style: A Meta-Analysis," *Psychological Bulletin* 108 (1990): 233–256. See John K. Hemphill and Alvin E. Coons, "Development of the Leader Behavior Description Questionnaire," in Ralph M. Stogdill and Alvin E. Coons, eds., *Leader Behavior: Its Description and Measurement* (Columbus, OH: Bureau of Business Research, Ohio State University, 1957), 6–38, for the distinction between task-oriented and interpersonally oriented styles, and Victor H. Vroom and Philip W. Yetton, *Leadership and Decision-Making* (Pittsburgh, PA: University of Pittsburgh Press, 1973), for work on democratic versus autocratic styles.

26. Marloes van Engen and Tineke Willemsen, "Sex and Leadership Styles: A Meta-Analysis of Research Published in the 1990s," *Psychological Reports* 94 (2004): 3–18.

27. Rosabeth Moss Kanter, *Rosabeth Moss Kanter on the Frontiers of Management* (Boston: Harvard Business School Press, 1997).

28. For transformational leadership, see James M. Burns, *Leadership* (New York: HarperCollins, 1978); Bruce J. Avolio, *Full Leadership Development: Building the Vital Forces in Organizations* (Thousand Oaks, CA: Sage, 1999); Bernard M. Bass, *Transformational Leadership: Industrial, Military, and Educational Impact* (Mahwah, NJ: Erlbaum, 1998). For charismatic leadership, see Jay A. Conger and Rabindra N. Kanungo, *Charismatic Leadership in Organizations* (Thousand Oaks, CA: Sage, 1998).

29. John Antonakis, Bruce J. Avolio, and Nagaraj Sivasubramaniam, "Context and Leadership: An Examination of the Nine-Factor Full-Range Leadership Theory Using the Multifactor Leadership Questionnaire," *Leadership Quarterly* 14 (2003): 261–295.

30. Timothy A. Judge and Ronald F. Piccolo, "Transformational and Transactional Leadership: A Meta-Analytic Test of Their Relative Validity," *Journal of Applied Psychology* 89 (2004): 901–910.

31. Alice H. Eagly, Mary C. Johannesen-Schmidt, and Marloes L. van Engen, "Transformational, Transactional, and Laissez-Faire Leadership Styles: A Meta-Analysis Comparing Women and Men," *Psychological Bulletin* 129 (2003): 569–591.

32. Antonakis, Avolio, and Sivasubramaniam, "Context and Leadership."

33. For example, Kanter, *Rosabeth Moss Kanter on the Frontiers of Management*; Jean Lipman-Blumen, *The Connective Edge: Leading in an Interdependent World* (San Francisco: Jossey-Bass, 1996).

34. See Michael Z. Hackman, Alison H. Furniss, Marylyn J. Hills, and Tracey J. Paterson, "Perceptions of Gender-Role Characteristics and Transformational and Transactional Leadership Behaviours," *Perceptual and Motor Skills* 75 (1992): 311–319; Biernat and Kobrynowicz, "Gender- and Race-Based Standards"; and Martha Foschi, "Double Standards for Competence: Theory and Research," *Annual Review of Sociology* 26 (2000): 21–42.

35. For sexual harassment, see Robert A. Jackson and Meredith A. Newman, "Sexual Harassment in the Federal Workplace Revisited: Influences on Sexual Harassment by Gender," *Public Administration Review* 64 (2004): 705–717; U.S. Merit Systems Protection Board, *Sexual Harassment in the Federal Workplace: Trends, Progress, Continuing Challenge* (Washington, DC: U.S. Government Printing Office, 1995). For effects of masculine domains on style, see Eagly and Johnson, "Gender and Leadership Style."

36. Avolio, *Full Leadership Development*; Kanter, *Rosabeth Moss Kanter on the Frontiers of Management*; Lipman-Blumen, *The Connective Edge*.

37. For evidence of changes in perceptions of managers, see Duehr and Bono, "Men, Women, and Managers"; Sczesny, Bosak, Neff, and Schyns, "Gender Stereotypes and the Attribution of Leadership Traits"; Schein, "A Global Look." For changes in perceptions of bosses and political leaders, respectively, see David W. Moore, "Americans More Accepting of Female Bosses Than Ever," May 10, 2002, available online: http://brain.gallup.com, access date: September 24, 2004; David W. Moore, "Little Prejudice Against a Woman, Jewish, Black, or Catholic Presidential Candidate, June 10, 2003, available online: http://brain.gallup.com, access date: September 6, 2004.

4

WOMEN, LEADERSHIP, AND THE NATURAL ORDER

Rosalind Chait Barnett

While the question of whether women have what it takes to be leaders continues to capture headlines in the United States, the same is not true in many other countries. In 2005, Michelle Bachelet was elected president of Chile, Angela Merkel was named chancellor of Germany, and Ellen Johnson-Sirleaf was elected president of Liberia. Politics is not the only realm in which women's capacity to lead is questioned: women's ability to lead in business and the military is also the topic of considerable public debate in the United States. Although this debate occurs at all levels of our society—our homes, classrooms, universities, legislatures, courtrooms—nowhere is it more visible and influential than in the media.

Another favorite theme of the American press concerns women's leadership style. Are women more democratic, empathic, and sensitive than men? Are women's leadership traits well designed for the cutthroat world of high-level statesmanship? This issue has been debated as long as anyone can remember. And it still goes on; witness the December 24, 2005, cover of *Newsweek* featuring Oprah Winfrey. The title story was "How Women Lead." This media obsession is totally unaffected by the wealth of social science data that find only minor gender differences in men's and women's leadership styles, as discussed by Kellerman and Rhode.[1] The data tell us that both men and women exhibit the traits that are associated with good leadership.[2] Nevertheless, the debate goes on, suggesting that there is still an open and serious question to be resolved.

When we conjure up images of business leaders, the people that come to mind are almost always male. Perhaps that is only natural because men predominate in leadership positions in corporate America. Yet many women have achieved great success in the business world, although their accomplishments are not heralded and the memories of their feats quickly fade. Thus when we are asked to name business leaders, Bill Gates, Jack Welch, and Steve Jobs all come to mind; they are household names. In contrast, few would name Meg Whitman, president and CEO of eBay; Brenda Barnes, president and chief executive of Sara Lee; or Patricia Russo, CEO of the merged Lucent-Alcatel telecommunications company that has earnings of roughly $25 billion per year.

The same scenario applies when we think of military leaders. Because of strong support for the belief in the natural order in this highly masculinized environment, leadership opportunities for women have until recently been limited. Over time, and especially since Operation Desert Storm in 1991, women in the U.S. military been given the opportunity to lead and are showing that they have "the right stuff."

The only time that the idea of a woman as a serious contender for president gets any attention in the press is once every four years, and then only if there is a woman who might be a credible candidate and has the gumption to put herself forward. While the media generally brush aside the possibility of a female president, the general population seems, in principle, more accepting. A January 2006 CBS News/*New York Times* Poll found that 92 percent of a national sample of 1,229 adults surveyed responded affirmatively when asked, "If your party nominated a woman for president, would you vote for her if she were qualified for the job?" Interestingly, there were no significant differences in the percentage of men (93 percent) and women (92 percent) who would consider casting their vote for a qualified woman.

Why is it that we know so little about the leadership accomplishments of women? Why is the United States so fixated on the gender issue when so many other countries are not? Obviously, not all women want to be leaders, but neither do all men. It is also true that not all women have what it takes to be leaders, but neither do all men. Some women are highly ambitious, whereas others are not; the same is true for men. Some women thrive on the pressure and spotlight of high office; others do not. The same is true for men. Some women relish the challenge of combat, others do not. The same is true for men. Nevertheless, leadership, whether it is in politics, business, the military, or in such professions as medicine, engineering, or academics, continues to be discussed as if it were the preserve of one gender or the other: We persist in gendering leadership. Why?

In this chapter, I argue that the underlying reason is the unspoken but firmly held belief that there is a natural order in which males are innately and uniquely endowed to take charge, whereas females are innately and uniquely endowed to take care. (It is possible, of course, to believe in a different natural order, but in this chapter, I assume the conventional gendered notion as just described.) The idea of a woman as the president of our country, the head of a major corporation, or a high-level military commander runs counter to our deeply held belief that men are rightly in charge; they have the wisdom and fortitude to make well-thought-out and difficult choices, enforce good but unpopular reforms, and take control when confronted with threat. Men, it is believed, are naturally equipped to do so, either through evolutionary pressures, innate traits that predispose them for dominance, or a history of male leadership. Think of a chest-thumping, aggressive alpha male chimp who has to dominate all members of his troop before assuming the leadership position. Think of Man the Hunter, the ape's evolutionary successor, who fights off enemies and risks everything to provide for his vulnerable mate and offspring. In contrast, women in this scenario are naturally (and therefore rightly) passive and submissive; they are better at following than leading, they are timid, risk averse, and by nature nonaggressive and ill suited for the demands of strong leadership. This myth, in spite of being discredited by modern anthropologists, has undeniable staying power.

Regardless of their actual abilities and historical contributions, women are rarely glorified as heroic characters who can accomplish grand feats of leadership.

If there is a natural-order explanation for males' propensity for leadership, perhaps it can be found in extrapolations from the world of our closest nonhuman primate relatives.[3] Certainly the media have latched on to such evidence, especially from the much-studied chimpanzees, one of our two closest primate relatives. Recent attention has also been paid to our other close primate relative, the bonobo.

Chimpanzees are patriarchal, hot-tempered, and often engage in physical violence, including infanticide and cannibalism. Chimps tend to resort to dominance displays and aggression to resolve conflicts. They have been described as warring, shrieking, stalking killing machines. In short, "Males are dominant and control with violence."[4] Many primatologists and other researchers have for a long time likened human behavior to that of chimps. They have, for example, drawn parallels between the naturally aggressive behavior of male chimps and that of human males. One of the most vivid examples was the opening scene of the film *2001: A Space Odyssey*. This scene dramatically depicts the evolution of male apes from weapon-wielding aggressors to humans circling the earth in a spaceship.

Bonobos, who look exactly like chimpanzees, are our other very close nonhuman primate relative. They are relatively less well studied and understood than chimpanzees. Yet we do know that these two species are dramatically different in temperament and behavior. Bonobos live in large matriarchal groups, tend to be friendly, peaceful, passive, socially accommodating, promiscuous, and nonviolent. Moreover, among bonobos, there is female dominance, infanticide does not occur, and sex is used to resolve conflict. In short, "Females are dominant and control with sex."[5]

Bonobo behavior presents a problem for those who argue that human male dominance is natural. The relatively new revelations about bonobo behavior that do not fit nicely into the natural-order

belief have not been readily accepted by many in the scientific community. According to University of Southern California zoologist
Amy Parish, who is also a scientific adviser to the Bonobo Conservation Initiative, "Not everybody's been willing to accept that
[bonobos are a matriarchal society] because it is so rare in mammals
to see patterns of female dominance."[6]

It appears that even trained scientists are vulnerable to the
omnipresent male-as-leader bias. Parish shares some examples of
how this bias affects primatologists' interpretations of their own
data on chimps and bonobos. So "unnatural" (in their terms) is
male-deferent behavior that male bonobos have been called "hen-
pecked" and "mama's boys." Anything but male dominance tends
to be treated as evidence of dysfunction, whether it occurs among
bonobos or human males. By pathologizing male bonobo behavior,
it is possible to retain belief in the natural order. As a further example of the lengths to which some researchers will go to preserve the
belief in the natural order, Parish noted that some of her colleagues
refuse to accept the bonobo pattern of female dominance. They call
it "strategic male deference,"[7] meaning that, of course, male bonobos could be in charge if they wanted to, but for strategic reasons,
like having more sex, they step back and let females have the upper
hand. Not surprisingly, signs of male dominance are never met with
the explanation that females could be dominant if they wanted to,
but for strategic reasons they are stepping back.

Parish notes that in one scientific publication, male deferent
behavior was described as "male chivalry"—not at all an empirical
term for a scientific paper.[8] She was quick to point out that the male
behavior in question was not chivalry, it was just that females had
the upper hand. In line with the argument of this chapter, male
take-charge behavior (leadership or aggression) toward females is
considered natural, whereas female take-charge behavior toward
males is not.

I contend that the belief in the natural order is in the air; it per-
meates our thinking, our expectations, our perceptions of the world,
and our pedagogy. The tenacity with which we embrace this belief

is reflected both in the often gargantuan efforts we make to preserve it even in the face of overwhelming evidence challenging it and in the severity of the penalties we exact when individuals dare to violate it. I focus on three areas of women's leadership: business, military, and politics. To make my case, I will draw on media accounts, the historical record, and social science research.

Women in Business

"Men and women equally aspire to be CEO. In addition, women who have children living with them are just as likely to want the corner office as women without children at home."[9]

With respect to women and leadership in business, the belief in the natural order takes two different but related forms: women don't want powerful careers, and women who have attained such positions drop out.

Do Women Want Power?

While women are making great strides in high-visibility leadership positions in the corporate world and academia, their motivation is still being questioned. For example, a *Fortune* cover story about the fifty most powerful women in America asked in 2003, "Power: Do Women Really Want It?" The implication, of course, is that women are naturally unsuited for such lofty positions and must, therefore, be ambivalent at best about their accomplishments. Yet numerous studies indicate that women are just as motivated as men to achieve the executive suite. In a survey of nine hundred senior-level women and men from Fortune 1000 companies, Catalyst found that women and men report "similar career aspirations and advancement strategies."[10]

A recent study suggests that the similarity between the sexes extends to their ratings of the importance to them of such work values as becoming recognized in your field, doing an excellent job no matter what field you are in, helping people, and making a lot of money.[11] The researchers surveyed eight hundred MBA graduates over a sixteen-year period. Contrary to the researchers' prediction, women and men MBAs did not differ on three of the four work values. The one significant gender difference was that women rated "wanting to do an excellent job, no matter what field you are in" higher in importance to them personally than did their male counterparts.

Are Women Opting Out?

Even in the absence of solid evidence, newspapers, magazines, and television stories continue to claim that the best and the brightest American women are dropping out of the workplace and going home to be housewives. Perhaps the biggest trend story about women opting out and not wanting powerful careers was a 2003 *New York Times* cover story by Lisa Belkin. The title read, "Q: Why don't more women get to the top? A: They choose not to." The anecdotal data upon which this trend story was based were gathered informally from a very small and nonrepresentative sample of highly atypical women—Princeton graduates who had dropped out, lived with husbands who were able to support them and their children on one income, and were book club members. Belkin wrongly used anecdotes as data to prove her thesis. Yet serious scholars, using data from representative samples, consistently show that women are not opting out.[12] According to census data, more than 78 percent of mothers with graduate or professional degrees are in the paid workforce, and they are three times as likely to work full time as part time. Indeed, a careful reading of Belkin's article shows that many of the women she profiled were pushed out of work, not pulled by the desire to be at home. Moreover, many of these women planned on resuming their careers in the future.

Despite considerable and solid data to the contrary, in 2005 the *New York Times* ran a highly visible front-page story titled "Many Women at Elite Colleges Set Career Path to Motherhood." The article was based on one small, nonrandom sample of Yale undergraduates and had a large nonresponse rate, yet the findings were reprinted in newspapers from Boston to Minneapolis and repeated on countless Web sites and radio talk shows. The research on which this blockbuster article was based was so shoddy that it was severely and publicly criticized by reputable social scientists and by other journalists.[13] It appears that the belief in the natural order overrides the growing body of research data suggesting that women intend to work and have families,[14] that they thrive when they combine work and motherhood,[15] and that their career ambitions mirror those of their male counterparts.[16]

When Women Fail

While the media rarely give women credit for their successes, their failures in the corporate world make headlines. For example, when Brenda Barnes resigned from a high-level position at PepsiCo, a media feeding frenzy ensued, full of stories saying that she, and by extension other women, couldn't handle work and family. Apparently the Sara Lee Corporation didn't buy the media take on Barnes. Sara Lee, a Fortune 100 company that is a global manufacturer and marketer of high-quality brand-name products for consumers throughout the world, offered Barnes the job of president. She now heads a corporation that has operations in fifty-eight countries, markets branded products in nearly two hundred nations, and employs 137,000 people worldwide. But when Barnes was hired to head Sara Lee, the media did not jump all over this story as proof that women could succeed at work and at home.

The media are eager to embrace any story about women who fail in high-level positions; Brenda Barnes is in good company. The same treatment was given to Carly Fiorina of Hewlett Packard, Jane Swift (lieutenant governor of Massachusetts), Carol Wallace (former editor of *People* magazine), and Rosie O'Donnell, when she taped her last talk show in May 2003. The headline of one such story was "They Conquered, They Left," and the tag line was "some say women have less psychic investment in careers." (Nowhere do we learn who the "some" are.)[17]

More generally, women who fail spark a national discussion about women's commitment to work; men who fail never ignite debate about men's commitment to work. It seems that women's failures in business are taken as proof that they can't manage a career and family responsibilities. Men's failures generate no such claim. When women succeed, they are viewed as having some special stroke of good fortune—a wonderful mentor, a lucky break, being at the right place at the right time. Their success is treated as a happenstance, an outcome over which they had no particular control. Not surprisingly, research shows that when women succeed, they rarely get credit for their success.[18] Perhaps more ominously, when women succeed, they are marginalized as anomalous and their accomplishments regarded as trivial. This tortured reasoning makes sense in the context of the belief in the natural order. Because of the belief, at least in the United States, that women are not naturally equipped to succeed in leadership, their failures are touted as proof of women's inherent inabilities.

Whereas the media often treat the failure of a high-level businesswoman as proof that women in general cannot excel in a man's world, no such generalizations are made when a woman succeeds. The story of Patricia Russo is a case in point. Russo, rated by *Fortune* magazine as the thirteenth most powerful woman in the world in 2005, was chairman and chief executive officer of Lucent Technologies. She now heads the new telecommunications giant formed by the merger of Lucent and Alcatel. This company will be one of the largest in the world and the largest in the world in terms of revenues (over $25 billion) run by a woman. The day the merger was announced, numerous stories described Russo's stellar accomplishments during her twenty-year career at Lucent. No mention was made of the obvious—women can clearly lead successfully in highly competitive business environments. Of course, unlike the response that would have occurred if she had failed, no gender generalizations were made. One can only hope that the next time a prominent businesswoman fails, the media will resist the temptation to ascribe her failure to her gender.

Belief in the natural order thus creates a Catch-22 situation for U.S. women. As members of an outgroup in the business world (that is, any group other than white males), women are seen as either liked but incompetent (think a blonde secretary), or as successful but disliked (think Margaret Thatcher).[19] Not only do women who achieve in the male world pay a high price socially, they also pay a steep price professionally. Such women are not readily offered special opportunities for advancement, nor are they likely to receive high salaries and other benefits.[20] Successful males pay no such price.

Women in the Military

"During wars, women are ubiquitous and highly visible; when wars are over and the war songs are sung, women disappear."[21]

With respect to women in the military, the dominant theme is that they are the invisible sex. Although women have always and everywhere been inextricably involved in war, their accomplishments—indeed, their very presence—has been hidden from history.

Although women have served in every war fought by the United States, it wasn't until the end of World War II that The Women's Armed Services Integration Act passed in Congress. The Act finally granted women rank and a permanent place in the services in wartime and in peacetime.[22] Yet limitations on women's advancement remained in place. Ceilings were set on the percentage of women in uniform and the number who could be army lieutenant colonels or navy captains and commanders. The situation for women improved in 1967 when President Lyndon Johnson signed a law lifting those ceilings. However, other limitations were left in place. For example, a woman could not have children and stay on active duty. Nor could a woman even marry a man who had children and stay on active duty. In addition, women could not be admitted to any of the armed service academies. In 1975, President Ford lifted this restriction and, in 1980, the first women graduated from the service academies. Not coincidentally, 1980 was the year in which the first woman, Wilma L. Vaught, was promoted to brigadier general—the highest rank a woman had ever been awarded. Clearly women's advancement in the military had far less to do with their gender than it had to do with onerous restrictions that reflected belief in the natural order.

Women's opportunities for leadership, although much improved, were still constrained by laws that restricted their participation in combat—a necessary stepping-stone for advancement to positions of high leadership. Women's positive performance in Operation Desert Storm in 1991 led to an intensification of the debate over women in combat. Finally, in 1994, what was known as "the risk rule" was rescinded, and women, while formerly excluded from any job that directly exposed them to hostile force or capture, were able to hold about 80 percent of all jobs in the military, even in support units alongside combat units.

As of 2004, there were over 210,000 women on active duty in the military (U.S. Army, Navy, Marine Corps, and Air Force). About 16 percent of these women were officers, a percentage similar to that of military men.[23] The percentage of women officers and enlisted personnel on active duty rose from 13 percent to 15 percent between 1995 and 2004. Today, top military leaders describe women as essential to the operation of the U.S. military.[24] In summarizing his exhaustive study of gender and war, Goldstein concludes: "The results of the U.S. experience indicate a broad, deep, and well-rounded capability of women to participate in the kinds of actions and operations required for combat, and to hold their own in combat itself when drawn into it."[25]

An Unsung Military Heroine

The history of women's early efforts to gain a toehold in the U.S. space program dramatizes the incredible injustices done in the service of preserving male leadership. Jerrie Cobb, unfortunately, is not a household name, but it should be. Geraldyn (Jerrie) was born in 1931 in Norman, Oklahoma, and grew up in an aviation-oriented environment. By age twelve she had learned to fly, and by sixteen, while a high-school student, she earned a private pilot's license. By eighteen she had her commercial and flight instructor's licenses and she made her living crop dusting and teaching navigation. In the 1950s, as a commercial pilot, Cobb set several world altitude and speed records; she was also the only female international ferry pilot in the United States.[26]

By the time she was twenty-one, Jerrie was setting world aviation records for speed, distance, and absolute altitude. In 1959, at age twenty-eight, she was named Pilot of the Year by the National Pilots Association, and her fellow airmen awarded her the Amelia Earhart Gold Medal of Achievement. President Nixon awarded her the Harmon Trophy for the best woman pilot in the world. In addition, she was one of the nine women *Life* magazine selected as among the "100 most important young people in the United States." In 1959, when NASA began operations, Jerrie thought she would have an opportunity to attain her life's ambition, namely to be the first woman in space. In 1960, she began secretly undergoing tests for the aerospace program. Nineteen top-notch women pilots applied to the space program; four of them had logged more flying hours than any of the seven men chosen two years earlier as Mercury astronauts.

The women underwent the same rigorous physical and psychological evaluations for fitness that the Mercury astronauts, including John Glenn and Alan Shepherd, had endured. Dr. William Randolph Lovelace II, the head of Life Sciences for NASA, helped select the Mercury astronauts and wanted to find out if top-flight women pilots might perform as well. In fact, they did. To the great surprise of many NASA officials, some of the women even surpassed the test scores of the men. Jerrie's scores were considered extraordinary. Thirteen of the nineteen women (later known as the Mercury 13) who applied to the space program qualified to be astronauts. Lovelace believed that because women weighed less and consumed less oxygen, they might actually make better astronauts than men.

In August 1960, *Life* magazine learned about the female astronauts and ran a photo essay showing how Jerrie trained for space. The media dubbed Jerrie and a few of the other women in the training program as the "astronettes." Not surprisingly, the press was not always so supportive. According to Sarah Gorelick, one of the Mercury 13 who had quit her engineering job to take part in the NASA testing, "At one point we even felt like we had been defeated in the press, because every time a woman was mentioned, like Jerrie Cobb, they'd give her [physical] dimensions." Gorelick went on say, "It was very demeaning. I felt we should be recognized not because we were women, but because of what we ourselves could do as individuals or what we could bring to the program."[27]

The Mercury 13's success and visibility notwithstanding, the system, entrenched as it was in the belief in natural male superiority, could not tolerate the idea of women succeeding in such a highly visible masculine role. This intolerance led to both an abrupt end of the women's training program and to Jerrie's dreams. Just as the women were about to begin final testing in Florida, NASA canceled the program. Why waste money on women, NASA argued, since it had no interest in women astronauts.

At that point, the Mercury 13 broke their silence. According to Martha Ackmann of Mount Holyoke College, who has chronicled their story, "After having risked jobs and marriages for the chance to fly into space, they were not about to let NASA's sexist attitude stand in their way."[28] They eventually got a meeting with Vice President Lyndon Johnson, head of the Space Council. After listening to their appeal, Johnson said his hands were tied: A women-in-space program was NASA's call. What the women did not know was that Johnson later penned his opinion at the bottom of a letter to NASA. When it came to the possibility of women in space, Johnson had just four words: "Let's stop this now."[29] Those words sealed the fate of women in the aerospace program for the next twenty years.

Lyndon Johnson's words, we later found out, reflected the broader sentiment within NASA. Here is how astronaut James Lovell put it in 1973: "We've never sent any woman into space because we haven't had a good reason to. We fully envision, however, that in the near future, we will fly women into space and use them the same way we use them on Earth—and for the same purpose."[30]

In congressional testimony, astronaut John Glenn (who later served for twenty-five years as a U.S. Senator) captured the indignation he and others felt when he said that men go off and fly the planes and fight the wars and women stay at home. "It's a fact of our social order."[31] When pressed, NASA said that they didn't want women to go forward because they believed all astronauts should come from the ranks of military jet test pilots. That, of course, was a splendid example of backwards reasoning, because in the early 1960s, women were not allowed to fly planes in the military.[32]

The next twenty years brought considerable change in attitudes and practice. In 1983, Sally Ride became the first U.S. woman astronaut to fly in space. In 1999, Eileen Collins was the first woman to command a space shuttle, a feat she repeated in 2005 just before she retired. As of 2006, 21 percent of NASA's active management astronauts were women. More room for progress remains, but women's positions at NASA have improved considerably since the days of the Mercury 13.[33]

Despite the improved recognition today's women in space are getting, the Mercury 13 are all but invisible. There are no exhibits chronicling their achievement at the Smithsonian, or at the Kennedy or Johnson space centers. On the contrary, science and history museums don't mention them. No college or university has ever awarded any of them an honorary degree. The White House has never acknowledged the women's sacrifice.

Much more than men, women's opportunity to demonstrate their leadership on the battlefield is highly dependent both on a nation's manpower needs and on the vicissitudes of social attitudes about women's place. When, as in ancient Egypt, women had high status, several women became pharaohs and led their country in battle. In contrast, in the United States, during the 1950s, '60s, and '70s, when traditional gender-role attitudes were dominant, women had very few opportunities for leadership in the military or other arenas thought to be appropriate for males only.

Women in Political Office: The U.S. Example

"Women audacious enough to seek political power are routinely dogged by gender-specific coverage that focuses on their looks, fashion sense, familial relationships, and other feminizing details that have nothing to do with their expertise."[34]

At present, women in other countries are earning the right to lead their countries by working their way through the political system, as men have always done. (This is not to imply that the situation of most women in these countries is anything but dismal with respect to most opportunities for leadership, as we are reminded by Rhode and Kellerman's Introduction to this volume.) In the United States, we are still wringing our hands about whether women have the right hormones, the right brains, the right motivation, or the right abilities to take on the leadership challenges of the modern world. Specifically, in 2007 there were only 71 women in the 435-member U.S. House of Representatives, sixteen women in the hundred-member Senate, and nine women governors in our fifty states.

While the rest of the world seems to accept the notion that women are fit to command a nation, in the United States, women who have the temerity to put themselves forward for the top job face harsh questioning. Hillary Clinton, for example, a leading contender for the Democratic nomination, has been called either a "witch" or "witchlike" in the media more than fifty times. There are constant innuendos about her sexuality, as evidenced by a book by former *New York Times* man Ed Klein, *The Truth About Hillary: What She Knew, When She Knew It, and How Far She'll Go to Become President*. As critic Tina Brown pointed out in the *Washington Post*, every time Klein describes anyone female in Hillary Clinton's circle, you hear the clump, clump, clump of stereotypical lesbian footwear. Aides are described as mannish, frumpy, and a little overweight with grayish hair.

As for Condoleezza Rice, mentioned as a Republican nominee for president, her single status is often commented upon as if her ambition were somehow unfeminine. There's also an inordinate amount of attention to her clothes and her style—her pearls, her southern accent, her size-six dresses, her high-heeled "dominatrix" boots.

When Elizabeth Dole threw her hat in the presidential ring in 2000, she was treated very differently from male candidates by the media, despite the fact that she was the only Republican who beat Al Gore in several head-to-head polls. Many men would have given their eyeteeth for her credentials: former cabinet member in the Reagan administration, head of a well-known national organization (the American Red Cross), and high name recognition. But researchers Caroline Heldman, Susan J. Carroll, and Stephanie Olson of Rutgers University note that while political insiders and the public regarded Dole as a strong contender, the media did not.[35] The press focused more on Dole's personality traits than those of other candidates. She was called "rehearsed, scripted, robotic, controlled, frozen, a 'Stepford Wife.'"[36] (Could these same qualities in a man be called "focused, stays on message, articulate"?) Dole never got the level of coverage that her polling indicates she should have had. In fact, she received about the same coverage as Gary Bauer and Steve Forbes, two decidedly uncharismatic men who lacked polling strength and had little chance of winning.

The Case of Jane Swift

Research shows that the media pay far more attention to the personal situation of women in public life than to that of men. Jane Swift, former governor of Massachusetts, arguably wins the prize for having endured the most relentless scrutiny of her family life. Why? Because she was the first person to run for statewide election while pregnant and the first elected lieutenant governor to give birth (to twin daughters) while in office. Journalists and other media types had a field day hashing and rehashing the pros and cons of women's combining work and family life. Almost without exception, every reference to her in the media began with the fact that she "was the first governor to give birth while in office" or that she "recently gave birth to twins." For example, an article recounting her record in office and announcing her decision to run for governor began with the following sentence: "Acting Gov. Jane M. Swift, who made history as the first governor to give birth while in office, said today that she would run for governor of Massachusetts in 2002."[37] Headlines read: "Campaigning for Office on the Mommy Track"; "The Year of the Stork"; "An Announcement: Candidate Has Baby"; "Massachusetts Delivers"; "A Mommy Track Derails, Mama's Delicate Condition"; and "Jane Swift: Motherhood in the Massachusetts Governor's Office."

On the surface the clamor was about whether she could perform her official duties while also taking some time for pregnancy-related medical issues. One would think that no previous governor had ever taken any time away from work for health or any other reason. In fact, there is plenty of evidence to the contrary. Earlier in 2001, the governor of Rhode Island was laid up at home for more than a month, recovering from surgery for prostate cancer. No one demanded he surrender his powers. Ronald Reagan recuperated from a gunshot wound while president. Dwight Eisenhower suffered a heart attack, a bout with ileitis, and a minor stroke. Moreover, these two were men with their fingers on the proverbial button. Closer to home, Swift's predecessor, Governor Paul Cellucci, underwent heart surgery while in office. And Cellucci's predecessor, Bill Weld, was often criticized for spending lots of time away from work. In Weld's words, "Getting to be governor is the hardest part, I used to go on vacation for a week at a time and I wouldn't even call in."[38]

The subtext of the coverage often implied that Swift's "crime" was her intent to hold on to power even if it meant abandoning her husband and children. In so doing, she was violating the most basic principle of the natural order, namely, that it is unnatural for women to seek power (especially over men). Men, for whom the pursuit of power is seen as natural, never receive such close scrutiny of their family lives. As one journalist asked: "Who knows how many male governors have children, or who takes care of them?"[39]

What was the real situation? Was she really rejecting her family to selfishly pursue her career? Not at all. Swift's husband had long before decided to support her political ambitions by quitting his job and caring for their children. As she put it when she decided to run for governor in 2002, "When you decide to have children, adults then arrange their lives around them, and that's what we've done." Only those who have never read a single article indicating that men can be as nurturing to children as women could honestly claim that the couple's young children were at risk.

Her wishes and ambitions notwithstanding, Swift decided not to run in 2002 after all; she bowed to Republican pressure to make way for the candidacy of Mitt Romney, who was considered a far stronger and much better-financed candidate. Unfortunately, her personal life created such a stir that her many political challenges, successes, and failures were completely overshadowed. She was well aware of her situation. As lieutenant governor, she was asked to talk to an audience of elementary-school students about her career in politics. After a few minutes, she pointed to the army of journalists, reporters, and TV-cameramen surrounding the auditorium and asked the fourth and fifth graders, "Does anybody know why they are following me?" One boy ventured the answer, "Because they want to know what you stand for?" An amused Swift responded, "I only wish that were true. It's because I am pregnant and all of these guys think that it's a great big deal."[40]

She was actually well qualified for a high-level leadership role in politics, having served as a state senator, an executive with the Massachusetts Port Authority, and as the commonwealth's consumer affairs secretary before being elected lieutenant governor in 1998. She became acting governor in 2001, when Governor Paul Cellucci became the U.S. ambassador to Canada. At thirty-eight, she was the youngest governor in the nation's history. Over the course of her tenure, her popularity ratings plummeted and then soared. By October 2001, her approval rating was 66 percent, considerably higher than the 20 percent she had in 2000. Whatever her failings, she will be remembered most for the disastrous results of her daring violation of deeply held views about the proper role of women. In her emotional address announcing her decision to drop out of the governor's race, she did what was expected, saying that she "could not successfully juggle the increasing—and often competing— duties of gubernatorial candidate, chief executive, and mother."[41] No one will ever know whether she could have successfully juggled the roles of wife, mother, and governor; the stranglehold of the natural order was too tight.

Are Women Innately Unsuited For Leadership?

The U.S. press seems fixated on gender differences. Recently, headline stories focused on whether women have the right brain structure for leadership, the right hormones to make decisions, or enough motivation to devote themselves to a high-powered career. An argument by psychologist Simon Baron-Cohen that men's brains were designed for understanding systems while female brains were suited for making friends, mothering, gossip, and "reading" one's partner has been quoted again and again. Despite the fact that scientific critics skewered the study on which this claim was based, his ideas were featured in the *New York Times*, a BBC documentary, a *Newsweek* cover, and numerous newspaper articles across the United States. The appeal of such gender-difference claims notwithstanding, women have in recent years proved themselves in very high political office in the United States. For example, Madeleine Albright was the first female Secretary of State, followed later by Condoleezza Rice.

In this country, the more we hear that women are unsuited for leadership, the more women and men will internalize this message. If this self-perpetuating process goes unchecked, we may never get to the place so many other countries (including Germany, Chile, and Liberia) have recently reached, where a woman running for high political office is judged not by some rigid sex-role stereotype but by the credentials she brings to the position.

Conclusion

"We have a tendency to see every instance that confirms our stereotypes and filter out all the counterexamples."[42]

The belief that men are naturally suited to take charge whereas women are naturally suited to take care is reinforced endlessly. This message reverberates throughout our society in popular movies, advertisements, songs, books. It is indifferent to age. From a child's earliest days onward, the message is the same—boys are active, girls are passive. Boys are the quarterbacks, girls are the cheerleaders. As members of this society, we too often unwittingly promulgate this belief. How?

One particularly well-documented way is through a process social psychologists call stereotype confirmation. This process has several manifestations. For example, once we have a stereotype in our heads—such as "women can't lead"—we tend to notice every instance that confirms our stereotype and to filter out counterexamples.[43] Thus we are more likely to remember that Brenda Barnes quit PepsiCo than we are to remember that she now heads the Sara Lee Corporation. In addition, we are also more likely to notice when a woman leaves a high-level position than we are to notice the same behavior in a man. And we are more likely to interpret her leave-taking as due to family constraints, whereas we are less likely to make the same interpretation when a high-level man steps down.

Not only does society do this to women, men do it to women and women do it to themselves. Women (as well as men) are more likely to ascribe a woman's success to chance or external factors rather than to innate ability or hard work.[44] Thus women are less likely than men to take personal credit for their own successes. In this way, women's cognitive attributions undercut their own abilities to build on their prior achievements.[45] It is hard to climb to the top of the corporate, military, or political ladder if you always feel that you have to start your next assignment on the first rung.

As long as belief in the natural order dictates how we understand our world, we and our children will remain caught in a loop.

When women and men believe that women cannot lead, women renounce leadership positions. Then their absence from leadership positions is taken as proof that they don't have the right stuff. Those who do succeed are marginalized; their successes are explained away as chance phenomena. In this climate, women's leadership ability will always be questioned and their success in high-powered positions suspect. We can and must do better by our women; fortunately, examples from our own history as well as the history of other contemporary and ancient societies point the way. At present, Women's History Month (first proclaimed in 1987) is almost the only time of the year in which women's accomplishments are front and center—at least in some media outlets. Clearly, the status quo is not going to change unless attention to women's accomplishments becomes a 24/7 phenomenon, not a one-month-a-year special event.

The evidence is in: Given the opportunity, women have in the past succeeded and will continue to succeed in leadership positions. Yet this information has not been incorporated meaningfully in the lessons our children are taught, the media messages they absorb, nor the aspirations and expectations they develop for their own lives. To remedy this situation we need to uproot the belief in the natural order. We need to notice when this belief creeps into discussions of leadership, we need to challenge those who assume this belief to be correct, and we need to use the information we have to assert a new belief, a belief that both men and women equally have the potential for leadership.

Endnotes

1. Barbara Kellerman and Deborah Rhode, "Viable Options: Rethinking Women and Leadership," *Compass: A Journal of Leadership*, Fall 2004, 14–17, 37.
2. Alice H. Eagly, Mona G. Makhijani, and Bruce G. Klonsky, "Gender and the Evaluation of Leaders: A Meta-Analysis." *Psychological Bulletin 111*, no. 1 (1992): 3–22.

3. Robert Ardrey, *African Genesis: A Personal Investigation into the Animal Origins and Nature of Man* (New York: Atheneum, 1963). See also Raymond Dart, *Adventures with the Missing Link* (New York: HarperCollins, 1959), 255; Sarah Blaffer Hrdy, "Adaptive and Nonadaptive Classes of Infanticide," in P. K. Seth (ed.), *Perspective in Primate Biology* (New Delhi: Today and Tomorrow, 1983), 11–17; Amy R. Parish and Frans B. M. DeWall, "The Other Closest Living Relative: How Bonobos *(Pan paniscus)* Challenge Traditional Assumptions About Females, Dominance, Intra- and Intersexual Interactions, and Hominid Evolution," *Annals of the New York Academy of Sciences* 907 (2000): 97–113.

4. C. MacDuffee, "Bonobos vs. Chimpanzees," in "Who Cares About the Issues? I Do," 2000, available online: www.webspawner .com/users/whocaresido/whocaresido2.html, access date: August 15, 2006.

5. Frans DeWaal, *Bonobo: The Forgotten Ape* (Los Angeles: University of California Press, 1997), 210.

6. Parish and DeWall, "The Other Closest Living Relative." See also Amy R. Parish, [review of the article "The Social Behavior of Chimpanzees and Bonobos"], *Current Anthropology* 39, no. 4 (1998): 413–414.

7. Craig B. Stanford, "The Social Behavior of Chimpanzees and Bonobos," *Current Anthropology* 39, no. 4 (1998): 399–407.

8. Frances J. White, Kimberley D. Wood, and Michelle Y. Merrill, [review of the article "The Social Behavior of Chimpanzees and Bonobos"], *Current Anthropology* 39, no. 4 (1998): 414–415.

9. Catalyst, "New Catalyst Study Reveals Financial Performance Is Higher for Companies with More Women at the Top" (news release), Catalyst, 2004, 2.

10. Catalyst, "New Catalyst Study Reveals Financial Performance Is Higher for Companies with More Women at the Top," 1.

11. Irene Frieze, Josephine Olson, Audrey Murrell, and Mano Selvan, "Work Values and Their Effect on Work Behavior and

Work Outcomes in Female and Male Managers," *Sex Roles 54*, no. 1–2 (2006): 83–93.

12. Katherine Bradbury and Jane Katz, "Women's Rise: A Work in Progress," *Regional Review 14*, no. 3 (2005): 58–68. See also Heather Boushey, *Are Mothers Really Leaving the Workplace?* (Chicago: Council on Contemporary Families and the Center for Economic and Policy Research, 2006), 1–3; and Claudia Goldin, "Working It Out," *New York Times*, Late edition, March 15, 2006, p. A27.

13. Boushey, "Are Mothers Really Leaving the Workplace?" See also Goldin, "Working It Out"; Jack Shafer, "Weasel-Words Rip My Flesh! Spotting a Bogus Trend Story on Page One of Today's *New York Times*," September 20, 2005, available online: www.slate.com/id/2126636/, access date: December 19, 2006.

14. Goldin, "Working It Out."

15. Rosalind C. Barnett and Caryl Rivers, *She Works/He Works: How Two-Income Families are Happier, Healthier, and Better Off* (Cambridge, MA: Harvard University Press, 1998).

16. Catalyst, "New Catalyst Study Reveals Financial Performance Is Higher for Companies with More Women at the Top."

17. Alex Kuczynski, "They Conquered, They Left," *New York Times*, Late Edition—Final, March 24, 2002, sec. 9, p. 1.

18. Madeline E. Heilman and Michelle C. Haynes, "No Credit Where Credit Is Due: Attributional Rationalization of Women's Success in Male-Female Teams," *Journal of Applied Psychology* 90, no. 5 (2005): 905–916.

19. Susan T. Fiske, "Stereotyping, Prejudice and Discrimination," in Daniel T. Gilbert, Susan T. Fiske, and Gardner Lindzey (eds.), *Handbook of Social Psychology*, 4th ed. (New York: McGraw-Hill, 1998), 357–411.

20. Madeline E. Heilman, Aaron S. Wallen, Daniella Fuchs, and Melinda M. Tamkins, "Penalties for Success: Reactions to Women Who Succeed at Male Gender-Typed Tasks," *Journal of Applied Psychology* 89, no. 3 (2004): 416–427. See also Heilman and Haynes, "No Credit Where Credit Is Due."

21. Joshua S. Goldstein, *War and Gender: How Gender Shapes the War System and Vice Versa* (Cambridge, UK: Cambridge University Press, 2001).

22. Goldstein, *War and Gender.*

23. Goldstein, *War and Gender.*

24. Goldstein, *War and Gender,* 93.

25. Goldstein, *War and Gender,* 105.

26. Irene Stuber, "NASA's Dirty Little Secret: Jerrie Cobb and the *Mercury 13,*" excerpted from *Women of Achievement and Herstory,* various dates, available online: www.thelizlibrary.org/liz/cobb.htm, access date: December 18, 2006.

27. Martha Ackmann, *The Mercury 13: The True Story of Thirteen Women and the Dream of Space Flight* (New York: Random House, 2003).

28. Ackmann, *The Mercury 13.*

29. Margaret A. Weitekamp, *Right Stuff, Wrong Sex: America's First Women in Space Program* (Baltimore: Johns Hopkins University Press, 2004), 232.

30. Stuber, "NASA's Dirty Little Secret."

31. Ackmann, *The Mercury 13,* 168.

32. Aaron Brown, "News; Domestic," *CNN Newsnight,* June 21, 2003, available online: http://transcripts.cnn.com/TRANSCRIPTS/0306/21/asb.00.html, access date: June 21, 2006.

33. Space Today Online, "Leaders Among Women in Space," 2003, available online: www.Spacetoday.org/History/SpaceWomen.html, access date: August 17, 2006.

34. Jennifer L. Pozner, "Commander in Chic," *Tom Paine Common Sense,* November 8, 2005, available online: www.tompaine.com/articles/2005/11/08/commander_in_chic.php, access date: December 18, 2006.

35. Caroline Heldman, Susan J. Carroll, and Stephanie Olson, "Gender Differences in Print Media Coverage of Presidential Candidates: Elizabeth Dole's Bid for the Republican Nomination," paper presented at the Annual Meeting of the American

Political Science Association, Washington, DC, August 31, 2000, available online: www.cawp.rutgers.edu/Research/Reports/dole.pdf, access date: March 5, 2007.

36. Heldman, Carroll, and Olson, "Gender Differences in Print Media Coverage of Presidential Candidates."

37. Pam Belluck, "Acting Governor Will Seek New Term in Massachusetts," *New York Times*, October 19, 2001.

38. Gail Collins, "Public Interest: Massachusetts Delivers," *New York Times*, February 16, 2001.

39. Carly Rivers, "Media Hillary Bashing Segues into Teresa Trashing," *Womens Enews*, June 18, 2003, available online by subscription: www.womensenews.org.

40. Center on Women and Public Policy, "Jane Swift: Motherhood in the Massachusetts Governor's Office," HHH Institute of Public Affairs, Minneapolis, MN, n.d.

41. Pamela Ferdinand and Dan Blaz, "Swift Drops Out of Mass. Governor's Race, GOP Applauds Surprise Move, Which Clears Path for Olympic's Romney," *Washington Post*, March 20, 2002.

42. Diane Halpern, "Work, Stress, and Health Linkages: How Does Working and Caring for Families Affect Health?" Session Coordinator at the Work and Families, Changing Realities Conference, Claremont, CA (2006). See also NPR: Diane Halpern, "Analysis: Gender Differences and Cognitive Abilities," *NPR: Talk of the Nation/Science Friday* (December 2, 2005).

43. Mark Snyder and Julie A. Haugen, "Why Does Behavioral Confirmation Occur? Perspective on the Role of the Perceiver," *Journal of Experimental Social Psychology 30*, no. 3 (1994): 218–246.

44. Heilman and Haynes, "No Credit Where Credit Is Due."

45. Fritz Heider, *The Psychology of Interpersonal Relations* (New York: Wiley, 1958). See also Harold H. Kelley, "Attribution Theory in Social Psychology," in D. Levine (ed.), *Nebraska Symposium on Motivation* (Lincoln: University of Nebraska Press, 1967).

5

WHAT DIFFERENCE WILL WOMEN JUDGES MAKE?

Looking Once More at the "Woman Question"

Anita F. Hill

For decades now, feminist legal theorists have been asking what has come to be known as the "woman question." It began as an examination of how the law fails to take into account women's experiences and how existing legal standards may disadvantage women.[1] Over the years, as courts have defined gender equality under the law and scholars have developed various theories for promoting equality and inclusion, the "woman question" has been applied to many aspects of gender relationship. In this chapter, I place the "woman question" in the context of judicial appointments. I look beyond issues of whether procedures for judicial selection exclude women and examine whether the gender of a judge really matters.

The relevance of the "woman question" today is clear in light of the recent appointments of Justices John Roberts and Samuel Alito to the Supreme Court of the United States. For the first time since Justice Ruth Bader Ginsburg took office in 1993, the Court has only one female justice. As we contemplate future appointments, it is important to consider whether in the twenty-first century the judiciary will be a body that looks more like the population it serves.

Justice Sandra Day O'Connor's appointment as the first woman on the U.S. Supreme Court was a historic event. So was her resignation.[2] It was greeted with widespread public speculation about the gender of her replacement. Immediately following her announcement, journalists began asking the "woman question": "Should Justice O'Connor's replacement be female?" Within days, First Lady Laura Bush expressed her desire that Justice O'Connor's replacement be a woman. This may have prompted President George W. Bush to suggest that he was interested in appointing a woman. The focus then shifted to which of the conservative women serving on the lower courts might be that replacement. There was, however, relatively little discussion about why choosing a woman would be desirable.[3]

When I was asked the question, my response was that the nominee's respect for gender equality was more important than the nominee's own gender—as though we had to choose between having a woman and having someone committed to gender equality. My sincere but uninspired response barely masked my ambivalence about being asked whether O'Connor's replacement had to meet a gender litmus test. My perception was that behind the question was the idea that the O'Connor seat was the woman's seat—just as many had assumed that the Thurgood Marshall years on the Court secured a seat for an African American. Few questioned what was behind such a presumption. The idea of setting aside a seat for a woman evoked memories of past special protections for women that often resulted in measures that limited rather than expanded women's opportunities. For me, the question hinted that a woman would only be chosen if she were given special consideration because the vacancy was left by a woman. Not even the Democrats on the judiciary committee were asking that Chief Justice William Rehnquist's replacement be a woman. All this suggested that, except when a woman resigned, the likely nominee would be male.

With a total of nine seats at stake, simply setting aside O'Connor's seat as a woman's seat seemed more likely to restrict women's interests than to advance them. Both historical experience and contemporary theory suggest that the key to women's advancement is not setting aside a single seat for women—it is rejecting the practice of setting aside others for men.

We have come a long way from the time when our only choice for including women was to have special protections or set-asides. We have also moved beyond an era where we believed that we had to ignore the differences in women's and men's experiences in order to treat them equitably and offer meaningful inclusion. This chapter examines the question of whether women judges will make a difference in light of the last decade of thinking about equality. It first looks at the experience of a Canadian justice, Bertha Wilson, in raising the question of whether women judges would make a difference and the impact it may have had on Canada's Supreme Court. Analysis then turns to the U.S. experience with a particular focus on gender and race in Supreme Court appointments. I argue that, for a variety of reasons with regard to substantive changes in the law as well as perceptions of fairness and the role the judiciary plays in our society, women judges do make a difference. Justice O'Connor, though generally seen as a conservative or moderate judge, has played a pathbreaking role in demonstrating the difference women judges can make. I conclude that equality and fairness demand greater diversity in race, ethnicity, and gender in judicial appointments.

The Canadian Experience

Though legal scholars have asked the "woman question" in many contexts, in 1990 Madame Justice Bertha Wilson, the first woman to sit on Canada's Supreme Court, gave that question new prominence. The title of her widely publicized lecture posed the issue directly: "Will Women Judges Really Make a Difference?"[4] According to Justice Wilson's assessment, the different life experiences of women and men cause them to think differently and to approach the law and legal decision making differently. Thus she concluded that including more women in the judiciary would change the substance of the law and the processes by which the law is decided.

Justice Wilson's treatment of the question was presented at Osgoode Hall Law School, and, not surprisingly, she approached the question as one approaches a legal issue. She carefully laid out her arguments for how the appointment of women to the bench would help "shatter stereotypes about the role of women in society that are held by male judges and lawyers as well as by litigants, jurors, and witnesses"; help preserve the public trust by fostering perceptions of diverse representation in the judiciary; reduce problems for women counsel; alter the process of judicial decision making, and reform legal doctrine particularly in such areas as tort, criminal, and family law.

Wilson's conclusions about women's potential to change the law fell into two categories. She first argued that the appointment of women judges would alter perceptions. In addition, she argued that the presence of women on the bench would modify law itself. According to Justice Wilson, the presence of women in the role of judicial decision makers and leaders would change the way fellow judges as well as lawyers and litigants saw all women in the judicial process. This, she concluded, would also change the behavior of women and men. So too, with more women as judges, the public at large would see the justice system as more representative and presumably more fair.

Justice Wilson's conclusions about women's potential to change the substance and processes of the law proved to be the most controversial of her claims. Wilson argued that, because of their gendered experiences, women were more willing to contextualize the law and its processes than were men, who were more formalistic in their approach to decision making. These assertions drew fire from critics who challenged many of Wilson's premises.[5] Her conclusions were understandably most offensive to those who view the law as gender, race, and class neutral, notwithstanding the different life experiences of women and men. For those who believe in the law's neutrality, Justice Wilson's arguments raise the question of whether any effort to appoint more women is misguided if it is done for the sake of adding the female perspective. For those with a particularly traditional view of the law, the appointment of women who are perceived as particularly "feminist" in their approach to the law and decision making remains very troublesome.[6]

Canadian law professor Constance Backhouse chronicles the response to one such judge in her 2003 article titled, "The Chilly Climate for Women Judges: Reflections on the Backlash from the Ewanchuk Case."[7] Justice L'Heureux-Dube of the Supreme Court of Canada came under fire for a concurring opinion she wrote in *R. v. Ewanchuk*, a criminal case involving the question of whether an alleged sexual assault was actually consensual sex. L'Heureux-Dube wrote a separate opinion in which she concurred with the full Court's decision to overturn the dismissal of the complaint and to enter a conviction of the defendant. The opinion criticized her colleague on the Supreme Court, Justice John Wesley McClung, who in voting to dismiss the conviction suggested that the "complainant's repeated 'no's'" during the alleged attack were irrelevant. He also implied that "a woman who had had a child out of wedlock, while living with a male partner, was not capable of refusing consent." Justice L'Heureux-Dube's opinion advised that judges should avoid the use of "language . . . which not only perpetuates archaic myths and stereotypes about the nature of sexual assaults but also ignores the law."[8] Even further, the opinion noted that judicial bias, such as that suggested in Justice McClung's opinion, adversely affected complainants' ability to rely "on a system free from myths and stereotypes" and on a reasonable expectation of judicial impartiality.

Although her colleague Justice Charles Doherty Gonthier also signed the opinion, Justice L'Heureux-Dube received the brunt of the public criticism. The first came in the form of a letter written by Justice McClung and published in a national newspaper, in which he accused her of "feminist bias" and suggested that her interjection of personal invective into the law could be "responsible for the 'disparate (and growing) number of male suicides being reported in [Quebec Province].'"[9] In the public attacks that followed, lawyers and representatives from national organizations criticized L'Heureux-Dube for feminist judicial activism.[10] Despite the criticism, Justice L'Heureux-Dube did not shy away from the feminist label.

Throughout their careers both Justice L'Heureux-Dube and Justice Wilson expressed opinions that were characterized as feminist, although L'Heureux-Dube came under particular scrutiny for challenging what she believed were sexist ideas.[11] While Justice Wilson certainly received public criticism for raising the "woman question," her willingness to do so may have had a notably positive, if somewhat delayed, effect.[12] At the time this chapter was written, of the nine justices on Canada's Supreme Court, four were women. Three of the appointments came between 2002 and 2004. The Chief Justice of that Court is Madame Justice Beverley McLachlin. In the context of advising President Bush on the appointment of women to the Supreme Court of the United States, Senator Patrick Leahy of Vermont pointed to the Canadian Supreme Court as an example of gender equity.[13] As many commentators have noted, the United States has much to learn about diversity on the bench from Canada's highest court.[14]

Equality in Theory in the United States

Scholars have identified several dominant theories that the U.S. Supreme Court has employed in gender discrimination cases that are relevant to judicial appointments.[15] One involves difference theory.[16] Justice Wilson's arguments, based largely on the differences in the way women and men experience life, fit squarely within difference frameworks. However, the U.S. Supreme Court has not incorporated difference theory in its jurisprudence. These are the primary theories relied on by the Court:

- Separate spheres, which allows different treatment based on cultural expectations and biological differences
- Formal equality, which requires that women and men be treated the same
- Substantive equality, which calls for rules such as affirmative action that can produce equality in results

Two more views, difference theory and nonsubordination theory, have been argued in recent years.

The separate spheres ideology dominated social thought until the mid-twentieth century and shaped legal decisions as well. It assumes women's inferiority in matters involving physical strength and intelligence, and superiority in matters concerning motherhood and related functions. Such assumptions served to justify special legislative protections of women, particularly those aimed at safeguarding women's reproductive capacities.[17] In addition, both courts and legislatures invoked separate spheres theory to rationalize women's exclusion from certain jobs and public positions. The most famous application of the separate spheres ideology appeared in a concurring opinion in *Bradwell v. Illinois,* a case in which the U.S. Supreme Court upheld the state's exclusion of women from the practice of law. In the court's view, woman's nature was to nurture, her "property-timidity and delicacy left her unfit for many of the occupations of civil life."[18] In response to the inequity that cases like *Bradwell* allowed, women's rights advocates proposed a theory of formal equality. This framework, modeled on theories of racial equality, assumes that women and men are fundamentally the same and deserve similar treatment. An important contribution of formal equality is its rejection of gender-based privileges for women because they have traditionally served to protect women out of positions desired by men.

Rather than look at whether a rule or law treats women and men the same or differently, substantive equality theory questions whether a law or rule has the effect of disadvantaging individuals due to their gender. Thus substantive equality frameworks acknowledge differences, but with the goal of eliminating or leveling them to encourage more equal outcomes. Affirmative action and pay equity are the kinds of strategies that advocates of substantive equality support.[19]

By contrast, difference theory emphasizes biological and cultural distinctions between men and women. But unlike the theories predicated on the sexes' separate spheres, difference frameworks insist on accommodating cultural or biological differences to avoid negative consequences. In effect, difference approaches demand that women's differences be valued.[20] Such differences include not only experiences and needs but also different priorities and concerns. Many feminist legal scholars have applied this idea to argue that women favor an ethic of care over an ethic based on individual rights. From this vantage, the law should draw on women's distinctive perspective to develop rules that value interconnectedness and interpersonal responsibility.[21]

Unlike substantive equality frameworks, difference theory maintains that "affirmative action or comparable worth schemes are ultimately insufficient in addressing root social and biological inequalities."[22] As law professor Christine Littleton puts it, substantive equality would merely require that a step stool be available to permit women to be seen from a podium. Difference theory requires designing podiums that adjust to both men's and women's heights. Compensation, then, is not enough; women's contributions and skills must be valued in the same way men's are.[23]

Instead of focusing on the question of whether men and women are different, nonsubordination theory looks at what meaning society attributes to those differences. Assuming that the consequences of male power are more significant than gender similarities or differences, nonsubordination frameworks concentrate on eliminating power imbalances. According to the theory's major proponent, Catharine A. MacKinnon, "A rule or practice is discriminatory . . . if it participates in the systemic social deprivation of one sex because of sex. The only question for litigation is whether the policy or practice in question integrally contributes to the maintenance of an underclass or a deprived position because of gender status."[24]

For example, under nonsubordination theory, sexual harassment violates principles of equality and should be prohibited because it reinforces men's power over women.[25] The violation flows from the domination it supports, not the boorish, bad, or even assaultive behavior itself.

Despite the opportunities that difference and nonsubordination theories offer for positive change, they are not without their feminist critics. Some commentators argue that difference theory risks reinforcing gender-based stereotypes that perpetuate gender-based inequality. By attempting to articulate an all-encompassing meta-narrative, both theories are criticized for denying class, racial, sexual orientation, and religious differences among women and making the experiences of white, middle-class women the model. In addition to criticizing MacKinnon's theory on the grounds that it promotes what amounts to gender essentialism, some feminists criticize Catharine MacKinnon for what they call "gender imperialism," namely the assumption that gender is the most important source of oppression.[26]

Just How Will Women Judges Make a Difference?

Though Justice Wilson relied on difference theory to support her position that women judges would change the law, a review of the research reveals no definitive evidence to confirm that assumption. Empirical and anecdotal accounts do not conclusively establish the idea that individual women judge differently or that women as a group judge differently from men. However, at least some research finds gender differences.[27] For example, political scientists Elaine Martin and Barry Pyle studied high courts in all fifty states, concluding that in divorce decisions "a judge's gender" tended "to be the primary predictor of a judge's vote."[28] In addition, Brenda Kruse's research has concluded that Justices Sandra Day O'Connor and Ruth Bader Ginsburg are also influenced by their gendered experiences in deciding employment cases.[29]

There is also considerable evidence that some male judges' perspectives cause them to view women's experiences very differently than women might. Professor Shirley Wiegand has chronicled numerous examples that demonstrate a judge's apparently limited vision.[30] One of her examples comes from the case that served as the basis for the 2005 movie North Country, a grim and painful, if sometimes fictionalized, account of sexual harassment at a mine in Minnesota. The fictionalized version was apparently no more grim and painful than the real experience the women in the suit faced in the mine or the hostility they faced in the court. According to Wiegand:

> The federal court, upon the recommendation of its appointed Special Master, awarded sixteen women who had been subjected to sexual harassment for more than a decade a total of $182,500, or about $11,400 each (compared to the average $250,000 in such cases). The Special Master's report (adopted fully by the federal district judge) revealed that he could not understand why one woman was fearful when a man who she said had exposed himself to her several years earlier began driving his truck in circles, over and over, around her work area. "This court has difficulty understanding why the appearance of a suspected flasher outside the building in which she was working . . . would cause great fear—of something—in a reasonable woman."[31]

The judge also could not understand why a woman would fear rape simply because "a man who had repeatedly and crudely propositioned her suddenly lunged at her one night at work with his arms spread, only stopping when she began screaming." When one woman found the clean clothes in her locker soiled by semen, three times, the judge determined that she confused "suspicions . . . with reality."[32]

(It is worth noting that the trial judge who adopted this language was overturned on appeal some eleven years later.)

Yet such decisions and other evidence of male bias do not establish sweeping gender differences in judging. And considerable evidence suggests that other factors, such as ideology, are better predictors than sex in accounting for judicial decisions. So, for example, commentators who have looked specifically at Justice O'Connor's and Justice Ginsburg's voting records generally find that gender is not a compelling factor in their judging.[33]

Unlike their Canadian counterpart Madame Justice Wilson, both Justice O'Connor and Justice Ginsburg reject the notion that their gender guides their judicial decision making. In responding to questions of whether women judges "speak with a different voice," Justice O'Connor refers to the lack of "empirical evidence that gender differences lead to discernible differences in rendering judgments." Moreover, she warns that such ideas may rely on troubling myths and stereotypes. Instead she suggests that male and female jurists alike should seek a collective wisdom gained through different struggles and different victories.[34]

Justice Ginsburg draws on her experiences as a judge and as a law teacher to conclude that there is no discernable difference in the way women and men reason: "In class or in grading papers . . . and now in reading briefs and listening to oral arguments in court . . . I have detected no reliable indicator of distinctly male or surely female thinking—or even penmanship."[35]

It is difficult to argue with these two women, in particular, about whether women judges speak with a different voice, especially given that there is no clear definition of what a "different voice" means. However, failure to reach consensus about the whether women jurists reach different conclusions or even reason differently does not resolve the question of whether there should be more women on the bench. Whether women judges will make a difference is a larger question than whether women and men will reach different outcomes in particular cases. Whether women judges make a difference depends on the role that judges and judging play in our legal system and must take into account a variety of professional and community activities in which judges participate. As the research from various judicial task forces suggests, judging involves collegiality, and a diverse bench enables members to influence each other.[36]

In addition, as noted later, the role of a judge also has significance in terms of perceptions about representation. The face of judging, in an emblematic way, matters as a reflection of access to justice; the diversity of the bench affects public perceptions of fairness. Finally, diversity among judges is a reflection of how power is distributed in the justice system. Professor Judith Resnik states the issue clearly: "In the contemporary world, where democratic commitments oblige equal access to power by persons of all colors whatever their identities, the composition of a judiciary—if all-white or all-male or all-upper class—becomes a problem of equality and legitimacy."[37] Equality and legitimacy require that we increase the inclusiveness of today's judiciary.

I call the model I would choose for including women and people of color on the bench the "representative perspective frame." My model borrows ideas from both difference and nonsubordination theories and attempts to address some of the criticisms of essentialism and gender imperialism. As applied to the appointment of judges, my representative perspective theory rests on three premises:

- Gender, racial, and ethnic experiences influence perspectives and worldviews, including one's sense of justice and how it should be achieved.
- The contribution of representative perspectives is substantial and reaffirms the promise of equality under the law by suggesting that all citizens have the chance to take part in our democracy.
- The failure to have a broad array of perspectives represented undermines judicial integrity and contributes to false ideas about intellect and competency.

Theories of equality—as well as the law adopted by the Supreme Court in recent years—support greater inclusion of women in the judiciary. A basic tenet of feminist critical theorists is that perspective matters. As Patricia Cain explains, understanding women's life experiences requires a different lens from the one most men use to take in the world; the feminist point of view comes "either from living life as a woman and developing critical consciousness about that experience or from listening carefully to the stories of female experience that come from others."[38]

Perspectives and experiences can also influence the outcome of a case as well as the overall direction the law takes. As Justice O'Connor stated in her concurring opinion in *J.E.B v. Alabama ex rel. T. B.*, a case that challenged the exclusion of women from juries, "One need not be a sexist to share the intuition that in certain cases a person's gender and resulting life experience will be relevant to his or her view of the case. . . . Individuals are not expected to ignore as jurors what they know as men—or women."[39] The idea that perspective matters is not limited to feminist scholars or female jurists. Jon Hanson and Adam Benforado made precisely that point in their recent *Boston Review* article: "Most legal scholars recognize that a judge's antecedent presumptions and perspectives often influence judicial decisions as much or more than her purported principles and precedents."[40] As noted earlier, gender is only one of the antecedents that influence judicial decisions and decision making; race, class, and sexual orientation, as well as previous areas of practice, are others.

Even conservative supporters of Judge Samuel Alito recognized the importance of a judge's perspective. During his confirmation hearing, they argued that his experience as the son of an Italian immigrant father would be a positive influence on his ability to relate to the little guy in cases that might come before him as a Supreme Court justice. It is hard to imagine that the experience of being an immigrant's son could be any more influential than the experience of being a man is for now eight of the nine members of the Court.

In considering whether women judges will make a difference, we also should not overlook the symbolic and representational role that members of the judiciary play. Beginning in the 1970s, the federal and state judicial systems launched initiatives on racial and gender bias. To date, no fewer than thirty-nine states and many of the federal judiciary circuit court systems have taken steps to respond to bias. The need for responses is well documented in task force reports. They found bias in a broad range of substantive areas such as family, domestic violence, and criminal law, as well as in administrative areas such as the appointment and election of judges.[41]

It is hard to deny, though perhaps impossible to measure, how bias against women and people of color undermines the integrity of the U.S. judicial system. However, a measurement of actual impact is not necessary. Justice O'Connor herself recognized that even the perception of bias does injury to the judicial system. As she wrote in the introduction to the Ninth Circuit task force: "When people perceive . . . bias in a legal system, whether they suffer from it or not, they lose respect for that system, as well as for the law."[42] Virtually all the task forces concluded that at least some reforms were necessary to reduce the potential for gender bias and better serve the ultimate objective of equal justice under law. In particular, many of the task force reports advocated measures that would increase the number of women on the bench. These reports cited the educational role women judges could play with their male counterparts in addition to the greater public confidence in the judiciary that can come from more diverse representation on the bench.

Given a history of gender and racial bias in our legal system, the overrepresentation of white male perspectives on the Court undermines the integrity of the American judicial system. Law professor Lani Guinier has noted that Supreme Court appointments have carried important symbolic messages. In *Grutter v. Bollinger*, a case in which the Court affirmed that a university had a compelling interest in a racially diverse student body, Justice O'Connor, writing for the Court, concluded that for "legitimacy in the eyes of the citizenry it is necessary that the path to leadership be visibly open to talented and qualified individuals of every race and ethnicity."[43] Professor Guinier argues that the same can be said for leadership in the judiciary, and that it too must be open regardless of race, ethnicity, and gender.[44] Professor Sylvia R. Lazos Vargas argues that the *Grutter* decision goes further and demands a critical mass of minority judges.[45] The Supreme Court itself recognized in the *J.E.B.* case that exclusion of women and people of color from juries causes harm to the litigants, the community, and the individual jurors who are excluded. So too, the failure to include diverse perspectives on the bench can have an adverse impact on litigants, the community, and the underrepresented groups that are excluded.

Given the large pool of qualified female and minority candidates in today's legal profession, the recent appointment of two white male justices carried a dispiriting message. When Harriet E. Miers, the sole female nominee, withdrew because of lack of confidence in her qualifications, the message of female inferiority was further reinforced. Yet for most women, the balance of family and work life makes it impossible to have the kind of distinguished career and traditional family that Justices Samuel Alito and John Roberts enjoy.

Throughout this chapter, I have been asking the "woman question." How does the judicial selection process disadvantage women or disregard their experiences? Perhaps one way to answer that question is to ask the "man question." How do the judicial selection process and unchallenged selection standards advantage typically white male experiences and perspectives? In this context it is important to note that most legal experts believe that ample numbers of women and people of color are qualified to sit on the Court.[46] Of course, that depends on how one determines qualifications. Much was made of John Roberts's Supreme Court clerkship and Samuel Alito's long experience on the federal bench, as well as the Ivy League education and law review experiences of both men. But surely state court experience or other forms of service to the profession and to the public would constitute equally valuable qualifications. Had the qualities that Roberts and Alito brought to the nomination process been the primary criteria in 1983, Justice O'Connor would not have been nominated to the Court. Her distinguished service makes clear that other, less traditional backgrounds can be equally valuable. The judicial process, in fact and in appearance, will be strengthened by members with diverse talents, backgrounds, and perspectives.[47]

Conclusion

Will women judges make a difference? In fact, they already have. Justice Bertha Wilson made a difference by raising the question and by unapologetically answering it in the affirmative. An example of true leadership, her speech moved the discussion of women's inclusion in the judiciary forward in an unprecedented manner. Justice Sandra Day O'Connor's legal opinions and public addresses provide language and ideas that legal scholars will continue to draw upon to support gender and racial inclusion in the courts. Other women judges provide similar inspiration. Constance Baker Motley, the first African American woman to be selected for the federal judiciary, is a fitting example on which to close. Her contributions were numerous, but perhaps her most famous decision came when she refused to excuse herself from a gender discrimination case involving an African American woman plaintiff.[48] In rejecting the defendants' claim that her general background and status as an African American female somehow prejudiced her in the matter, Judge Motley noted that she was not the only member of the judiciary who possessed both race and gender. "It is beyond dispute that for much of my legal career I worked on behalf of blacks who suffered race discrimination. I am a woman, and before being elevated to the bench, was a woman lawyer. These obvious facts, however, clearly do not, *ipso facto*, indicate or even suggest [heightened] personal bias or prejudice. . . . Indeed, if background or sex or race of each judge were, by definition, sufficient grounds for removal, no judge on this court could hear the case. . . ."[49] To her credit, Judge Motley unapologetically embraced both her race and her gender as well as the wisdom she had gained through her particular struggles.

Judges like Motley, Wilson, and O'Connor are notable examples of how women judges in different ways can and do make a difference. They give us a greater appreciation for having women as members of the judiciary and bring us further along the path of achieving a judiciary of which we can be proud.

Endnotes

1. Katherine T. Bartlett, "Feminist Legal Methods," *Harvard Law Review 103*, no. 829 (1990): 836–837.
2. Adam Liptak, "O'Connor Leap Moved Women Up the Bench," *New York Times*, Late Edition—Final, July 5, 2005, Section A.
3. Elisabeth Bumiller, "Pillow-Talk Call for a Woman to Fill O'Connor Seat," *New York Times*, Late Edition—Final, July 18, 2005, Section A.

4. Bertha Wilson, "Will Women Judges Really Make a Difference?" Fourth Annual Barbara Betcherman Memorial Lecture given at Osgoode Hall Law School, Toronto, Canada, February 8, 1990; printed in *Osgoode Hall Law Journal 28* (1990): 507.

5. See Robert E. Hawkins and Robert Martin, "Democracy, Judging and Bertha Wilson," *McGill Law Journal 41*, no. 1 (1995).

6. Lynne Cohen, "Gender Irrelevant When Judging a Judge," *Ottawa Citizen*, Final Edition, June 2, 1998, C4.

7. Constance Backhouse, "The Chilly Climate for Women Judges: Reflections on the Backlash from the Ewanchuk Case," *Canadian Journal of Women and the Law 15* (2003): 167–193.

8. Backhouse, "The Chilly Climate for Women Judges," 170.

9. Backhouse, "The Chilly Climate for Women Judges," 171.

10. Backhouse, "The Chilly Climate for Women Judges," 173.

11. Claire L'Heureux-Dube, "Lecture: Conversations on Equality," *Manitoba Law Journal 26*, no. 273 (1999).

12. Hawkins and Martin, "Democracy, Judging and Bertha Wilson."

13. Richard Foot, "Canadian Top Court Held as Example in U.S.: Vermont Senator Advising Bush on Supreme Court Pick," *Gazette* (Montreal), Final Edition, July 13, 2005, A13.

14. Clare Dyer, "Law: Where Are the Women? Our Judges Are Still Overwhelmingly Male, White and Public School-Educated, but It Is Possible to Create a Judiciary More Like the Population—Just Ask the Canadians." *Guardian* (London), July 8, 2003, Guardian Features Pages, 16.

15. See generally Katharine T. Bartlett, "Essay: Gender Law," *Duke Journal of Gender Law & Policy 1*, no. 1 (1994), and Vicki Lens, "Supreme Court Narratives on Equality and Gender Discrimination in Employment: 1971-2002," *Cardozo Women's Law Journal 10* (2004): 501.

16. See Martha Minow, "Making All the Difference: Inclusion, Exclusion, and the American Law" 20 (1990), and Christine

A. Littleton, "Reconstructing Sexual Equality," *California Law Review 75*, no. 1279 (1987).

17. See *Muller v. Oregon*, 208 U.S. 412 (1908).

18. *Bradwell v. Illinois*, 83 U.S. 130 (1873) (Bradley, J., concurring).

19. Bartlett, "Essay: Gender Law," note 16.

20. Lens, "Supreme Court Narratives on Equality and Gender Discrimination in Employment," note 16.

21. Leslie Bender, "Changing the Values in Tort Law," *Tulsa Law Journal 25*, no. 759 (1990): 767–773.

22. Lens, "Supreme Court Narratives on Equality and Gender Discrimination in Employment," note 16.

23. Littleton, "Reconstructing Sexual Equality."

24. Catharine A. MacKinnon, *Feminism Unmodified: Discourses on Life and Law* (Cambridge, MA: Harvard University Press, 1987).

25. Catharine A. MacKinnon, *Sexual Harassment of Working Women* (New York: Houghton-Mifflin, 1979).

26. Angela P. Harris, "Race and Essentialism in Feminist Legal Theory," *Stanford Law Review 42* (1990): 581.

27. For an overview, see Katherine Bartlett and Deborah L. Rhode, *Gender and Law: Theory, Doctrine, Commentary*, 4th ed. (Boston: Aspen, 2006).

28. "Women of the Courts Symposium: State High Courts and Divorce: The Impact of Judicial Gender," *University of Toledo Law Review 36* (2005): 923.

29. "Comment: Women on the Highest Court: Does Gender Bias or Personal Life Experience Influence Their Opinions," *University Toledo Law Review 36* (2005): 995.

30. Shirley A. Wiegand, "Deception and Artifice: Thelma, Louise, and the Legal Hermeneutic," *Oklahoma City University Law Review 22* (1997): 25.

31. Wiegand, "Deception and Artifice," at 47.

32. Wiegand, "Deception and Artifice."

33. See Tony Mauro, "O'Connor and Ginsburg, Together and Apart," *Legal Times*, June 9, 2003. Mauro notes that Justice O'Connor and Justice Ginsburg voted for the same result approximately 75 percent of the time. Justice O'Connor agreed with Justice Kennedy 83 percent of the time, while Justice Ginsburg agreed with Breyer and Souter in 94 percent of the decisions.

34. Sandra Day O'Connor, *The Majesty of the Law* (New York: Random House, 2003).

35. Ruth Bader Ginsburg, "United States Supreme Court Justice Ruth Bader Ginsburg Address: Remarks for California Women Lawyers," September 22, 1994, *Pepperdine Law Review 22* (1994): 4.

36. See note 41 in this chapter, citing a number of judicial task force reports from around the country.

37. Judith Resnik, "Judicial Selection and Democratic Theory: Demand, Supply, and Life Tenure," *Cardoza Law Review 26* (2005): 1.

38. Patricia Cain, "Feminist Jurisprudence: Grounding the Theories," *Berkeley Women's Law Journal 4* (1990): 191.

39. *J.E.B v. Alabama ex rel. T. B.*, 511 U.S. 127 (1994).

40. Jon Hanson and Adam Benforado, "The Drifters: Why the Supreme Court Makes Justices More Liberal," *Boston Review*, January/February 2006.

41. See, for example, Federal Courts Study Commission, "Report of the Federal Courts Study Commission 167" (1990); "Report of the Working Committees to the Second Circuit Task Force on Gender, Racial and Ethnic Fairness in the Courts," *New York University School of Law Annual Survey of American Law* (1997); and The Missouri Task Force on Gender and Justice, "Report of the Missouri Task Force on Gender and Justice," *Missouri Law Review 58* (1993): 485.

42. "The Effects of Gender in the Federal Courts: The Final Report of the Ninth Circuit Gender Bias Task Force" (July

1993), reprinted in *Southern California Law Review* 67 (1994): 745.

43. *Grutter v. Bollinger*, 539 U.S. at 332.

44. Lani Guinier, "Admissions Rituals as Political Acts: Guardians at the Gates of Our Democratic Ideals," *Harvard Law Review* 117 (2003): 113.

45. Sylvia R. Lazos Vargas, "Diversity, Impartiality, and Representation on the Bench Symposium: Does a Diverse Judiciary Attain a Rule of Law That Is Inclusive? What *Grutter v. Bollinger* Has to Say About Diversity on the Bench," *Michigan Journal of Race & Law* 10 (2004): 101.

46. See Carl Tobias, "Fostering Balance on the Federal Courts," *University Law Review* 47 (1998): 935, and Marcia Coyle, "How Deep Is the Pool for Supreme Court Picks," *Fulton County Daily Report*, September 28, 2005.

47. See, for example, Wilson Ray Huhn, "The Constitutional Jurisprudence of Sandra Day O'Connor: A Refusal to 'Foreclose the Unanticipated,'" *Akron Law Review* 39 (2006): 373.

48. *Blank v. Sullivan & Cromwell*, 418 F. Supp. 1 (1975).

49. *Blank v. Sullivan & Cromwell* at 9 & 10.

Part Two

Leadership in Context: Women in Politics

6

OPENING THE DOOR

Women Leaders and Constitution Building in Iraq and Afghanistan

Pippa Norris

Recent decades have witnessed growing demands for the inclusion and empowerment of women leaders as elected representatives. Women representatives have made important strides in some nations, but progress worldwide has proved sluggish. A global comparison shows that on average women are one-sixth of all members of the lower houses of parliament today (16.6 percent), a proportion that has risen by less than five percentage points during the last two decades.[1] A question arising from this situation is whether fast-track strategies are effective in accelerating the pace of change? These strategies include the use of reserved seats, which mandates offices for women members of parliament, statutory gender quotas that regulate the proportion of women candidates nominated by all parties, and voluntary gender quotas, which are adopted in rule books that govern nomination processes within specific parties. These reforms have been adopted and implemented for local and

This research would not have been possible without the generous funding of the Kuwait Program Research Fund/Middle East Initiative, the Woman and Public Policy Program (WAPPP), and the Women's Leadership Board at John F. Kennedy School of Government. I am also most grateful for invaluable research assistance provided by Sepideh Yousefzadeh and Andrew Vogt in conducting interviews and assembling background information, for the cooperation of all the individuals who were willing to be interviewed as part of this project, and for supplementary data provided by Julie Ballington and the Inter-Parliamentary Union.

national office in many places during recent decades, but their effects are by no means straightforward. In some cases, formal rule changes appear to generate a rapid and immediate stepped shift in the number of women in office, whereas elsewhere, similar policies seem to produce a minimal difference to the outcome. Moreover, even where more women attain legislative office through fast-track strategies, achieving greater descriptive representation in parliaments, this gain should not necessarily be equated automatically with women's substantive empowerment in decision-making processes.[2]

The rapid diffusion of fast-track strategies since the early 1990s raises questions about the overall trends in the proportion of women leaders in parliaments and governments. What types of fast-track strategies are available? Where and why have these policies been adopted—and in some cases abandoned? And what can we learn about the conditions that lead to the adoption of strategies designed to ratchet up the number of women in elected office? The first section of this chapter compares the detailed case studies of Iraq (illustrating the implementation of statutory gender quotas) and Afghanistan (illustrating the use of reserved seats). These qualitative cases exemplify the process of adopting two alternative fast-track strategies in recent postconflict constitutional settlements. The second section considers the underlying conditions leading to the effectiveness of these arrangements, and the third summarizes the conclusions.

The broader lessons of the comparison are that mechanisms aiming to bring women into representative office have now spread throughout the world, but policies are not all equally effective. The choice of mechanism is conditioned by the broader context, including the country's prior level of democracy, the degree of constitutional rigidity, the type of electoral system, global and regional patterns of diffusion, the existence of positive action policies for minority communities, and the levels of party institutionalization. No single policy is optimal in all contexts, and considerable care is needed to craft and implement the measures that will work best to promote the involvement of women in national decision-making processes.

Overall, the study concludes that new constitutions in postconflict peace settlements represent a critical opportunity to secure the voices of women leaders in the reconstruction of a society.

What Types of Fast-Track Strategies Are Available?

Many parties and national legislatures, recognizing the slow pace of change occurring worldwide, have adopted fast-track strategies during the past decade designed to raise the number of women in elected office.[3] How far are the national contrasts in the proportion of women in parliament evident today due to fast-track policy interventions rather than attributable to differences in the cultural or structural barriers facing women in elected office? Fast-track strategies fall into three main categories:

- *Reserved seats* are allocated to women legislators either by appointment or election, established by constitutional provision or electoral law.
- *Statutory gender quotas* regulate the specific proportion of women and men nominated as parliamentary candidates by all parties seeking election.
- *Voluntary gender quotas* have been adopted by specific parties, as specified in the internal regulations, party constitutions, and party rule books governing candidate recruitment processes, which control the pool of those eligible for nomination as well as those selected as parliamentary candidates.

Often these alternative policies are discussed indiscriminately as quotas, but this practice obscures the way rules differ in their design and implementation. Reserved seats established in the constitution or by electoral law provide the strongest external constraints on the parties' and electorate's choice of members of parliament, especially where members are indirectly elected or appointed to office. Statutory gender quotas, usually monitored by electoral commissions, limit the choice of legislative candidates nominated by all parties contesting an election. Voluntary gender quotas within particular parties provide the weakest external regulation of the candidate nomination process. These categories may also overlap: for example, the introduction of legal regulations governing the nomination process can encourage parties to amend their rule books and selection procedures. The use of these policies has been monitored in a comprehensive global database assembled by International IDEA and Stockholm University.[4] The database documents the ways that reserved seats for women in national parliaments are now used in more than a dozen countries. Statutory gender quotas for the lower houses of national assemblies exist in at least two dozen nations. Voluntary gender quotas governing nomination procedures have spread to parties in more than seventy nations. The diffusion of these mechanisms since the early 1990s has been remarkably swift and extensive, but their impact has varied. What explains the choice of one or another of these mechanisms by different states, what are the pros and cons of each of these fast-track strategies, and how do they work? It is useful to compare their global use and focus on Iraq and Afghanistan to consider these issues in the context of postconflict constitutional settlements.

Reserved Seats

By constitutional decree or electoral law, some countries have stipulated that a number of reserved seats are open only to women or to members of specified underrepresented ethnic minority groups. Such a policy has been adopted most commonly by developing nations to strengthen women's representation in single-member district majoritarian electoral systems, particularly in African and South Asian nations.[5] Reserved seats have been used in the lower house of the national legislature in Morocco (30 women members elected from a national list among 325 representatives), Bangladesh (30/300), Pakistan (60/357), Botswana (2 women appointed by the president out of 44 members), Taiwan (elected), Lesotho (3 women appointed out of 80 seats), and Tanzania (37 women out of 274 members, the seats distributed to parties according to their share in the House of Representatives).[6] Similar policies have been used at the subnational level with considerable success, including 30 percent of seats reserved for women in local village councils in India, Bangladesh, and Pakistan.[7]

The idea of reserved seats for women follows similar practices designed to elect representatives from regional, linguistic, ethnic, or religious minority communities. The effect depends on the size and geographic concentration of such groups.[8] Reserved seats for ethnic minorities have been used in about two dozen countries: in New Zealand, Pakistan, and Fiji, for example, where the seats are filled by appointees of a recognized group or elected by voters from a communal roll.[9] There is nothing particularly novel about these arrangements; after World War II separate communal rolls with reserved seats became integral parts of power-sharing solutions to end internal conflicts in Lebanon in 1943, Cyprus in 1960, and Zimbabwe in 1980. During the last decade, these strategies were evident in the compartmentalized ethnic arrangements of peace pacts in Bosnia, Croatia, and Kosovo. In Croatia, for example, which uses party list proportional representation (List PR) for most seats, specific districts are reserved for members of Hungarian, Czech and Slovak, Ruthenian and Ukrainian, and German and Austrian minorities. India reserves a certain number of seats in each state for Scheduled Castes and Tribes. In Uganda, 53 of 292 parliamentary seats are reserved for women (18 percent), via indirect election, along with seats set aside for representatives drawn from such groups as the army, the disabled, the trade unions, and youth. The stated aim there is to ensure an inclusive Movement party despite a legal ban to prevent opposition movements' standing for parliamentary election.[10] Most countries using reserved seats for women or minority communities have majoritarian electoral systems, but countries with PR and combined electoral systems can also include this mechanism.

Afghanistan. The adoption of reserved seats for women in postconflict constitutional settlements, and their impact in traditional cultures, is exemplified by the case of Afghanistan.[11] Afghanistan had not had a functioning parliament since 1973, and even during the decade of the New Democracy (1963–1973) the king usually ruled by decree. The breakdown of Taliban rule, international pressures for democratization and human rights, and the development of the new constitution presented a critical opportunity to develop new political institutions and to incorporate women into the public arena. The new constitution was crafted by the Constitutional Drafting Commission and the Constitutional Review Commission, before finally being debated in December 2003 by the emergency Loya Jirga (Grand Assembly). Women had a voice in each of these commissions, representing 12 percent of the delegates in the Loya Jirga, while two women sat on the nine-member Drafting Commission. The international community, led by the United Nations, the U.S. State Department, and the Afghanistan Reconstruction Project, also provided expert advice and information about constitutional design, including possible measures for the inclusion of women.[12] This process was part of a larger debate about the desirability of adopting either a presidential or parliamentary democracy, making federal and local arrangements, choosing the type of electoral system, and determining the role of Islamic law in the new constitution. Women's groups in Afghanistan also mobilized, including those who had been exiled, to call for 25 percent female representation in the new assembly and a women's Bill of Rights.[13] The new Afghan constitution, agreed on in January 2004, established that women would be included in both houses of the national assembly. The constitution specified that for the Wolesi Jirga (lower house):

> Members of the Wolesi Jirga are elected by the people through free, general, secret, and direct elections.
>
> Their mandate ends on the first of Saratan of the fifth year after the elections, and the new assembly starts its work.

The number of members of the Wolesi Jirga, proportionate to the population of each region, shall be not more than 250.

Electoral constituency and other related issues shall be determined by election laws.

In the election law, measures should be adopted so the election system shall provide general and just representation for all the people of the country, and at least two female delegates should be elected from each province.

In practice, the requirement that at least two women should be directly elected to the Wolesi Jirga from each of the thirty-four existing provinces meant that sixty-eight women would be included in the lower house, or 27.3 percent of the total. But the constitution did not specify either the type of electoral system or how to guarantee the inclusion of women. For the Meshrano Jirga (upper house), the president was empowered under the constitution to appoint one-third of the members, of whom half were to be women. At least one-quarter of the seats on provincial councils were also reserved for women.

The May 2005 Electoral Law and the Electoral Commission determined how these requirements would be implemented. Afghanistan chose the single non-transferable voting (SNTV) electoral system for the Wolesi Jirga, with multimember constituencies and simple plurality voting.[14] In this system, used previously in Japan until 1993, Vanuatu, Jordan, and (partially) for Taiwan, electors cast a single vote for one candidate in a multimember district. The candidates with the highest vote totals are declared elected. This system was adopted because it is technically simple to administer and count, and it works even in the absence of organized parties and any other political groupings. Multimember districts based on existing provincial boundaries are also advantageous, given the practical limitations of insufficient population data and time to draw single-member constituency boundaries. The system allows independent candidates to nominate themselves, without requiring prior party endorsement. The system also encourages local elected members to serve their provincial constituency, since individual candidates compete for popular support within as well as among parties. The disadvantages of this system, however, are that candidate-centered voting encourages weak party organizations, with potential problems for coordination within the new legislature. It is one of the most disproportional electoral systems, as candidates can be elected with an extremely modest plurality of the vote, and even a small shift in votes may tip the outcome in an unpredictable direction. SNTV also encourages strategic party nominations, in deciding how many candidates to nominate in each district, and strategic voting.[15] Electors faced long lists of candidates: for example, 390 candidates were listed on a seven-page ballot in Kabul, without any familiar party cues to simplify their choices. This system may have reinforced voting for local leaders along ethnic lines with minimal incentive for cooperation in the parliament.[16]

In terms of Afghanistan's constitutional requirement for the inclusion of women, the choice of the SNTV electoral system constrained the available options.[17] The system ruled out the type of statutory gender quotas that specify a proportion of women candidates in List PR. The use of voluntary party quotas would not achieve the constitutional guarantee in Article Eighty-Three. Moreover, majoritarian elections in neighboring Pakistan and Bangladesh, as well as for village elections in India, had long employed reserved seats for women and minority communities, which may have influenced the Afghan decision makers.[18] As a result, the Commission specified reserved seats within each province, varying the number allocated in each area according to population size until the total reflected the constitutional provisions. Two women could not have been allocated in every province, as in the smaller provinces—with only two seats— only women would be returned. The Electoral Commission implemented the constitutional requirements and designated the number of Wolesi Jirga seats per province according to population size, allocating, for example, thirty-three seats for Kabul, of which nine were reserved for women. This system meant that all general seats were filled, irrespective of gender, by the candidates with the most votes in each province. If the specified minimum number of women were not returned under the general competition, then the women who achieved the most votes in each province were elected to the reserved women's seats. As a result, women were often elected with dramatically fewer votes than men, which may lead to questions about the fairness of the outcome.[19]

Afghanistan's first legislative contests in September 2005 attracted 2,835 candidates for the Wolesi Jirga, of whom 344 were women (12.1 percent). The results saw the election of 68 women out of 249 members (27.3 percent). The country now ranks twenty-fourth in the Inter-Parliamentary Union's global comparison of the proportion of women in parliament, well ahead of many established democracies and affluent states such as France, Italy, and the United States. This situation is all the more remarkable given its traditional social and political context: Afghan women have long lacked many basic human rights, including access to education, health care, and freedom of movement, and many of the women candidates who stood for office were subject to serious threats, harassment, and violent intimidation during the campaign.[20]

Statutory Gender Quotas

An alternative strategy uses statutory gender quotas applied to all political parties, specifying that women must constitute a minimal proportion of parliamentary candidates within each party. Quotas are an instrument to introduce specific formal selection criteria into nomination procedures. They can be used for elected or appointed office in the public sphere or for personnel recruitment in the private sector, such as for trade-union office. There is an important distinction drawn between statutory gender quotas introduced by law, which apply to all parties within a country, and voluntary gender quotas, which are implemented by internal regulations and rule books within each party. Quotas can be specified for women and men, or for other selection criteria such as ethnicity, language, social sector, or religion. Statutory gender quota laws have been applied to elections in Belgium, France, Italy, and to many nations in Latin America (see Table 6.1).[21] Quotas

Table 6.1   Examples of Statutory Gender Quotas Used Worldwide

Country	Date of Law	Gender Quota %	Legislative Body	Electoral System	List Open or Closed	% Women MPs Before Law (1i)	% Women MPs After Law (2ii)	Change (1i)-(1ii)	% Women Elected in Latest Election	Date of Latest Election
France	1999	50	Lower	Majoritarian	—	11	12	+1	12.2	2002
Costa Rica	1997	40	Unicameral	Proportional	Closed	14	19	+5	35.1	2006
Belgium	1994	33	Lower	Proportional	Open	18	23	+5	34.7	2003
Bosnia-Herzegovina	2001	33	Lower	Proportional	Open	—	14.3	—	16.7	2002
Argentina	1991	30	Lower	Proportional	Closed	6	27	+21	35.0	2005
Peru	1997	30	Unicameral	Proportional	Open	11	18	+7	18.3	2001
Venezuela	1998	30	Lower	Combined	Closed	6	13	+7	17.4	2005
Panama	1997	30	Unicameral	Combined	Closed	8	10	+2	16.7	2004
Venezuela	1998	30	Senate	Combined	Closed	8	9	+2	—	2005
Bolivia	1997	30	Lower	Combined	Closed	11	12	+1	16.9	2005

Country	Year		Chamber	System	List					Year
Mexico	1996	30	Senate	Combined	Closed	15	16	+1	24.2	2003
Bolivia	1997	30	Senate	Combined	Closed	4	4	0	16.9	2005
Brazil	1997	30	Lower	Proportional	Open	7	6	-1	8.6	2002
Mexico	1996	30	Lower	Combined	Closed	17	16	-1	24.2	2003
Indonesia	2003	30	Lower	Proportional	Closed	9	11.3	+2	11.3	2004
Macedonia	2001	30	Lower	Combined	Closed	—	17.5	—	19.2	2002
Serbia	2002	30	Lower	Proportional	Open	7.5	7.9	—	7.9	2003
Dominican Republic	1997	25	Lower	Proportional	Closed	12	16	+4	17.3	2002
Ecuador	1997	20	Unicameral	Combined	Open	4	15	+11	8.9	2002
Paraguay	1996	20	Senate	Proportional	Closed	11	18	+7	10.0	2003
Paraguay	1996	20	Lower	Proportional	Closed	3	3	0	10.0	
Korea, North	—	20	Lower	Majoritarian	—	—	20.1	—	20.1	2003
Philippines	1995	20	Lower	Combined	Closed	—	17.8	—	15.7	2004
Armenia	1999	5	Lower	Combined	Closed	—	3.1	—	5.3	2003
Nepal	1990	5	Lower	Majoritarian	—	—	5.9	—	0.0	1999

Continued

Table 6.1 Examples of Statutory Gender Quotas Used Worldwide (Continued)

Country	Date of Law	Gender Quota %	Legislative Body	Electoral System	List Open or Closed	% Women MPs Before Law (1i)	% Women MPs After Law (2ii)	Change (1i)-(1ii)	% Women Elected in Latest Election	Date of Latest Election
Iraq TNA (*)	1/2005	25	Lower	Proportional	Closed	—	31.5	—	—	2005
Iraq	12/2005	25	Lower	Proportional	Closed	—	25.5	—	—	2006
Average		**30**				**10**	**14**	**+4**		

Note: Statutory gender quotas for the lower house of national parliaments are defined as legal regulations specifying that each party must include a minimum proportion of women in their candidate lists. Change is estimated based on the percentage of women MPs in the parliamentary election held immediately before and after implementation of the gender quota law.

* The Iraqi Transitional National Assembly.

Sources: Mala Htun, "Electoral Rules, Parties, and the Election of Women in Latin America," paper presented at the Annual Meeting of the American Political Science Association, San Francisco, August 30, 2001; Mala Htun and Mark Jones, "Engendering the Right to Participate in Decision-Making: Electoral Quotas and Women's Leadership in Latin America," in Nikki Craske and Maxine Molyneux, eds., *Gender and the Politics of Rights and Democracy in Latin America* (London: Palgrave, 2002); International IDEA/Stockholm University Global Database of Quotas for Women, available online: www.quotaproject.org.

have also been used for appointments to public bodies and consultative committees in countries such as Finland and Norway.[22]

Iraq. Iraq's use of quotas provides an example. A range of constitutional and legal options were considered for including women in elected office.[23] Historically the country was more egalitarian toward women than many Arab states, achieving relatively high levels of female education, literacy, and participation in the workforce during the 1960s and 1970s as part of the economic development program of the secular Baathist regime.[24] The 1970 Iraqi Constitution formally guaranteed equal rights to women, and in 1986 Iraq became one of the first countries to ratify CEDAW. Employment and labor laws were passed to give maternity benefits, equal pay, and freedom from harassment in the workplace.[25] In practice, these laws were often not enforced, but nevertheless the legal climate was considerably more liberal than many others in the region. In 1980 Iraqi women got the right to vote, and in the first parliamentary elections that year women won 16 out of 250 seats (6.4 percent) on the National Council; this proportion doubled to 13.2 percent in 1985, before falling to 10.8 percent in 1990 and 8 percent in 2003, immediately before the war.

In the post-Saddam era, Iraq developed a new constitution and electoral laws through a multistage process. After the fall of Saddam Hussein, in May 2003 the Coalition Provisional Authority (CPA), under Ambassador Paul Bremer, was established by the U.S.-led coalition to administer Iraq. In July 2003, the CPA created the Iraqi Governing Council, with twenty-five appointed Iraqi representatives from five ethnic groups, including three women (12 percent). On March 8, 2004, the Transitional Administrative Law (TAL) was approved as a provisional constitution. In June 2004, the U.S.-led coalition handed over power to Prime Minister Ilad Allawi's interim government, which consisted of thirty ministers, among them six women and the newly created post of Minister of Women's Affairs. The Iraqi Governing Council was in turn replaced in August 2004 by a larger (100-person) appointed national assembly, a body that was subsequently replaced by the 275-member transitional National Assembly, following the January 2005 elections. The primary responsibility of the Assembly was to design the new Iraqi Constitution, which was proposed in August 2005 and finally approved by a public referendum in October 2005. On December 15, 2005, Iraqis went to the polls to elect the 275-member permanent House of Representatives, with the results announced in late January 2006.

With the United Nations pressing for the representation of women and minority communities in any new constitution, the process of constitutional design drew on advice from many international experts, including agencies such as IFES, NED, and USAID. The process stimulated considerable debate within Iraq. Prior to agreement about the TAL, in early spring 2004 public meetings were held around the country to debate the proposed contents, including the role of women's rights in the document. Iraqi women mobilized strongly though a series of meetings, conferences, and workshops, with debate on the level of quota to adopt and whether 20 percent, 30 percent, or 40 percent of all elected positions should be allocated to women. For example, in January 2004, women in Hilla, Divsania, Karbala, and Najaf organized a major conference in Basra, attended by four hundred delegates. The Iraqi Higher Women's Council, a body containing a diverse cross-section of Iraqi women, presented Ambassador Bremer with a letter supporting a 40 percent quota for women in legislative bodies. The U.S.-led coalition was divided about this issue; Tony Blair and the British representative in Baghdad favored introducing gender quotas for Iraqi elections.[26] By contrast, Paul Bremer and CPA preferred equal opportunity policies over quotas, although it was hard to argue against them for Iraq after reserved seats had been adopted in Afghanistan.[27] The Shiite religious parties were also strongly opposed to any quotas, in part because they were concerned about whether they could nominate a sufficient number of women candidates, but secular Iraqis supported the idea. The TAL did not adopt the 40 percent quota that some had lobbied for, but Article 30c did specify that the electoral law governing contests for the National Assembly "shall aim to achieve the goal of having women constitute no less than one quarter of the members."[28] The TAL also ensured fair representation of all communities in Iraq, including Turkoman and other minorities, although it did not specify the mechanism to achieve this aim.

To implement these policies, the Electoral Law (CPA 96) that passed in June 2004 specified that a system of nationwide closed-list PR would be used (with a Hare quota) for elections to the transitional National Assembly.[29] Parties could present a list of at least twelve candidates in ranked order, with positions filled from the top of the list downward according to their share of the vote. To guarantee the inclusion of women in the new body, the Electoral Law specified that any party seeking to contest the election had to include women candidates ranked ("zippered") as one among every third name included in the party list: "No fewer than one out of the first three candidates on the list must be [a] woman; no fewer than two out of the first six candidates on the list must be [a] woman; and so forth until the end of the list."[30] Individual candidates could also stand for office. Although there was debate about the use of reserved seats for minorities, insufficient time prior to the election to identify and classify minority electorates and candidates, especially given the displaced populations, hampered the implementation of this policy. Criticisms about the legitimacy of reserved seats were also expressed.[31] The use of smaller electoral districts was considered and rejected on the grounds that implementation would delay the process, given the lack of credible population figures to allocate seats.[32]

The direct elections to the transitional National Assembly on January 30, 2005, returned 86 women out of 273 members (31.5 percent), a remarkable proportion given the history of women's representation in Arab states; it exceeded the 25 percent target set in the TAL. Moreover, the women who were elected came from all communities, some favoring a secular government and legislation dealing with women's rights, others preferring an Islamic state and Sharia law. A similar quota system was used for elections to the Kurdistan National Assembly and for the Governorate Councils.

The contents of the final Iraqi constitution were debated in the new National Assembly, and Article Forty-Seven in the final document retained a 25 percent quota for women in the lower house: "The elections law aims to achieve a percentage of women representation not less than one-quarter of the Council of Representatives members."[33] To implement this goal, the second Electoral Law, adopted in September 2005, required parties seeking election to implement the same process followed earlier, with at least one women candidate included among the first three names on party lists, two in the first six names, and so on. The second Electoral Law also continued to use the List PR electoral system, but with regional, not national, districts. In total, 230 seats were allocated proportionally, divided among eighteen governorates (provinces) based on the size of the registered electorate in each. In addition, forty-five so-called compensatory seats were allocated for parties and groupings that achieved a minimum threshold of votes nationwide to reinforce the strength of larger parties.

The results, following the general elections held on December 15, 2005, for permanent members of the National Council of Representatives, are that women are now more than one-quarter (25.5 percent) of the legislature, distributed across all major parties and communities. For reasons that are unclear, this is less than the 31.5 percent elected to the transitional National Assembly. This is probably due, at least in part, to the use of regional electoral districts rather than a nationwide contest. This situation is a striking outcome given that women are usually marginalized in legislative office in Arab states; indeed in Saudi Arabia and the United Arab Emirates women continue to be denied the right to vote and to stand for election, and societies in the Middle East also display some of the most traditional cultural attitudes toward the roles of women and men.[34] As a result of the election, Iraq now ranks twenty-sixth worldwide in the proportion of women in the new parliament, comparable to Switzerland, Australia, and Mexico, and well above the United Kingdom and the United States.

Voluntary Gender Quotas

An alternative policy concerns the use of voluntary gender quotas within specific parties. While party activists and leaders can take the initiative, this is not a matter that is implemented through electoral law. Rules, constitutions, and internal regulations within each party are distinct from electoral statutes enforceable by the courts. Voluntary gender quotas have been widely used by multiple parties in Scandinavia, Western Europe, and Latin America. At the same time, Communist parties employed them in the past in Central and Eastern Europe but these policies were abandoned as redolent of the Soviet era in the transition to democracy during the early 1990s.[35]

Assessing the Impact of Fast-Track Strategies

What has been the impact of fast-track initiatives? Reserved seats, statutory gender quotas, and voluntary gender quotas all have an impact, but none offers a panacea for the underrepresentation of women in decisions that affect their lives.

Reserved Seats

The use of reserved seats guarantees a minimum number of women in elected office. Table 6.2 illustrates how the proportion of women elected in the most recent election in the countries using these strategies exceeded the statutory minimum. In this regard, the policy works, setting a minimum floor. Yet the full impact of these mechanisms is difficult to assess, given their relatively recent adoption in many countries, and the policy remains controversial for a number of reasons. Some have argued that this mechanism may be a way to appease women—and ultimately sideline them.[36] Women, where appointed to office, may be marginalized from exercising any independent power and responsibility if they lack an independent electoral or organizational base, and the ruling party can reinforce control of parliament by patronage. This is particularly the case in regimes

Table 6.2 Worldwide Reserved Seats for Women in the Lower House of Parliament

	Election	Electoral System	Number of Seats Reserved for Women	Percentage of Seats Reserved for Women (11)	Percentage of Women Elected in Latest Election (1i2)	Difference Between (11) and (2ii)	Appointed or Elected
Rwanda	2003	List PR	24/80	30.0	48.8	+18.8	Elected
Tanzania	2000	FPTP	48/295	16.2	30.4	+14.2	Appointed
Afghanistan	2005	SNTV	64/249	25.0	27.3	+2.3	Elected
Uganda	2001	FPTP	56/292	19.1	23.9	+4.8	Indirectly elected
Taiwan	1996	SNTV/List PR	Varies/334	Varies	22.2	—	Elected
Pakistan	2002	FPTP/List PR	60/357	16.8	21.3	+4.5	Elected
Zimbabwe	2000	FPTP	37/274	13.5	16.0	+2.5	Appointed
Bangladesh	2004	FPTP	45/345	13.0	14.8	+1.8	Appointed
Sudan	2000	FPTP	35/360	9.7	14.7	+5.0	Elected
Lesotho	1998	FPTP/List PR	3/80	3.8	11.7	+7.9	Appointed
Botswana	1999	FPTP	2/44	4.5	11.1	+6.6	Appointed
Djibouti	2003	PBV	7/65	10.7	10.8	+0.1	Elected

Morocco	2002	List PR	30/325	9.2	10.8	+1.6	Elected
Somalia	2004	—	25/245	10.2	—	—	Appointed
Jordan	2003	SNTV	6/110	5.5	—	—	Elected

Note: *Reserved seats for women* in the lower house of the national parliament are defined as those that by law can only be filled by women, either by appointment or election. It should be noted that the parliament in Eritrea is currently suspended and also Egypt used reserved seats (8.3 percent for women) from 1979 to 1984.

Electoral systems: *List PR* is Party list proportional representation; *FPT* is first-past-the-post; *SNTV* is single non-transferable vote; *PBV* is party block vote.

Sources: The Electoral Institute of Southern Africa (EISA) www.eisa.org.za; *Elections Around the World;* www.quotaproject.org.

that have limited institutional checks and balances, weak legislatures, and power concentrated in the hands of the executive. If the level of reserved seats is set too low, it may result in token representation.[37] Reserved seats also need organizations to develop effective training programs for women leaders who are considering running for office, so they can develop skills, knowledge, and confidence.

Nevertheless, against these arguments, women who gain reserved seats through free and fair elections have the opportunity to develop an independent political base and the experience of political leadership. If electoral law implements reserved seats, it guarantees a minimum number of women in elected office without the uncertainty of statutory and voluntary gender quotas. Moreover, reserved seats have been adopted in many countries that share a common Muslim cultural heritage and where traditional attitudes prevail concerning the roles of women and men.[38] Thus, this strategy may boost the number of women in leadership positions, a process that may also change attitudes toward sex roles more generally.

Statutory Gender Quotas

How well have statutory gender quotas worked? Table 6.1 showed the proportion of women returned in the election held immediately before passage of the law, the election held immediately after passage, and the summary short-term change. The pattern shows that statutory gender quotas appear to have worked more effectively in some countries and elections than in others: hence the substantial short-term rise in the number of women in parliament found in Argentina and the modest short-term growth in Peru and Belgium, but minimal progress evident in France, Mexico, or Brazil. The comparison of the number of women in the latest election to date also shows that many countries are falling far short of the specified legal quota.

To determine the cause, the next step is to research the relative importance of the institutional conditions that operate in different contexts. Case studies suggest that the effective implementation of statutory gender quotas can plausibly vary according to several factors:

- The type of electoral system
- The mean district magnitude
- The implementation of the statutory mechanisms
- The level of the gender quota specified by law
- Whether the rules for party lists regulate the rank order of women and men candidates
- Whether party lists are open or closed
- The strength of women's organizations within parties
- Good-faith compliance by parties
- The penalties associated with any failure to comply with the law

Legal regulations are designed to alter the balance of incentives for the party gatekeepers who nominate candidates. Where these laws are implemented, selectors need to weigh the potential penalties and benefits of compliance. Selectors may still prefer the default option of traditionally nominating a male candidate under certain circumstances: for example, if the laws are seen as symbolic window-dressing more than as good-faith regulations; if the regulation specifies that a certain proportion of women have to be selected for party lists but they fail to specify their rank order so that female candidates cluster in unwinnable positions at the bottom of the list; or if sanctions for noncompliance are weak or nonexistent. Delayed effects may also occur, as parties adapt gradually to the new regulatory environment and as incumbents retire. As in many attempts to alter incentive structures, the devil lies in the practical details, and superficially similar policies may have diverse consequences in different contexts.

Voluntary Gender Quotas

Similar observations can be made about specific parties' implementation of voluntary gender quotas. Building on the growing case-study literature and developing systematic cross-national analysis, the next step is to research the relative weight given to a number of conditions that could generate variations in the effectiveness of these measures among different parties.[39] These differences can be explained by factors such as these:

- The specific type of electoral system
- The degree of party institutionalization in its nomination procedures
- The implementation of formal party rules
- The penalties associated with any failure to comply with the rules
- The level of the gender quota specified by party rules
- The strength of women's organizations within parties
- The regulation of rank order of women and men candidates by party lists
- The good faith compliance and the informal cultural norms operating within parties

Case studies suggest that gender quotas can effectively constrain the choices of the selectorate in mass branch-party bureaucratic organizations, where rules are strictly implemented in nomination processes. The adoption of all-women shortlists within the British Labour Party in the run-up to the 1997 British general election illustrates this process most dramatically. The proportion of women MPs at Westminster doubled overnight as a result of this shortlisting, coupled with the Blair landslide.[40] Set against that result, other cases suggest that gender quotas can be regarded as ideal targets rather than binding resolutions in highly personalist parties, where the party leadership determines nominations primarily on a patronage basis.[41]

Conclusions: Do Fast-Track Strategies Work?

This study concludes that alternative fast-track strategies should not be treated as functionally equivalent, as they differ substantially in their workings and impact. Of the three main types, reserved seats involve the most radical intervention in the electoral process; it constrains the autonomy of parties to nominate candidates and of the electorate to choose. Reserved seats can increase the number of women in office, as demonstrated by the case of the 2005 elections in Afghanistan, although the independence of the women holding these seats can be curtailed in the case of appointment by patronage. This plan has most commonly been adopted in transitional democracies characterized by single-member district majoritarian electoral systems and weak party organizations, and it has also been adopted in many societies with deeply traditional cultural attitudes toward gender equality. By contrast, statutory gender quotas have most commonly been used in consolidating democracies, especially those already undergoing processes of constitutional change.

The short-term impact of statutory quotas in subsequent elections depends on many specific factors, as illustrated by the contrasting results in France, Iraq, and Argentina. Their design is critical to their effect. Last, voluntary gender quotas are the most popular and flexible strategy adopted by parties to govern their own nomination procedures, and they are now widely used throughout the world. In bureaucratic extra-parliamentary party organizations where internal rules matter, and where women's internal party organizations are mobilized around these measures, voluntary quotas can prove very effective in electing more women to office. But under many conditions, writing voluntary gender quotas into party rulebooks may prove more symbolic than substantive—for example, in party cultures with traditional attitudes toward sex roles, in legislatures where incumbents rarely lose, and in poorly institutionalized parties whose formal organizations remain weak and whose nomination processes are dominated by patronage.

The broader lessons are that fast-track strategies have become increasingly popular during recent decades as a way to increase the number of women in office. Where implemented effectively, under certain conditions these policies can generate substantial short-term change in the proportion of women parliamentarians, reducing the barriers to legislative office. Fast-track strategies have their limitations, and they should not be seen as panaceas to improve the political position and power of women overnight. But these policies can be remarkably effective in giving women a stronger public voice in parliament, with important consequences for articulating the wide range of women's concerns, for the role of women leaders in higher government office, for strengthening the democratic legitimacy of elected bodies, and for modifying cultural attitudes toward women leaders.

Endnotes

1. Inter-Parliamentary Union, "Women in National Parliaments, January 31, 2006, available online: www.ipu.org/wmn-e/world-arc.htm, access date: December 21, 2006; Inter-Parliamentary Union, *Women in Parliaments, 1945–1995* (IPU: Geneva, 1995).

2. Hanna Pitkin, *The Concept of Representation* (Berkeley: University of California Press, 1967); Anne Phillips, *The Politics of Presence* (Oxford: Clarendon Press, 1995); Anne Phillips, ed., *Feminism and Politics* (New York: Oxford University Press, 1998); Jane Mansbridge, "Should Blacks Represent Blacks and Women Represent Women? A Contingent 'Yes.'" *Journal of Politics 61*, no. 3 (1999): 628–657; Irene Tinker, "Quotas for Women in Elected Legislatures: Do They Really Empower Women?" *Women's Studies International Forum 27*, no. 5–6 (2004): 531–546; Leslie A. Schwindt-Bayer and William Mishler, "An Integrated Model of Women's Representation," *Journal of Politics 67*, no. 2 (2005): 407–428.

3. For an overview of developments, see Drude Dahlerup, ed., *Women, Quotas and Politics* (New York: Routledge, 2005); Mona Krook, "Politicizing Representation: Campaigns for Candidate Gender Quotas Worldwide," Ph.D. dissertation, Columbia University, 2004; Drude Dahlerup and Lenita Freidenvall, "Quotas as a Fast Track to Equal Representation for Women," *International Feminist Journal of Politics 7*, no. 1 (2005): 26–48.

4. International IDEA and Stockholm University, "Global Database of Quotas for Women," 2006, available online: www.quotaproject.org, access date: December 21, 2006.

5. Richard Matland, "Electoral Quotas: Frequency and Effectiveness," in Dahlerup, *Women, Quotas and Politics.*

6. For details of the African cases, see International IDEA, *The Implementation of Quotas: The African Experience* (Stockholm, Sweden: International IDEA, 2004). Reserved seats for women have also been used in the past in Eritrea, but the parliament is currently suspended in this country.

7. International IDEA, *The Implementation of Quotas;* L. D. Jenkins, "Competing Inequalities: The Struggle Over Reserved Seats for Women in India," *International Review of Social History 44* (1999): 53–75.

8. Andrew Reynolds, "Reserved Seats in National Legislatures," *Legislative Studies Quarterly 30*, no. 2 (2005): 301–310.

9. Anna Jarstad, *Changing the Game: Consociational Theory and Ethnic Quotas in Cyprus and New Zealand* (Uppsala, Sweden: Department of Peace and Conflict, Uppsala University, 2001); Andy Reynolds, "Reserved Seats in National Legislatures," *Legislative Studies Quarterly 30*, no. 2 (2005): 301–310; Lisa Handley, "Comparative Redistricting Practices," paper presented at the annual meeting of the American Political Science Association, Washington, DC, 2005.

10. D. Pankhurst, "Women and Politics in Africa: The Case of Uganda," *Parliamentary Affairs 55*, no. 1 (2002): 119–125.

11. For more details, see Julie Ballington and Drude Dahlerup, "Gender Quotas in Post-Conflict States: East Timor, Afghanistan and Iraq," in Dahlerup, *Women, Quotas and Politics*.

12. Pippa Norris, "Increasing Women's Representation in Government: What Options Would Work Best for Afghanistan?" paper prepared for the Afghanistan Reconstruction Project Center on International Cooperation, New York University, 2003; Larry Goodson, "Afghanistan's Long Road to Reconstruction," *Journal of Democracy 14*, no. 1 (2003): 82–99; Barnett R. Rubin, "Peace Building and State-Building in Afghanistan: Constructing Sovereignty for Whose Security?" *Third World Quarterly 27*, no. 1 (2006): 175–185; Barnett R. Rubin, "Crafting a Constitution in Afghanistan," *Journal of Democracy 15*, no. 3 (2004): 5–19; Barnett R. Rubin, "(Re)building Afghanistan: The Folly of Stateless Democracy," *Current History 103* (2004): 165–170; C. J. Riphenburg, "Post-Taliban Afghanistan— Changes Outlook for Women?" *Asian Survey 44*, no. 3 (2004): 401–421.

13. Drude Dahlerup and Anja Taarup Nordlund, "Gender Quotas: A Key to Equality? A Case Study of Iraq and Afghanistan," *European Political Science* (2004): 91–98.

14. Dahlerup and Nordlund, "Gender Quotas."

15. Bernard Grofman, Sung-Chull Lee, Edwin A. Winckler, and Broan Woodall, eds., *Elections in Japan, Korea, and Taiwan Under the Single Non-Transferable Vote* (Ann Arbor: University of Michigan Press, 1999).

16. Barnett R. Rubin, "The Wrong Voting System," *International Herald Tribune*, March 16, 2005.

17. Pippa Norris, "Implementing Women's Representation in Afghanistan Electoral Law: Options for Reserved Seats," paper prepared for the Afghanistan Reconstruction Project Center on International Cooperation, New York University, 2004.

18. International IDEA, *The Implementation of Quotas*.

19. Andrew Reynolds and Andrew Wilder, "Free, Fair or Flawed: Challenges for Legitimate Elections in Afghanistan," *Afghanistan Research and Evaluation Unit* (September 2004): 14.

20. There were many journalistic reports of harassment against women candidates and this may have encouraged a disproportionate number of women candidates (58 out of 344) to withdraw prior to election. For the position of women under the Taliban, see Valentine M. Moghadam, "Patriarchy, the Taleban, and Politics of Public Space in Afghanistan," *Women's Studies International Forum 25*, no. 1 (2002): 19–31.

21. Mark P. Jones, "Increasing Women's Representation via Gender Quotas: The Argentine Ley de Cupos," *Women and Politics 16* (1996): 4, 75–98; Mark P. Jones, "Gender Quotas, Electoral Laws, and the Election of Women: Lessons from the Argentine Provinces," *Comparative Political Studies 31*, no. 1 (1998): 3–21; Liza Baldez, "Elected Bodies: Gender Quota Law for Legislative Candidates in Mexico," *Legislative Studies Quarterly 29* (2004): 2, 231–258; Miki Caul, "Political Parties and the Adoption of Candidate Gender Quotas: A Cross-National Analysis," *Journal of Politics 63*, no. 4 (2001): 1214–1229; Mala Htun and Mark P. Jones, "Engendering the Right to Participate in Decision-Making: Electoral Quotas and Women's Leadership in Latin America," in N. Craske and M. Molyneux, eds., *Gender and the Politics of Rights and Democracy in Latin America* (New York: Palgrave, 2002), 32–56.

22. Council of Europe, *Positive Action in the Field of Equality Between Women and Men*, Final Report of the Group of Specialists on Positive Acton in the Field of Equality Between Women and Men (EG-S-PA), 2000; Anne Peters, Robert Seidman, and Ann Seidman, *Women, Quotas, and Constitutions: A Comparative Study of Affirmative Action for Women Under American, German and European Community and International Law* (The Hague: Kluwer Law International, 1999).

23. Pippa Norris, "Women's Representation in Iraq: Strategies and Options," Report for National Endowment for Democracy International Forum for Democratic Development, 2004.

24. United Nations Development Fund for Women, "Gender Profile of the Conflict in Iraq," 2005, available online: www. WomenWarPeace.org.

25. Human Rights Watch, "Background on Women's Status in Iraq Prior to the Fall of the Saddam Hussein Government," November 2003, available online: hrw.org/backgrounder/wrd/iraq-women.htm, access date: December 21, 2006.

26. See Larry Diamond, *Squandered Victory* (New York: Times Books, 2005), 145.

27. Personal interview with Lesley Abdela, chief executive of Project Parity and international consultant who worked on training women in Iraq. On November 3, 2003, the CPA spokesman said: "There are no plans for quotas, but we are planning on empowering women through . . . women's organizations, democracy trainings, and involving them in the political process." Annia Ciezadlo, "Iraqi Women Raise Voices for Quotas," *Christian Science Monitor,* December 17, 2003.

28. The Law for the Administration of Iraq During the Transition Period, available online: www.ieciraq.org.

29. CPA Orders 92, 96 and 97. available online: www.ieciraq.org.

30. Coalition Provisional Authority Order Number 96, "The Electoral Law," June 7, 2004, available online: www.iraqcoalition.org/regulations/index.html#Regulations, access date: December 21, 2006.

31. The Independent Electoral Commission of Iraq, 2005. Note: *FAQ: 15th December Electoral System;* available online: www.ieciraq.org.

32. United Nations, "Iraq Electoral Fact Sheet," available online: www.un.org/news/dh/infocus/iraq/election-fact-sht.htm, access date: December 21, 2006.

33. Available online: www.ieciraq.org/final%20cand/Constitution_Eng_UNs-13.pdf.

34. Ronald Inglehart and Pippa Norris, *Rising Tide: Gender Equality and Cultural Change Around the World* (New York: Cambridge University Press, 2003); UNDP, *Arab Development Report, 2004* (New York: UNDP, 2004); Amal Sabbagh, "The Arab States: Enhancing Women's Political Participation," in International IDEA, *Women in Parliament: Beyond Numbers*, rev. ed. (Stockholm, Sweden: International IDEA, 2006).

35. Marilyn Rueschemeyer, *Women in the Politics of Post-Communist Eastern Europe* (New York: Sharpe, 1998); Richard E. Matland and Kathleen Montgomery, *Women's Access to Political Power in Post-Communist Europe* (New York: Oxford University Press, 2003).

36. Irene Tinker, "Quotas for Women in Elected Legislatures: Do They Really Empower Women?" *Women's Studies International Forum 27*, no. 5–6 (2004): 531–546.

37. Najma Chowdhury, "The Implementation of Quotas: Bangladesh Experience—Dependence and Marginality in Politics," International IDEA Regional Workshop on the Implementation of Quotas, 2002, available online: www.idea.int/quota/CS/CS_Bangladesh.pdf.

38. Inglehart and Norris, *Rising Tide*.

39. See, however, Caul, "Political Parties and the Adoption of Candidate Gender Quotas"; Krook, "Politicizing Representation"; Dahlerup, *Women, Quotas and Politics*.

40. For details, see Joni Lovenduski, *Feminizing Politics* (Cambridge, England: Polity, 2005).

41. Joni Lovenduski and Pippa Norris, eds., *Gender and Party Politics* (London: Sage, 1993).

7

WILL GENDER BALANCE IN POLITICS COME BY ITSELF?

Drude Dahlerup

When it comes to gender quotas, some see this development as a specter haunting the world; others welcome it. The fact is that in spite of all controversies, gender quotas for public positions are being introduced all over the world at an amazing speed. During the last fifteen years about 100 out of the world's 192 countries have introduced some kind of quota provision in an effort to remedy women's underrepresentation in political institutions.[1]

All over the world, concern is growing about women's lack of influence in political decision making. The widespread use of electoral gender quotas illustrates increasing impatience with the slow speed of improvements in women's representation. Quotas certainly do not solve all problems for women in politics, but they may create unprecedented historical advances in women's representation. In 1999 women occupied 13 percent of the seats in the parliaments of the world (single or lower houses), in 2003 it was 15 percent, and in 2007 the figure increased to 17 percent.[2] One can hardly label this good news. According to Pippa Norris's calculation, with change occurring at its present rate, gender balance will not be reached until the turn of the twenty-second century.[3]

But even the time-lag theory, which proposes that equality between women and men will come in due time with development—even if it may take some time—is losing credibility. Also, our previous theories that unambiguously linked an increase in women's public representation to women's enhanced civic resources seem increasingly obsolete. Today, through the introduction of gender quotas, some countries are making historical and unforeseen advances in the number of women in their political institutions. This is in fact a very exciting development for those of us who have researched women's political representation for several decades.

This chapter is based on the results of "Electoral Gender Quotas—A Key to Equality?"—a research project in which we studied the introduction of electoral gender quotas all over the world. We looked at the discursive controversies around quotas, policy processes, actual quota rules, and their troublesome implementation. We have analyzed the effects of electoral gender quotas in quantitative as well as qualitative terms—the effect on the numbers as well as on the actual influence of women. The book *Women, Quotas and Politics*, which gives the first worldwide overview of the introduction of gender quotas into public elections, was written in cooperation with researchers from most major regions of the world.[4] My many travels around the globe confirm that something new is happening, and admittedly by our being invited to so many countries to tell the exciting story of these changes and by making the news available through a global Web site, we as researchers may in fact be part of spreading this new discourse on women's representation.

In a narrow technical sense, electoral gender quotas are simply a type of affirmative action that forces the political parties and other nominating bodies to recruit, nominate, and select a certain number or percentage of women for political positions. However, quotas touch upon many fundamental principles in feminist theory, in democratic theory, and in contemporary political debates, such as the contested construction of women as a political category and the principles of representation and of equality.

Those resisting gender quotas and other forms of affirmative action seem to be most outspoken in the Western world, not least in the United States.[5] This chapter argues that as a consequence, in the future, the West may no longer be found at the top of the world rank order in terms of women's political representation. Even the Scandinavian countries, which led for many decades in women's political representation, are challenged today. Recently, dramatic rotations have occurred at the top of the world rank order, with Rwanda number one before Sweden, and Costa Rica number three—ahead of Finland, Norway, Denmark, and the Netherlands—in terms of the percentage of women in national parliaments.[6]

The chapter discusses the recent global trend to introduce some form of electoral gender quotas, and it analyzes the newest discourses on women's political representation and the use of quotas. In particular, The Beijing Platform for Action from the UN Women's Conference of 1995, which has been and still is very influential for feminist advocacy, promotes an alternative perspective on the causes of women's underrepresentation to the usual story about women's lack of resources and commitment. The declaration has had important consequences for many countries' choices of strategy to reach gender balance in public life.

Changing the Acceptable Minimum of Women

Fifty years ago male leadership was the norm. Outside feminist circles very few people questioned the democratic legitimacy of an all-male assembly or board. Photos of governments and world leaders, all men, inspired confidence and respect. This attitude has changed dramatically, and today an assembly without women will meet severe public criticism. As a result of feminist pressure, an all-male assembly or board has lost its democratic legitimacy in most parts of the world, despite some exceptions depending on the country and area. But how many women are needed to guarantee legitimacy?

One may talk about the "acceptable minimum" of women, defined as the number or share or women that appointing or nominating bodies, at a given time in history at a given location, consider necessary to avoid public criticism. The relevance of this concept is based on the realistic assumption that those already in power control recruitment. A woman does not get a chance simply because she is good; she gets it because someone in power lifts her up.[7]

The first woman minister in a democratic country was the Danish minister of education, Nina Bang, appointed in 1924 as member of the country's first social democratic government.[8] But it was not until after 1947 that a new norm was established: every Danish government, no matter which political color, always had one woman minister. Later, the acceptable minimum was increased to two or three women ministers, and today the acceptable minimum of women ministers in the country is around 25 percent. In Norway and Sweden, both of which got their first women cabinet ministers later than Denmark and Finland, the acceptable minimum is, however, higher—40 to 50 percent. The present Norwegian social democratic prime minister, not just to avoid public criticism but also to look modern and progressive, has equally divided appointments to the cabinet between women and men. In the United States, ever since Sandra Day O'Connor took the oath in 1981, one female judge, or maybe two, has been established as the acceptable minimum on the Supreme Court.

In many other parts of the world, similar gradual increases in the acceptable minimum of women have occurred, from the one obligatory woman to 10 percent women, maybe later to 30 percent. These improvements in women's representation reflect gradual changes in cultural perceptions of gender, and the feminist movement has been one of the main actors behind the changes everywhere.

It would, however, be wrong to assume that no backlash can occur. The cultural changes behind any increase in the acceptable minimum of women can, unfortunately, not be considered irreversible. Political regime change may lead to backlash, as seen in many parts of the world. Consequently, the feminist movement must keep pressure on the leaders in politics and organizations. Even if the introduction of gender quotas usually is an attempt to increase women's representation rapidly and substantially, in countries with a high representation of women it may represent an assurance against temporary backlash to the acceptable minimum of women.[9] Today, the historically dominant incremental track for more women in politics is being challenged by an alternative fast track model.[10]

The Connection Between Problem-Diagnosis and Choice of Strategies

Any serious choice of strategy for enhancing women's political representation must start with an analysis of the problem: why are women underrepresented and men overrepresented? Despite some exceptions, there is often an intimate relation between the perception of the problem and the strategies chosen. In the following discussion, I look at the strategic choices of those who want to increase women's representation, and omit those who do not consider women's underrepresentation a problem. Inspired by the "What's the problem?" approach of the Australian political scientist Carol Bacchi, I phrase the problem as a question of how women's underrepresentation is understood, that is, the diagnosis of the problem.[11]

If the problem of women's underrepresentation is understood first and foremost as a consequence of women's lack of resources, then the strategy to enhance women's political representation will typically offer educational opportunities for present or future women politicians, that is, establishing programs to build capacity.[12]

If, however, the main problem is understood to be discrimination against women, in which direct and indirect mechanisms of exclusion are at work in the political system, then the strategy must be to change the ways the political institutions function and work. One such institution is the nomination process; further, the political culture and in general the political institutions in a workplace perspective may come under scrutiny. The Beijing Platform for Action of 1995 represents an important change of discourse toward this second understanding that focuses on structural discrimination. Women's movements all over the world have attempted to give the controversial demand for gender quotas legitimacy by referring to the presentation of the problem in the Platform for Action.

The Diagnosis

The Beijing Platform talks about "discriminatory attitudes and practices" and "unequal power relations" that lead to the underrepresentation of women in arenas of political decision making. These actions and relations may be labeled a discourse of exclusion.[13] Whereas the focus was previously on women's lack of resources or lack of will to participate in politics, attention is now directed toward those institutional and cultural mechanisms that prevent women from obtaining an equal share of positions in most political institutions in the world. In this new discourse, the responsibility for promoting change shifts from the individual woman to the institutions themselves, which are consequently expected to take action to identify and correct the causes of women's underrepresentation.

The Goal

The demand for a certain minimum level of representation for women is being challenged by a new discourse of equal representation, often expressed by the term "gender balance." WeDo's 50/50 Campaign is a good example of this new discourse.[14] The goal is no longer described as "more women in politics" but rather as "equal participation" and "equitable distribution of power and decision making at all levels."[15] Somewhat contradictorily, however, the Beijing Platform also speaks of securing a minority representation, a so-called critical mass, often associated with figures of 20 or 30 percent women.[16]

The Strategy

The Beijing Platform for Action suggests affirmative action as a possible means of attaining the goal of women's equal participation in political decision making, although it does not directly use the controversial word *quotas*. For governmental and public administration positions, the Platform recommends that the world's governments use "specific targets and implementing measures . . . if necessary through positive action."[17] Concerning elections, the Platform states that governments should commit themselves to "take measures, including, where appropriate, in electoral systems that encourage political parties to integrate women in elective and non-elective public positions in the same proportion and at the same levels as men."[18] Political parties should "consider examining party structures and procedures to remove all barriers that directly or indirectly discriminate against the participation of women."[19] Even if the language is cautious, the Beijing Platform represents, on the whole, a new discourse focusing on the mechanisms of exclusion through institutional practices, setting the goal of gender balance, and demanding commitment to affirmative action from governments and political parties.[20] This new discourse implies a fast track model for gender balance in political decision making, in contrast to the incremental track model so well known in the Western world.[21] By applying this fast track model, several developing countries are now challenging the Western world and even the Scandinavian countries when it comes to the number of women in parliaments.

New Countries at the Top of the World Rank Order

Table 7.1, which shows the top rank order in terms of the number of women in parliaments, reveals some interesting new trends in world politics. Three main features can be read from this table. First, the Scandinavian countries, for so long at the top of the world rank order in terms of women's representation, are being challenged by several developing countries such as Rwanda, Costa Rica, and Argentina, as mentioned earlier. Second, many of the countries that have more than 30 percent women in parliament do make use of some kind of quota, either legal or voluntary, by parties. However, the cases of Finland and Denmark, numbers four and six on the list, indicate that quotas are not a necessary condition for a high number of women representatives. However, the previous line of increase seems to have come to a halt in these countries. Third, the

Table 7.1   The Top of the World Rank Order of Women in Parliament (Single House or Lower House)

Country	Women in National Parliament (percentage)	Quota Type	Electoral System
Rwanda	48.8 (2003)	Legal quotas (C)	List PR
Sweden	47.3 (2006)	Party quotas	List PR
Costa Rica	38.6 (2006)	Legal Quotas (L)	List PR
Finland	38.0 (2003)	No quotas	List PR
Norway	37.9 (2005)	Party quotas	List PR
Denmark	36.9 (2005)	No quotas	List PR
Netherlands	36.7 (2006)	Party quotas	List PR
Cuba	36.0 (2003)	No quotas	Two Rounds
Spain	36.0 (2004)	Party quotas	List PR
Argentina	35.0 (2005)	Legal quotas (C)	List PR
Mozambique	34.8 (2004)	Party quotas	List PR
Belgium	34.7 (2003)	Legal quotas (L)	List PR
Iceland	33.3 (2003)	Party quotas	List PR
South Africa	32.8 (2004)	Party quotas	List PR
United Kingdom	19.7 (2005)	No Quotas	FPP
United States	16.2 (2006)	No Quotas	FPP

List PR: Proportional Representation system with party lists including several candidates.

MMP: Mixed Member Proportional, a combination of List PR and single member constituencies.

FPP: First past the post, single member constituencies.

Key to quota types:

Legal quotas are written into the constitutions (C) or/and the electoral law (L).

Party quotas are voluntary measures by individual political parties.

Sources: Interparliamentary Union (2007): www.ipu.org (as of January 31, 2007); International IDEA and Stockholm University (2007: www.quotaproject.org (as of February 21, 2007); official statistics. Election day figures.

table shows that most of the countries with the highest women's representation elect their representatives under the proportional representation system, usually with party lists containing many candidates for each party in every constituency.

The majoritarian electoral system is no doubt one of the major reasons for the relatively low representation of women in the United Kingdom (19.7 percent in the House of Commons, fifty-second in world rank order) and the United States (16.2 percent in the House of Representatives, sixty-seventh). It is a well-known fact that political systems based on proportional representation (PR) tend to have a higher representation of women than majoritarian systems. A PR system does not guarantee a high political representation of women, but it may definitely help.[22]

When it comes to isolating the effect of the electoral system, the ideal test cases are those countries that operate a mixed electoral system, combining the PR system with single-member constituencies. Electoral statistics from Germany, Hungary, and New Zealand show that women's representation tends to be higher among the parts of parliament elected under PR than among those elected from single-member districts.[23]

In PR elections, where each party list contains many names, the local party organization will try to attract as many voters as possible by composing a list with many different candidate profiles: young as well as veteran candidates, candidates who represent different geographical parts of the constituency and different occupations, and women as well as men. However, historically important changes in the composition of the lists have followed changes in the cultural construct of the ideal politician in terms of gender, ethnicity, and class.

This historical perspective is crucial. Diane Sainsbury has pointed out that the electoral system in itself cannot explain the remarkable increase in women's political representation over time in the Nordic countries, since all five countries have used PR systems all through the twentieth century.[24] In my opinion, it is relevant to rephrase the thesis of the favorable effects on women's representation in the PR system into this new thesis: The PR system is more open to change than the majoritarian system, because it can include new categories of candidates, such as women or immigrants, without replacing old and well-known political profiles. This discussion has focused on gender, but the lack of openness to new groups in the majority system is also highly relevant for the underrepresentation of immigrants, ethnic groups, and other marginalized groups.

Because it is very difficult to apply a quota system within a majoritarian electoral system—how can you demand 30 or 40 percent of a single candidate?—the gap between women's representation in PR versus majoritarian systems will tend to widen in the future with the new trend of introducing gender quotas in politics.

Which Gender Quota System to Apply?

In our present research on electoral gender quotas around the world, my colleagues and I have identified many different quota systems. In general, quota systems differ widely depending on the area of application (education, labor market, company boards, public committees and boards, elections). The research on gender quotas for public elections shows that it is crucial that the quota provisions chosen match the electoral system in place, otherwise the gender quotas are purely symbolic. Table 7.2 shows the various types of quota systems preferred in different parts of the world.

Quotas in politics involve setting up a number, most often in the form of a minimum percentage, typically 20, 30, or 40 percent, for the representation of a specific group. Quotas are a means for increasing the representation of historically excluded or underrepresented groups. Gender quotas may be constructed so as to require a minimum representation for women, or they may state a maximum-minimum representation for both sexes. For instance, they may require no more than 60 and no less than 40 percent for each sex. This provision is a gender-neutral regulation that sets a maximum for both sexes, which quotas for women do not.

Table 7.2   Regional Variations in Preferred Quota Type[a]

Mandate by	Aspirants Quotas	Candidate Quotas	Reserved Seats Quotas
Legal quotas (constitutional or law)	n/a	Latin America The Balkans	Arab region South Asia Africa[b]
Voluntary party quotas	Women's short lists	The "West" Nordic region Africa The Balkans	Morocco's Charter

[a] According to the predominant type of quota. A region placed in two categories indicates that two quota types are used equally or almost equally. No clear pattern is found in the Pacific region.

[b] Reserved seats in one-party states are categorized as legal quotas.

Source: Drude Dahlerup, Women, Quotas and Politics (London: Routledge, 2006), p. 294, minor revisions.

Quotas and the Level of the Electoral Process

In the study of different quota regimes in politics, a distinction must be made between regulations aimed at changing the composition of the pool of potential candidates, the aspirants; the people who stand for election, the candidates; and those elected, the serving officers. Electoral quotas may be defined as regulations that in public elections require a certain minimum in numbers or a percentage of a specific group at one of these levels.

Examples of quota requirements can be found at all three levels, but most quota systems concern the second level: setting up minimum requirements for the percentage of candidates from a certain group on the electoral ballot, or candidate quotas. EMILY's List in the United States and the heavily challenged "all-women shortlists" in England are examples of a type of quota system targeting the first level: aspirant quotas. At this level, the aim of quotas is to broaden the pool from which the selection committee or the primary will choose candidates. On the third level, certain groups are guaranteed a certain number of seats: *reserved seat quotas*. Increasingly, reserved seat systems involve election rather than appointment, as in Jordan, Uganda, Rwanda, Afghanistan, Taiwan, and at the local level India, Bangladesh, and Pakistan.

Quota Mandates

Quotas may be mandated in a country's constitution or electoral law, that is, *legal quotas*. Legal quotas regulate the proceedings of all political parties in a country and may also prescribe sanctions in case of noncompliance, as in Costa Rica—where the electoral commission has the authority, and uses it, to reject lists that do not comply with the rather radical requirement of having 40 percent women on each party's list for election and very specific rules for the rank order of women and men on these lists. In contrast, voluntary party quotas are decided by one or more political parties in a country. In such cases some political parties may have quotas, typically parties at the center or left, while other parties in the same country may reject the idea of quotas.

Table 7.2 shows the combination of using quota level and mandating. While quotas to enlarge the pool of aspirants (first level) are usually decided on by the parties themselves, as in the United Kingdom, Canada and New Zealand, candidate quotas for party lists at elections (second level) may be mandated either by the parties themselves (voluntary party quotas) or by the constitution or law (legal quotas). The third level of quotas, reserved seats, usually comes from a legal quota system mandated by the constitution or the law (or both), by decree from the ruling party in a one-party system, or from the monarch. However, in Morocco, an agreement between all political parties reserved all thirty seats on a special "National list" for women candidates. Moreover, a political party may also apply quotas for its internal organizations such as steering committees or nomination committees.

Table 7.2 shows variations in the preferred quota type in major regions of the world. Legal candidate quotas are preferred in Latin America, in general the leading region in the use of quotas. In the Balkans, voluntary candidate quotas were introduced in the first period after the civil wars, but because of a lack of results, legal quotas are now in place in several countries of this region. The West, including the Nordic region, typically applies voluntary party quotas for candidate lists, more prominently among social democratic, green, and left parties as in Sweden (50 percent), Norway (40 percent), Spain (40 percent), Austria (33 to 50 percent), and South Africa (ANC, 30 percent). The successful electoral gender quotas in Belgium and the less successful ones in France at the national level are exceptions to the rule that the liberal democracies of the West prefer voluntary quotas, if any. In sub-Saharan Africa, the countries Rwanda, Uganda, Burundi, and Tanzania, for example, have introduced reserved seats for women, while other countries like South Africa and Senegal prefer voluntary party quotas. Reserved seats are the most widespread gender quota type found in South Asia and in the Arab region, where reservations for other groups are also known. Almost all political systems use some kind of geographical quota to ensure a minimum level of representation for a densely populated area. That type of quota is usually not considered as controversial as a gender quota.

Yet most of the world's political parties do not employ any kind of quota at all. An increasing number of parties all over the world operate more or less vague targets and recommendations, sometimes labeled *soft quotas*, because they are just a recommendation for the nominating bodies and usually not specified either in numbers or in time. A target might in some cases be just as effective as a formally written quota provision, but its use is more vulnerable to temporary setbacks and requires continuous pressure from women's groups to be fulfilled.[25]

In the United States, electoral gender quotas are not a prominent issue, and the central role of the primaries, the outrageous financial requirements, and the weakness of the political parties make it difficult to apply a quota system. Consequently, gender quotas have primarily been discussed and in a few cases applied to party conventions.[26]

Even if electoral gender quotas are most easily introduced in a List PR system and other multi-list systems, small parties and parties in small constituencies experience difficulties in implementing quotas without the central party organization's interference in the usual prerogative of local party organizations or local primaries to nominate candidates of their own choice.

Finally, electoral gender quotas have been introduced in democratic political systems, as well as in systems with limited democratic freedoms or even in nondemocratic or authoritarian political systems. Many postconflict countries like Rwanda, which has a quota of two women to be elected per district, Bosnia-Herzegovina, which has a candidate quota of one-third of the underrepresented gender, Afghanistan, whose quota is two women per province, and Iraq, which has a minimum of 30 percent women on the lists, are introducing quotas in order to make historic advances toward gender balance in politics while the countries are being reconstructed.[27] But what are the arguments used in the debates about quotas?

Discursive Controversies

Do those who advocate electoral gender quotas and those who oppose them agree at any points when it comes to the diagnosis of the reason women are underrepresented? Do they have the same goals but just disagree upon the means to reach this goal?

Advocates of electoral gender quotas argue that if women are underrepresented because of open or indirect mechanisms of exclusion and discrimination, then a program of educating women is not enough and may result in little change unless institutions are changed simultaneously. If the problem is not women's lack of resources but lack of acknowledgment of those resources and the experiences that women actually bring with them into political life, then there is no need to wait for women to be more educated or experienced.

The opponents of quotas sometimes describe gender quotas as preferential treatment of women or even as discrimination against men. Those who hold these views argue that people should be treated equally. This position, however, cannot be discussed solely in abstract, the quota advocates maintain.[28] If everything were fair in society, gender quotas would surely be discrimination against men. But if the diagnosis is that real equal opportunities do not exist, and that direct as well as structural discrimination is present in a society, then quotas should be considered compensation for present and future discrimination.

Some argue that when all impediments against women are removed, quotas will no longer be necessary. From this perspective, quotas are a temporary measure. It may take decades, though, before all social, cultural, and political barriers preventing equal women's representation are eradicated. Today, the very concept of a linear progressive development toward gender equality is challenged by the actual experiences of backlash or lack of progress when it comes to women's representation in formal political institutions.

Four different categories of quota opponents can be identified in quota discourses around the world: the traditional "politics-is-a-male business" opponent, the post-communist opponent, the liberal opponent, and, finally, the feminist opponent.[29] Only the latter two are discussed in this chapter.

The Liberal Opposition to Quotas

The strong resistance to affirmative action and to formal quota provisions in the West, especially in the United States, is closely connected to the liberal notions of representation and meritocracy.[30] Those who hold this view feel that increased representation for women should come by itself, not by any unnatural intervention. Further, representation to them is about representing ideas, not social classes or categories, and it should be based on the principle of "let the best candidate win."[31] Quotas are seen as a violation of the principle of merit, unacceptable even if the cause is a good one.

The principle of equal opportunity comes first, not the principle of equality of results. In terms of diagnosis, goals, and strategy, the strong resistance to quotas in the United States and partly in Western Europe does not rest on a general rejection of gender balance as the goal. Rather, the resistance is based on a different diagnosis of the problem from the one used by the advocates of quotas.

In contemporary American and European societies, women are as well educated as men. Consequently, the old argument is very seldom heard that politics is dominated by males simply because women are less qualified than men. So what diagnosis would those arguing against active equality measures such as quotas make?

The dominant contemporary argument seems to be that women's underrepresentation is principally due to women's lack of willingness to enter into politics or other leadership positions. Women do not want leadership positions because women have other priorities. This premise is, the gender quota advocates would reply, both true and false. True, because surveys in many countries have shown that more men than women express an interest in moving into positions of leadership, and false (or at any rate problematic) because people tend to neglect the many problems women meet in politics because of the way politics is conducted: the recruitment process, the amount of money needed for campaigning, the political jargon, culture, and so on. This perspective again turns the burden of proof to the political institutions themselves. In conclusion, the liberal opponents to gender quotas may share the goal with the advocates of quotas, gender balance in politics, but reject the strategy based on a different understanding of why women are underrepresented.[32]

The Feminist Opposition to Gender Quotas

Feminist opponents of electoral gender quotas share the quota advocates' goal as well as their diagnosis that women are subject to direct as well as structural discrimination, but they discard quotas as a relevant means. Two different types of arguments can be identified under this anti-quota discourse: first, many women would emphasize that they personally never want to be chosen just because they are women; second, opponents fear that women elected or appointed on the basis of gender quotas will be stigmatized.

A well-known example of the first type of objection is the woman top manager who firmly argues that she did it all by herself, and she would certainly not want to be appointed just because of her sex. This is a relevant consideration. So what is the answer to those many women who so strongly dissociate themselves from ever being elected or appointed because of gender quotas? One answer is that nobody forces them to take such a job, and consequently they could step down on being appointed and leave space for other women. A second answer is that perhaps they should consider that this is not a matter of just an individual women's private career, but rather of historical changes in the gender structure of political institutions.

The second—and very relevant consideration—is that "quota women" may meet stigmatization that will hamper their effectiveness. Since quota provisions are relatively new, very little research is available on this question. It has been argued, for instance, that the actual stigmatization of Egyptian women politicians during the short period of quota use probably was primarily an effect of a general distrust and dislike of women in public life, not of the quota system per se.[33]

Women politicians who reject the notion that they have met any stigmatization usually argue that, after the election, all votes in the assembly count as equal when it comes to gathering votes for building a majority.[34] Some of these parliamentarians point out that men throughout history have been elected or appointed partly because of their male gender without being stigmatized. However, it should not be denied that cases of stigmatization of women elected on gender quotas have been recorded, just as examples of puppet or proxy women politicians. Such records originate primarily from strong patriarchal societies.[35]

One of the conclusions of our research on the use of electoral gender quotas worldwide is that the crucial question for the performance and effectiveness of women politicians, once they are elected, is the level of support from their constituencies. It may constitute a serious problem for the elected women if the quota system is constructed in such a way that they lack clearly distinctive districts of their own. Some of the problems for women politicians elected on a quota basis in India and Bangladesh at the local level, for example, derive from the difficulties in combining a majoritarian electoral system with any quota system.[36]

Feminist opponents also sometimes argue that there will not be enough women to fill the positions, and there is some truth in this. We all know of the many demands on prominent women to join this or that committee to get the gender balance right. However, it is important to note that for the highest positions in governments, parliaments, or top company boards around the world, very few women are needed in absolute numbers to fill 50 percent of the seats. Some problems of recruiting a sufficient number of women are, however, found at the local level. Such problems may be temporary. It is worth remembering that just after women's suffrage was passed, the political parties argued that they were unable to find more than a handful of women who were willing to stand for election!

Feminist Advocacy of Quotas

The feminist arguments for gender quotas are often based on principles like those found in the Beijing Platform statement concerning exclusionary practices that must be overcome. Quotas force organizations to start recruiting women seriously. The principle of justice is frequently used as an argument; that is, women constitute half the population and are therefore entitled to half the seats of political power. In that case no further arguments are needed and gender balance is a goal in itself. But around the world, and not least in postconflict societies and societies in transition to democracy, the experience and interest arguments are still widespread for electoral gender quotas: women should be selected because women better than men represent women's experiences and interests. Further, it is argued that a larger number of women can bring the diversity of female experience into political institutions. Supporters say that women are needed in politics to better the education of girls, improve the water supply, and work against violence against women and children. The postmodern discussion on whether women can, will, and should make a difference in politics is more dominant in the Western world than elsewhere. Maybe this is a consequence of the actual integration, although unequal, of women and men in the workplace in highly industrialized societies.

This chapter has discussed the justifications and actual consequences of electoral gender quotas. Let me end with quoting the British political scientist Anne Phillips: "What we can more usefully do is to turn the argument around, and ask by what 'natural' superiority of talent or experience men could claim a right to dominate assemblies?"[37]

Endnotes

1. Together with International IDEA, we in the research project "Electoral Gender Quotas—A Key to Equality" at the Department of Political Science at Stockholm University have constructed a global Web site containing information about the various quota types used in countries with electoral gender quotas: www.quotaproject.org.
2. "Women in National Parliaments," www.ipu.org/wmn-e/world.htm, access date: February 21, 2007.
3. Pippa Norris, *Electoral Engineering* (New York: Cambridge University Press, 2004), 180.
4. Drude Dahlerup, ed., *Women, Quotas and Politics* (London: Routledge, 2006). As for the research project on quotas in general, see "Quotas: A Key to Equality?" available online: www.statsvet.su.se/quotas, access date: December 23, 2006.
5. The concept of "the West," so broadly used previously, is becoming more and more problematic. In relation to the quota discourse, the concept of the West is however still relevant, as

argued by Mona Lena Krook, Joni Lovenduski, and Judith Squires, "Western Europe, North America, Australia and New Zealand: Gender Quotas in the Context of Citizenship Models," in Dahlerup, *Women, Quotas and Politics*, 194.

6. "Women in National Parliaments (as of January 31, 2007)" www.ipu.org/wmn-e/classif.htm, access date: February 21, 2007.

7. In electoral politics in most, although not all, parts of the world, the political parties are the real gatekeepers to political posts. The influence of the voters is, unfortunately, lower than generally believed.

8. Alexandra Kollontai, minister for social affairs in the Soviet Union from 1917, was the first female minister in the world.

9. The "high echelon quotas" in some of the Nordic countries illustrate the latter; see "The Nordic Countries: An Incremental Model," in Dahlerup, *Women, Quotas and Politics*, 78.

10. The fast track model versus the incremental track model, constructed as ideal types, was first presented in Drude Dahlerup and Lenita Freidenvall, "Quotas as a 'Fast Track' to Equal Representation for Women: Why Scandinavia Is No Longer the Model," *International Feminist Journal of Politics* (March 2005): 26–48.

11. Carol Bacchi, *Women, Politics and Policy: The Construction of Policy Problems* (London: Sage, 1999).

12. Dahlerup and Freidenvall, "Quotas as a 'Fast Track' to Equal Representation for Women."

13. A *discourse* is here defined as interlinked constructions of meanings, which includes perceptions of possible actions (but not actual actions).

14. Women's Environment and Development Organization (WeDo). "The '50/50 Campaign.' Get the Balance Right!" available online: www.wedo.org/campaigns.aspx?mode=5050 main, access date: December 23, 2006.

15. *Platform for Action*, adopted at United Nation's Fourth World Conference on Women (FWCW), Beijing 1995, Art. 181–195.

16. See Drude Dahlerup, "From a Small to a Large Minority: Women in Scandinavian Politics," *Scandinavian Political Studies 11*, no. 4 (1988): 275–298, and Drude Dahlerup, "The Story of the Theory of Critical Mass," *Politics & Gender 2*, no. 4 (2006): 511–522.

17. FWCW 1995: Art. 190. a.

18. FWCW 1995: Art. 190. b.

19. FWCW 1995: Art. 191. a.

20. Some of these formulations may in fact be found in the CEDAW convention from 1979. The convention recommends that states adopt "temporary special measures" (*Convention on the Elimination of All Forms of Discrimination Against Women*, CEDAW, UN 1979: Art. 4). Also, the Interparliamentary Union, IPU, and other international and regional organizations early on formulated new claims for women's representation. However, it is the Beijing Platform that is most often referred to in the quota debate.

21. Dahlerup and Freidenvall, "Quotas as a 'Fast Track' to Equal Representation for Women."

22. Focusing on structural variations, Pippa Norris is able to show that the differences between the outcome in proportional representation systems versus plurality-majority systems are much more distinct in postindustrial societies, whereas the differences between these two electoral systems in terms of women's representation are much smaller in industrial societies and minimal in poorer agrarian societies (Norris, *Electoral Engineering*, 188); see also Richard Matland and D. T. Studlar, "The Contagion of Women Candidates in Single and Multimember District Systems: Canada and Norway," *Journal of Politics 58*, no. 3 (1996): 707–733.

23. Scotland is an exception to this rule, but this is first and foremost due to the quota system applied by the Scottish Labour Party.

24. Diane Sainsbury, "The Politics of Increased Women's Representation: The Swedish Case," in Joni Lovenduski and

Pippa Norris, *Gender and Party Politics* (London: Sage, 1993), 263–290.

25. In her Ph.D. thesis, Lenita Freidenvall compares Swedish political parties with and without formally written quota provisions: *Vägen till Varannan damernas. Om kvinnorepresentation, kvotering och kandidaturval i svensk politik 1970–2002 (Every Other for the Ladies. Women's Political Representation, Gender Quotas and Candidate Selection in Swedish Parties 1970–2002)*, Department of Political Science, Stockholm University, 2006.

26. See Krook, Lovenduski, and Squires, "Western Europe, North America, Australia and New Zealand," 214–216.

27. In Bosnia-Herzegovina additional rules about the rank order state that among the first two candidates one must represent the underrepresented sex, two among the first five, three among the first eight; all in all one-third must be women. In spite of these radical rules for constructing the lists, the open list election of 2002 resulted in election of only 16.7 percent women, in 2006 only 14.3 percent. In Iraq one out of the first three and two out of the first six must be a woman, and so forth, to the end of the list. The result was 25.5 percent women elected in the 2005 election.

28. See Carol Bacchi, "Arguing for and Against Quotas," in Dahlerup, *Women, Quotas and Politics*, 32–51.

29. Dahlerup, *Women, Quotas and Politics*, 297–299.

30. See Jytte Clausen and C. S. Maier, eds., *Has Liberalism Failed Women?* (New York: Palgrave, 2001).

31. See Krook, Lovenduski, and Squires, "Western Europe, North America, Australia and New Zealand."

32. Many different arguments can be found among the opponents of electoral gender quotas, and there are of course overlaps between the liberal and the feminist opponents. Consequently, the categorization used here is analytical.

33. Gihan Abou-Zeid, "The Arab Region: Women's Access to the Decision-Making Process Across the Arab Nation," in Dahlerup, *Women, Quotas and Politics*, 169–193.

34. It should be noted that a fifty-fifty gender quota as practiced in the Swedish Social Democratic Party makes women no more "quota women" than the men are "quota men"!

35. Shirin M. Rai, Farzana Bari, Nazmunessa Mahtab, and Bidyut Mohanty, "South Asia: Gender Quotas and the Politics of Empowerment—A Comparative Study," in Dahlerup, *Women, Quotas and Politics*, 223–245.

36. Rai, Bari, Mahtab, and Mohanty, "South Asia."

37. Anne Phillips, *The Politics of Presence* (Oxford, England: Oxford University Press, 1995), 65.

8

THE FUTURE OF WOMEN'S POLITICAL LEADERSHIP

Gender and the Decision
to Run for Elective Office

Richard L. Fox

Will women seize the reins of political leadership in the United States? To the casual observer glancing at the political landscape early in the twenty-first century, it might appear that the era of women's leadership is already upon us. In 2007 Nancy Pelosi was elected Speaker of the U.S. House of Representatives, and heading into the 2008 presidential election, two of the highest-profile political figures in the United States are Secretary of State Condoleezza Rice and New York Senator Hillary Clinton. Former political-strategist-turned-media-pundit Dick Morris has even written a best-selling speculative book titled *Hillary vs. Condi: The Next Great Presidential Race.* But the media frenzy—particularly surrounding Hillary Clinton, the first woman to ever enter a presidential campaign season as the frontrunner for her party's nomination—obscures the deep gender disparities that pervade the political system in the United States. A quick glance at the numbers of

This is a revised and updated version of a report that was published online by the Center for American Women and Politics (CAWP): Richard L. Fox, "Gender, Political Ambition, and the Decision Not to Run for Office," CAWP, 2003, available online: www.rci. rutgers.edu/~cawp/Research/Reports/Fox2003.pdf. For more detailed reporting on the Citizen Political Ambition Study, see Jennifer Lawless and Richard Fox, *It Takes a Candidate: Why Women Don't Run for Office* (New York: Cambridge University Press, 2005).

women serving in top elected positions will reveal the gender gap in political leadership: 84 percent of U.S. Senators, 84 percent of the members of the House of Representatives, 82 percent of state governors, 88 percent of big city mayors, and 76 percent of state legislators are men.[1] From an international perspective, the United States lags far behind many nations in the world in the integration of women into the national government. As of early 2007, the United States ranks eighty-second in the world in the percentage of women serving in the national legislature and behind roughly forty countries that the Freedom House organization regards as fully democratic.[2]

Since the early 1980s, scholars of gender and politics have produced an impressive and expanding body of work exploring the role gender plays in the U.S. electoral system. Much of this work has been motivated by the underlying premise that a government dominated by male elected officials is biased against the election of women and, accordingly, does not fairly represent the public, particularly the interests of women. Studies of the policy preferences of national and state legislators have found that the representation of women's interests requires a greater inclusion of women leaders in public office.[3] Further, there are critical descriptive and symbolic benefits to having more women political leaders. A recent study by David Campbell and Christina Wolbrecht, for instance, found that the presence of highly visible political women increases the political engagement of adolescent girls.[4]

Surprisingly, though, much of the recent research that examines the performance of women candidates in the electoral arena finds no evidence of bias against them. More specifically, in terms of fundraising and vote totals, often considered the two most important indicators of electoral success, investigators find that women fare just as well as their male counterparts, if not better. In fact, in a comprehensive study of voting in general elections, Richard Seltzer, Jody Newman, and Melissa Leighton conclude: "A candidate's sex does not affect his or her chances of winning an election. . . . Winning elections has *nothing* to do with the sex of the candidate" (emphasis added).[5]

What emerges then, is the puzzle of a political system that does not appear to directly discriminate against the election of women, yet still seems to produce few women leaders. To explain this puzzle, researchers have offered two institutional explanations for the continuing gender disparities in office holding. First, scholars point to the incumbency advantage. In most legislative bodies in the United States, incumbents are reelected over 90 percent of the time. Researchers Barbara Palmer and Dennis Simon, focusing on the U.S. House of Representatives, demonstrate how low turnover in seats and increasingly noncompetitive elections converge to make dramatic change in the makeup of Congress unlikely.[6] Second, other researchers point to the eligibility pool as the most important explanation for the small number of women candidates and elected officials. Writing in the early 1990s, political scientist Janet Clark summarizes this view: "Women are not found in the professions from which politicians inordinately are chosen—the law and other broker-type businesses. Therefore, they do not achieve the higher socioeconomic status that forms the eligibility pool for elective office."[7] Under this explanation, it follows that as the number of women in the fields of law and business increases, so too will their economic status and likelihood of seeking elected positions. Common to both of these explanations, incumbency and the eligibility pool, is the conclusion that gender parity will occur in U.S. electoral institutions as more opportunities become available and when more women enter careers that have historically prepared those who decide to run for office.

To assess prospects for gender parity in the U.S. electoral system based on these institutional explanations, however, is to fail to consider a critical piece of the puzzle: the manner in which gender interacts with the initial decision to run for office. In fact, we know very little about how gender affects political ambition for elective office. Are professionally accomplished women and men equally likely to consider a run for elective office? If we are to understand women's prospects for fuller representation in high-level office, then we must first determine whether well-situated women have the same desire and interest in holding elective office as similarly situated men. With the exception of one poll conducted by the National Women's Political Caucus in 1994 and a study of potential candidates in New York State in the late 1990s, prior to the findings presented here, no research specifically examines the manner in which men and women initially consider seeking public office.[8]

In this chapter I report and summarize some of the key findings of the Citizen Political Ambition Study, the first broad-based national survey of potential men and women candidates. My central goal in this chapter is to shed light on how women and men think about running for office and the manner in which their attitudes will affect the future prospects for gender parity in U.S. governing bodies.

The Citizen Political Ambition Study

Although why candidates run for office is a critically important question, an empirical study of how people choose to run for office is very difficult to execute. Many undocumented considerations enter the decision to run. When a potential candidate decides not to enter a race, for example, the decision is often unknown and, thus, that individual is difficult to locate and interview. In addition, many individuals who ultimately run for office may never have considered themselves potential candidates prior to being recruited. Further, attempts to identify potential candidates through research may even cause political controversies. A study by Sandy Maisel and Walt Stone moved members of Congress to try to persuade the National Science Foundation not to fund their project on candidates' decisions to run for Congress for fear of spurring qualified challengers to enter races they would otherwise have not considered.[9]

In an attempt to examine gender differences in political ambition, we carried out the Citizen Political Ambition Study.[10] The study is composed of a national sample of what might be considered the candidate eligibility pool. We defined the eligibility pool for elective office as men and women in the three professions that tend to yield the highest proportion of political candidacies. Examinations of the career paths of members of state legislatures and the U.S. House of Representatives reveal that law, business, and education are the most common professions.[11] Within each occupational group, we surveyed an equal number of men and women.

Ultimately, we mailed a four-page survey to a national sample of 2,700 men and 2,700 women, each of whom could be considered part of the eligibility pool. We asked respondents about their sociodemographic backgrounds, familial arrangements, political activism, political outlook, political experience, and perceptions of and willingness to run for office.[12] After taking into account respondents who refused to complete the questionnaire or filled in very few answers, we were left with a 55 percent response rate, which is higher than that of similar elite sample mail surveys.[13] The pool of potential candidates responding to the Citizen Political Ambition Study is a broad cross-section of highly credentialed and professionally similar men and women who are well positioned to serve as future candidates for elective office. The pools of women and men are roughly equal in terms of race, place of residence, region, education level, and household income. As might be expected, women in the sample were more likely to be Democrats, while men were more likely to be Republicans and Independents, a finding consistent with recent polls showing a partisan gender gap among the general U.S. population. Further, women in the sample, on average, are four years younger than men, a result probably based on women's relatively recent entry into the fields of law and business.

The Results: A Substantial Gender Gap in Interest in Running for Office

Do men and women have equal interest in seeking elective office?[14] We asked potential candidates a number of questions to determine their level of interest in seeking political office. First, men and women were asked directly whether they ever considered running for office. Table 8.1 presents the results of this question, broken

Table 8.1 Gender Differences in Interest in Running for Office

	Women (percentage)	Men (percentage)
Has "ever" considered running for office	36	55
Has "seriously" considered running for office	7	16
Discussed running with party leaders	4	8
Discussed running with friends and family	17	29
Discussed running with community leaders	6	12
Solicited contributions from potential donors	2	4
Investigated how to place name on ballot	4	10
Combined Sample Size of (Lawyers, Educators, and Businesspeople)	(1,248)	(1,454)

Note: All comparisons between men and women are statistically significant.

down by sex. In presenting the results I combine the professions because the gender differences across the three occupations are remarkably similar. The findings clearly show that women are substantially less likely than men to have ever considered running for office. Further, men were more than twice as likely as women to say that they have seriously considered running for office. To make certain that the results were not merely picking up a gender difference in interest in politics, we also asked survey respondents about their overall level of political participation in such activities as voting, interest-group membership, and community involvement. For all of the other types of political participation, we found no significant gender differences: the women and men we surveyed were equally likely to participate in or follow politics. It was only on the question of interest in running for office that a large gender gap emerged.

To measure interest in office holding in a manner that does not rely entirely on self-perceptions of whether a respondent considered running, we also asked potential candidates whether they ever took any of the steps required to mount a political campaign. More specifically, respondents were asked whether they ever discussed a candidacy with party leaders, community leaders, family members, or friends. In addition, they were asked if they ever discussed or solicited financial contributions from potential donors and whether they investigated how to place their names on the ballot. Comparisons between men's and women's answers to all of these questions again highlight stark gender differences in political ambition (see Table 8.1). Men are substantially more likely than women to have undertaken any of these fundamental campaign steps.

Beyond the gender difference in political ambition, it is also important to determine what elective offices potential women and men candidates are interested in seeking. Table 8.2 shows the office-specific interests of those members of the sample who would

Table 8.2   Office-Specific Interests of Prospective Women and Men Candidates

	Women (percentage)	Men (percentage)
What is the first office you would most likely seek?		
Local Offices:		
School Board	53*	37
City, County, or Town Council	23	24
Mayor	3	5
State Offices:		
State Legislator	11 *	18
Statewide Office (i.e. Attorney General)	2	1
Governor	1	1
Federal Offices:		
U.S. House of Representatives	5 *	10
U.S. Senate	2 *	4
President	0	1
Combined Sample Size (Lawyers, Educators, and Businesspeople with Some Interest in Seeking Electoral Office)	(1,022)	(816)

Note: Sample sizes represent respondents willing to consider a candidacy; individuals who said they would never run were dropped from the analysis. Asterisk (*) indicates difference for men and women is statistically significant.

consider running at some point in the future. Some analysis suggests that women will be more likely to focus their political involvement at the local level or in positions that match their stereotypic strengths, such as education or health care. Accordingly, Table 8.2 divides the offices into local, state, and federal levels; in assessing office interests, respondents were asked to identify which office they would most likely seek first. As might be expected, women demonstrate greater interest in local offices; women are more likely than men to select a school board position as the first office for which they might run. Men are more likely to identify a state office. Further, 15 percent of men compared to only 7 percent of women identify a federal office as their first choice.

Before examining possible explanations for the great gender disparity in interest in running for office, it is important to determine whether certain key political and demographic variables are driving the differences. One common assumption about the evolution of women in politics is that gender disparities in electoral office are generational. In other words, traditional attitudes about women's proper place in society which would have precluded women from serving in high-level elected politics, undoubtedly affected previous generations of women, but younger professional women should not face the same obstacles. The findings presented in Table 8.3 do not support this assumption. While women under forty years of age are slightly more likely to be interested in seeking office than older women, younger men are also more interested than older men. There is a gender gap in political ambition that exists in roughly equal proportions across all age groups. The lack of any significant generational gap suggests that if vestiges of traditional gender socialization deter women from considering a candidacy, then these vestiges continue to affect women of all generations.[15]

The gender gap in political ambition also persists across all three party identifications. Among Democrats, Republicans, and Independents, men are much more likely than women to have considered running for office. Nonetheless, Democratic women are slightly more likely to think about seeking office than are their Republican and

Table 8.3 Gender Differences in Interest in Running for Office (by Age, Party, and Personal Income)

	Women (percentage)	Men (percentage)
Age:		
Under 40 years of age	41	59
40–59 years of age	33	53
60 and older	38	55
Political Party:		
Democrat	39	58
Republican	35	51
Independent	33	52
Income Level (per year):		
Less than $50,000	29	54
$50,001–$100,000	36	56
Over $100,000	41	55
Combined Sample Size (Lawyers, Educators, and Businesspeople)	(1,209)	(1,404)

Note: Sample sizes vary slightly, as some respondents omitted some questions. All comparisons between men and women are statistically significant.

Independent counterparts. This difference can be generally explained by the Democratic party's agenda, which embraces policy priorities more closely allied with self-identified feminists. Women who self-identify as feminists are more likely than nonfeminists (41 percent to 30 percent) to have considered running for office. In terms of party affiliation and interest in office seeking, though, there are no significant differences among men of different partisan affiliations.

Finally, personal wealth and income is regarded as a potential predictor in running for office. An increasing number of candidates are financing themselves; two high-profile examples are New York City Mayor Michael Bloomberg and New Jersey Governor Jon Corzine. Both spent tens of millions of their own money on their campaigns. There are very few examples of similarly situated women financing their own electoral campaigns. Further, the Citizen Political

Ambition Study revealed that women across all categories of personal income are less likely than their male counterparts to have considered running for office. It is important to note that among women, personal income and interest in seeking elective office are positively correlated. Women with higher personal incomes are more likely to be interested in running for office, but even in the highest income category there is still a significant gender gap. This finding suggests that if women's incomes become equal with men's, women's interest in running for office may increase as well.

The findings presented in Tables 8.1, 8.2, and 8.3 clearly indicate that women, even in the top tier of professional accomplishment, are far less likely to consider a run for public office than are their similarly situated male counterparts. As these results suggest, there is far more to consider than the incumbency advantage and the eligibility pool in explaining women's slow ascension into top positions of political power. Further, men's greater interest in high-level offices suggests that gender parity, particularly for the most important elective offices, will be difficult to achieve in the foreseeable future.

Explaining Gender Differences in Ambition for Office Seeking

What explains lower levels of political ambition among potential women candidates? Examining the results of the Citizen Political Ambition Study provides three possible explanations for the gender gap in interest in holding elected office: lower levels of external support for women, prevalence of traditional family dynamics, and gendered self-perceptions of electoral viability.

Gender Differences in External Support to Run for Office

Studies of congressional candidates and state legislative candidates have identified recruitment as one of the most important factors in an individual's decision to seek elective office. Clearly, having an elected official or someone associated with the local, state, or national party organization encourage a run for office makes the prospect of seeking office much more serious. Recruitment and encouragement leads many individuals to become candidates who otherwise might never have run for public office.[16] For instance, Colleen Rowley, the FBI agent who was a 9/11 whistleblower, had never thought about running for office until Democrats approached her to seek a seat in Congress; she ultimately decided to run for a seat in Minnesota in 2006. But are women just as likely to receive support and encouragement to run? To measure whether men and women received the same levels of external support, respondents of the Citizen Political Ambition Study were asked whether anyone ever suggested that they launch a candidacy. More specifically, respondents were presented with a list of seven types of individuals who might have suggested or encouraged a candidacy. Three of the sources could be considered formal political actors: party officials, elected officials, and nonelected political activists. The other four sources, friends, spouses, family members, and coworkers, are informal sources, but certainly also important to the decision to run for office.

Table 8.4 reveals that women are less likely to have received the suggestion to run for office, regardless of the source. The differences are particularly stark in terms of formal political actors. This is a powerful explanation for why women are less likely than men to consider running for office. In fact, among women and men who have received a suggestion to run for office, especially from a formal political actor, the gender gap in interest in running for office narrows substantially. When women and men are recruited to run for office, they both respond favorably and are almost equally likely to consider a candidacy. That electoral gatekeepers' preferred candidates continue to be men highlights a masculine ethos pervading the political environment. These results corroborate the findings of political scientist Kira Sanbonmatsu, who in a 2006 study of party officials found that those who are charged with the task of recruiting candidates to run for elective office tend to prefer male candidates.[17]

Table 8.4   Gender Differences in External Support for Running for Office

	Women (percentage)	Men (percentage)
Have any of the following individuals ever suggested that you run for office?		
Formal Political Actors:		
Official from a political party	12	20
Elected official	14	23
Non-elected political activist	14	22
Informal Actors:		
Friend or acquaintance	46	56
Spouse or partner	23	27
Family member	30	35
Coworker or business associate	37	44
Combined Sample Size of (Lawyers, Educators, and Businesspeople)	(1,226)	(1,429)

Note: Entries represent the percentage responding "yes" to each question. Sample sizes vary slightly, as some respondents omitted questions. All comparisons between men and women are statistically significant.

Family Arrangements and Interest in Office Holding

The extent to which socialized norms and traditional family structures persist among professional women and men is not entirely evident. Many of the barriers to women's advancement in formerly male fields have changed drastically from the 1970s. Correspondingly, the conception of a rigid set of gender roles has dissipated with the increasing number of two-career families. Yet surveys of two-income households continue to find that women spend twice as many hours as men working on household tasks such as cleaning and laundry. Married women also continue to perform significantly more of the cooking and child care than do their husbands. This pattern holds true even when women are the primary breadwinners in a family.[18]

As a result, when women do enter the public sphere, they often face what noted scholar Kathleen Hall Jamieson calls the "double bind." The essence of the bind is that women must prove themselves to be accomplished in both their professions and as mothers and caretakers of the home.[19] In order to be successful public citizens, women must also be successful private citizens. Thus, if questions arise about the effectiveness of a woman in fulfilling her traditional role, then assessments of her professional performance are affected. In other words, women in the public eye have to meet higher standards to function effectively. Former Texas governor Ann Richards famously captured this sentiment in her speech at the 1988 Democratic Party National Convention, commenting: "Ginger Rogers did everything Fred Astaire did. She just did it backwards and in high heels."

As might be expected, there were distinct gender differences in family arrangements among members of the sample. Women respondents were significantly less likely to be married and have children. Clearly, some women who become top-level professionals are not as likely to pursue a traditional family life. Further, when we consider the household division of labor among those with traditional family arrangements, we find that women are nine times more likely than men to be responsible for more of the household tasks; the numbers are similar for child care duties. For individuals in the sample, being married and having children result in a different set of responsibilities for men and women.

While the degree to which traditional family dynamics continue to prevail among respondents to the Citizen Political Ambition Study, and in American culture more generally, is perhaps striking, the important question for our purposes is whether these dynamics affect whether men and women are equally likely to consider running for office. On this point, the results from the study were not entirely clear. Empirical analysis revealed that family structures and roles did not result in women's being less interested in running for office. Traditional family dynamics do not significantly affect whether women and men think about running for office. It may be that we have entered an era where family responsibilities are no longer a critical determinant of whether successful and qualified women consider running for office.

To gain some perspective on the role of family dynamics and political ambition we conducted in-depth interviews with two hundred of the participants of the Citizen Political Ambition Study. The women we spoke with were far more likely than men to explicitly state that family responsibilities prevent running for office from being a feasible option in their lives. Thus the continuation of traditional family roles, while no longer precluding women from thinking about running for office, still makes it less likely that women will actually decide to run for office.

Gender Differences and Self-Perceptions of Electoral Viability

In most cases individuals who make the often difficult decision to run for office are very confident about their ability to hold the position they are seeking. Moreover, they usually believe that they have a good chance of winning if they do run for office. Do women and men view themselves as equally viable candidates for elective office? While little prior research concerns the initial decision to run, we can extrapolate from the typical behavior of ambitious politicians that candidates' self-perceived qualifications are an important aspect of the decision to run for office. The primary task of a politician in a campaign, after all, is to be perpetually self-promoting. Along these lines, the literature on social psychology provides evidence that gender might play a role in potential candidates' self-assessed qualifications to run for office. For instance, researchers find that males tend to be more self-congratulatory, whereas females tend to be more modest about their achievements.[20] Women also tend to underestimate their own intelligence, whereas men tend to overestimate theirs.[21] In other words, males are more likely to express confidence in skills they may not possess and overconfidence in skills they do possess. These kinds of misperceptions tend to be exacerbated for women when the task at hand is considered to be typically masculine, such as electoral politics.[22]

Women in the sample of the candidate eligibility pool are, objectively speaking, just as qualified as men to hold elective positions. They have achieved comparable levels of professional success in the fields that precede political candidacies. Having matched samples of men and women allows us to test more clearly whether the self-perceptions of women and men are equal. To test this proposition, we asked respondents two questions: how they rated their qualifications to run for elective office and how they rated their chances of winning their first election (see Table 8.5).

By a margin of over 20 percent, women rate themselves less qualified than men to run for office. Women in the sample are twice as likely as men to rate themselves unequivocally as not qualified. Considering that potential candidates who perceive themselves as more qualified are more likely to consider running for office, the gender gap in self-perception is critically important. The same result holds true for respondents' belief that they would win their

Table 8.5   Self-Perceptions of Qualifications and Likelihood of Winning an Electoral Office

	Women (percentge)	Men (percentage)
Overall, how qualified do you feel you are to run for office?		
Qualified or Very Qualified	36	57
Somewhat Qualified	34	29
Not Qualified	30	14
If you were to become a candidate for public office, how likely is it that you would win your first campaign?		
Likely or Very Likely	25	37
Unlikely	43	44
Very Unlikely	31	20
Combined Sample Size of (Lawyers, Educators, and Businesspeople)	(1,202)	(1,397)

Note: Comparisons of men and women on each question are statistically significant. Columns do not total 100 percent due to rounding.

first election. Again, men were significantly more likely to think that they would win their first race.

Across the board, women in the sample, regardless of profession, income level, party affiliation, and age, are significantly less likely than their male counterparts to view themselves as qualified to enter the electoral arena. As a result, women are substantially less likely than men to consider running for office. Because women's self-assessments are a complex phenomenon, the responses to the survey were not able to capture the roots of the gender differences in these self-assessments. This is certainly an important area for the exploration of future researchers.

Conclusion and Discussion

In this chapter I have attempted to address two questions. First, are men and women in the eligibility pool of potential candidates equally likely to consider running for office? And second, if there are gender differences in levels of political ambition, what accounts for the gender gap? Turning to the first question, the evidence is clear: Well-qualified women are less likely than their male counterparts to consider running for office, and when women do think of running, they are more likely to be interested in lower-level offices. Explaining gender differences in political ambition is clearly a complex convergence of external support, traditional family roles, and self-perceptions of electoral viability.

These results have broad implications for both the academic study of gender politics and for practitioners and advocates who hope to increase the number of women serving in electoral politics. In terms of academic research, we must reassess the general explanations for women's underrepresentation. The explanations of incumbency and lack of women in the pool of eligible candidates both assume that similarly situated men and women will be equally interested in running for office. The findings presented here suggest that is not the case. Moreover, the findings presented in this chapter point to the importance of investigating candidate recruitment processes and the manner in which women and men in contemporary society come to be socialized about politics and the acquisition of political power.

At a practical level, these results suggest that we are a long way from a political reality in which women and men are equally likely to aspire to attain high-level elective office. For political actors interested in increasing the numbers of women serving in office, though, these findings offer some direction. Foremost, the evidence reveals that recruitment and encouragement to run for office is effective. When women are solicited to become candidates, the gender gap in political ambition almost entirely disappears. This suggests that organizations such as Emerge, EMILY's List, and the White House Project are on the right track with their recruitment efforts for potential women candidates.

In a final measure of women's and men's interest in office holding, we asked respondents to assess their future attitudes toward running for office. While women are still significantly more likely than men to say they would never run, the differences are small. And the number of women who say they would definitely be interested in running "someday" is equal to that of men. These results suggest that while women have been less likely than men to have considered running for office in the past, they are almost equally receptive to thinking about running in the future. This attitude should offer some hope to organizations seeking to increase the number of women in elective positions.

Endnotes

1. CAWP Fact Sheet, "Women in Elective Office 2006" (New Brunswick, NJ: Center for American Women and Politics, 2006).
2. "Women in National Parliaments," *Inter-Parliamentary Union*, January 31, 2007, available online: www.ipu.org/wmn-e/classif.htm, access date: February 17, 2007.
3. A good example of gender differences in policy priorities at the congressional level is Michele L. Swers, *The Difference Women Make* (Chicago: University of Chicago, 2002).

4. David E. Campbell and Christina Wolbrecht, "See Jane Run: Women Politicians as Role Models for Adolescents," *Journal of Politics* 68 (2006): 233–247.

5. Richard A. Seltzer, Jody Newman, and Melissa Leighton, *Sex as a Political Variable* (Boulder: Lynne Reinner, 1997), 79. This is not to suggest, however, that candidate sex has become irrelevant in the electoral arena. To the contrary, many scholars find that gender stereotyping, linked to traditional sex roles, continues to pervade the electoral environment. While the assumption that women do not belong in politics has dissipated, vestiges of traditional sex-role orientations continue. Many actors in the electoral arena—voters, party officials, candidates, journalists—transfer their stereotypical expectations about men and women to male and female candidates. Despite the apparent role of gender, these studies are usually not linked to the final question of whether women win or lose elections.

6. Barbara Palmer and Denis Simon, *Breaking the Political Glass Ceiling: Women and Congressional Elections* (New York: Routledge, 2006).

7. Janet Clark, "Getting There: Women in Political Office," in Marianne Githens, Pippa Norris, and Joni Lovenduski, eds., *Different Roles, Different Voices* (New York: HarperCollins, 1994), 106.

8. For the study of potential candidates in New York, see Richard L. Fox, Jennifer Lawless, and Courtney Feeley, "Gender and the Decision to Run for Office," *Legislative Studies Quarterly* 26 (2001): 411–435.

9. Sandy L. Maisel and Walter J. Stone, "The Politics of Government-Funded Research: Notes from the Experience of the Candidate Emergence Study," *PS: Political Science and Politics* 31 (1998): 811–817.

10. The data for this project was collected in collaboration with Jennifer L. Lawless, an assistant professor of political science at Brown University. Thus, in describing the methods

of the study and the presentation of the findings, I often refer to "we."

11. Gary F. Moncrief, Peverill Squire, and Malcolm E. Jewell, *Who Runs for Legislature?* (Upper Saddle River, NJ: Prentice Hall, 2001).

12. For a detailed description of the study and the methods employed see Jennifer Lawless and Richard Fox, *It Takes a Candidate: Why Women Don't Run for Office* (New York: Cambridge University Press, 2005), 32–35, and Appendices A, B, and C.

13. Response rates within the three subsamples: lawyers—67 percent, business executives and leaders—45 percent, educators—61 percent. We attribute the relatively lower response rate of the business executives and leaders both to the fact that this group would seem to have the least interest in participating in an academic survey and to the fact that we could not follow up with them by sending personalized e-mail messages, since e-mail addresses are not listed in the national directory from which the sample was chosen.

14. Throughout this presentation of the findings from the Citizen Political Ambition Study, the results are presented as simple percentages with significance tests comparing women and men. This was done to make the results clear and accessible to a wide range of academics and practitioners. For a more sophisticated empirical analysis of the findings, see Richard L. Fox and Jennifer L. Lawless, "Entering the Arena: Gender and the Initial Decision to Run for Office," *American Journal of Political Science* 48 (2004): 264–280.

15. The age variable was broken down into a number of different categories. Regardless of the manner in which age was examined, the findings hold; women of all ages are less interested in running for office than men of all ages. We display the results in terms of three generations for ease of exposition.

16. See, for instance, David Niven, "Party Elites and Women Candidates: The Shape of Bias," *Women and Politics* 19 (1998):

57–80; Linda L. Fowler and Robert McClure, *Political Ambition* (New Haven, CT: Yale University Press, 1989).

17. Kira Sanbonmatsu, *Where Women Run: Gender and Party in American States* (Ann Arbor: University of Michigan Press, 2006).

18. See Nancy Burns, Kay Lehman Schlozman, and Sidney Verba, *The Private Roots of Public Action: Gender, Equality, and Political Representation* (Cambridge, MA: Harvard University Press, 2001); Nancy E. McGlen, Karen O'Connor, Laura Van Assendelft, and Wendy Gunther-Canada, *Women, Politics, and American Society*, 4th ed. (New York: Longman, 2004) for additional evidence of the gendered division of household labor and child care responsibilities.

19. Kathleen Hall Jamieson, *Beyond the Double Bind* (New York: Oxford University Press, 1995), 4.

20. Allan Wigfield, Jacquelynne S. Eccles, and Paul R. Pintrich, "Development Between the Ages of 11 and 25," in D. C. Berliner and R. C. Calfee, eds., *Handbook of Educational Psychology* (New York: Macmillan, 1996).

21. Adrian Furnham and Richard Rawles, "Sex Differences in the Estimation of Intelligence," *Journal of Social Behavior and Personality 10* (1995): 741–748; H. Beloff, "Mother, Father and Me: Our IQ," *Psychologist 5* (1992): 309–311.

22. Silvia Beyer and Edward M. Bowden, "Gender Differences in Self-Perceptions: Convergent Evidence from Measures of Accuracy and Bias," *Personality and Social Psychology Bulletin 23* (1997): 157–172.

9

IT'S WOMAN TIME

Marie C. Wilson

Almost a decade ago, I attended a women-and-power conference in Salzburg, Austria. During a seminar there, a majestic African rose slowly to address the group. "Sisters," she said, sweeping the auditorium with an imaginary broom, "we will lead. When things get really messy, we always get to clean up."

How prophetic. In 2006, women heads of state have emerged from some of the world's historically messiest places: Angela Merkel, chancellor of Germany; Han Myung-Sook, prime minister of South Korea; Ellen Johnson-Sirleaf, president of Liberia; Michelle Bachelet, president of Chile. Even in macho France, Marie Ségolène Royal, an unmarried mother (like Bachelet), has entered the political fray and might just become the first woman to lead there. Portia Simpson-Miller's reggae campaign song is clearly right: "It's Woman Time." That time is long overdue in this country. We still rank an embarrassing seventieth in the world when it comes to women's political participation.

Soon after that Salzburg seminar in 1998, the White House Project (which I founded and still lead) began its mission to advance the leadership of progressive women across all sectors, with particular focus on that last glass ceiling, the U.S. presidency (hence our name). The sheer immensity of the goal invited broad cynicism in those early years. But that has changed. And so have I. Back then, getting women into leadership seemed to me the fair thing to do; now I see it as the only thing to do—the only leadership alternative not tried in this world of calamity.

I'm not the only one ready for change: 66 percent of Americans say the country has a leadership crisis, according to the National Study of Confidence in Leadership (2005), conducted by the Center for Public Leadership at Harvard's Kennedy School of Government. Well over half the respondents said they believe we would be better off with more women in leadership.

We are also witnessing a marked change of acceptance regarding women's ability to handle traditionally male issues, such as foreign policy and the economy. In an Omnitel poll conducted for the White House Project in 2005, over half the respondents felt a woman president would do the same job as a man on those two key issues and also on homeland security. (No surprise that over half see a woman president as better at what are perceived as women's issues: health care, human rights, and education.)

This newfound comfort regarding women and foreign policy has to be inspired at least partially by Madeleine K. Albright and Condoleezza Rice. Albright served as U.S. delegate to the United Nations for four years under President Bill Clinton, then served as his secretary of state for another four years. Rice, national security advisor for four years under President George W. Bush, is now two years into her term as secretary of state. Whether you agree with their politics or not, their very presence in news photos and on the nightly network broadcasts has made such a role more normal for women.

A February 2006 poll by CBS News found 92 percent of Americans willing to put a woman in the Oval Office, the highest number ever found by CBS on that question. What a difference half a century makes: Gallup polls conducted in 1955 found 52 percent supportive (surprisingly high for that era); in 1975, that number increased to 73 percent. More than a decade later, in 1987, 82 percent declared their readiness.[1]

In the end, though, the story is richer than polling numbers. We hunger as a nation for authentic leaders—men and women who bring all of themselves to decision making and who don't act into the stereotypes of party or gender. The more women we put at the policy tables of government and industry, the more options we'll get; plus, men are more likely to act beyond masculine expectations.

The rising confidence in women's leadership, our desire for authenticity at the top, the continual appearance of female heads of state on the world stage, and the national prominence of our first-name-only female political rock stars (Hillary and Condi) have set American tongues wagging with "Why not a woman here?" The problem embedded in this question is the phrase "a woman." One woman can't carry the water for a thirsty nation: She'll be too busy proving she's man enough for the job. We need many women in the pipeline, up and down government and industry, able to help that top female leader succeed differently. Just because Americans see two prominent women in the spotlight, they think we're a nation with an equal playing field for women. We're not.

Here are the facts: In addition to our seventieth-place world ranking in women's political representation, we have only nine women governors (a traditional pipeline to the presidency), sixteen out of a hundred women senators, and only 16 percent of the 435-seat House of Representatives. Elsewhere around the globe, women in seventeen countries hold at least 30 percent of the seats in parliament, and twenty-two women are speakers. Currently, there are seventeen women heads of state. Wales recently reached full parity between women and men in the legislature. Among the countries that have achieved critical mass of about a third women in their parliaments are Denmark, Finland, Norway, Iceland, the Netherlands, Germany, Belgium, Austria, Spain, and Sudan (which obviously needs all the help it can get from women).[2]

By contrast, the percentage of women in our state legislatures, a stepping-stone to national office, has hovered at 20 percent for close to a decade, going down yet again just this past year.[3] Only fourteen mayors in the hundred largest cities are women, and women hold only about 25 percent of statewide executive offices.[4] The story is similar for women in corporate America: there are only twelve female CEOs of Fortune 500 companies (only one in the top hundred), and only 10.6 percent in line-officer positions (those with responsibility for profit and loss) are women.[5] When you add race to the mix in the political arena, it gets even worse. Women of color make up only 4.5 percent of state legislators and 1.6 percent of statewide executive leaders. Of the hundred largest cities in the United States, only one Latina and one African American woman serve as mayors.[6]

These gender inequalities carry a cost. Research institutions like the Center for American Women and Politics at Rutgers and the Women and Politics Institute at American University have spent decades studying the values women bring to the legislative process and their distinctive priorities that shape the resulting policies. Among the findings: Women tend to include more diverse viewpoints in decision making, conceive of public policy more broadly, and offer new solutions to intractable problems. These tendencies, not to mention a propensity to think outside the box (kind of easy, since they were never in the box), are precisely what we need in critical mass.

How did women develop a leadership style without truly getting to lead? The answer is what Harvard professor Ronald A. Heifetz calls "leadership without authority." He says it's possible to lead "from the foot of the table," but it "requires trust, respect and moral force in order to sustain progress. . . . [The leader] may need people across boundaries to believe that she represents something significant, that she embodies a perspective that merits attention."[7] Throughout history, women have been forced to lead this way. Margaret Sanger, for instance, formed a collaboration that brought us the birth-control pill. Gloria Steinem did it before she became a feminist icon, gaining both positional and moral authority amassed from decades of travel and conversation, as she organized the modern women's movement. Like the leaders Heifetz describes, Steinem had no choice but to work within and across communities, teaching and being taught, using her ability to place her struggles "in the context of the day's dominant values and concerns,"[8] working toward change by casting the net wide and deep.

This very trait, this capacity for community building, is one of the significant factors increasing the odds that women will lead. Our communities and our country have now recognized the worth of women's leadership and they want it. They want integrity, they want an end to partisan bickering, they need a guarantee that their voices (and their votes) actually count. Women have vision and values that are urgently needed in today's world. But how do we put them to work?

Gender in politics is a risky business. Although polling shows that the vast majority of Americans would vote for a qualified woman for president, they aren't sure their neighbors would, which could reflect an ambivalence they are reluctant to publicly acknowledge. Interestingly, a similar dynamic happens when corporate leadership approaches the edge. Many talented female executives are still banging at the glass ceiling, being consistently passed over as CEOs because their boards just can't seem to take that critical final step.[9] Why all this hedging? Why do we say we want women, but our neighbors don't? Why do we advance women, but only so far? It starts with understanding what still needs to change: the perception of women as leaders.

Part of that change in perception is happening as a result of powerful women at the top of government, such as Senator Hillary Rodham Clinton, Secretary Rice, and Secretary Albright, all of whom have altered the landscape for women in traditionally male areas of leadership. But, as Connie Buchanan, former associate dean of the Harvard Divinity School, wrote in *Choosing to Lead*, the cultural ideal of woman hasn't truly changed in the United States: It's still wife and mother. It doesn't matter that women are now 47 percent of the labor force—that private role still holds sway over the public one.[10] We still have work to do in changing the conversation and the culture to advance women's leadership.

For starters, numbers matter: As Associate Justice Sandra Day O'Connor said when Ruth Bader Ginsburg joined the court, "The minute Justice Ginsburg came to the court, we were nine justices. It wasn't seven and then 'the women.' We became nine. And it was a great relief to me."[11] Only numbers will allow women to be themselves and to help normalize women as potential CEOs or senators or presidents. That's why the White House Project joined with *Parade Magazine* to reach its 80 million readers in March 2006 with a straw poll called "8 for '08"—eight women leaders who could be president. The poll included the usual suspects, but we also wanted the public to meet some great potential candidates they might not know, such as Shirley Franklin, Atlanta's African American mayor, and Governor Kathleen Sebelius of Kansas, both of whom tied for third in the poll, behind Senator Clinton (first) and Secretary Rice (second).

Without numbers, women are scrutinized for all the wrong reasons. Our White House Project research, *Framing Gender on the Campaign Trail* (not so affectionately called our "hair, hemlines, and husbands" study), looked at media coverage of women running for governor in 2002, a record year for contenders for the top state job. The research found that if one woman is in a race, she is viewed only through a gender lens; two women constitute a catfight. But if there are three or more women in the race, the focus shifts from gender to agenda, which is obviously where we want to be.[12]

So how do we get a critical mass of progressive women running for office? We certainly can't depend on the parties to find them, nor can we depend on women to self-identify, as men do. We need to fuel each other's ambition, to give women the encouragement they need, and the courage embedded in that word. With our help, they can and will step forward and say, "I'm here. I can do this, and I want to lead."

I'm a good example. More than twenty years ago, I ran for (and won) a seat on the city council in Des Moines, Iowa. But I would never have done it if a woman friend on the council had not called and threatened to leave her seat if I didn't run. I was thrilled to be invited, but I wouldn't have put myself out there without her call. If we want to see more women political leaders, we need to urge more women to take the first step. We all know someone to call, to e-mail, to take to lunch. We need to ask her to step up to the plate, whether it's for the school board, the city council, the state legislature, or the Congress. As studies like *Who Runs for the Legislature* make clear, significantly more women than men reported that they had to be invited to run for office: 37 percent of male candidates who were polled indicated that it was their own idea to run, while only 11 percent of female candidates made the same claim; 37 percent of female candidates said they hadn't given serious thought to running until someone else brought it up, an experience they shared with only 18 percent of male candidates.[13] We need to help create the ambition in women that comes so naturally to men.

Numbers matter, but culture also matters. The constant call for Oprah Winfrey to run for office is understandable in light of career paths like those of President Ronald Reagan and Governor Arnold Schwarzenegger. Not only does popular culture confer power, it also suggests what a different kind of leader would look like: Dennis Haysbert's African American president on Fox's *24*, Glenn Close as the vice president in the movie *Air Force One*, and Geena Davis as the president on ABC's *Commander in Chief*. Haysbert has spoken eloquently of art imitating life, of testifying on the Hill about Hollywood's portrayal of Washington, where everyone from limo drivers to congressional pages, Secret Service agents to guards, called him "Mr. President."[14] As Marion Wright Edelman, founder and president of the Children's Defense Fund says, "You can't be what you can't see." If we want to see these alternative models of leadership, we can let the networks, advertisers, and producers know. With Hollywood, you can vote with your feet or your TiVo, and it works.

We can also do more to increase the visibility of existing female leaders who still need to struggle to make their voices heard. Consider, for example, Sunday morning political talk shows, which frequently set America's agenda for the coming week. Except for Condi and Hillary, you rarely see a female face. White House Project studies of shows such as *Meet the Press* and *Face the Nation* have shown a profound lack of diversity among scheduled guests. As a result of those studies and continued pressure, the numbers of women have somewhat improved, increasing from 11 percent in 2001 to 14 percent in 2005. But that's a slow climb over four years.[15] Mostly, it's all men all the time.

One complaint of producers: they don't know who's out there. So the White House Project invented "SheSource.org," an online database of women experts formed in partnership with Fenton Communications and the Women's Funding Network. The database is organic, growing daily, and being used constantly, especially in the areas of foreign policy and the economy, where women experts are less well known.

We need more of these ways to give talented women the push they need and the authority they deserve. However, we also have to stop demanding perfection of our women leaders—a perfection we demand of no man. Every time we say a woman can't win (often before she's even announced she's running), we belittle her authority and decrease her chances of making it. We want the perfect mother, harkening back to our ideal of women: someone who does everything right and nothing wrong. I'm not arguing that we shouldn't hold women as accountable as men; we should. But we should then hold men as accountable as we do women. We need to level the field, give women a chance to misspeak, to misstep, to not know everything about everything when they enter the fray.

Above all, we have to demonstrate our political will. That's how South Africa and India, Norway and France got women into power. In 1994 South African women had to threaten the men they had fought alongside to end apartheid when these same men denied their request for 30 percent of the seats in parliament. Women's groups linked arms and threatened to vote against their own new African National Congress. The men changed their minds.

In 1996, five political women from the left and five from the right formed their "Manifesto of the Ten," and called for equal numbers of men and women in French politics. Three years later, the "Ten" and its allies got a constitutional amendment that required parity, forcing the parties to either include women on their ballots or incur a financial penalty. After the amendment passed, female representation on French city councils nearly doubled, going from 25.5 percent to 47.5 percent.[16]

In 1989, after fifty-five years of democracy, India still had a parliament with only 8 percent women. Ranjana Kumari, director of the Centre for Social Research in India, gathered allies and traveled the vast country by train, spreading colorful cloths on tables and collecting signatures for a constitutional amendment that would reserve a third of all village council seats for women. It passed in 2001, and 1.3 million women now serve their villages in a whole new way.

These are great stories of will and courage, with profound implications for gender equality. As research by scholars such as Pippa Norris makes clear, the only way women have managed to achieve anything close to political parity with men is through enforceable quotas. Although we are reluctant to embrace quotas in the United States, having a political system where the leaders are more than 90 percent white and male is a de facto quota.[17]

It can't stay like this forever. As the wise African woman said, we will undoubtedly get to clean the place up. The political movement to make this happen is clearly growing, built from the bottom up, intent on bringing a new voice to leadership. It has, of course, been a long time coming, with much vacillation. The suffragettes of the early twentieth century built vibrant membership organizations that were slowly abandoned when the vote was secured in 1919. Early activists thought that the vote itself would bring power to women. It mostly hasn't. And we now know better what else is required.

A wave of feminism that started in the 1970s brought with it organizations intent on making the world more equitable for women. In 1971, the Center for American Women and Politics began supporting these efforts with rich resources. The Women's Campaign Fund emerged in 1974, shortly after the *Roe v. Wade* abortion victory in the Supreme Court. The second wave built other large organizations such as the National Organization for Women and the National Women's Political Caucus, streaming women into the political pipeline at the local level and helping

them move up. EMILY's List came along in 1985 to provide early
money for pro-choice Democratic women in the Senate, and Wish
List arrived in 1992 for progressive Republican women.

But just as the money began to flow for women candidates, the
resources of local groups were siphoned off to secure prior legislative
gains, particularly around reproductive freedom, as the right wing
of the Republican party ascended. What's worse, term limits (which
many thought might help women) actually eroded the numbers of
women in the state legislatures.

But that was then and this is now. A fresh breed has stepped forward: literally dozens of progressive state and local women's groups
are beginning to close the leadership gap. Some are local chapters of
older national groups, like the Women's Campaign Fund in Minnesota and the National Organization for Women in Washington
State. Some are new, like Emerge, which is strategically moving into
the states and preparing young women to run for public office. Others are on campuses, affiliated with organizations like the Center for
American Women and Politics at Rutgers. Some are stand-alones,
like the CREW (Coalition to Recruit and Elect Women) program
out of the Center for Women in Politics and Public Policy at the
University of Massachusetts. This organization fields "ambassadors"
to scour communities, recruiting women to run at all levels and
steering them to local and national campaign-skills training. Some
are political action committees like Future Pac, which describes itself
as the "first national political action with the goal of electing more
African American women to public office both at the federal and
state level by creating a network of support and funding."[18] The
White House Project's "Vote, Run, Lead"™ campaign is training
close to a hundred very diverse women at each session we hold in
four regions around the country. And this is just a sampling of the
work that is thriving at the local level, intent on establishing a true,
permanent pipeline to political power for women in America.

In these past three years, as I have traveled the country espous-
ing the idea of my book, *Closing the Leadership Gap: Why Women
Can and Must Help Run the World*, I have witnessed firsthand the

yearning for women as leaders, especially in politics. It's time, to be sure, for today's young women to live out the promise that earlier activists made: That women can run the world alongside men. That they can run a corporation, a state, and, ultimately, a country. That their voices will be heard.

We know that women often bring different priorities to the leadership process. We want to make sure that women's voices matter when they favor diplomacy over war, when they insist that true security does not come in the form of bombs and bullets but in education, health care, and employment opportunities.

John Naisbitt's book *Megatrends* speaks eloquently of the failure of the railroad industry. As he says, the railroads didn't recognize that they were no longer in the railroad business, that they were now in the transportation business.[19] We, too, are at a moment of change when we are no longer in the gender-equity business but in the business of transformation. Our problems, national and global, are urgent. Women need to be part of fundamental institutional changes. The time is now. And not a moment too soon.

Endnotes

1. CBS News/*New York Times* Poll, "A Woman for President," January 20–25, 2006, press release of February 5, 2006, available online: www.cbsnews.com/htdocs/pdf/020306woman.pdf, access date: December 29, 2006.

2. Inter-Parliamentary Union Web site, Women in National Parliaments, www.ipu.org/wmn-e/classif.htm, last updated July 31, 2006.

3. Center for American Women in Politics, "Women in State Legislatures 2006: Fact Sheet," Center for American Women in Politics, Eagleton Institute of Politics, Rutgers, New Jersey, 2006.

4. Center for American Women in Politics, "Statewide Elective Executive 2006: Fact Sheet," Center for American Women in Politics, Eagleton Institute of Politics, Rutgers, New Jersey, 2006.

5. Judith H. Dobryznski, "Cherchez la Femme," *Wall Street Journal*, August 4, 2006, A16.

6. Center for American Women in Politics, "Women of Color in Elective Office 2006: Fact Sheet," Center for American Women in Politics, Eagleton Institute of Politics, Rutgers, New Jersey, 2006.

7. Ronald A. Heifetz, *Leadership Without Easy Answers* (Cambridge, MA: Harvard University Press, 1994).

8. Heifetz, *Leadership Without Easy Answers*.

9. Dobryznski, "Cherchez la Femme," A16.

10. Constance Buchanan, *Choosing to Lead: Women and the Crisis of American Values* (Boston: Beacon Press, 1996).

11. Interview with Sandra Day O'Connor, "Live from . . . with Judy Woodruff," aired on CNN May 19, 2003; transcript available online: http://transcripts.cnn.com/TRANSCRIPTS/0305/19/lol.14.html, access date: December 29, 2006.

12. James Devitt, *Framing Gender on the Campaign Trail: Women's Executive Leadership and the Press* (New York: Women's Leadership Fund, 1999).

13. Gary F. Moncrief, Peverill Squire, and Malcom E. Jewell, *Who Runs for the Legislature?* (Upper Saddle River, NJ: Prentice Hall, 2001).

14. Wilson, 131.

15. The White House Project, *Who's Talking Now: A Followup Analysis of Guest Appearances by Women on the Sunday Morning Talk Shows* (New York: White House Project, October 2005).

16. Pippa Norris, *Electoral Engineering: Voting Rules and Political Behavior* (New York: Cambridge University Press, 2003).

17. Center for American Women in Politics, "Women in Elective Office 2006: Fact Sheet," Center for American Women in Politics, Eagleton Institute of Politics, Rutgers, New Jersey, 2006.

18. Wilson, 175.

19. John Naisbitt, *Megatrends: Ten New Directions Transforming Our Lives* (New York: Warner Books, 1986).

10

SHE'S THE CANDIDATE!

A Woman for President

Ruth B. Mandel

This chapter is divided into two major sections: the first is a brief descriptive summary of historical and quantitative information about women as candidates for the presidency of the United States; the second is an essay contemplating the question of a woman for president from the vantage point of 2007, the moment when the first woman to be a serious contender for the highest office in the world's most powerful nation announced her candidacy for the 2008 presidential election.

A Woman for President?

"Why not me?"

A song sheet from 1961 captures the social context in which women who might have dreamt of running for president have found themselves. In large print above the freckled face of an intense little boy with tousled hair, the song's title proclaims, "Every Little Boy Can Be President."[1] At the end, he sings: "Every little boy can be President, Why not me? Why not me? Why not me? Why not me? Why not me?" A few bold women did ask themselves just that and considered presidential races both before and after that song was written. But the dominant cultural presumption through the centuries weighed in on the little boy's side; the women candidates' side was fantasyland.

For the record, some women have run. They merit a place in the annals of women's political history. We might call them proto-candidates. In the course of 132 years—between 1872 and 2004—perhaps a few dozen women presented themselves as presidential candidates: some sought major party nominations, and the rest ran as candidates representing minor parties.[2] No matter how impressive, determined, or putatively qualified some of them might have been, it seems important to emphasize that not one was ever considered a serious contender for a major party nomination, much less a winner of a national presidential election. None of these women could have been self-deluded about winning, but most had an audience to reach, a message to send, or a point to make about the value of the candidacy itself. A number of them enjoyed enthusiastic national followings.

Victoria Woodhull was the first, nominated in 1872 as the presidential candidate of the Equal Rights Party, a party she had conceived and organized.[3] Twelve and sixteen years later (1884 and 1888), Belva Lockwood ran as the nominee of the same party. Between them, Woodhull and Lockwood chalked up a remarkable string of firsts for women in the United States. Lockwood, an attorney, was the first woman to argue before the Supreme Court. Woodhull, the first woman stockbroker and newspaper publisher, also broke ground as the first woman to testify before Congress. As an outspoken, flamboyant personality who was involved in a major scandal of the time and as a proponent of what were considered outrageous views about sex and marriage, her record as a pathbreaker was overshadowed by her notoriety. Controversies notwithstanding, both Woodhull and Lockwood were extraordinary women, exhibiting courage and daring. Their sense of entitlement to options most women had not yet begun to imagine for themselves made them vulnerable to easy dismissal or ridicule.

It does seem fitting that the first two women to make active bids for the U.S. presidency should do so as feminists under a banner of equal rights, which sent a message still relevant a full century later when the next audacious woman launched a visible but doomed national presidential campaign on behalf of women. The hundred-year distance from 1872 to 1972 took U.S. feminists from the fight for the ballot box to the fight for political leadership. But it was all of a piece—a struggle to gain full citizenship for women in the democracy.

Congresswoman Shirley Chisholm's 1972 run for the Democratic nomination remains the most sustained, visible, and passionate campaign ever organized by a woman bidding for the presidency. The campaign attracted dedicated supporters who saw Chisholm as a crusader delivering a challenge to America. An elementary school teacher from Brooklyn, New York, and in 1968 the first black woman ever elected to Congress, Shirley Chisholm told the world in no uncertain terms that a woman—a black woman at that—had every right to aspire to the nation's most powerful political position.[4]

A year after the race, Chisholm wrote a memoir of the campaign in which she offered her view of its achievement: "The mere fact that a black woman dared to run for President, *seriously,* not expecting to win but sincerely trying to, is what it was all about. 'It can be done'; that was what I was trying to say, by doing it. . . . At any rate, I feel the Chisholm candidacy accomplished one thing. The next time a woman of whatever color, or a dark-skinned person of whatever sex aspires to be President, the way should be a little smoother because I helped pave it."[5] Thirty years later, she believed her run for the nomination had sent an overdue message: "I knew I could not become president. But the time had come when persons other than males could run for the presidency of this country. Why couldn't a woman run? Why couldn't a black person run? I was angry that everything always, always redounded to the benefit of white males."[6] Chisholm was always clear that she would not be nominated and elected, but she fought stubbornly and audaciously to make herself heard and to be taken seriously as a contender for center-stage leadership.

Resisting pressure from African American male political leaders to withdraw her candidacy and creating an uncomfortable situation for activist feminists who very much wanted to gain Democratic party influence by supporting a winner that year, Chisholm remained in the contest. She entered primaries in twelve states and campaigned nationwide until the Miami nominating convention, where she won 151.25 delegate votes, a record no woman has bested thirty-five years later.

Actually, the name of another trailblazing elected official had garnered votes at a presidential nominating convention eight years before Chisholm's quest. This time on the Republican side, Senator Margaret Chase Smith of Maine was nominated for president in July 1964 at the Republican convention in San Francisco. Her name was placed in nomination by Senator George D. Aiken of Vermont who, recalling her famous Senate floor "Declaration of Conscience" speech denouncing Senator Joe McCarthy, described her as someone with the "courage to stand for the right when it may not be popular to do so—courage to stand for decency in the conduct of public affairs—courage to stand alone if necessary against formidable odds."[7] The first woman to achieve the distinction of having her name placed in nomination on the floor of a major political party's national presidential nominating convention, Smith withdrew after winning twenty-seven delegate votes on the first ballot.

A groundbreaker in political history, Margaret Chase Smith had been the first woman elected to both houses of Congress. As a congressional widow, in 1940 she won the House seat vacated by her husband's death; eight years later, she moved up to the U.S. Senate, where she served until 1973. But Senator Smith did not view herself as a champion or symbol of progress for women. She did not wish to travel the country asking for money and organizing to mount a national campaign, and she fully understood that the political realities of the time were not on the side of her achieving the presidency. But make no mistake about it, Margaret Chase Smith, a woman who began professional life as a secretary and ended her career as a member of the Senate Armed Services Committee and the Senate Appropriations Committee, believed that she had what it took to be president of the United States. To her, the nomination was not just symbolic, a courtesy with a wink and a nod. It spoke to her sense of being qualified and fully prepared. A deeply ambitious woman who did not hesitate to say "I like to win," Smith wanted the nomination and she wanted the presidency. She believed that she had earned and deserved it.[8] A biographer who grew close to Smith during years of interviewing writes, "She wanted to be president because it was the top job in her business, because it was the capstone to a lengthy and distinguished political career, because she loved the limelight, because she thought she could do a good job."[9]

In 1988 in the Democratic party and in 2000 on the Republican side, highly accomplished and nationally prominent political women, each with a law degree from Harvard University, emerged as possible presidential contenders. After sixteen years in the U.S. House of Representatives, Congresswoman Patricia Schroeder of Colorado spent the summer of 1988 exploring whether she could become a viable candidate in her party's primaries. The exploration ended in an emotional press conference at which she announced that she could not raise the money required for a serious race. Remaining in Congress for another eight years, Schroeder continued to play a vocal role as a national spokesperson for women's rights and for a progressive policy agenda. In her 1988 exploration, Schroeder contributed to the record set by previous women who knew that they could not win the presidency but that someone must sound the call and call attention to the importance of beginning the long march to the White House.

More than a decade later, Elizabeth Hanford Dole spent the better part of 1999 exploring a race for the presidency in 2000. She had not yet held elective office; but she had a long history of high-level government service, having worked for four presidents in major roles, including cabinet positions as secretary of transportation (1983–1987) and secretary of labor (1989–1991). Moreover, she was married to Republican Senate leader Bob Dole, himself a previous presidential contender. She could also claim executive leadership credentials based on eight years as president of the American Red

Cross. By virtue of her own professional and political experience, as well as a vast network of connections, Elizabeth Dole might have been expected to become a serious candidate for the presidency. Yet after nine months, she dropped out without ever developing as a contender on the campaign trail.[10] She cited the difficulty of raising money as a major barrier to building a viable presidential candidacy and gave her support to George W. Bush, who had a campaign chest with tens of millions of dollars.[11]

The same obstacle was cited as insurmountable four years later when Carol Moseley Braun, another political woman with a law degree, ran for the Democratic presidential nomination. She came to the race after serving for one term as the first African American woman in the U.S. Senate and for a brief time as President Clinton's Ambassador to New Zealand. While Braun was one of two African American Democrats to announce for president in 2004, she remained the sole female among her party's ten candidates during primary season. She maintained her profile as a candidate by taking advantage of the free media attention offered by debates. From May 2003 to January 2004, Braun appeared on stage with her fellow candidates in six debates that were televised locally in various primary states and aired nationally on C-Span. Notwithstanding the platform provided by this visibility, Braun was never able to attract the funding and voter support required for creating a serious campaign organization. Reading the tea leaves, she withdrew four days before the first 2004 primary votes were cast in the Iowa caucuses and threw her support to former Vermont governor Howard Dean, who was viewed as a leading candidate at that time.

To a greater or lesser extent, these five accomplished and well-known political women—Smith, Chisholm, Schroeder, Dole, and Moseley Braun—all of whom expressed presidential aspirations in the forty years between 1964 and 2004, lamented that a lack of money defeated their efforts. The dollar deficit probably did not surprise any of them. Politically savvy as they were, they knew that hot contests in America survive on cold cash, and that in turn, money is organization, staff, message, and media time—every ingredient in the lifeblood of a successful campaign beyond the candidate herself. Without personal fortunes to spend on political ambitions, women and men seek votes by buying the means to contact voters, the funds coming from donors comfortable with a candidate's vision and viability. Racing enthusiasts do not bet on untrained, untested horses, and political supporters rarely risk money on unfamiliar candidate breeds. In the period that these five women tested the presidential waters, women were (and continue to be) an unfamiliar breed in the rarefied realms of national executive leadership.

None of these women broke through to the stature that made them serious contenders in the eyes of party leaders, power brokers, or the national media. All five women lacked a vast national base of party support and the organizational structure required for mounting a sustained campaign. They had not laid the groundwork for building a credible race in modern presidential politics. It would have been unrealistic for any of them to undertake the task at that level. The time had not come when a woman candidate had a real chance to break through the historic barriers that being female added to the enormous, grinding burdens of presidential candidacy. And they knew it.

Each one had other points to make or other objectives to pursue. The early equal rights candidates Victoria Woodhull and Belva Lockwood were running to express the sense of entitlement they believed women should assert. Senator Smith and Congresswoman Chisholm conveyed important messages to women who would later take the presidential path. Margaret Chase Smith knew she was no mere symbolic figure. She could raise her hand to take an oath to become the nation's chief executive convinced she had the ability to fulfill the requirements of the office. Shirley Chisholm knew that a right unclaimed might as well be a right not granted. She would run to make a statement that power and tradition will not yield to change without being challenged by those who seek to claim their rights. Patricia Schroeder ran largely to call attention to an agenda that included the gender issue, a platform of progressive family and feminist issues that she and her supporters wanted to keep before the public's eyes during the national election season. At a moment when Republicans were intent on recapturing the White House, Elizabeth Dole might have liked her heightened visibility and a demonstration of widespread support to boost her chances for consideration as the first female vice-presidential nominee on her party's national ticket. Carol Moseley Braun, still suffering the effects of controversial stories during her Senate years that questioned her conduct and character, held her own in the primary debates, impressing audiences with her knowledge, poise, and articulateness. She used the presidential primary stage to rehabilitate her public image and position herself for an appointment if her party won the White House.

While it was never in the cards for Smith, Chisholm, Schroeder, Dole, or Moseley Braun to win a major party nomination, much less become president of the United States, their races remain of interest. Each woman individually and all collectively left a legacy of daring, a mark on women's political history. At a minimum, other women could absorb the message that these political leaders' behavior sent into the public consciousness. They made a claim on public awareness by attaching voices and living images of accomplished women leaders to the idea that one day a woman could conceivably become president. Their actions made the idea less outrageous to conceive. Now the time has come when there should no longer be a need to establish the point that women can consider themselves presidential candidates. The time has come for a dead serious run on the White House. To be sure, gender will not be beside the point, but we are well past the time when it should be viewed as the central point.

From "If" to "When"—Public Consciousness, Public Attitudes

Until the issue has been tested in a real contest, there is no certainty about whether a majority of U.S. voters will press the presidential lever for anyone other than a Caucasian man. Since the option has not yet been presented by the two major parties, we know only what voters say they would be prepared to do.[12] Public opinion data about women and the presidency have told a relatively consistent, unsurprising story over time: the closer we come to the present day, the more people say they would be willing to vote for a woman.

The increase in positive attitudes toward a woman for president coincides with the impact of the feminist movement on a period of vast social change in women's and men's lives beginning in the 1970s. In the political arena, U.S. women held fewer than 5 percent of all elective offices in the early 1970s. By the early years of the new century women had broken age-old barriers throughout the system. Still accounting for only a relatively small minority of public leaders, women had achieved a visible and significant presence in political life across the country, as elected and appointed officials, political party activists, campaign organizers and professionals, high-level strategists, political staff, donors, and fundraisers. Federal and state offices that had been almost the exclusive province of men—governor, secretary of state, attorney general, treasurer, supreme court justice—had been occupied by more than one woman. Furthermore, beginning in the 1980s, the political community developed a keen interest in women's voting power after discovering that women, the majority of the voting electorate, turned out at the polls at higher rates than men and often voted differently from men. These and other changes in late twentieth-century society opened minds and doors to women's leadership.[13]

The Gallup Poll is the familiar early source of information about national attitudes on the matter of a woman's being president, with data collected as far back as the 1930s—when only a third of Americans said they would consider voting for a qualified woman for president. By mid-century, a change in attitude had taken place, and the majority switched to the positive side, backing the idea of a woman as president. Between 1958 and 1969, both women and men were positive, but there was a gap, with men more positive: 50 percent to 53 percent of women and 55 percent to 60 percent of men answered

"Yes" to the question of whether they would vote for a woman if she were their party's nominee. A big leap forward took place in the early 1970s, just when the women's rights movement had reached a pitch of activist intensity. Both the Gallup Poll and the National Opinion Research Center's General Social Surveys throughout the 1970s found that large majorities (from over two-thirds to over three-quarters) of both women and men said they were willing to vote for a woman for president.[14] By the early twenty-first century—about seventy years after the public's opinion on the matter of a woman for president began to be measured—positive responses had climbed toward the heights of unanimity. In a news release, the CBS News/*New York Times* Poll noted that support had increased steadily over half a century and reported that 92 percent of respondents in their January 2006 poll said "they would vote for a woman for president from their party if she were qualified for the job."[15]

Because the media are full of stories about a woman or two who might actually seek the presidency in the near future, the question is no longer simply abstract. A woman's candidacy has become far more interesting and complex than its being a simple gauge of broad societal attitudes about women in charge. By 2006, polling organizations were regularly including more than one question about the issue as they sought to tease out nuances in the public's views. Having been tracked for many decades, attitudes about the public's willingness seem to be known, but what about its readiness? When it comes to the kind of change represented by a woman head of state, it seems that openness and readiness are a distance apart.

This question has attracted interest. While overwhelming majorities of respondents say they would vote for a woman, much smaller percentages say that the country is ready for a woman president (92 percent versus 55 percent in the CBS News/*New York Times* Poll).[16] Analyzing responses by variables such as gender (60 percent of men versus 51 percent of women think the country is ready), age (younger citizens see the country as readier than senior citizens do), partisan affiliation (a 61 percent majority of Democrats versus a 48 percent minority of Republicans consider America ready), and ideological orientation (declining majorities of liberals, moderates, and conservatives all see the country ready for a woman president), the CBS News/*New York Times* Poll and other survey organizations are building a trove of information as the country heads closer to the inevitable day when the attitudinal database will be enriched with information about actual voting behavior.

It takes a bit of social psychology to interpret what people say about readiness and timing. For example, a 2005 CNN/*USA Today*/Gallup poll found large majorities of citizens (94 percent of Democrats and 76 percent of Republicans) saying they themselves would vote for a woman, but they did not think their neighbors were quite as enlightened. The numbers took a deep dive—twenty to thirty points—when people were asked whether their neighbors would vote for a woman: only 72 percent of Democrats and 47 percent of Republicans believed that their neighbors would pull the lever for a woman. As for timing, while a large majority of respondents expressed their own willingness to vote for a qualified woman for president, less than a majority thought a woman would be elected to the White House in the next decade. A quarter of a century appears to be a safe distance from which to contemplate change, with most respondents predicting that within twenty-five years a woman would be elected.[17]

Answers to an informal poll taken at a bipartisan conference of women state legislators in late 2005 are of interest here. Women's progress in political leadership generally has taken the arduous step-by-step route, and expectations about the next big breakthrough seem to reflect an awareness of that course. The group was asked to respond anonymously in writing to two questions: In what year would a major party nominate a woman for president? In what year would the first woman be elected president? Of thirty respondents, almost everyone selected 2008 as the year when the United States would reach the milestone of nominating a woman for president (twenty-eight answered 2008; the other two chose 2012). But when it came to winning, only ten people attending a conference of elected women had confidence that the first nominee would win the first race. Oddly, another ten said that while a woman would be nominated in 2008, the first woman would win in 2012. Was this group of experienced people predicting the defeat of an incumbent president? Did they assume that the man who won against the first woman nominee in 2008 would become a one-term president by being challenged and defeated in a primary by a woman from his own party in 2012, or lose the general election to a woman nominated by the opposing party? It is easy to speculate confidently that almost every woman attending this conference believed that the most obvious potential candidate in 2008, Hillary Rodham Clinton, would be nominated. But was it hard political calculus that led only one-third to think she would win? Like the Gallup poll respondents, did these elected women reveal their own willingness to support a woman in their answers about a nomination date, and then their projection of their neighbors' hesitation in their answers about a victory date? Or were they unable to cross the psychological hurdle between knowing and feeling that the time is right for change and believing that it can actually happen? Interpreting their puzzling answers obviously requires more information than this playful, informal poll offers.

Whether we review findings from large, national, scientifically drawn samples or from playful, informal polls, whether we listen to talk radio or watch talking heads on television, whether we read analysis in political journals or check out *Parade* magazine (inserted for mass circulation in Sunday papers), it is obvious that the matter of a woman for president has entered the national consciousness and everyday discourse. The focus of inquiry has shifted: the question is no longer "If"; it is "When."

The Closer We Come, the More Interesting It Gets

From the vantage point of 2007, "When" may very well be now. For the first time in over half a century, the door to the Oval Office is wide open, with neither an incumbent president nor an incumbent vice president a candidate for the presidency in 2008. At the same time, this unusually open election year shows signs of becoming unique by producing the first woman to win a nomination for president of the United States.

It is remarkable, really, that in the history of the republic not one woman has been a serious candidate for a nomination, much less a nominee in a general election. Equally mind-boggling is the fact that as late as 2007, still only one woman in the entire land is considered viable as a potential candidate. After more than thirty-five years of major breakthroughs in politics, accounting for this paucity presents a monumental challenge to those who believed that parity for women in leadership positions would flow from the social reforms and new educational and professional opportunities gained in the twentieth century's latter decades.

If for no other reason, that granite fact alone makes the subject interesting. Yet, upon hearing that I was planning to write something about women as candidates for the presidency, a highly regarded political scientist dismissed the topic as lacking interest. He offered, "I don't like the topic. It suggests that gender is the qualification. People should not vote for or against someone because of gender." I found this comment surprising because I had no intention to argue a proposition that being a man or a woman should be the reason for running or winning votes. While gender, race, religion, and ethnicity are not qualifying characteristics one way or the other, these identity markers have been relevant historically. Their entrance as characters with growing speaking parts on the stage of electoral politics late in the twentieth century and their visible presence in the twenty-first elevate them to relevancy in considering the evolution of political leadership. In the calculus of constituency power and campaign dynamics, they influence political viability no less than geography or other traditional variables.

My colleague elaborated that people should be talking about real qualifications, tactics, and policy positions, and explained that his vote for a woman for president would be driven by party and policy, not gender. I agree; all of that makes sense. I disagree with his hot-button and, in my view, defensive reduction of the gender issue to a nonsubject. It reminded me of a comment made in the early 1970s by another prominent political scientist in response to the news that a colleague was beginning research for a book about women in politics. "But you don't have a subject there," he pronounced.

Are these opinions packed with weighty knowledge, or is there less here than meets the eye? Since I suspect that a version of these views is held by more people than these two individual scholars, I want to pause over them. Both opinions suggest a lack of curiosity about aspects of a subject that might not be immediately apparent. While the reactions are not the same, both objections raise the issues of the legitimacy of a candidate and her being taken seriously. Both seem instantly and unabashedly dismissive. Such an unqualified, outspoken response could arise from distaste or discomfort— swat the idea to get rid of it quickly—or more likely the opposite, that response could emerge from confidence in a time-honored framework of accepted assumptions and well-established grounds for inquiry that grant gender no conceivable standing as a serious topic.

I find it hard to understand that these topics are either threatening or unworthy. That 1970s opinion has been rendered obsolete and irrelevant by the many volumes written about women's political participation in the intervening thirty years. The 2006 response seems to assume, even after thirty years of change and interest in women's leadership, that the only angle of interest in a gender question would be polemic or simplistic advocacy. ("If you're writing about the topic, your point must be that a woman should run and be elected president simply because she's a woman. What else is there to say about the subject?") But even if gender were being advocated as a qualification in and of itself, which has never been the case, it would not be surprising if it stimulated interesting discussions.

Having no body of empirical data to examine, social science research understandably rejects the subject of women as presidential candidates. That situation will change in the face of events to come. The closer the day comes to witnessing a viable female presidential candidate who can mount a competitive race for the White

House, the more interest will heighten. The media will be interested, as will pollsters and pundits, party leaders, businesspeople and interest groups, foreign leaders, and allies and enemies. Voters will be curious and have opinions on the matter because a female candidate's gender is not (yet) an invisible characteristic and because heretofore the office of president has become identified with its male occupants. People will want to know whether and how the gender difference will make a difference.

How will a woman hold the reins and exercise power in a job no woman has ever held? Will a woman in the Oval Office think differently or face crises differently, govern differently, and serve differently as a commander in chief? Because the overwhelming majority of people firmly believe that women and men are not the same, they do not know if a woman holding the nation's top leadership position will bring about change that is somehow influenced by her gender. People tend to fear change. When a friend who says he is more than willing to vote for a woman president was asked whether he has negative feelings or concerns, he admitted, "Honestly, I'm a little leery. I haven't had an experience or good example of a woman as a leader. If anything gives me pause, it's the unknown." Needless to say, every newly elected male president is an unknown in that role. But the man is still one among the fifty-seven varieties, not a different brand name.

The nature of the interest in a woman running for president will, of course, depend on the individual candidate. Its intensity will decline markedly after the first woman has made a run of it and won. Soon after the first woman joined the Supreme Court or became secretary of state or won election as governor or other official in a previously all-male office, the extraordinary converted to the ordinary in public life—so, too, at the peaks of political leadership. After the first breakthroughs, it will not take forever before having a woman at the top of the ticket or in the White House becomes merely the way things are. The first woman will be tasked with clearing the path from the extraordinary to the ordinary. Predictably, some percentage of voters who claim to support the idea of women running for president will demur, "but not this one." It might be vexing for them to find precisely the right woman they would trust to carry the banner of this particular historic change.

Naturally, whoever is the first nominee will meet and probably exceed the basic qualifications of competency, ambition, experience, preparedness, organization, and resources. If she also identifies with the societal transformations for U.S. women in recent decades and relates to liberal feminist thinking, the discussion about her candidacy and what she symbolizes will intensify. Because the most obvious potential first female presidential nominee, Senator Hillary Rodham Clinton, is just such a woman, this scenario is the most likely and is fascinating to imagine.

Here the curtain rises on familiar plot twists. First female candidates have often faced the double bind that if they are "outsiders," breaking ground for newcomers to electoral politics, their "outsiderness" looms as a hurdle to political acceptability and viability. Yet those who have stood for progressive social change for women and have themselves broken barriers into the political system can find themselves in a no-win situation. Having succeeded in acquiring the credentials and gaining the support to mount winning races, they become suspect and may even forfeit the trust of outside constituencies who are wary of the accommodations and inevitable compromises a newcomer makes along the road to becoming a tenable candidate in our two-party system. Like other women leaders who have pioneered in new territory since the 1970s, the former First Lady and now Senator from New York is not an "either-or" in this matter, neither an outsider nor an insider. She is both—at once a unique newcomer and a recognizable political type.

A Hillary Rodham Clinton presidential candidacy simultaneously offers the nation a historic outsider and a consummate insider. On one side of the coin, here is a former First Lady, a wife publicly betrayed and humiliated, a proud mother, an "uppity" feminist baby boomer, a successful lawyer, an outspoken voice for women's rights, a strong children's rights advocate: as a presidential candidate, Hillary Rodham Clinton is uniquely different, "other," and pathbreaking. On the other side, Senator Clinton is as well-known, pre-pared, well-positioned, organized, and formidable a Democrat to approach presidential politics as any in recent memory, a senator who works with people across the political spectrum, attracting part-ners and adherents from various backgrounds, with a strong state and national network of supporters. In a lengthy *New York Times Maga-zine* cover story appearing more than two and a half years before the 2008 presidential election, journalist Matt Bai variously tagged her as the "establishment candidate," the Democrat who could be chal-lenged in her party's primaries by an outsider. Describing the then possible primary campaign of former Virginia Governor Mark Warner as an insurgency, Bai concludes: "You have to be ready, as an earlier generation of Democrats would have put it, to take on the Man—even if the Man this time happens to be a woman."[18]

A Hillary Rodham Clinton candidacy for president of the United States provokes discussions and encounters far removed from the electoral arena itself. Variations on the following campus scene will play out elsewhere, among all ages and groupings around the country and across the oceans. In late 2005, a college student described an incident in which she and several other campus lead-ers (female and male) went out to celebrate the conclusion of a demanding semester's work in student government. The women represented different points of view, including an apolitical student, a liberal feminist, and a more conservative Republican. When someone mentioned Hillary Clinton's name, one of the male stu-dents offered, "Well, she's not smart; she's just stupid." Offended, the women rose in unison to challenge this insult. A Clinton race for the White House will set off conversations within generations, within and across genders, classes, and races. Her running will prompt confrontations with the unfinished work of men and women moving to a twenty-first-century way of being together. It will stim-ulate conversations and arguments about who we are as women and men and how we view one another.

Most of these exchanges will be rooted in specific reactions to this specific candidate, the woman who repeatedly has been characterized in the media as controversial, a woman who elicits strong feelings and has been described as someone some people love to hate. Many men will be uncomfortable with any woman who is the first presidential nominee and commander in chief, but they will consciously or unconsciously feel more threatened by a woman who is not only brilliant and tough but who also voices and represents a special interest in progress for women. For other reasons, many women will also feel uncomfortable about such a woman. Nonetheless, women in droves will develop personal pride in her and will find themselves defending her. Office workers, service workers, professionals, retirees, and stay-at-home moms—all manner of women will be as offended as the college students who didn't share political affiliations but expressed mutual anger at hearing some guy friend dismiss Hillary Clinton as "stupid."

Except for the intense historic moment provoked by Anita Hill's nationally televised testimony at the confirmation hearings for Supreme Court Justice Clarence Thomas in late 1991, nothing like a sustained, widespread, charged national conversation about gender has taken place since the activist phase of the women's movement, which had cooled down by the mid-1980s.[19]

As to the broader subject of women's leadership, the nomination of the first woman for president of the United States is of major interest. The event will signal an unprecedented change in the nation's political history, symbolizing acceptance for women at a height of public leadership never before scaled, and representing a decisive break with the view that men and women cannot cross centuries-old boundaries defined by stereotypes of maleness and femaleness.

That interest is slated to play out with Hillary Rodham Clinton. If not then with her, in 2008, the question appears moot for the foreseeable future. Fed up with historic limitations on women's public roles, activists in the early 1970s announced a claim on leadership and the intention to acquire it.[20] Notwithstanding all the hurdles leapt in the interim and the changes in how women are viewed and behave in political life, no more than one woman in the entire country is positioned, prepared, and has the vaunted fire in the belly to make a serious run for the White House at the close of the twenty-first century's first decade.

Yet this is the situation: a single woman in the United States stands with two feet firmly planted at the entrance to the arena of a presidential race. Popular magazines, running stories on the subject of a woman for president, have profiled several high-placed political women as potential candidates.[21] Women's organizations, seeking to stimulate interest in the idea and required to present more than one name, have carefully offered lists balanced in racial, geographic, and partisan composition. People speculating about the issue bandy about names of female politicians, military officials, business leaders, and celebrities. But extraordinary as she is, Oprah Winfrey is not going to run for president. Neither is Condoleezza Rice. All of that is image and media sport, useful for popularizing the issue and perhaps especially for capturing the attention of girls and women who might otherwise be unaware that when it comes to leadership at even the highest levels, gender history should not have to be political destiny.

Some hard facts come into consideration. The fact is that we do not nominate state cabinet officers, mayors, or even congresspeople for the presidency. Nor do we nominate corporate or foundation executives, university presidents, newspaper editors, or any number of other influential leaders whom we might admire. For largely good reasons—although resulting perhaps in some interesting missed opportunities over time—the structures of our political system have evolved to sift out presidential candidates from among a relatively small group of highly experienced public leaders capable of running a brutally difficult gauntlet to capture a nomination. A number of presidents over the past hundred years began life as elected officials in local or state positions, or in the U.S. House of Representatives, but by the time they won the presidency, the overwhelming majority had held at least one of three offices: the vice presidency, a U.S. Senate seat, a governorship. Only three twentieth-century presidents (two cabinet secretaries and one wartime general) came from other positions.

At one level, therefore, the straightforward answer to the question of why women have not yet been nominated and elected president is that as late as 2007 only twenty-five women, sixteen senators and nine governors, stood in the right line that leads to the White House.[22] Eliminating those who are not native born, or consider themselves too old to run, or do not have a strong political or geographic base for fundraising, organization, delegate votes, and electoral college strength, or plainly have no burning desire to become president, the line just about disappears. Hillary Rodham Clinton is not at the head of a line. She is the line. The real question about women and the presidency is the pipeline question, not only for the highest office in the land but for those offices below it that are short of women.

The reason that only one woman stands at the threshold of a presidential nomination is that only one woman prepared herself to run, and everyone knows it. Heightened journalistic coverage is no random matter. Without a credible, serious candidate in place, the media show little interest in whether and when women break the presidential glass ceiling. Carol Moseley Braun recalls that in 2004, the *New York Times* editorial board interviewed all her male opponents for the Democratic presidential nomination but "did not bother" to give her an interview despite the fact that she had qualified for all the primaries.[23] During the long approach to 2008, the proliferation of print and electronic stories was linked specifically to speculation about a Clinton race.[24] While media attention could provoke musing about whether and when a woman will be elected president—and why it hasn't happened yet—without a credible candidate at the center of the story, too few people would care to make the subject newsworthy.

In the long trek forward and upward, a Hillary Rodham Clinton campaign for the presidency in 2008 bespeaks at least one certainty: she does not run with the organizational, structural, and financial disadvantages of the women who preceded her. They each raised an issue, an image, a challenge, a claim, a conversation, a lament, an item on the nation's political agenda; still, not one of them was truly prepared in the way one must be in modern American presidential politics. Not one of them had built and placed an organization on the ground; not one of them benefited from a blueprint that included a systematic, strategic plan for wresting the nomination from competitors, or for preempting potential would-be competitors. To a greater or lesser extent, all five women who dared to see themselves as presidential material in the forty years between 1964 and 2004 lamented that a lack of money defeated their presidential aspirations. Hillary Rodham Clinton, relentless in raising money, will have a campaign treasury for any political contest she enters; so, too, she enjoys the benefits of a team of tested advisers and loyal staff, a strong organization, and long-range planning. Describing her political organization in early 2006, one journalist went so far as to call it a "vast political empire . . . that, in its scale and ambition, is unrivaled in Democratic politics."[25]

Preparedness is necessary; yet it is never sufficient. The rest is about the political and historic moment at home and around the globe, about personality issues, about the strength of the competition and the forces of opposition, and about timing, chance, accident, and luck; and as always, about the unforeseeable hand of fate.

Endnotes

1. "Every Little Boy Can Be President," music by David Saxon, lyrics by Diane Lampert and Peter Farrow (New York: Sam Fox and Sewanee Music, 1961).

2. Information about the most visible candidates is presented in "Women Presidential and Vice Presidential Candidates," fact sheet from the Center for American Women and Politics, Eagleton Institute of Politics, Rutgers University (www.cawp.rutgers.edu). See the fact sheet for basic information about each of these women, including dates, party affiliations, and brief profiles of the better-known candidates. This sheet is the source of the factual information incorporated in the following thumbnail sketches of several women who ran for

president. It is likely that many additional women put their names forward in local areas or under minor party labels for brief periods during one campaign or another without rising to a level of broad visibility or political significance.

3. The extraordinary life of Victoria Woodhull (1838–1927), an audacious, flamboyant, and notoriously controversial early feminist, is described in Lois Beachy Underhill's *The Woman Who Ran for President: The Many Lives of Victoria Woodhull* (New York: Penguin Books, 1996).

4. Chisholm often repeated her view that her gender had been a bigger obstacle than her race. In an interview with journalists many years later, she confirmed: "'I suffered from two obstacles— I was a black person and I was a woman. . . . I met far more discrimination as a woman in the field of politics. That was a revelation to me. Black men got together to talk about stopping me. . . . They said I was an intellectual person, that I had the ability, but that this was no place for a woman. If a black person were to run, it should be a man.'" Quoted in Eleanor Clift and Tom Brazaitis, *Madam President* (New York: Scribner, 2000), 28.

5. Shirley Chisholm, *The Good Fight* (New York: HarperCollins, 1973; Bantam Books, 1974), 151. *Unbought and Unbossed*, a film documenting the campaign, directed and produced by Shola Lynch, was released in 2004 and premiered on PBS February 2, 2005.

6. Videotaped interview with the author on the occasion of Chisholm's receiving an honorary doctorate from Rutgers University, May 2002.

7. Quoted in Janann Sherman, *No Place for a Woman: A Life of Senator Margaret Chase Smith* (New Brunswick, NJ: Rutgers University Press, 2000), 197.

8. These impressions and the quote ("I like to win") are recorded in notes from a December 9, 1985, interview with Margaret Chase Smith conducted by Ruth B. Mandel and Katherine E. Kleeman at Smith's home in Skowhegan, Maine.

9. Sherman, *No Place for a Woman*, 199.

10. Dole's credibility as a serious candidate was not helped by her husband's comment during a national television interview that he was interested in supporting a different candidate for the presidential nomination.

11. In 2002, Elizabeth Dole did succeed in winning elective office, this time as a U.S. Senator from North Carolina.

12. Congresswoman Geraldine Ferraro's name did appear on the ballot as the Democratic vice presidential nominee in 1984, but voting data have not demonstrated that she made a substantial difference one way or another to the election outcome. American presidential elections have always been about the top of the ticket, with the second slot used to balance the ticket geographically or shore up the loyalty of particular constituencies.

13. A variety of fact sheets with current and historical information about the numbers and status of women holding public office and women as voters are available from the Center for American Women and Politics at the Eagleton Institute of Politics, Rutgers University (www.cawp.rutgers.edu or www.eagleton.rutgers.edu).

14. For discussions of these public opinion data, see among others Hazel Erskine, "The Polls: Women's Role," *Public Opinion Quarterly 35*, no. 2 (Summer 1971): 275–290; Myra Marx Ferree, "A Woman for President? Changing Responses: 1958–1972," *Public Opinion Quarterly 38*, no. 3 (1974): 390–399; E. M. Schreiber, "Education and Change in American Opinions on a Woman for President," *Public Opinion Quarterly 42*, no. 2 (1978): 171–182.

15. CBS News/*New York Times* Poll, "A Woman for President," January 20–25, 2006, press release of February 5, 2006, available online: www.cbsnews.com/htdocs/pdf/020306woman.pdf, access date: December 29, 2006.

16. Perhaps people feel under pressure to express a perceived socially desirable opinion that reflects well on them but

believe their neighbors to be less enlightened. Perhaps they are projecting their real opinions onto their neighbors. However, even with the drop of almost forty points, respondents still believed that a majority of Americans are ready for a woman in the White House.

17. Based on a poll of 1,005 adults conducted September 8–11, 2005, these findings were released by the Gallup Organization on October 4, 2005.

18. Matt Bai, "The Fallback," *New York Times Magazine*, March 12, 2006, 75.

19. While interest in women's roles and status and in changing relations between women and men is now woven into the fabric of contemporary life, it is more at the level of polite social conversation and TV sitcom material than it is a fulcrum for change. After the ERA failed in 1982 to win the last three states for passage of the constitutional amendment, and in 1984 the Democratic ticket with Geraldine Ferraro as vice presidential nominee was defeated, social change issues and progressive activism receded from center stage as the country moved in a conservative direction.

20. I mark the founding of the National Women's Political Caucus in July 1971 as the moment signaling that U.S. women had set a new collective goal for themselves as public citizens—that of seeking their own empowerment in politics and government.

21. In "A Woman for President?" the February 19, 2006, issue of *Parade* magazine included thumbnail sketches of eight experienced political women and encouraged readers to view them as potential presidential candidates.

22. Several former senators and governors would bring the total number up by only single digits.

23. Videotaped interview with the author during Braun's visit to the Center for American Women and Politics at the Eagleton Institute of Politics, Rutgers University, December 8, 2004.

24. Throughout 2006, newspapers and magazines across the country kept tabs on Clinton and regularly reported public opinion polls. *Time* magazine devoted its August 28, 2006, cover story to Hillary Clinton's presidential ambitions. In addition, general stories focusing on the subject of a woman for president have been appearing. See, for example, Anne E. Kornblut, "The Ascent of a Woman: After a Fictional Female President, Are Americans Ready for the Real Thing?" *New York Times*, June 11, 2006, Section 9, 1.

25. Ryan Lizza, "A Guide to the Clinton Juggernaut: Welcome to Hillaryland," *New Republic* online, February 20, 2006. Available online by subscription.

Part Three

Leadership Redefined: Authority, Authenticity, Power

11

LEADERSHIP, AUTHORITY, AND WOMEN

A Man's Challenge

Ronald A. Heifetz

Men who join discussions of leadership and authority in the context of women, however careful and nonpolemical, may encounter outrage. The profound injustices that fuel this outrage go back many lifetimes. Women who today seek equal opportunity and traditionally male roles of prominence and authority often carry both their own experience of injustice and the injustices of the past on their shoulders. They have become repositories for the pent-up frustrations of our ancestors as they champion change in essential elements of our social order. This outrage appears close to the surface particularly when women gather to discuss issues of authority, power, and leadership. It's like static electricity in the air.

A man who steps into this force field is, with the slightest misstep, quite likely to receive an electric jolt. I have seen it happen to many men, even more gentle souls than I, when they are trying their utmost to "get it right." (Yes, I know, Poor Darlings.) Of course, the men who remain hostile to the human rights of women, along with those who haven't thought about it much or who just don't care, do not show up to engage, so they are not around to be challenged. They do not go where this electricity is in the air. Unfortunately, the "friendlies," when they do show up, too often become lightning rods for it and are shocked to be treated as enemies.

This dynamic sometimes takes place in other settings, for example, when a white person works to assist black people or Native Americans, or when young Germans encounter Israelis or American Jews. They often get an earful. It happened to the first prime minister of Poland to visit Israel, Wlodzimierz Cimoszewicz, in January 1997.[1] He expected to be warmly greeted for his heartfelt and singular action, and many people, including Holocaust survivors from Poland, did indeed receive him with sincere and deep appreciation. But he also became the lightning rod for the pent-up outrage of some of the survivors and was taken aback. After all, he was born after the Holocaust and had been demonstrating through courageous political action that he cared deeply about the injustices of that history.

Perhaps when a victimized and suppressed group rediscovers its voice and demands that it be heard, and then encounters someone sympathetic to its experience and views, the resemblance of that person to the enemy makes it likely that he will be placed in a role we might call "the reconstructed, but not yet trustworthy, enemy." Until that person passes several tests of trust, primarily by his capacity to remain graceful as he receives anger and listens with the intent to learn, he remains suspect. It is a worthy role to play in social progress, but not an easy one for men. Most men, I think, do not appreciate the demands of that role, and some recoil when they find out what those demands are.

Moreover, the challenge to men participating in discussions with women on leadership, authority, and power increases because we too easily get caught in a bind between two paradigms of feminism. In one tradition of feminism, prevalent when I came of age in the 1960s, the fight for equal opportunity meant the eradication of differences. Men and women were presumed equal, and the socialization practices that made them look different were targets of activism. When this paradigm frames the discussion, it seems taboo, at least for a man, to talk about the existence of any interesting differences between men and women. In contrast, in a second feminist tradition, the challenge for our social order is to honor the differences, learn and make good use of the differences, create a new order that takes advantage of them, and yet also encourages the complete freedom and right of expression beyond any characterization of difference to whatever extent necessary to achieve human rights.[2] Women, too, it seems to me, are caught between these conflicting paradigms; but perhaps because women trust each other sufficiently, they give themselves permission when these conflicts emerge to stay engaged with each other in spite of the difficulty. In my experience, however, women do not seem predisposed to trust men in these discussions.

I am often caught in this bind. For example, when engaging with women in discussions that draw upon my reflections as a teacher on the challenges men and women face in the practice of leadership and authority, the air of distrust that ensues frequently derails the conversation. Indeed, because I think that there are interesting gender differences to the practice of leadership and authority and that men and women can have much to teach one another, I often trigger the outrage and distrust of the women who subscribe to the "no interesting differences" paradigm. I find that the women representing the second paradigm, the "interesting differences" one, stay quiet, perhaps not wanting to undermine their peers—often their pioneering elders—and the conversation transforms into a symbolic fight in which I represent the typical bad guy who stereotypes women and limits their options. Occasionally, a heroic man will jump in, defending the women who express grievance and competing with me for some form of primal authority. It's usually downhill from there. I cannot recall ever recovering either the topic of conversation or the participation of the whole group when this happens.

For both of these reasons—outrage and paradigmatic conflict—men may find it challenging to speak and write on this subject, and I hope my experience as a teacher, scholar, and consultant will serve to move forward a set of long-overdue conversations. My impressions are meant as suggestions based on my years of working with men and women on the practices of leadership and authority across sectors and regions of the world.

Distinguishing Leadership from Authority

In my reading of the literature on leadership and women, I see authors trapped by the inadequacy of our language. This seems enormously important, because language shapes our thinking, research, and practice.

Our language fails us in the study of leadership as a topic in itself. Nearly every study I have read on leadership in general, and women and leadership in particular, makes the mistake of equating leadership with authority. We make this mistake because our common language has not yet developed a refined set of understandings that distinguish the social phenomena of formal authority, informal authority, and leadership. For example, when we commonly refer to the leaders of a company, a school system, a government, or a nonprofit, we generally mean the people with formal authority. And when we refer to the movers and shakers behind the scenes, or the real sources of influence in an organization or community, we generally mean the people with informal authority. We know intuitively that there is a difference between leadership and authority because we complain frequently about the lack of leadership we get from people in these formal and informal authority positions. But writers and scholars have not yet gained precision in the use of these terms, with significant costs to the identification and analysis of women's leadership.

The benefits of these distinctions are profound. First, distinguishing leadership from authority enables us to engage in "recovering our capacity for authority."[3] Second, we can then draw more usefully on decades of research analyzing the uses of the powers of formal authority, distinguishing them from the persuasive and soft powers of informal authority.[4] Third, these distinctions enable us to analyze the resources and constraints of formal and informal authority on the practice of leadership. And fourth, they enable us to celebrate, learn from, and affirm the vital practice of leadership without and beyond one's authority.

Nearly all studies that refer to leadership and women have little to do with leadership in itself and can be more usefully understood as studies of women in relationship to forms of power and structures of authority.[5] In the study of women, power, and authority, we need to understand the anthropology, sociology, and psychology of authority relationships. To change how power and authority are distributed and practiced, we need to comprehend the value and function of authority structures and relationships so that we begin to understand what we want to change and what we want to conserve. In my midcareer and executive courses on leadership, men and women in every culture have a great deal to teach each other about this question. In a postcolonial society, for example, women may have critically important perspectives on the useful and mistaken practices of authority and can help men generate new models for themselves so that they do not repeat the behaviors of the only models they know, the colonial administrators and the peddlers of influence.

On the other hand, men have important practices that they can teach women because they have been holding positions of formal authority for centuries, often in a trustworthy way. For many men, the demands of serving in roles of authority are ingrained in their socialization. But learning across genders is not easy in either direction and often not readily welcomed. For example, a colleague once described her consulting effort to a prominent women's organization during its 2004 presidential campaign to unseat George Bush. They were trying to figure out, among other things, "How are we going to work the system in Washington?" Of course, a lot of men do, in their bones, understand the workings of Washington, but the organization seemed allergic to asking men for help.

We need to value and to study authority, including ways that women and men practice authority. How can women's insights expand and improve our society's traditional practices? Why have women been excluded from positions of authority? In what ways, and with what kind of training and socialization, can girls and women negotiate and claim more formal and informal authority in environments where boys and men traditionally fill these roles?[6] These are all critically important questions, not only for the welfare of women ambitious for authority and power but also for the welfare of a world that desperately needs new, better, and more trustworthy modes for the exercise of power.

In my experience, women often hesitate, sometimes with shame, to discuss or admit (even to themselves) their ambitions for the hard powers of formal authority and the soft power of informal authority. They hide these ambitions in the more noble-sounding word *leadership*. But keeping these desires under wraps generates a self-defeating dynamic in which many women remain inhibited in trying to get the power they want. This, too, is a critically important subject for study. How do the feelings of guilt or shame regarding power and authority generate paralysis or burnout? How do women use indirect means to get what they want—sometimes successfully but sometimes at great cost to their integrity?

For example, in my classroom I find it very important, though extremely sensitive, to generate discussions about how both men and women compete for proximity to people in high positions of authority. They compete for legitimacy and they compete for attention. Men and women do different dances as they sidle up to authorities in their efforts to bask in reflected glory and draw on referred sources of power. Both risk abusing themselves. For example, one of the techniques women use is beauty and sexual presence. But rarely do women practitioners have the opportunity to discuss the uses and misuses of their physical capacity to draw attention. This, too, should be studied and taken out of the shadows.

All these questions, which seem to me related to the current research on women and what many often think of as leadership, would be advanced considerably by referring to power as power, and by clarifying the concept of authority, its functions and options for practice, and the differences, challenges, and potential contributions within a culture of each gender.

Leadership With and Without Authority

However crucial are their study and practice, neither formal nor informal authority is leadership. My colleagues and I define *leadership* as the activity of mobilizing progress, and we define progress as the work of mobilizing people's adaptive capacity to tackle tough problems and thrive.[7] The concept of *thriving* is a metaphor drawn from adaptation in evolutionary biology, in which a successful adaptation accomplishes three tasks: it preserves essential DNA—the accumulated wisdom of generations; it discards the DNA that no longer serves the current need, and it innovates to develop capacity that enables the organism to thrive in new ways and in challenging environments.[8] A successful adaptation enables a living system to take the best from its history into the future. It is conservative as well as progressive.

Anchoring a conception of leadership in the work of progress—resolving contradictions within our cultural DNA, or between our cultural DNA and the demands of our environment—enables us to view authority and various forms of power as a set of tools and constraints, rather than as ends. They do not define leadership, though they are often central to its practice. The tools are rich and varied, yet the constraints are significant. Clearly, too many individuals in positions of power are not exercising much leadership, and we need to understand far more deeply than we do how the acquiring of authority limits, not just enables, leadership.

In our teaching and consulting, my colleagues and I find that people in authority are generally under enormous pressure to treat adaptive challenges as if they were technical problems to be solved through current structures, norms, and expertise. So common is this source of leadership failure that we call it the *classic error*.[9] Countering these pressures is an art form, which begins to explain why leading from an authority position is difficult, dangerous, and not nearly as common as we might hope.

Aspects of this are gendered. As discussed in the Introduction, what in a man is thought to be assertive can be perceived in a woman to be presumptuous, or harsh.[10] Conversely, a woman who invites inquiry may seem open-minded, whereas a man who invites inquiry may seem confused. Similarly, age and charismatic presence may have different appearances for gender and cultural context and serve different uses to mobilize adaptive work. These generalizations may be inaccurate, but the point is that cultures define the expectations upon which one gains authority, and these may be different for men and women. Women who gain authority will need to understand how to work with their newly won resources and constraints as they vary by gender and culture. And scholars need to help them by studying in context these operational variables to leadership.

In addition to anchoring a conception of leadership in the collective work of progress, rather than in transactional processes of power, influence, and authority, we also find it most useful to view leadership as an activity rather than as a set of personal characteristics, styles, or talents. This view permits a focus on the ways that individuals lead for moments in time, sometimes rarely but significantly, rather than consistently across sectors and eras of a life. Indeed, I don't know of anyone, currently or historically, who has been a leader for all seasons. When leadership is viewed as an activity, we can examine how leadership is distributed, often shared, and how it overlaps, rather than being defined by and limited to the structures of formal and informal authority.

These conceptual clarifications provide the basis then for what is perhaps an even more significant reason for women to distinguish leadership from authority: to highlight, learn from, and encourage the extraordinary number of women who exercise leadership every day, yet do not have any authority. Indeed, if there is anything that women have understood for countless generations, it is leadership without authority.

When we equate and confuse leadership with authority, what are we doing to all of those women and to all of those examples of leadership from which to inspire and learn? As of now, historians and journalists rarely write about them. There are genetic and socialization reasons that explain why we tend to direct our attention upward toward authority in organizational and political structures, but we cannot afford to be entrapped by these patterns of attention.[11] Ignoring leadership without authority does an enormous disservice to the distributed intelligences that make a society adaptive and able to thrive over time.

For example, during her doctoral research on Native American poverty in 1997, Sousan Abadian tried to understand why some tribes had gone from nearly 100 percent alcoholism to 95 percent sobriety. She spoke with a woman I'll call Maggie, who had exercised leadership during the previous ten years in turning her band around. In their conversation, Sousan asked Maggie, "How did you come to think that it would be possible to turn your tribe around, when so many around you were drinking? How did you step out of the box?"

And Maggie told her the following story: "Many years ago I used to baby-sit for Lois, who lived in a neighboring band within our tribe. Once a week I'd go the few miles to her community and take care of Lois's little ones. But after about two months, I started to wonder, 'What could Lois possibly be doing every Tuesday night? There's not much to do around here.' So one evening after Lois left to go to the meeting lodge, I packed up the children and went over there. We looked through a window into the lodge and saw a big circle of chairs, all neatly set in place, with Lois sitting in a chair all by herself. The chairs in the circle were empty.

"I was really curious, you know, so when Lois came home that evening, I asked her, 'Lois, what are you doing every Tuesday night?' And she said, 'I thought I told you weeks ago, I've been holding AA [Alcoholics Anonymous] meetings.' So I asked her again, 'What do you mean you're holding meetings? I went over there tonight with the children and we looked through the window. We watched you sitting there in a circle of chairs, all alone.' Lois got quiet—'I wasn't alone,' she said. 'I was there with the spirits and the ancestors; and one day, our people will come.' "

Lois never gave up. Maggie continued, "Every week Lois set up those chairs neatly in a circle, and for two hours, she just sat there. No one came to those meetings for a long time, and even after three years, there were only a few people in the room. But ten years later, the room was filled with people. The community began turning around. People began ridding themselves of alcohol. I felt so inspired by Lois that I couldn't sit still watching us poison ourselves."

In their leadership, the two women were initially mocked and marginalized. They acted before they had any collaborators or so-called followers; for stretches of time, they had none. They spent years feeling out of place in their own communities, unwelcome at parties and gatherings where alcohol flowed. Indeed, they spent weekends off the reservation to find people with whom they could talk. They had put themselves, as well as significant relationships with neighbors, friends, and family, at risk. They led without authority and, eventually, they succeeded. But for a long time, they could not know.[12]

The world is full of people like Maggie and Lois. And I expect that many readers will recognize themselves and others in stories like theirs. Jane Mansbridge, in her research on "everyday feminism," is showing us that the world is full of women who have exercised leadership, sometimes only at key moments, and sometimes in sustained efforts, but quietly without notice, until they happened to bump into Jane Mansbridge and her notebook.[13] So to equate leadership with authority, as if the highest aspiration for women should somehow be calibrated by levels of political or organizational authority and the traditional values of men competing for them, does injustice to all of these not just heroic people, but people practicing necessary everyday leadership.

If the health of a society requires enlightened leadership only from the people at the top of organizations, or at the top of our political apparatus, we are in trouble. We are then in what Dr. Seuss describes as "The Waiting Room," waiting for the occasional philosopher-queen or philosopher-king who can pull rabbits out of the hat.[14] That mode of dependency and waiting is dangerous. Adaptability requires variability, because you never know who, in a changing environment, has the capacity to take us into the future. In many businesses, for example, the chief bottlenecks to growth and adaptability are the quality and distribution of leadership. Our organizations and communities need leadership with and without authority.

Women have practiced leadership without authority forever, and if the lessons from this rich experience were identified and articulated, an enormous contribution to the practice of leadership would be available to inspire women anew and to teach men to lead in a flattening world.

Learning Further Across the Boundaries of Gender Difference

Men and women have much to teach one another in many additional areas of practice. For example, the idea that leadership is about developing the adaptive capacity of others—so that people in groups and communities can shoulder problems, organize themselves, and independently meet an ongoing stream of challenges in the future—often sits more naturally with women than men. Men seem often to operate with the cultural assumption that leadership is about authoritative action and the decisive and subtle mobilization of what needs to be done. Men often operate with the notion that leadership means "having a vision," and the rest is a sales problem in motivation, inspiration, negotiation, and sometimes command. The idea that leadership operates in situations that demand adaptability—pulling people together, not having the answers, not rushing to closure, listening carefully, generating creative ideas, and nurturing the capacity of people to take collective responsibility to solve problems—falls more naturally in my experience with women than with men. Women have a lot to teach men about getting comfortable with a feeling of "not knowing," having the patience to listen, and not rushing to decision.

Moreover, women have something to teach men about the value of relationships as an end rather than as a means—the wisdom that women have long known—that men have begun to legitimize for themselves through language by calling it "social capital."

Of course, in pulling people together across boundaries to engage in adaptive work, one is also begging for conflict. The tough issues are tough because they often involve losses when roles need redefinition, areas of incompetence need exposure, and loyalties require refashioning. Those stakes generate conflict, because adaptive solutions are often not wholly positive in sum. As Rhode and Kellerman discuss in the Introduction, a wide variety of research suggests that men are more comfortable with conflict than women in most settings relevant for leadership.[15] Men are more comfortable competing in games, in work, and in the marketplace. Women do not as commonly see conflict as a source of creativity, innovation, change, and learning. They often perceive conflict as a threat to relationships, rather than as a resource in relationships. So in the practice of orchestrating conflict, men have something to teach women.

Both men and women, in my experience, tend sometimes to compartmentalize the lessons from different facets of their lives and fail to apply them across sectors within their lives. Both have difficulty, for example, distinguishing role from self, and therefore knowing when not to take both idealization and hostility personally. Men seem to have more trouble not taking it personally when their kids misbehave and turn nasty at home. Women seem to have more trouble not taking it personally as they enter the traditional men's organization and take grief there. Each can help the other. Of course, women have always helped men calm down and regain perspective when the kids are tough to be around. What's new is that women have a lot to learn from men about doing this at work: how not to take it personally when your project is tossed out, your presentation critiqued, or you lose the argument. At the same time, women could do one another an enormous service by helping each other translate what they know from the traditional role sectors of their lives to the new.

Finally, to continue with my initial theme—a man's challenge— I suggest that women spend more time understanding men. At the risk of sounding like a typically narcissistic male, I think that research on leadership, authority, and women is sorely in need of investigating, to use a cardboard phrase, "the opposition." At a minimum, if this were a military strategy session in which we were planning a campaign to increase the opportunities for women in roles men traditionally inhabit, we would want to know the enemy very, very well. In my reading of the research on women's rights and social action, I see many outstanding and insightful studies about women, but very few about men. How can we prepare women to compete with men for positions of authority without more deeply appreciating the context in which men operate?

I am surprised at how little discussion or curiosity there seems to be about the nature of the changes women want men to make. It is as if women assume they understand men already. But men are not as simple as women sometimes suggest, and the functions men serve in anchoring authority systems across sectors, institutions, and cultures are complex and demand sophistication. Do women understand these demands, and the costs to men of the social changes they seek? The justice of the cause should not lead us to discount as trivial the demands of replacing or reinventing the functions men serve, or the set of losses and disloyalties we are asking men to accept and manage. If these demands and losses were trivial, the desired changes would not take decades. At its extreme, the frequent violence by men against women as women find their voices suggests that the perceived and real losses women are asking men to take, here and around the world, are profound. You and I might see the benefit to mankind, once we get over the mountain pass, but most men haven't seen that new land, and they also know that some of them are not going to make it over that pass. Women need to invite men into their circle, at least as objects of study.

Let me give an example from a pivotal moment in my own career when I began to discover these pains of change from a woman's experience. Early on, as a doctor, I worked in the King's County Hospital emergency room in Brooklyn, New York. One night, a woman named Alice came in beat-up and bruised by her boyfriend. I did what I knew how to do: I patched her up and gave her the obvious solution. I said to her, "Leave your boyfriend. Leave the guy." A month later, she came back bruised again, and I did the same thing.

The third time Alice came in, six weeks later, her head was injured, and we held her in the emergency room overnight for observation. Again, she was lucky: nothing was broken. When it became quiet after midnight, I sat down at her bedside and this time, instead of telling her to leave her boyfriend, I asked Alice, "Why are you with him?" And she told me. She gave me three clear, powerful reasons that made me realize how hard a change this was going to be, and why the remedy was way beyond my expertise—the experiences of direct loss, disloyalty, and incompetence.

First she said, "He loves me." And I said, "Well maybe you could find a guy who can love you just as well, but doesn't drink and get violent." And she said, "Well, where am I supposed to find him?"

I began to see that to change her ways, Alice was going to have to go through a sustained period of direct loss with no guarantee of finding anyone better. And in the hope of finding someone better, who was going to hold her through the uncertainty and loneliness and help her learn to find new resources in herself and in new relationships to make life worthwhile?

And then Alice gave me the second reason. She said, "You know, my mother has stayed true to my father for thirty years. And he gets drunk and beats her once in a while. *But she's never gotten that badly hurt*. Isn't that the right thing to do, to be true to your man?"

I began to realize what is going to happen if Alice breaks up with her boyfriend, Jack, and then goes home to visit her parents on a Sunday morning? Her mother is going to say, "Where's Jack? He's such a nice guy. We love having him around." How can Alice learn to say to her mother, "You loved me really well. You taught me so much. But you also modeled tolerating abuse I should never tolerate." Those are hard words to discover and say in any way, let alone effectively. In her heart, Alice would probably go through an experience of betrayal. And she might in fact be accused of betrayal by her mother, until she found a way to reconnect with her and refashion their loyalty. And what would happen if Alice goes into the living room that morning to visit with her father? And her father says, "Where is Jack? We refilled the ice chest yesterday, and I was looking forward to having some beers and watching the game with him later." What is she going to say? "Dad, you never abused me, but you abused Mother. She should have kicked you out until you got better."

Alice and I kept talking for a while longer, and she gave me the third reason she stayed with Jack. She said, "I know how to go into a bar and meet a guy. You're telling me to talk to a guy who just drinks coffee. I don't know how to talk to a guy like that. I don't know how to act." I think she was telling me that she was going to feel incompetent. I was telling her to learn new moves, but during her first two visits to the Emergency Room, I hadn't a clue to the nature of this challenge. Who was going to teach Alice these moves and help sustain her confidence when she felt, perhaps for a long time, incompetent?

Alice taught me that people don't resist change—what they resist is *loss*. When we think change is a good thing for us, we don't tend to resist. Nobody gives back a winning lottery ticket. People resist the various forms of loss that sometimes accompany change. Alice taught me how to begin to know and disaggregate these forms of loss. Practitioners of leadership need also to comprehend the losses they are asking people to sustain in order to achieve a better way.

In my reading of the women's literature on leadership, and in my participation at conferences on women and leadership, I do not think women scholars have achieved a deep understanding of, or any real compassion for, the nature of the change women are asking men to sustain. Nor have they generated an adequate theory of authority to replace or improve the traditional practices of men. Perhaps the outrage gets in the way, coupled with the prevailing assumption, "Men are simple creatures; we know what we're dealing with."

I cannot blame women for losing compassion. The injustices are searing. And we all fall prey to confusing familiarity with comprehension. But nothing justifies, morally or strategically, arrogant assumptions. I do not see how women can change men and social structure if they do not deeply understand the social functions that ride on men's shoulders, and the losses, disloyalties, and incompetence men would need to move through. We need ethnographic and statistical studies where we get to know and to understand, with our heads, analytically, and with our hearts, compassionately, what we are asking to be changed, both in women and in men. Women claiming power and positions of authority need strategies to lead men to move through disorientation into a world that, in retrospect, men might want, too.

Endnotes

1. Personal communication, Warsaw, May 1999.
2. Betty Friedan, *The Second Wave* (New York: Summit, 1981).
3. Teresa Monroe at the University of San Diego designed a course that we co-taught at Harvard from 1992 through 1995: "Exercising Authority: Power, Strategy, and Voice." These concepts were central to her design.
4. See Richard E. Neustadt, *Presidential Power and the Modern Presidents*, 3rd ed. (New York: Free Press, 1991); Joseph S. Nye Jr., *Soft Power: The Means to Succeed in World Politics* (New York: Perseus BBS Public Affairs, 2004); the large tradition of management literature spurred by Chester Barnard's *The Functions of the Executive* (Cambridge, MA: Harvard University Press, 1938), or the many curricular materials from the Department of Behavioral Science and Leadership, U.S. Military Academy at West Point.
5. For examples, see Deborah L. Rhode, ed., *The Difference "Difference" Makes: Women and Leadership* (Stanford, CA: Stanford University Press, 2003).
6. See Kathleen McGinn and Hannah Riley Bowles, "Claiming Authority: Negotiating Challenges for Women Leaders," in Devid Messick and Roderick M. Kramer, eds., *The Psychology of Leadership: New Perspectives and Approaches* (Mahwah, NJ: Erlbaum, 2004).
7. See Dean Williams, *Real Leadership* (San Francisco: Berrett-Koehler, 2005); Ronald A. Heifetz and Marty Linsky, *Leadership on the Line: Staying Alive Through the Dangers of Leading* (Boston: Harvard Business School Press, 2002); Ronald A. Heifetz, *Leadership Without Easy Answers* (Cambridge, MA: Belknap/Harvard University Press, 1994), and Ronald Heifetz and Riley Sinder, "Political Leadership: Mobilizing the Pub-

lic's Problem-Solving," in Robert Reich, ed., *The Power of Public Ideas* (Boston: Ballinger, 1988; Cambridge, MA: Harvard University Press, 1990).

8. The terms *discard* and *innovate* are simplifying metaphors to describe a variety of biological processes that change genetic material and how it's regulated. See "An Analysis of the Concept of Natural Selection," in Ernst Mayr, *Toward a New Philosophy of Biology: Observations of an Evolutionist* (Cambridge, MA: Belknap/Harvard University Press, 1988), 95–115, or Marc W. Kirschner and John C. Gerhart, *The Plausibility of Life: Resolving Darwin's Dilemma* (New Haven, CT: Yale University Press, 2005).

9. Ronald A. Heifetz and Donald L. Laurie, "The Work of Leadership," *Harvard Business Review*, January-February 1997.

10. See also Alice H. Eagly, Mona G. Makhijani, and Bruce G. Klonsky, "Gender and the Evaluation of Leaders," *Psychological Bulletin 111* (1992): 17; Jeanette N. Cleveland, Margaret Stockdale, and Kevin R. Murphy, *Women and Men in Organizations: Sex and Gender Issues at Work* (Mawah, NJ: Erlbaum, 2000), 106, 107.

11. See Heifetz, *Leadership Without Easy Answers*, Chapter 3: "The Roots of Authority."

12. This story is adapted from Sousan Abadian, "From Wasteland to Homeland: Trauma and the Renewal of Indigenous Communities in North America," doctoral dissertation, Harvard University, 1999. The names have been changed and the story altered to maintain confidentiality. It was published in Heifetz and Linsky, *Leadership on the Line*, 9–11.

13. Jane Mansbridge, *Everyday Feminism*, currently in manuscript.

14. Dr. Seuss, *Oh, the Places You'll Go!* (New York: Random House, 1990).

15. See also Linda Babcock and Sara Leschever, *Women Don't Ask: Negotiation and the Gender Divide* (Princeton, NJ: Princeton University Press, 2003); Pat Heim, *Hardball for Women: Winning at the Game of Business* (New York: Penguin, 1992).

12

BRINGING YOUR WHOLE SELF TO WORK

Lessons in Authentic Engagement from Women Leaders

Laura Morgan Roberts

In the twenty-first-century U.S. business world, authenticity has become one of the highest virtues. A 2001 *Ad Week* poll asked adults to choose—from a list of positive qualities—what they would most like to be known for, and half the respondents said "being authentic" was the most desired personal quality, with "being intelligent" and "having a sense of humor" each drawing only 22 percent of the votes. The single most important trait that 61 percent of adults reported they would require in a lifelong companion was "authenticity"; "intelligence" was named in only 24 percent of responses. Capturing the quality of this phenomenon, Lionel Billing referred to authenticity as the "moral slang of our day."[1]

Indeed, the notion of authenticity has become a symbol of self-knowledge and moral integrity. *Authenticity* refers to the degree of congruence between internal values and external expressions. As a psychological construct, authenticity reflects general values of knowing, accepting, and remaining true to one's self by acting in accord with one's principles.[2] Some researchers see authenticity as especially important for women's and minorities' position in groups and have extended the definition to include the act of countering pressures to suppress one's social identity, and openly claiming one's race, gender, sexual orientation, religious background, or social class, among other social categories.[3]

Recent academic literature finds value in authenticity, particularly in current U.S. personal and professional life.[4] Authenticity for women in the workplace offers both benefits and disadvantages. Authenticity facilitates the development of intimate relationships, as it helps people to build more complex, accurate, and appreciative understandings of each other's characteristics, experiences, feelings, values, and cultural backgrounds.[5] Moreover, bringing one's "whole self" to a welcoming work environment enables individuals to reach maximal effectiveness, productivity, and performance.[6] When people fail to express their true feelings and beliefs, they may suffer psychological and relational costs including tension, anxiety, and alienation.[7] Hewlett and her colleagues at the Center for Work Life Policy conclude from their research on minority executives: "For many [professionals of color], the need to 'render invisible' their real identities has exacted a huge toll. For a substantial number, covering up and staying below the radar has produced isolation, alienation and disengagement—with predictable effects on commitment and performance."[8] Suppressing one's authentic self can have dramatic consequences, so it is important to uncover strategies for enhancing authenticity in the workplace.

The goal of this chapter is to illustrate the ways in which many women leaders have overcome these struggles and authentically engage their identities as a source of strength. First, I describe the potential conflict between individuals' desire for authenticity and corporations' need for cohesion. I then propose that individuals and organizations might mutually benefit through focusing on sources of strength and offering a constructive opportunity for authentic engagement at work. To illustrate authentic engagement, I feature three women leaders who drew upon aspects of their professional and cultural identities as sources of strength. By authentically engaging many facets of their identities, these women were able to contribute in unique and valuable ways to organizations in the for-profit and not-for-profit sectors. Based on these case studies, I propose directions for future research and practice that might enhance authentic engagement at work. To conclude, I propose what is needed to create an organization that authentically engages the strengths of women and men of all cultural backgrounds.

A Premium on Authenticity in the Twenty-First Century

The changing nature of work has heightened the value of authenticity. Increasing competition in a global marketplace has led to organizational restructuring and shorter-term staffing arrangements.[9] In response, the terms of the psychological contract between American workers and their employers have shifted from conformity and security to flexibility and fulfillment. During the mid to late twentieth century, for example, workers were expected to conform to corporate culture, prioritizing the company's interests above their own while keeping personal and family interests separate and subordinate to their work role. In exchange, workers were offered long-term job security, stability, and opportunities for advancement within a single organization.

Work practices in the twenty-first century, in contrast, are characterized by fewer boundaries between one's job and one's life outside work. Flexible work arrangements, global teams, and technological innovations create the possibility for contact between workers and their employing organizations at any time of the day or night. Organizations offer considerably less job security, as mergers and acquisitions, downsizing, outsourcing, and the use of contingent workers have decreased the average tenure of employees. With these new work practices, a new psychological contract is emerging that places a higher premium on generating short-term results than on demonstrating lifelong loyalty to one's employer. In exchange, more workers expect to gain opportunities for personal growth and career advancement by developing transferable skills and experiencing fulfillment in each position they hold.[10]

The emerging psychological contract is based on a delicate balance of authenticity, conformity, diversity, and homogeneity. Employees' growing need for self-expression and self-fulfillment may challenge the organization's need for control, standardization, and predictability. Norms, standards, and routines facilitate collaboration among workers from diverse backgrounds.[11] Yet authenticity, diversity, and positive deviance foster maximal engagement, flexibility, and innovation.[12] Under this new psychological contract, employers and employees alike can find common ground by strategically engaging the unique strengths that individuals bring to their diverse workforce and customer base.

Authentic Engagement Through Strategic Use of Strengths

Strategically applying strengths provides a constructive opportunity for individuals to experience authentic engagement in their work; it lessens the focus on fitting into standardized job and organizational requirements so employees can focus more on making unique and valuable contributions to their workplaces.[13] This focus on identifying and making the most of strengths is rooted in the paradigm of "positive scholarship."[14] Positive scholarship is an organizing frame for research in various social science disciplines (for example, psychology, organizational behavior, and social work) that invites scholars to critically examine positive states, outcomes, dynamics, and generative mechanisms to learn from what is working well.[15] Much of this work on positive scholarship emphasizes the development of individual and collective strengths and how they allow humans to flourish.[16]

Scholars and practitioners suggest that it is not only important for leaders to make the most of their employees' unique strengths, they also need to bring their own unique strengths and authentic selves to their leadership roles.[17] Authentic leadership has numerous positive connotations, including self-confidence, genuineness, reliability, trustworthiness, a deep awareness of one's values and beliefs, a focus on building followers' strengths, and an ability to create a positive and engaging organizational context.[18] Goffee and Jones claim authenticity is the attribute that uniquely defines great leaders.[19] As a result, they encourage leaders to painstakingly earn and carefully manage their reputation for authenticity. This literature suggests that authentic leadership requires more than just doing what comes naturally. Rather, leaders must be intentional about bringing their whole selves to work as a source of strength.

Women Leaders and Authentic Engagement

Authentic engagement with work and people is especially important for women leaders. Many women leaders add value to organizations by strategically applying the strengths they have cultivated through their professional, gendered, and cultural experiences. Certain feminist scholars emphasize the unique attributes women leaders bring to the traditionally masculine workplace.[20] For instance, in *Closing the Leadership Gap*, Wilson writes: "Women will add [to government and business] their own recipe of strong values—inclusion, communication across lines of authority, the work of caring, relationship building—all of which would increase satisfaction and productivity everywhere."[21]

Other scholars have chosen to deemphasize the role that gendered and sociocultural experiences play in shaping leadership competencies, focusing instead on personality attributes and professional experiences.[22] I posit that all aspects of identity influence work goals, style, and practices. It is difficult to disentangle the strengths or core competencies one has developed as a function of work experiences from those that have been formed through socialization as a member of social identity groups. Given the embedded nature of interpersonal and intergroup encounters, social identity categories are inextricably linked to the ways in which people define themselves and one another in the workplace.[23] Moreover, social identity group memberships offer an interpretive framework for individuals to view problems, envision possibilities, and approach tasks at work. Organizations will fall short of making full use of their diverse talent pool if they do not recognize these social identities as a source of strength. Discounting strengths constrains the potential for authentic engagement at work.

Yet, in making this claim, I would caution against setting rigid standards and norms for behavior that all women leaders should embody. Such norms create unrealistic expectations that are based upon idealized images of womanhood and femininity.[24] The unqualified reification of these images may pressure women to lead lives that emphasize dependency, nurturance, and compliance even when those are not authentic qualities of the individual. Moreover, as Rhode argues, these traditionally valued traits may perpetuate inequality; while these assets are valued in the home, they are used as reasons to marginalize women in the workplace.[25]

Femininity, when not idealized, can be empowering.[26] Research on aspiring women leaders reveals that they feel empowered and are "at their best" when they engage their strengths in a way that brings them personal gratification and generates a constructive experience or outcome for others.[27] The personal experience of gratification can be an indicator that one takes joy or pride in developing her strengths to rise above challenges and generate desired results.[28] Some experiences are characterized by the feeling of elation, entering into a flow state of effortless engagement, where one loses all sense of time and boundaries.[29] Even if the experience is challenging, as when dealing with illness, loss, or conflict, one may take pride in one's own conduct in the wake of failure or difficulty.

Best-self moments reach beyond personal gratification or fulfillment to qualify the impact of one's actions on others. To engage one's strengths constructively, an external or *ecocentric* orientation is critical.[30] In contrast to an egocentric orientation, where people are driven primarily by the need to protect their self-image, those with an ecocentric orientation act to protect or contribute to a system that is larger than they are. They do not view their own success or happiness in zero-sum terms, feeling that they can only experience happiness at the expense of others. Rather, when they operate in this best-self zone, they envision their success as inextricably linked to the success of those around them.

Common examples of women at their best are those who work in the media and entertainment industry. These women are able to brand and showcase their unique talents of singing (Jessica Simpson), acting (Hilary Swank), dancing (Paula Abdul), modeling (Tyra Banks), decorating (Martha Stewart), and public speaking (Oprah Winfrey). In the ways in which they present themselves, they authentically engage their identities as a source of strength to generate personal gratification and social impact. For example, Oprah Winfrey states,

> When you get me, you are not getting an image. You are not getting a figurehead. You're not getting a theme song. You're getting all of me. And I bring all of my stuff with me: my history, my past, Mississippi, Nashville. I'm coming in with the sistahs in the church, I'm bringing Sojourner Truth with me. . . . The greatest thing about what I do is that I'm in a position to change people's lives. It is the most incredible platform for influence that you could imagine. [I want] people to see within each show that you are responsible for your life, that although there may be tragedy in your life, there's always a possibility to triumph. The ability to triumph begins with you.[31]

Oprah speaks of how her authenticity is reinforced by her willingness to embrace all aspects of her identity. For example, her strengths in public speaking are grounded in her personal history as an African American woman from the South. Intertwining her identity with her work enables her to inspire people to transform their lives.

How do women who aren't employed in the media and entertainment industry create opportunities to bring their whole selves to work? I offer three case studies of women leaders at their best to illustrate how they authentically engaged their professional, gendered, and cultural experiences to inspire their leadership vision and inform their leadership practice. Each woman's career is characterized by remarkable accomplishment: Jeanette Clough, a hospital CEO, led a dramatic turnaround from the brink of bankruptcy to expansion; Bennie Wiley, a nonprofit CEO, built a nationally renowned organization around her passion for inclusion and holism; and Josie Esquivel, a star research analyst, was considered among the top 5 percent of analysts in her sector for thirteen consecutive years on Wall Street.[32]

I employ case studies to provide concrete examples of how these three women led authentically during periods in their careers. These examples help to anchor the positive descriptions of authentic leaders in the business and career challenges they face. By focusing on these leadership cases, we are better able to understand how women can draw upon aspects of their personal identity to define who they are and what they do as leaders of an organization, community, profession, or industry. The following descriptions of Clough, Wiley, and Esquivel illustrate how women leaders take actions that build on their strengths by mobilizing others to achieve joint successes, connecting with others to foster high-quality relationships, and passionately pursuing their goals.[33] Each woman led authentically by engaging aspects of her professional background, gender, culture, and social location to direct her vision, strategy, and style.

Jeanette Clough: The Mobilizer

Jeanette Clough, CEO of Mount Auburn Hospital in Cambridge, Massachusetts, was called upon to mobilize all of the hospital's key constituents to turn the struggling community-based teaching hospital around. Clough was a surprise choice to lead the hospital, as she had a nontraditional background as a registered nurse rather than as a medical doctor. Born in Manhattan and raised in New Jersey, Clough had always been interested in medicine. She graduated from the Boston University School of Nursing in 1975 and began working as a staff nurse in the surgical and later in the cardiac surgical departments at Massachusetts General Hospital (MGH). She was promoted to nursing manager in 1978 and then to staff development specialist by 1982. Clough also completed two master's degrees in science and health administration during that time.

In 1988, Clough left MGH to become director of nursing at Waltham Hospital, a community hospital located in a western suburb of Boston. Clough became acting CEO of the hospital when the president was let go in 1991. A permanent CEO was appointed, and Clough directed the hospital's operations as COO from 1992 to 1995. In 1995, she was selected to be the new chief executive officer of Waltham Hospital by the Board of CareGroup, the health care management organization that oversaw Waltham and other hospitals in the Boston area. Clough remained CEO at Waltham Hospital until 1998.

That same year, Clough was invited to apply for the CEO position at Mount Auburn Hospital. When she applied, the hospital reported a $10 million deficit. Several CareGroup executives thought that the hospital could not sustain itself for much longer; some predicted that it would go bankrupt within thirty-six months. The physical plant was aging and areas of the hospital had become dilapidated. Clough was asked to take control of this dire situation, in part because of her medical background and ability to work well with physicians.

Clough experienced numerous challenges to her credibility as CEO. To start, she succeeded an interim CEO who was very well regarded by the medical and administrative staff of the hospital. The chief of Emergency Medicine said of the interim CEO, "He was a physician, he spoke the language, he knew the problems. Nothing came easy. We still had the deficits and the like, but he had a way of communicating with everybody that was much different than with the previous regime."

Clough found the hospital staff to be just as skeptical as the rest of the medical staff, who were upset that they had lost a CEO who had actually listened to them. During her first six months, several members of the senior leadership team quit, including the CFO, the VP of Nursing, the head of Development, the head of Human Resources, the head of Volunteers, and the head of Security. Clough also encountered doubts surrounding her identity as a woman and nurse. She remembers: "There was a lot of, 'Who is this lady? She's a nurse. She's young, and she's from Waltham for God's sake.' They thought that Waltham was absolutely no comparison to Mount Auburn, a Harvard teaching hospital in Cambridge. So my previous leadership experience didn't really win me any points with a lot of the people here." Thus the very factors that build credibility for many new leaders—prior CEO experience and technical expertise in medicine—were potential liabilities for Clough, due to her association with what others perceived to be lower-status institutions and occupations.

From the moment she accepted the position, Clough worked actively to establish her credibility using open and honest communication. Her opening speech included the following statements:

> Here are some of the things you can expect from me: I will communicate with you often and I will tell you the truth. The truth will sometimes be difficult to hear but it will be the truth. I will set very high expectations within the organization, and I will do whatever it takes to help you achieve these high standards. I will advocate for you and for the care that you provide the community to anyone and everyone.
>
> Here are some things I expect from you: treat your patients and their families as you would like to see your own family members treated. We have the honor of serving patients in their times of greatest need and we must constantly remember that amidst all the clatter of health care these days, that they come first. . . . Maintain a positive attitude about your work and your role in the organization. It's not easy in health care these days, but over time we will find the answers and try to have some fun along the way.

Clough's speech set the stage for her transparent, collaborative approach to change, focusing first and foremost on patient care. She emphasized that financial viability is a means to improving patient care, rather than an end unto itself, which was consistent with her experience as an RN. Clough brought the same careful, detail-oriented approach to resuscitating the struggling hospital that she would have used to manage a patient in cardiac arrest as an RN. From her background, she was also very skilled at building trust and credibility with key constituents: the trustees, the medical staff, and the employees. Every month after her arrival, Clough worked in a different area of the hospital. She rotated through many departments, including medical records, radiology, critical care, and even the kitchen. Every Wednesday, Clough convened the medical leadership, including the VP of Nursing, the COO, and the chiefs of departments, to have an ongoing dialogue on medical issues at the hospital. The business metrics of every department were put on the table, and each department chair was made aware of challenges across the various departments.

Soon, Clough's colleagues began to sing her praises. For example, the chief of Emergency Medicine commented: "Jeanette has been able to understand the strategic needs of the hospital and she has a unique ability to pull people together. At the same time, it's not always warm and fuzzy; sometimes it's pretty cold and direct. In a meeting she'll say, 'Why are we going on diversion at times when the hospital has open beds?' I will be held personally accountable though it may not be my personal problem, but I'm the department chair and I'm expected to fix that."[34] The chief of Radiology remarked: "Of at least five CEOs that I've seen at this hospital, Jeanette is the most effective. The reason she was more effective than her predecessors is because she would listen to the doctors and try to get a sense from them how they saw the hospital and what they thought they needed to be more successful doing their work. It doesn't require a huge amount of brainpower to figure out that you [the hospital CEO] will be more successful if your doctors are more successful."

Clough's mobilizing efforts paid off. By rallying the medical and administrative staff, she reduced Mount Auburn's deficit by 50 percent in the first year. By 2004, the hospital reported three consecutive years of multimillion-dollar operating margins. Clough had revitalized the organization, repairing and building new relationships between the administration and physicians, and forming strategic alliances with organizations outside the hospital. Moreover, the hospital gained community support for its capital campaign to fund renovation and expansion.

Clough's leadership is indicative of the power of authenticity; she maintains her integrity by drawing upon her professional identity as a former nurse to enhance her role as a change agent. Clough's gender is also a relevant dimension of the identity that she brings to work. In Alvesson and Billing's words, "Gender is not simply imported into the workplace; gender itself is constructed in part through work."[35]

To fully appreciate Clough's authenticity, it is important to note the gendered and status implications of her nursing background, which is that of a subordinated role in the masculine context of an elite teaching hospital. The fact that she was a former nurse probably amplified the salience of her gender and widened the gap between Clough and typical hospital CEOs. Yet through her nursing experience, she had learned how to marshal resources and influence decisions for patient care, even if she didn't have the highest status or credentials within the hospital. As CEO, Clough used these mobilizing practices to lead the hospital authentically through its dramatic turnaround.

Benaree "Bennie" Wiley: The Bridge Builder

Bennie Wiley was appointed CEO and president of The Partnership, Inc., in March 1991. The Partnership began in 1987 with a group of civic and business leaders who were united by a desire to reduce racial tension in Boston and increase diversity among Boston's business leaders. When Wiley took office, The Partnership suffered from a lack of unity on its Board and an unclear mission. In addition, Wiley inherited a number of financial challenges, including a $100,000 debt to the landlord of the office.

Like Clough, Wiley had a personal and professional background that shaped her change agenda and leadership style. As one of the few African American graduates of the Harvard Business School (MBA 1972), Wiley brought a wealth of management consulting and entrepreneurial experience when she joined The Partnership. She had worked for both private and nonprofit organizations to build their capacity and refine their program delivery, and had served on a number of nonprofit boards. With a staff of one (an administrative assistant), Wiley built the organization from the ground up, using her ability to build relationships as the basis for growth. She spent hours meeting with more than seventy board members, sponsors, and participants in The Partnership's programs during her first ninety days on the job. Step by step, she helped clarify the mission and build the infrastructure necessary for the organization to expand its services and articulate the value added to sponsoring partners. She recalls: "I listened a lot and used my consulting skills, coupled with a heavy dose of market research. As a result of my Cambridge-centered management consulting focus, I felt somewhat disconnected from the Boston business community. I think this worked to my advantage as I didn't bring any baggage with me or have any preconceived ideas. I used this period of research to start building relationships and a rapport with a very large network of supporters."

Wiley saw her inexperience in the Boston business community as an opportunity for her to put her bridge-building skills into action. Next, she turned her attention to strategy, applying her consulting and entrepreneurial skills to change the brand and core programs of The Partnership. Before Wiley came to The Partnership, its programs were funded by charitable donations. Under Wiley's direction, The Partnership began to charge corporations for its leadership development programs. It gained recognition as a resource for local corporations who were willing to invest in recruiting, developing, and retaining a racially diverse workforce. Former participants lauded The Partnership's year-long leadership development programs, naming them as a primary reason they remained in the Boston area.

Along with her business experience, Wiley's respect for living an authentic, balanced life shaped her career decisions, leadership style, and The Partnership's programming. For example, when her first child was born, Wiley opted to work part time, an unorthodox request for women in business in 1976. Wiley was attracted to The Partnership because of its close alignment with her own values and experiences. For Wiley, success began with having a strong and healthy family life, being intellectually engaged, and having an impact. She built her own life on what she termed a holistic basis, blending the importance of professional, personal, and civic involvement.

She took the same holistic approach as she started to build The Partnership's program offerings. She explains:

> I lost my mother when I was only two years old, which had a profound impact on me. I knew that having a balance between being intellectually challenged yet having my children be an important part of whatever I did was very important. I wanted to experience what my mother had not had an opportunity to experience. During that period, while I was primarily focused on raising my children, I was able to negotiate flexible schedules with consulting firms and was very active as a volunteer where I ultimately took on leadership roles, such as becoming chair of The Children's Museum. I believe I developed more leadership skills from my volunteer work than my involvement with business. By 1991 my children were in high school and the opportunity to do something more intense felt right. The Partnership was the right opportunity at the right time. I knew I liked working with young people, I liked running my own operation, and I liked building things.

One Board member, who was also a former Partnership program participant, reflects on Wiley's authentic leadership:

> Bennie has provided The Partnership with what I would call "real authentic leadership." She has been very interested in creating substance and integrity for all the programs. For Bennie there are no "quick hits." She is methodical; she understands that good things

need to be developed over time and evolve. She has developed and raised The Partnership with all of the care that she has shown in raising her own children! Bennie is very giving of herself. Not only of her time, but also of her ideas and experience. She would readily share her life story and some of the tradeoffs that she has made. I think of her philosophy as being "stay true to your values; work hard and good things will happen." She pushed us to think about life in all of its complexity, rather than just focusing on our work. For each career decision, she encouraged us to think about the impact it would have on our life.

As a woman of color, Wiley appreciated the value of inclusion and social networks for ethnic minorities' career success and quality of life. She emphasized the relational benefits of Partnership participation, and also modeled these practices of inclusion and networking in her leadership style.

Wiley was even able to unify the Board of Directors, several of whom saw themselves as having competing interests when Wiley joined The Partnership. Another Board member attested to Wiley's strengths in connecting with program participants, corporate sponsors, Board members, and staff: "One of Bennie's real strengths is that she knows how to build coalitions and just zoom in on what drives people to get things done. Bennie truly knows how to engage her Board members. She knows each of us intimately. She will enter a Board meeting with a strong, well-developed strategic point of view and lead the Board to consensus. She can anticipate our individual reactions and address our questions because she has talked with each of us in advance, depending on the topic and expertise, to make sure we understand the context, associated drivers, and impact."

In reflecting on the search ahead of them for a new president after Wiley retired in 2004, another Board member remarked that Wiley's presence would be sorely missed: "The Partnership is very much about community building. It is based in business and is business-centric, but it can end up touching on all facets of a participant's life. Bennie is a connector with people; she is very much the center of the wheel. People want Bennie Wiley around their table. People return her calls because they know that a call from Bennie is important. She will not be easy to replace."

Much of The Partnership's growth from 1991 to 2005 was due to Wiley's ability to build bridges. Wiley deeply understood cultural differences and used this understanding to facilitate collaboration among dissimilar others. In other words, she possessed a rare set of relational skills in multicultural competence: conflict management, interpersonal communication, feedback seeking, and role-modeling her commitment to diversity and inclusion.[36] These skills uniquely positioned Wiley to garner the support of her key constituents of varying status positions, racial and ethnic backgrounds, and political ideologies so they could grow The Partnership together.

Josephine "Josie" Esquivel: The Passionate Pursuer

Unlike Jeanette Clough and Bennie Wiley, Josie Esquivel did not lead with the formal authority afforded by a CEO title. Instead, Esquivel distinguished herself as an industry leader when she became a star research analyst on Wall Street. Along her journey to Wall Street, Esquivel achieved numerous successes, consistently exceeding performance standards even in the face of what she felt may have been lowered expectations and opportunities for promotion because of her gender. Her first job was as a sales associate in the Juniors apparel department of Burdines department store. She was soon promoted to department manager; in this position she increased profitability by 55 percent, and her department became one of the top in the state (ranked number three out of twenty stores), generating $1 million in revenue. Esquivel then took a job as a sales account manager for Borden, moving her brand from fourth to third position in dairy and to second in frozen food in one year. After graduating from the Harvard Business School, Esquivel became a product manager for J.P. Stevens, a textile company. In this position, she increased sales 50 percent and brought profits to

10 percent on a brand of department store towels that had previously lost money.

Esquivel's most notable career accomplishments occurred during her tenure as a research analyst on Wall Street. In 1989, just eighteen months after she joined Lehman Brothers, *Institutional Investor (II)* listed Esquivel as a top-ranking research analyst for the textiles and apparel industry. Esquivel's climb to this star position was one of the most rapid in Wall Street history. She remained ranked for thirteen out of her fourteen years on Wall Street, when only 5 percent of all research analysts are ranked in a given year. Had anyone considered Esquivel's likely career trajectory after leaving college, becoming a star analyst probably wouldn't have made the list; yet it is clear how each job prepared her for that role. She drew upon her deep industry knowledge, which she gained through her work experiences, to become a liaison between her company's senior executives and the institutional sales force. By the early 1990s, Esquivel had become a gatekeeper to the industry.

More than her professional background, Esquivel's authenticity differentiated her from other analysts on Wall Street. Throughout her career, Esquivel rejected counsel that she should suppress her femininity to advance as a business leader. Esquivel describes her reaction to the advice that she should act like a man if she wanted to succeed at Borden: "As I was one of the first female sales representatives, the store managers were surprised when I began to call on their accounts. I had always been told that, in order to meet this challenge, I had to think like a woman but act like a man. I thought that advice was ridiculous. What would I bring to the table if I acted like a man? I learned to continue acting like a woman, and I did so professionally." Before she joined Wall Street, one of her Harvard Business School classmates advised her to change her appearance to look more conservative. Yet Esquivel maintained her own style. Her classmate recalls:

> I remember thinking Josie was more exotic and fashion-forward than anyone on the Street. In 1987 on Wall Street, women wore very

conservative business suits. Josie didn't look like Wall Street. For example, she had really long nails with red nail polish. Nails fit in textiles, but not on Wall Street. I recommended that she be more conservative. I told her she needed to cut her nails and lose the red polish. Josie's initial reaction to my suggestion about her nails was "absolutely not." She did trim her nails for the interview, but she kept the red nail polish. She modified it a bit, but not much. That was Josie's style. She wouldn't totally conform. She would go part of the way.

One might consider Esquivel to be a tempered radical, or someone who works quietly from within to effect change in the organization, often through small acts.[37] Esquivel was willing to modify some aspects of her self-presentation to achieve her goals, but she did not violate her core beliefs and identity in the process. Instead, she used her creativity and style to change gendered norms of professionalism, so that corporate America better fit her needs. Esquivel's formula for success was to apply her strengths of industry experience, creativity, and style. An investment banker at Lehman Brothers comments on Esquivel's approach to her work:

Like nobody else, Josie knew her strengths and weaknesses. Analysts need to learn so many skills. Many try to be the best in everything. Josie was very strategic in building her franchise. Very early on I think she understood that, with her background, she would not necessarily be the best in stock picking or creating sophisticated financial models. Knowing the apparel industry and understanding fashion trends was her thing. She came from the industry. So she spent the first three years becoming indispensable for the apparel companies. Starting with middle managers, she built relationships to the CEOs of major apparel firms, many of whom asked her for strategic advice.

Esquivel packaged her industry knowledge and creativity into a research product that institutional investors found valuable. Her creative research reports provided rich data with an innovative title or marketing slant, and even featured her twins, mirroring industry growth with updates from their stage of life. An analyst from another firm recalls: "Josie understood that there was no value in reporting what everyone else was reporting. So she always tried to differentiate herself from the competition. If everyone else emphasized X, Josie would write about Y. Clients had to read Josie's reports because they were different from the rest of Wall Street."

In January 1990, just a few months after *II* had ranked her as a star analyst in the textile and apparel industry for the first time, Esquivel stood alone in her "buy" recommendation for Nike, a footwear company that had been ignored by most of Esquivel's counterparts in top firms. In fact, all the other analysts who covered this sector had released a "hold" recommendation on Nike's stock. Esquivel remembers this episode as one of the moments during her research career when she was truly at her best:

> When I made the Nike "buy" recommendation, I had just become ranked, so my name wasn't really out there yet. I caught a lot of flak for my Nike recommendation over the next few months. I was lambasted by the Lehman sales force as the stock continued to decline for several weeks. The stock price didn't start to rise for another five months. This was the kind of pressure that could make or break an analyst. Many analysts would hide when their prediction about a company was not confirmed. But during this time, I stood my ground. I had confidence in my analysis, and I had the courage to face the salespeople who didn't agree with my call. I truly believed that Reebok's marketing success and stock price had peaked at that time, and Nike had gotten its act together with a strong product lineup and clear brand strategy that were worth considering. It turned out that 1990 was the beginning of a seven-year run for Nike.

Esquivel remained ranked for thirteen years, even after leaving Lehman Brothers to assume the position of head of Global Research in textiles at Morgan Stanley. Like Clough and Wiley,

Esquivel maintained her authenticity; she was courageous and unconventional. Clough, Wiley, and Esquivel each envisioned success in accordance with their personal values and principles of honesty, inclusion, and integrity. Clough's leadership drew upon her ability to marshal resources and mobilize people to act on behalf of the hospital. Wiley's leadership was enriched by her capacity to build personal relationships with her key constituents. Esquivel's leadership was fueled by her passionate pursuit of her goals, and her intense focus and determination. When asked how she was able to achieve such career success, Esquivel replies:

> I attribute my success to the fact that I was always extremely goal-oriented. I seemed to be able to establish a clear objective and a strategy to attain this objective. I wouldn't take no for an answer. I would always find different ways of going about getting something accomplished. My parents were immigrants, so we were raised under extremely hard-working ethics. Also, I always knew my strengths and weaknesses. I didn't ignore my weaknesses, but I didn't concentrate on them either. I didn't try to be what I wasn't. I don't think you can go very far doing that. You need to play to your strengths.

Lessons from Women Leaders on Enhancing Authentic Engagement at Work

The leadership journeys of Clough, Wiley, and Esquivel offer key insights about authentically engaging strengths to benefit organizations and society. Each woman's source of strength was the alignment she experienced between her identity (professional, gender, and cultural) and the work in which she fully engaged. For these leaders, authenticity was about more than self-expression or personal gratification. In a me-centered society, individuals may seek only to express themselves and meet their own needs and hedonic desires, while disregarding the destructive impact of their actions on others.[38] Clough, Wiley, and Esquivel aspired to make a difference, not only for their own edification but for society as well by providing quality health care, advocating for inclusion, and feminizing Wall Street. Goffee and Jones's description of authentic leaders is well suited to Clough, Wiley, and Esquivel: "Authentic leaders are comfortable in their skin; they know where they come from and who they are, and they know how to use their backgrounds to build a rapport with followers. Authentic leaders are not threatened by people with other origins; they welcome them. They are sensitive in communicating their origins and are aware of the differences in cultural attitudes toward their backgrounds. Authentic leaders know how to strike a balance between their distinctiveness and the cultures in which they operate."[39]

These are but three stories of three women. Clough, Wiley, and Esquivel, as leaders, have had greater autonomy than most women to set a personal and collective agenda for their work and for the organization. Yet the case studies of these women leaders point to new directions for researching and practicing authentic engagement at work. They invite us to inquire into new possibilities for creating organizational contexts where women and men of diverse backgrounds and hierarchical levels can engage their strengths more effectively. These cases demonstrate the process by which individuals can draw upon their professional, gender, and cultural backgrounds to contribute maximally to their colleagues, organizations, and societies.

The experiences of Clough, Wiley, and Esquivel illustrate how people might cultivate strengths through experiences of marginalization and social disadvantage based on race, gender, and occupational background. Carefully examining linkages between identity and effective work practices may reveal hidden (or unknown) strengths that are developed as a function of personal or historical disadvantage. For example, marginalized groups frequently unify around collective mobilizing efforts, such as advocacy groups, affinity networks, and professional organizations, to advance common interests within organizations and societies. Moreover, members of marginalized groups (such as immigrants and other ethnic minorities) must learn to operate in multiple cultural contexts and develop skills in multicultural competence. Leaders might use such mobilizing and connecting skills to enrich the quality of relationships across differences within organizations. Individuals who have struggled with oppression and discrimination have much to share about how to remain passionate in pursuing goals, even in the face of obstacles. Leaders might look to members of historically disadvantaged groups to glean cognitive, emotional, and behavioral practices of resilience and determination.

The case studies of Clough, Wiley, and Esquivel also counter underlying assumptions regarding sources of strength. Through these stories, we learn that strengths—or the characteristics that enable people to consistently produce desired results—are a function of talents, core competencies, principles, and identity. This broadened definition of strengths encompasses the perspectives and values that are shaped by sociocultural, gender, economic, and other group memberships. Indeed, for Clough, Wiley, and Esquivel, their experiences as women became a source of strength in their respective fields.

To view identity as a source of strength contrasts with many discussions of gender, race, diversity, and leadership, in which cultural difference is considered irrelevant at best or problematic at worst.[40] The color-blind and problem-focused discussions of race, gender, and diversity "overlook the fact that biological and cultural differences are both a fact of life and a source of pride and identity to many individuals."[41] Instead, fear overwhelms discussions of identity and difference, fostering an environment in which the unique strengths and contributions of marginalized groups are often discounted and ignored. Women and people of color may begin to suppress their strengths rather than direct them toward personal and organizational growth and productivity. Angela Williams, VP and deputy general counsel for Sears Holdings Corporation, speaks of how minority women must relate to white colleagues in a way that makes them feel comfortable. "Minority women are denying their authenticity. A highly qualified woman of color feels she can't be overly assertive, or show her cards, or use her strengths—doing so may undermine her professionally or be used against her. For example, women of color will refrain from making presentations together in order not to overwhelm upper management."[42] The suppression of strengths and the denial of authenticity undermines the promise of diversity; differences should be a source of strength for the organization, bringing latent skills and insights that challenge majority culture norms and lead to creativity, learning, and growth.[43]

To benefit from the qualities that women and other members of historically disadvantaged groups bring to organizations, researchers and practitioners must understand and appreciate their personal experiences. Offering them the freedom to authentically engage their identities as a source of strength requires a shift away from the focus on weakness that dominates organizational research and practice, and a shift toward an exploration of their strengths.[44] A deeper investigation into positive states and dynamics might offer greater insight into the origins of strengths, the process of applying strengths constructively, and the experience of authentic engagement at work. It would also provoke scholars and practitioners to reject uniform expectations of what women bring, and inquire into the simultaneity of multiple identity group memberships that uniquely define authenticity and inform work practices for each individual.[45] For example, a white male university president from a working-class background may differ from a president from a privileged background in supporting aggressive, need-based financial aid policies. Likewise, a black female physician has a qualitatively different experience from that of a black female nurse or janitor, given the gender composition of nursing staffs and the racial composition of janitorial staffs. These differences do not discount class, race, or gender; rather, the experience of occupational status is always processed in unique ways depending on how multiple social statuses intersect with a person's position in an organization.

As individuals and organizations honor the diversity that exists in the workplace, both between groups and within groups, they can mutually construct a psychological contract that affords each their desired options and ends. Employers and employees gain the benefits of authentic engagement, not only for self-expression but for strategic contribution. By looking to the experiences of women leaders who have carefully and deliberately carved a space for their whole selves to thrive within their work environment, we can learn how to become more authentic—and how to create systems in which identity is a source of strength that fosters growth and flourishing.

Endnotes

1. Lionel Billing, quoted in Mark Dolliver, "It's Popular, But Authenticity Isn't What It Used to Be," *Ad Week*, July 2, 2001, 19.

2. Bruce Avolio and William Gardner, "Authentic Leadership Development: Getting to the Root of Positive Forms of Leadership," *Leadership Quarterly 16* (2005): 315–338; Susan Harter, "Authenticity," in C. R. Snyder and Shane J. Lopez, eds., *Handbook of Positive Psychology* (New York: Oxford University Press, 2001), 382–394; Remus Ilies, Frederick P. Morgeson, and Jennifer D. Nahrgang, "Authentic Leadership and Eudaemonic Well-Being: Understanding Leader-Follower Outcomes," *Leadership Quarterly 16* (2005): 373–394; Michael Kernis, "Toward a Conceptualization of Optimal Self-Esteem," *Psychological Inquiry 14* (2003): 1–26; Christopher Peterson and Martin E. P. Seligman, *Character Strengths and Virtues: A Handbook and Classification* (New York: Oxford University Press, 2004).

3. Ella Louise Bell, "The Bicultural Life Experience of Career-Oriented Black Women," *Journal of Organizational Behavior 11* (1990): 459–477; Ella Louise Bell and Stella M. Nkomo, *Our Separate Ways: Black and White Women and the Struggle for Professional Identity* (Boston: Harvard Business School Press, 2001); Devon W. Carbado and Mitu Gulati, "Working Identity," *Cornell Law Review 85* (2000): 1260–1308; Prudence Carter, *Keepin' It Real* (New York: Oxford University Press, 2005); Judith A. Clair, Joy E. Beatty, and Tammy L.

Maclean, "Out of Sight But Not Out of Mind: Managing Invisible Social Identities in the Workplace," *Academy of Management Review* 30 (2005): 78–95; Belle Rose Ragins, "Disclosure Disconnects: Antecedents and Consequences of Disclosing Invisible Stigmas Across Life Domains," *Academy of Management Review* (in press); Laura Morgan Roberts, "Changing Faces: Professional Image Construction in Diverse Organizational Settings," *Academy of Management Review* 30 (2005): 685–711.

4. Patricia Faison Hewlin, "And the Award for Best Actor Goes to . . . : Facades of Conformity in Organizational Settings," *Academy of Management Review* 28 (2003): 633–642; Herminia Ibarra, "Provisional Selves: Experimenting with Image and Identity in Professional Adaptation," *Administrative Science Quarterly* 44 (1999): 764–791; Parker Palmer, *A Hidden Wholeness: The Journey Toward an Undivided Life* (San Francisco: Jossey-Bass, 2004); Marian N. Ruderman and Patricia J. Ohlott, *Standing at the Crossroads: Next Steps for High-Achieving Women* (San Francisco: Jossey-Bass, 2002); Martin Seligman, *Authentic Happiness* (New York: Free Press, 2002).

5. Martin N. Davidson and Erika Hayes James, "The Engines of Positive Relationships Across Difference: Learning and Conflict," in Jane E. Dutton and Belle Rose Ragins, eds., *Exploring Positive Relationships at Work: Building a Theoretical and Research Foundation* (Mahwah, NJ: Erlbaum, 2006); Jane E. Dutton and Emily Heaphy, "Coming to Life: The Power of High Quality Connections at Work," in Kim S. Cameron, Jane E. Dutton, and Robert E. Quinn, eds., *Positive Organizational Scholarship* (San Francisco: Berrett-Koehler, 2003), 263–278; Robin J. Ely, Debra E. Meyerson, and Martin N. Davidson, "Rethinking Political Correctness," *Harvard Business Review* 84 (2006): 79–87; Jeffrey T. Polzer, Laurie P. Milton, and William B. Swann Jr., "Capitalizing on Diversity: Interpersonal Congruence in Small Work Groups," *Administrative Science Quarterly* 47 (2002): 296–324; Laura Morgan

Roberts, "From Proving to Becoming: How Positive Relationships Create a Context for Self-Discovery and Self-Actualization," in Jane E. Dutton and Belle Rose Ragins, eds., *Exploring Positive Relationships at Work: Building a Theoretical and Research Foundation* (Mahwah, NJ: Erlbaum, 2006); David Thomas, "Racial Dynamics in Cross-Race Developmental Relationships," *Administrative Science Quarterly* 38 (1993): 169–194.

6. Michael H. Hoppe and George Houston, "A Question of Leadership: How Much of Themselves Should Leaders Bring to Their Work?" *Leadership in Action* 24 (2004): 13.

7. Carrie Yang Costello, *Professional Identity Crisis* (Nashville, TN: Vanderbilt University Press, 2005); Hewlin, "And the Award for Best Actor Goes to . . ."; Laura Morgan Roberts, "Changing Faces: Professional Image Construction in Diverse Organizational Settings," *Academy of Management Review* 30 (2005): 685–711.

8. Sylvia Ann Hewlett, Carolyn Buck Luce, Cornel West, Helen Chernikoff, Danielle Samalin, and Peggy Shiller, *Invisible Lives: Celebrating and Leveraging Diversity in the Executive Suite* (New York: Center for Work Life Policy, 2005).

9. Rosemary Hays-Thomas, "Why Now? The Contemporary Focus on Managing Diversity," in Margaret Stockdale and Faye J. Crosby, *The Psychology and Management of Workplace Diversity* (Malden, MA: Blackwell, 2004), 1–30.

10. Michael B. Arthur and Denise M. Rousseau, *The Boundaryless Career: A New Employment Principle for a New Organizational Era* (New York: Oxford University Press, 1996); Gian Vittorio Caprara and Daniel Cervone, "A Conception of Personality for a Psychology of Human Strengths: Personality as an Agentic, Self-Regulating System," in Lisa Aspinwall and Ursula Staudinger, eds., *A Psychology of Human Strengths: Fundamental Questions and Future Directions for a Positive Psychology* (San Francisco: Berrett-Koehler, 2003), 61–74; Katherine Stone, "The New Psychological Contract: Implications of the

Changing Workplace for Labor and Employment Law," *UCLA Law Review 48* (2004): 519–662; Denise M. Rousseau, "Changing the Deal While Keeping the People," *Academy of Management Executive 10* (1996): 50–59.

11. Katherine Y. Williams and Charles A. O'Reilly III, "Diversity in Organizations: A Review of 40 Years of Research," in Barry Staw and L. L. Cummings, eds., *Research in Organizational Behavior 20* (Greenwich, CT: JAI Press, 1998), 77–140.

12. Taylor Cox, *Cultural Diversity in Organizations: Theory, Research and Practice* (San Francisco: Berrett-Koehler, 1994); Taylor Cox and Stacy Blake, "Managing Cultural Diversity: Implications for Organizational Competitiveness," *Academy of Management Executive 5* (1991): 45–57.

13. Marcus Buckingham and Donald O. Clifton, *Now, Discover Your Strengths* (New York: Free Press, 2001); Marcus Buckingham, *The One Thing You Need to Know: About Great Managing, Great Leading, and Sustained Individual Success* (New York: Free Press, 2005).

14. Laura Morgan Roberts, "Shifting the Lens on Organizational Life: The Added Value of Positive Scholarship," *Academy of Management Review 31* (2006): 241–260.

15. Kim S. Cameron, Jane E. Dutton, and Robert E. Quinn, "Foundations of Positive Organizational Scholarship," in Cameron, Dutton, and Quinn, eds., *Positive Organizational Scholarship*, 3–13.

16. Aspinwall and Staudinger, *Psychology of Human Strengths*; Peterson and Seligman, *Character Strengths and Virtues*.

17. Bill George, *Authentic Leadership: Rediscovering the Secrets to Creating Lasting Value* (San Francisco: Jossey-Bass, 2003); Robert E. Quinn, "Moments of Greatness: Entering the Fundamental State of Leadership," *Harvard Business Review 83* (2005): 74–83.

18. Bruce Avolio and William Gardner, "Authentic Leadership Development: Getting to the Root of Positive Forms of Leadership," *Leadership Quarterly 16* (2005): 315–338; Bruce J.

Avolio, William L. Gardner, Fred O. Walumbwa, Fred Luthans, and Douglas R. May, "Unlocking the Mask: A Look at the Process by Which Authentic Leaders Impact Follower Attitudes and Behaviors," *Leadership Quarterly* 15 (2004): 801–823; William L. Gardner, Bruce J. Avolio, Fred Luthans, Douglas R. May, and Fred Walumbwa, "Can You See the Real Me? A Self-Based Model of Authentic Leader and Follower Development," *Leadership Quarterly* 16 (2005): 343–372; Ilies, Morgeson, and Nahrgang, "Authentic Leadership and Eudaemonic Well-Being."

19. Rob Goffee and Gareth Jones, "Managing Authenticity: The Paradox of Great Leadership," *Harvard Business Review* 83 (2005): 86–94.

20. Sally Helgesen, *The Female Advantage: Women's Ways of Leadership* (New York: Doubleday, 1995); Joyce K. Fletcher, *Disappearing Acts: Gender, Power, and Relational Practice at Work* (Cambridge, MA: MIT Press, 2001); Joyce K. Fletcher, "The Greatly Exaggerated Demise of Heroic Leadership: Gender, Power, and the Myth of the Female Advantage," in Robin J. Ely, Erica G. Foldy, and Maureen A. Scully, eds., *Reader in Gender, Work, and Organization* (Victoria, Australia: Blackwell, 2003), 204–210; Betty Freidan, *The Feminine Mystique* (New York: Norton, 1963).

21. Marie C. Wilson, *Closing the Leadership Gap: Why Women Can and Must Help Run the World* (New York: Penguin Books, 2004), xiii.

22. Buckingham, *The One Thing You Need to Know.*

23. Clayton P. Alderfer and Kenwyn K. Smith, "Studying Intergroup Relations Embedded in Organizations," *Administrative Science Quarterly* 27 (1982): 35–65; Mats Alvesson and Yvonne Billing, *Understanding Gender and Organizations* (London: Sage, 1997); Bell and Nkomo, *Our Separate Ways;* Robin J. Ely and David A. Thomas, "Cultural Diversity at Work: The Effects of Diversity Perspectives on Work Group Processes and Outcomes," *Administrative Science Quarterly* 46

(2001): 229–273; Irene Padavic, "The Re-Creation of Gender in a Male Workplace," *Symbolic Interaction 14* (1991): 279–294; David A. Thomas and Clayton P. Alderfer, "The Influence of Race on Career Dynamics: Theory and Research on Minority Career Experiences," in Michael B. Arthur, Douglas T. Hall, and Barbara S. Lawrence, eds., *Handbook of Career Theory* (New York: Cambridge University Press, 1989), 133–158.

24. Yvonne Due Billing and Mats Alvesson Billing, "Four Ways of Looking at Women and Leadership," *Scandinavian Journal of Management 5* (1989): 63–80; Robin Ely and Irene Padavic, "A Feminist Analysis of Organizational Research on Sex Differences," *Academy of Management Review* (in press).

25. Deborah Rhode quoted in Wilson, *Closing the Leadership Gap*, 17.

26. Janet Holmes and Stephanie Schnurr, "'Doing Femininity' at Work: More Than Just Relational Practice." *Journal of Sociolinguistics 10* (2006): 31–51.

27. Laura Morgan Roberts, Jane E. Dutton, Gretchen Spreitzer, Emily Heaphy, and Robert Quinn, "Composing the Reflected Best-Self Portrait: Building Pathways for Becoming Extraordinary in Work Organizations," *Academy of Management Review 30* (2005): 712–736. See also Seligman and Peterson, who differentiate between strengths and fulfillments. Fulfillments are likely consequences of strengths. They can include positive outcomes for an individual, relationships, institutions, and communities. Martin Seligman and Christopher Peterson, "Positive Clinical Psychology," in Aspinwall and Staudinger, eds., *A Psychology of Human Strengths*.

28. Charles Carver and Michael Scheier, "Three Human Strengths," in Aspinwall and Staudinger, eds., *A Psychology of Human Strengths*; Morgan W. McCall Jr., Michael M. Lombardo, and Ann M. Morrison, *Lessons of Experience: How Successful Executives Develop on the Job* (Lexington, MA: Lexington Books, 1988); Cynthia D. McCauley, Marian N.

Ruderman, and Patricia J. Ohlott, "Assessing the Developmental Components of Managerial Jobs," *Journal of Applied Psychology* 79 (1994): 544–560.

29. Mihaly Csikszentmihalyi, *The Evolving Self: A Psychology for the Third Millennium* (New York: HarperCollins, 1993).

30. Jennifer Crocker, Noah Nuer, Marc-Andre Olivier, and Sam Cohen, *Egosystem and Ecosystem: Two Motivational Orientations for the Self*, unpublished manuscript (Ann Arbor: University of Michigan, 2006); Quinn, "Moments of Greatness."

31. Quoted in Lynette Clemetson, "'It Is Constant Work': Oprah on Staying Centered, Ambition, Letting Go—and Pajamas," *Newsweek*, January 8, 2001, 44.

32. Boris Groysberg and Laura Morgan Roberts, "Leading the Josie Esquivel Franchise (A)," Harvard Business School (2004) Case 404-054; Laura Morgan Roberts and Ayesha Kanji, "Jeanette Clough at Mount Auburn Hospital," Harvard Business School (2005) Case 406-068; Laura Morgan Roberts and Victoria Winston, "Bennie Wiley at The Partnership, Inc.," Harvard Business School (2005) Case 406-012.

33. Laura Morgan Roberts, Brianna Barker Caza, Emily Heaphy, Gretchen Spreitzer, and Jane Dutton, *Strengths in Action: Themes in Best-Self Portraits*, Unpublished manuscript (Boston: Harvard Business School, 2006).

34. Diversion occurs when the emergency department is full and closes to ambulance traffic, and the patients are sent to neighboring hospitals.

35. Alvesson and Billing, *Understanding Gender and Organizations*, 108.

36. Donna Chrobot-Mason and Marion Ruderman, "Leadership in a Diverse Workplace," in Stockdale and Crosby, eds., *The Psychology and Management of Workplace Diversity*, 100–121.

37. Debra Meyerson and Maureen Scully, "Tempered Radicalism and the Politics of Ambivalence and Change," *Organization Science* 6 (1995): 585–600; Debra Meyerson, *Tempered Radi-*

cals: How People Use Difference to Inspire Change at Work (Boston: Harvard Business School Press, 2001).

38. Crocker, Nuer, Olivier, and Cohen, *Egosystem and Ecosystem;* Robin J. Ely, Debra E. Meyerson, and Martin N. Davidson, "Rethinking Political Correctness"; Quinn, "Moments of Greatness."

39. Goffee and Jones, "Managing Authenticity," 95.

40. Laura Morgan Roberts and L. Wooten, "Exploring Black Greek Letter Organizations Through a Positive Organizing Lens," in Gregory Parks, ed., *Our Fight Has Just Begun: The Relevance of Black Greek Fraternities and Sororities in the 21st Century* (Lexington: University of Kentucky Press, in press); Cornell West, *Race Matters* (New York: Random House, 1994); Wilson, *Closing the Leadership Gap.*

41. Pushkala Prasad, Judith Pringle, and Alison Konrad, "Examining the Contours of Workplace Diversity: Concepts, Contexts and Challenges," in Alison Konrad, Pushkala Prasad, and Judith Pringle, eds., *Handbook of Workplace Diversity* (Thousand Oaks, CA: Sage, 2006), 1–22; quote on p. 9.

42. Hewlett, Luce, West, Chernikoff, Samalin, and Shiller, *Invisible Lives,* 7.

43. Cox and Blake, "Managing Cultural Diversity"; Stockdale and Crosby, eds., *The Psychology and Management of Workplace Diversity;* David A. Thomas and Robin J. Ely, "Making Differences Matter: A New Paradigm for Managing Diversity," *Harvard Business Review* 74 (1996): 79–90; Williams and O'Reilly, "Diversity in Organizations."

44. Roberts, "Shifting the Lens on Organizational Life."

45. Patricia Hill Collins, "Towards a New Vision: Race, Class and Gender as Categories of Analysis and Connection," in Patricia Hill Collins, ed., *Race, Sex, Class* (Memphis, TN: Center of Research on Women, University of Memphis, 1993), 25–46; Kimberle Crenshaw, "Intersectionality and Identity Politics: Learning from Violence Against Women of Color," in

Mary Lyndon Shanley and Uma Narayan, eds., *Reconstructing Political Theory: Feminist Perspectives* (University Park: Pennsylvania State University Press, 1997), 178–193; Evangelina Holvino, "Complicating Gender: The Simultaneity of Race, Gender, and Class in Organizational Change(ing)," Working Paper No. 14 (Boston: Center for Gender in Organizations, Simmons School of Management, 2001).

13

WOMEN AND POWER

New Perspectives on Old Challenges

Evangelina Holvino

A few years ago I conducted a training program for high-potential managers on leadership and power at a Fortune 500 company. A workshop activity involved a panel of top-level executives of the corporation providing their perspectives on this theme. One of the invited vice presidents started her presentation by acknowledging that she had never thought about power until this occasion. "Is she serious?" I asked myself then. Today, she is one of the few women of color who have held the title of CEO at a major U.S. company. How can it be that a CEO of a corporation has never thought about power?

In this chapter I explore the complexity of the phrase "women, power, and leadership" by drawing from different feminist traditions with their embedded definitions of power. As an organizational consultant interested in the application of any theory to the practice of organizational change, I translate the complexity of these feminists' theories into ways of intervening that are useful for women in organizations. Although I still don't think it is possible that the CEO from my story has never thought about power, I believe that she, like many organizational women, may be confused and torn about how to talk about it.[1]

The Problem of Power: Current Debates

In mainstream theories, the debate over the meaning of power is ongoing. Is power an individual or a collective property? A relation, a process, or a possession? Is it intrinsically good or bad? Does its effectiveness reside more in its capacity to make things happen (produce), or in preventing things from happening (coerce)? Is there a difference between legitimate and illegitimate power? And the questions go on.[2]

Traditional definitions of power, such as "the ability to impose one's will on others, or control others, including against their will,"[3] have been particularly problematic for women, as these definitions are associated with male power and domination as opposed to a gentler type of power more congruent with women's role in society. For women, the question of power is very much tied to the question of leadership, since exercising leadership inevitably requires some exercise of power. And there is a long tradition of redefining the relationship between power, leadership, and women, as Jill Ker Conway reminds us when she asks women to "work steadily and deliberately to forge images of female power that can inform notions of leadership."[4]

The meaning of power for women has not proven any easier to resolve than are the mainstream debates on power. For example, while gender-role congruency would have us believe in a kind of female power that is indirect and personal as opposed to a male type of power that is direct, authoritative, and status-derived, studies have found that when the effects of gender and power are disentangled, the differences between men's and women's power disappear. It is the amount of power that an individual has, not gender, that makes for the different power behaviors and motivations attributed to women and men.[5]

More recently, the controversy over women's power and leadership has surfaced in the form of the opt-out revolution discussion, where the trend of women's leaving positions of power and leadership is explained by their supposed rejection of power and leadership. Yet a recent study by the Center for Gender in Organizations at the Simmons School of Management argues that the opt-out phenomenon is overplayed. Instead, the authors highlight three findings: first, women want leadership and power; second, women are redefining leadership and power in collaborative and inclusive ways and toward positive ends for society; and third, women are still not satisfied with their opportunities to exercise power and leadership in organizations.[6] So the debate continues.

In their review of the literature on women and power, Patricia Darlington and Becky Mulvaney summarize four types of power: traditional power, meaning power over; empowerment, meaning mutual empowerment focused on giving power to others or enhancing others' power; personal authority, the power to be self-determining and make independent choices based on knowledge; and reciprocal empowerment, a combination of personal authority and empowerment.[7] The authors conclude that women associate traditional power with masculine constructs, which they see as undesirable, and struggle to conceptualize power in new ways that embody their values. In addition, women of various racial, ethnic, and cultural backgrounds already practice a combination of personal authority and empowerment, which suggests a new model of reciprocal empowerment for women. Nevertheless, their findings are also contradictory in that the women they studied identified with traditional definitions of power, although they preferred reciprocal empowerment when it was presented as an alternative. In addition, they faced the challenge of recognizing and applying different forms of power, especially in public life. So it seems that we are back to the paradox and ambiguity of the power of women.[8]

The Problem of Power: Different Feminists' Contributions

Thanks to feminism we have come a long way in understanding the many dimensions of power that influence women's lives, because power is central to feminists' analyses of the relations between the sexes.[9] Most feminists agree that women's and men's situations differ because of women's lack of power, and they seek to change this situation in order to improve women's lives. On the other hand, feminists disagree on the extent, causes, and impact of these differences and on the means and strategies for changing and improving the situation of women. The difficulties we experience in understanding the relationship between women's power and leadership is a result of the various ways in which feminists have conceptualized gender, gender differences, the roots of gender oppression, and the goals of feminist change since the first feminist wave in the nineteenth century. Consequently, I explore a multi-lens approach to power and women's leadership that takes into account these different perspectives.

In this section, I review various strands of feminism, not as a way of categorizing women scholars into particular ways of thinking about gender but as a heuristic to bring to the fore the many ways in which we can look at women, power, and leadership. Implicit in each of these feminist frameworks is a different definition of power. It is essential to clarify how these definitions differ in order to strengthen our conceptual clarity and to increase our range of interventions when working with women, particularly in organizational settings. My intention is not to advocate for one particular perspective but to go beyond the traditional women-and-power debates by engaging in more nuanced explorations of the meaning of power from these different feminist traditions. I briefly review the following five feminist frameworks: liberal, cultural, socialist, poststructuralist, and transnational feminism.[10]

Liberal Feminism

Liberal feminism understands gender as a characteristic derived from the biological and socialized sexual differences between women and men. Drawing from the Enlightenment's belief in abstract individualism, rationality, and mind-body dualism, liberal feminism focuses on achieving the same individual rights for women as those of (white) men. The liberal perspective aims to guarantee a level playing field where women have the same access and opportunities as men and their differences do not matter. Its focus is on personal power and the ability of individual women to be self-determining—to get what they need and want in organizations, their families, communities, and life in general; in other words, the pursuit of individual happiness.

Two perspectives on women and power derive from this framework. First, the focus is on overcoming barriers to advancement for individual women and addressing issues of family work-life balance that hinder individual women's access to positions of leadership and power. A favorite measure of progress is the number of women in management positions, in political office, and in top leadership positions—CEOs and board members of Fortune 500 corporations.[11] The second focus is on helping women "act powerfully," which has usually meant to act like white men, from dressing for success to being appropriately authoritative.[12]

In organizations, the liberal framework translates into training programs and individual coaching of women to become self-empowered, which in turn promotes their access to leadership and gender equality. A how-to, individualistic approach frames this perspective. For example, I was recently interviewed as an expert on the topic of discrimination. One of the questions asked was, "How does a woman know she is being discriminated against and what can she do about it?" Even though I believe that discrimination is a structurally determined phenomenon, to my surprise, I found myself using the liberal feminist framework to offer concrete suggestions for individual women on how to address discriminatory behavior and perceived organizational inequalities.

The liberal framework, with its focus on individual responsibility and access to opportunities, is one of the most popular approaches to women's power and leadership in today's organizations.

Cultural Feminism

Cultural feminism also sees gender as derived from the sexual differences between men and women, but here male dominance and patriarchy, the rule of the father, is the source of women's oppression. However, proponents of this approach do not advocate the elimination of differences between women and men; on the contrary, they seek to enhance and celebrate those differences. The differences are deemed to be positive, making women more effective than men and more enlightened, better fitting them for contemporary leadership. For example, the experience of motherhood provides them with a heightened sense of morality that contributes to using power and authority more responsibly.[13]

The application of this framework in organizations has explored women's "relational practice"—their apparent preference for focusing on relationships rather than tasks and on collaboration rather than competition. This view results in definitions of leadership as being "at the center of things" rather than "on top."[14] Scholars in this tradition suggest that there is a difference between traditionally masculine power, which is defined as "power-over," and feminine power, which is defined as "power-with" or "power-to." Thus this framework focuses on shared power, relational power, collaboration, feminist collectives, and the mutual empowerment of women. For example, Darlington and Mulvaney define mutual empowerment as "a discursive and behavioral style of interaction grounded in reciprocity initiated by people who feel a sense of personal authority."[15] Power in this context is circular, with women at the center, as opposed to hierarchical, with women at the top.

The contributions of scholars of the Stone Center at Wellesley Centers for Women are particularly important within this framework, especially their Relational-Cultural Theory, with its focus on "power in connection."[16] Power is defined as "the capacity to produce change." It is experienced as a kind of energy that flows from the skills of empathic attunement, authenticity, and accountability, and the application of those skills in everyday living.[17] In her study of relational power in the workplace, Joyce Fletcher highlights mutual empowerment as one of its key practices. Mutual empowerment is intended to enable others to achieve more by contributing to work-related goals with activities such as empathic teaching and keeping people connected. The concept of power is thus expanded to include a type of expertise that is fluid and based on interdependence, very contrary to dominant images of leadership and power.

Yet Fletcher goes on to discuss how these relational practices "are disappeared" in workplace environments that are driven by competition, heroic leadership, individualism, hierarchy, and technical outcomes and expertise. Instead, relational practices are reinterpreted as expressions of essential femaleness and thus devalued, confirming prevalent stereotypes of women.[18]

In spite of the difficulties of shifting the dominant discourse to one of mutual empowerment and relational power, a cultural feminist perspective on power remains popular and attractive, especially for women looking for alternatives to power that value and exalt the feminine.

Socialist Feminism

Socialist feminism pays attention to the material dimensions of women's oppression under capitalism. In particular, it focuses on the structures and relations of power that sustain oppression and the ideologies that produce and replicate it. The sexual division of labor characteristic of capitalist society, which excludes women from wage labor and relegates them to the private and domestic sphere, is seen as a fundamental pillar of women's subordination. This gender structure of the labor market positions men and women in different jobs and different industries, with different salaries.[19] Also, gender is understood to be a historically determined difference that should not be studied in isolation from other social processes such as race, ethnicity, and class.

A socialist feminist framework pays attention to structural and societal power inequalities and seeks to eliminate them for all people, not just women. In this tradition, then, power has to do with access to and control of valuable and needed resources, a definition that brings us closer to more traditional definitions of power, such as "the capacity to produce a desired result," "act upon others," or "make things happen."[20] For example, in their feminist framing of women and empowerment, Bookman and Morgen define power as "a social relationship between groups that determines access to, use of, and control over the basic material and ideological resources in society."[21] Empowerment is the process and the variety of political activities that try to change the nature and distribution of power in a particular cultural context. Ultimately, this idea means challenging and changing power relations in a society. Thus the focus of women's power in this framework is collective, societal, and material.

In organizations, this structure of power is revealed by analyzing advancement opportunities, salaries, mentoring, job segregation, the particular positions women hold, job descriptions, and performance appraisal systems, and by examining other organizational processes that produce particular outcomes and disadvantages for women. In addition, one looks at how these organizational arrangements reflect and in a way reaffirm the structures and processes of inequality in the larger society. For example, socialist feminism helps us look at the structure of power through the lens of race and ethnicity to study the differences between the considerable gains made by white women in organizations compared to those made by women of color.[22]

Because of its emphasis on the interlocking structures of power and difference in organizations and society, the socialist feminist perspective has proven more difficult than other frameworks to consistently integrate into analyses and interventions for women in organizations. More recently though, Joan Acker has proposed a model for looking at "regimes of inequality . . . the particular, historically specific configurations of class, race, and gender patterns within specific organizations" through case studies on the differential impact that class and race have on men and women. She enumerates various forms in which these patterns can be made visible through detailed descriptions of the characteristics of the inequality regimes in an organization. She asks, for example: What constitutes the dimensions of inequality that form the basis of the regime? How are the patterns of inequality visible or not, and to whom? What is the legitimacy of these forms of inequality, and how is this legitimacy accomplished? And what are the practices and the organizational structures by which inequality is sustained, including methods of control and compliance?[23] It is my experience that it is possible to engage organizational members in this kind of analysis if the appropriate conditions for inquiry are created.

Poststructuralist Feminism

Poststructuralist feminism uses theories of language, subjectivity, and the history of institutions and social practices to understand and question existing power relations, especially as they are constructed through differences, knowledge, discourse, and the symbolic. For example, societal discourses typically constitute men and women as different. These discourses are in a binary and oppositional relation, but one side, the masculine, is privileged. One of the goals of this approach is to unpack and deconstruct those assumptions, images, and practices that are taken for granted. Once these dichotomies are identified, we can destabilize the knowledge claims that sustain these ways of framing and constructing the world, which are a form of power.

In organizations, poststructuralist feminism helps us pay attention to the discursive dimension of power—the ways in which meaning is created in organizations, yielding particular effects and identities of power.[24] For example, images of women's femininity and their proper place are continually changing and are also different for white women, Latinas, African American women, and Asian women. White women's femininity seems to fit images of the new international midlevel manager, while Latinas seem to fit the image of the good factory worker with their docile bodies and nimble fingers.[25]

Poststructuralist feminism also helps us pay attention to the discourses, rules, and practices that produce and reproduce unequal power relations in organizations. How do these practices come to be accepted and become legitimate? How do these practices and identities originate? How are practices and identities sustained by knowledge-producing mechanisms such as the academy and the media? What other informal structures support these practices and to what effect?[26] For example, when theories of leadership are produced and disseminated as scientific truth, and when these theories equate leadership with a certain kind of rugged masculine individualism, the leadership of women and people of color remains understudied and is treated as a kind of organizational oxymoron.[27]

With its questioning of all categories and knowledge claims, including gender, poststructuralist feminism has been critiqued as not being able to support a feminist agenda of change on behalf of women's power and women's agency. Still, the attention this perspective brings to the subjects of discourse and the symbolic in organizations is an important contribution, suggesting that women's power is not just a matter of access to resources, it is embedded in the very language of power itself.

Transnational and Third-World Feminism

Transnational and third-world feminism combines insights of the various feminists' frameworks mentioned thus far to explicate gender differences in relation to other social differences such as class, race, sexuality, ethnicity, and nationality. These differences reflect complex social processes and discursive constructions, which are historical. Today, more than ever, this historical context is global. The processes and structures of globalization bring to the fore an analysis of both the macro- and the micro-political economics of power, including the role of the state in circumscribing the daily lives and survival struggles of women. Thus it is important to analyze the role of the state, which is implicated in a complex nexus of power and domination that is gendered, patriarchal, racialized, and (hetero)sexualized.[28]

For example, in an analysis of child care and its impact on women in organizations, transnational feminists analyze the global chain of care—"a series of personal links between people across the globe based on the paid or unpaid work of caring."[29] This chain is a complex outcome of global capitalism and the unequal relations between rich and poor countries; the first with market demands for care and the latter with a surplus of migrant women to meet the care needs of career women. The ultimate beneficiaries of this chain may be the multinational companies, as both working mothers and their families in the North and domestic workers and their families of the South are the losers in this global arrangement.[30]

Transnational feminism helps us analyze power from a variety of positions and directions that flow in complex ways. Therefore we must consider not just the powerful but also the agency of those who are less powerful and who by a variety of means challenge, disrupt, or invert prevailing discourses and power relations in everyday practices.

Because of the analytical and subjective complexity this perspective demands, including its critique of Western discourses, the application of transnational feminism to organizations has been done mostly by women scholars of color working at the intersection of first- and third-world theory and practice.[31] The challenge posed by transnational feminism to incorporate more inclusive and global analyses of power of women (and men) in organizations remains to be expanded.

Feminism, Power, and Women's Leadership: Applications in Organizations

Once the idea of power has been complicated by applying the feminist theories we have explored, how do we translate this complexity into useful concepts and concrete interventions to increase and support women's leadership in organizations? From a practical standpoint, women are unlikely to be interested in theoretical complexity unless it comes with specific strategies for addressing the issues of power and leadership they face in everyday organizational life. I will use an example from my consulting practice with a woman manager at a major corporation in Puerto Rico to illustrate how the feminist frameworks discussed earlier can provide such concrete guidance.

I have been consulting to Ana, here given a fictitious name, in the last year and a half to support her leadership as a division director of a successful corporation with a good reputation in the island. What started as individual coaching has grown into a series of organizational consulting interventions that can be directly linked to the liberal, socialist, poststructuralist, and transnational feminist frameworks. While there might be advantages to applying the cultural framework in this organization, we have not yet found the occasion to do so.

To work with Ana, though, I have translated the feminist frameworks into familiar management and organizational terms, which she is more likely to embrace. Thus, four levels of analysis and intervention have guided the work with Ana: personal and individual power, personal and organizational authority, organizational culture and discourse, and the national sociocultural context. I use these levels of analysis as lenses to diagnose and make recommendations about the issue at hand for the organizational system and find myself shifting my gaze from lens to lens as I work with Ana.

Analyses at the level of personal and individual power derive from the liberal feminist framework. Focusing at this level meant providing Ana tools so that she felt able to act on her own behalf, express her needs and goals, and take the calculated risks necessary to achieve what she believes is most important. For example, much of the initial coaching with Ana centered on helping her become more assertive in her dealings with others, especially her supervisors and subordinates. Her goals included getting clear on her vision of the division, practicing communicating this vision to others with clarity, and engaging in discussions about her expectations. We also worked on increasing Ana's confidence in her own vision, competencies, and goals, helping her feel and act more empowered as a woman manager in her organization.

Second, Ana and I worked on the issue of her personal and organizational authority. This perspective derives from the socialist framework with its focus on formal structures and material processes and outcomes in an organization. Using this framework, Ana and I were able to concentrate on her organizational role, in addition to her personal power, and the interface of that formal role with the rest of the organization. For example, one question is: What is her role as division manager, and how does being a woman impact Ana's capacity to exercise formal and informal power in that role?

I define authority as "the capacity or right to perform work (utilize resources and make decisions) in the service of an organizational task."[32] Thus, besides focusing on personal or individual power, with this lens we were able to focus on the issue of organizational authority—that is, Ana's capacity to take up her formal and informal roles in the organization and use them to advance her task of managing her division.[33] I find that the concept of authority can be more productive than that of power when working in organizational settings, partly because of the negative implications of the concept of power. Ryan Smith argues that job authority has proven to be a useful lens by which to observe the contours of inequality, especially for women and racial minorities.[34]

The organizational authority lens helped focus the consultation on Ana's role as unit director and the ways in which her ability to accomplish her managerial role and tasks are supported, or not, by her position and formal role in the organizational structure and by the authority and influence her peers, boss, and subordinates give to that role. Working on these two elements led to a long-term team-building intervention to clarify roles and interdependencies among her unit's leadership group. The objective was to clarify the boundaries of authority and decision making among the team and Ana, to align the unit's task with Ana's vision of the task, to gain commitment from her team for that vision, and to restructure the unit so that Ana's vision could be reinforced by the unit's formal structure and the roles of her immediate team members.

I also worked with Ana to understand the power dynamics in the context of the organizational hierarchy and the positions women hold as a group in that hierarchy. For example, this business is well-established, family-founded, and male-dominated. Although it is one of the largest employers in the country, it still has no woman in a business-line position as a member of the chairman's team and no woman as a member of the CEO's team. It has no processes and structures in place to support affirmative action initiatives, and gender and race differences or inequalities are not discussed. Informal conversations and observations suggest a strong dynamic of benevolent sexism at work. Women themselves, the majority in Ana's unit, collude with men by their silence on gender inequities and gendered norms throughout the system.[35]

This dynamic brings us to the use of the organizational culture and discourse as a lens, which is tied to the feminist poststructuralist framework. For example, in an effort to address the informal, symbolic, linguistic, and discursive elements of power in this organization, I have encouraged Ana and her leadership team to identify and discuss more than thirty organizational norms—ways of talking, doing, and being in this organization—that hinder the ability of the team and its leader to act, and be perceived as acting, with authority. It has been much slower, though, to encourage and find the mechanisms and the will to enact and reinforce alternative norms that support women's roles and authority. Cultural norms likely to hinder women's authority and leadership are common in this organization, including not starting and ending meetings on time, valuing notions like "face time" and "putting out fires" rather than job outcomes, and rewarding individualistic and heroic accomplishments as opposed to team, collaborative, and support-giving behaviors, all of which are tasks women are more likely to perform.[36]

A poststructuralist feminist framework also helps us pay attention to the images of women in the organization and try to identify sources of organizational influence and power that go beyond those expected and sanctioned by the culture for its women leaders. For example, I was recently struck by a picture in an internal company brochure dedicated to leadership that portrayed the highest-ranking woman in Ana's organization with her arms extended, a happy smile, and serving a platter of lasagna. The image of a nurturing mother and dutiful housewife seemed to overshadow that of the woman executive. These are some of the discursive elements that we must pay attention to from a poststructuralist feminist perspective.

Finally, transnational feminism helps us pay attention to the national sociocultural context in which Ana lives, works, and exercises leadership and power beyond the confines of her particular organization. It helps us analyze how her situation is affected by larger processes such as the impact of globalization on the Puerto Rican economy and the ongoing issue of Puerto Rico's colonial status and relationship with the United States. For example, Ana is under increasing economic pressure to secure her position and income in the corporation, as she has become the sole breadwinner in her family after her husband lost his job and her two children started college on the mainland. The loss of jobs in the island is increasingly evident and the per capita income is about half that of the poorest U.S. state. The perceived need of the middle classes to send their children to the mainland for higher education and job opportunities is another outcome of a precarious socioeconomic context of high unemployment, increasing income disparities, and rampant consumerism.[37] Thus Ana's options for exercising power and leadership as division manager, which I analyze as very much related to her ability to rock the organizational boat, are embedded in the larger national context in which jobs are hard to find and economic security is considered a luxury of sorts.

While gendered, patriarchal, racialized, and (hetero)sexualized norms dominate, the pressure to change from inside is also strong, so that organizational actors, and especially women, find themselves needing to create new paths at the same time they try to honor past ones. For example, Ana is trying to maneuver between the sexist and patriarchal norms and expectations of her culture and organization at the same time that her material reality demands that she take on responsibilities previously reserved for her husband, and thus needing to challenge her own internalized sexism in a way that is manageable and acceptable to her, her family, and the organization. It is a constant challenge for me as a U.S.-based Latina consultant, now well trained in the Western discourse of leadership and management, to assess whether Ana's strategies, which others might consider disempowering, are actually subverting or creating alternatives for her—and thus whether they need changing or reinforcing.

Expanding Our Notions of Women's Power and Leadership

The perspectives on power and leadership I have discussed take account of the considerable contributions that feminist scholars have made to these topics throughout the past fifty years. By working through a case study where these feminist frameworks were applied, I suggest specific ways in which we can explore and help women in organizations enhance their exercise of power and leadership without pitting diverse perspectives on power one against the other, using them instead to complement and expand each other. Doing so also increases women's options for understanding, seeking, and enacting power in institutions at the same time that it honors the feminist traditions that continue to support women's equality in organizations today.

On many occasions I have observed how women discuss power and leadership as if one type of power was the most important or the one women should try to secure first. This dynamic does not serve us well. Instead, I suggest we embrace two principles of organizational change: start where the energy for change is, and "light many fires."[38] I believe applying the feminist frameworks I have reviewed allows us to do just that: to start where the energy of the individual woman and her organization is and to use all the ways we have of looking at power to attempt to make real change happen. I also propose that we add the concept of authority to our discussions and that we continue to seek ways of connecting the theory and practice of leadership to women in organizations.

Endnotes

1. Recent media articles have brought to the public's attention the apparent ambivalence of women toward power and to

serving in the highest leadership positions of corporations. See, for example, Patricia Sellers, "Most Powerful Women in Business—Power: Do Women Really Want It?" *Fortune*, September 29, 2003, and Lisa Belkin, "The Opt-Out Revolution," *New York Times*, October 26, 2003. But more than a new development, this seems to be an old controversy resurfacing, since "a conflicted female relation to power" is recurrently mentioned in the literature. See for example, S. J. M. Freeman and S. C. Bourque, "Leadership and Power: New Conceptions," in S. J. M. Freeman, S. C. Bourque, and C. M. Sheton, eds., *Women on Power: Leadership Redefined* (Boston: Northeastern University Press, 2001), 9.

2. See C. Hardy and S. R. Clegg, "Some Dare Call It Power," in S. R. Clegg and C. Hardy, eds., *Studying Organization: Theory and Method* (London: Sage, 1999), 368–387; T. Ball, "Power," in R. E. Goodin and P. Pettit, eds., *A Companion to Contemporary Political Philosophy* (Cambridge, MA: Blackwell, 1993), 548–557.

3. "Encyclopedia of Political Information," Power (sociology), available online: www.politicalinformation.net/encyclopedia/Power_(sociology).htm, access date: March 5, 2007.

4. J. K. Conway, "Amazons and Warriors: The Image of the Powerful Woman" (foreword), in Freeman, Bourque, and Sheton, eds., *Women on Power*, xix.

5. Freeman and Bourque, "Leadership and Power."

6. D. Merrill-Sands, J. Kickul, and C. Ingols, "Women Pursuing Leadership and Power: Challenging the Myth of the 'Opt Out Revolution,'" *CGO Insights #20*, 2005. (Publication of the Center for Gender in Organizations, Simmons School of Management, Boston.)

7. P. S. E. Darlington and B. M. Mulvaney, *Women, Power, and Ethnicity: Working Toward Reciprocal Empowerment* (New York: Haworth Press, 2003).

8. J. B. Elshtain, "The Power and Powerlessness of Women," in G. Bock and S. James, eds., *Beyond Equality and Difference* (London: Routledge, 1992), 110–125.

9. K. Davis and S. Fisher, "Power and the Female Subject," in S. Fisher and K. Davis, eds., *Negotiating at the Margins: The Gendered Discourse of Power and Resistance* (New Brunswick, NJ: Rutgers University Press, 1993), 3–20.

10. For an expanded discussion of these frameworks in organizations, see M. B. Calás and L. Smircich, "From 'the Woman's' Point of View: Feminist Approaches to Organization Studies," in S. Clegg, C. Hardy, and W. Nord, eds., *Handbook of Organization Studies* (London: Sage, 1996), 212–251; M. B. Calás and L. Smircich, "From 'the Woman's Point of View' Ten Years Later: Toward a Feminist Organization Studies," in S. Clegg, C. Hardy, T. B. Lawrence, and W. Nord, eds., *Handbook of Organization Studies*, 2nd ed. (London: Sage, 2006), 284–346; E. Holvino, "Intersections: The Simultaneity of Race, Gender and Class in Organization Studies," in M. B. Calás, L. Smircich, J. Tienari, and C. F. Ellehave, eds., *Gender, Work and Organizations;* special issue on gender and ethnicity (Oxford, UK: Blackwell, in press).

11. See, for example, *The 2005 Catalyst Census of Women Corporate Officers and Top Earners of the Fortune 500* (New York: Catalyst, 2006); "The Glass Ceiling: The Federal Glass Ceiling Commission," in D. Dunn, ed., *Workplace/Women's Place* (Los Angeles: Roxbury, 1997), 226–233.

12. J. Martin and D. Meyerson, "Women and Power: Conformity, Resistance and Disorganized Coaction," in R. M. Kramer and M. A. Neale eds., *Power and Influence in Organizations* (Thousand Oaks, CA: Sage, 1998), 311–348.

13. See, for example, M. F. Belenky, B. M. Clincy, N. R. Goldberger, and J. M. Tarule, *Women's Ways of Knowing* (New York: Basic Books, 1986); C. Gilligan, *In a Different Voice* (Cambridge, MA: Harvard University Press, 1982); A. Sinclair, *Doing Leadership Differently: Gender, Power and Sexuality in a Changing Business Culture* (Melbourne, Australia: Melbourne University Press, 1998).

14. L. M. Calvert and F. J. Ramsey, "Bringing Women's Voice to Research on Women in Management: A Feminist Perspective," *Journal of Management Inquiry* 1 (1992): 79–88; J. Fletcher, "Relational Practice: A Feminist Reconstruction of Work," *Journal of Management Inquiry* 7 (1998): 163–186; S. Helgesen, *The Female Advantage: Women's Ways of Leadership* (New York: Doubleday, 1990).

15. P. S. E. Darlington and B. M. Mulvaney, *Women, Power, and Ethnicity* (New York: Haworth Press, 2003), 2–3.

16. J. V. Jordan, A. G. Kaplan, J. B. Miller, I. P. Stiver, and J. L. Surrey, *Women's Growth in Connection: Writings from the Stone Center* (New York: Guilford Press, 1991); J. V. Jordan, ed., *Women's Growth in Diversity: More Writings from the Stone Center* (New York: Guilford Press, 1997); J. V. Jordan, M. Walker, and L. M. Hartling, eds., *The Complexity of Connection: Writings from the Stone Center's Jean Baker Miller Training Institute* (New York: Guilford Press, 2004).

17. M. Walker, *Power and Effectiveness: Envisioning an Alternate Paradigm*, Work in Progress No. 94. (Wellesley, MA: Stone Center, Wellesley Centers for Women, 2002).

18. J. K. Fletcher, "Relational Theory in the Workplace," in Jordan, Walker, and Hartling, eds., *The Complexity of Connection*, 270–298; J. K. Fletcher, "The Greatly Exaggerated Demise of Heroic Leadership: Gender, Power, and the Myth of the Female Advantage," in R. J. Ely, E. G. Foldy, M. A. Scully, and the Center for Gender in Organizations, *Reader in Gender, Work and Organization* (Malden, MA: Blackwell, 2003), 204–210.

19. H. Hartmann, "Internal Labor Markets and Gender: A Case Study of Promotion," in C. Brown and J. A. Peckman, eds., *Gender in the Workplace* (Washington, DC: Brookings Institution, 1987), 59–105; B. F. Reskin and P. A. Phipps, "Women in Male-Dominated Professional and Managerial Occupations," in A. H. Stomberg and S. Harkess, eds., *Women*

Working: Theories and Facts in Perspective, 2nd ed. (Mountain View, CA: Mayfield, 1988), 190–205.

20. S. Radford-Hill, *Further to Fly: Black Women and the Politics of Empowerment* (Minneapolis: University of Minnesota Press, 2000), 19; D. Noumair, "How to Manage Power and Influence More Effectively: Getting Things Done in a Changing Demographic Context," presentation at Working Mother Media Women of Color Conference, New York, June 2004.

21. A. Bookman and S. Morgen, *Women and the Politics of Empowerment* (Philadelphia: Temple University Press, 1988), 4.

22. Catalyst, *Women of Color in Corporate Management: Opportunities and Barriers* (New York: Catalyst, 1999); Catalyst, *Women of Color Executives: Their Voices, Their Journeys* (New York: Catalyst, 2001).

23. J. Acker, *Class Questions: Feminist Answers* (Lanham, MD: Rowman & Littlefield, 2004).

24. N. Gavey, "Feminist Poststructuralism and Discourse Analysis," in M. M. Gergen and S. N. Davis, eds., *Toward a New Psychology of Gender: A Reader* (New York: Routledge, 1997), 49–64; W. Hollway, "Gender Differences and the Production of Subjectivity," in J. Henriques, W. Hollway, C. Urwin, C. Venn, and V. Walkerdine, *Changing the Subject* (London: Methuen, 1984), 26–59.

25. M. B. Calás, "An/Other Silent Voice? Representing 'Hispanic Woman' in Organizational Texts," in A. J. Mill and P. Tancred, eds., *Gendering Organizational Analysis* (Thousand Oaks, CA: Sage, 1992), 201–221; M. B. Calás and L. Smircich, "Dangerous Liaisons: The Feminine-in-Management Meets Globalization," *Business Horizons 36*, no. 2 (1993): 71–81.

26. J. Martin, "The Organization of Exclusion: Institutionalization of Sex Inequality, Gendered Faculty Jobs and Gendered Knowledge in Organizational Theory and Research" *Organization 1* (1994): 401–431.

27. M. B. Calás and L. Smircich, "Voicing Seduction to Silence Leadership," *Organization Studies 12* (1992): 567–602; C. L.

Jennings and L. Wells, "The Wells-Jennings Analysis: A New Diagnostic Window on Race Relations in American Organizations" in W. Sikes, A. B. Drexler, and J. Gant, eds., *The Emerging Practice of Organization Development* (Alexandria, VA, and San Diego, CA: NTL Institute and University Associates, 1989), 105–118.

28. B. Mendoza, "Transnational Feminism in Question," *Feminist Theory 3* (2002): 295–314; E. Holvino, "Globalization: Overview," in Ely, Foldy, Scully, and Center for Gender in Organizations, Simmons College School of Management, eds., *Reader in Gender, Work and Organization*, 381–386.

29. A. R. Hochschild, "The Nanny Chain," *American Prospect*, January 2000, 32–36.

30. R. S. Parreñas, *Servants of Globalization: Women Migration, and Domestic Work* (Stanford, CA: Stanford University Press, 2001).

31. See, for example, V. Chio, *Malaysia and the Development Process: Globalization, Knowledge Transfers and Postcolonial Dilemmas* (New York: Routledge, 2005); M. P. Fernandez-Kelly, "Making Sense of Gender in the World Economy: Focus on Latin America," *Organization 1* (1994): 249–275; A. Ong, *Spirits of Resistance and Capitalist Discipline: Factory Women in Malaysia* (Albany: State University of New York Press, 1987).

32. This definition is shared by scholars and practitioners in The Tavistock Institute's tradition of group relations and differs from common sociological definitions, which equate authority with legitimate power. For example, Weber defines authority as the "probability that a command with a given specific content will be obeyed by a given group of persons" based on their legitimate position or role, as quoted in R. Smith, "Race, Gender, and Authority in the Workplace: Theory and Research," *Annual Review of Sociology 28* (2002): 535.

33. S. Brazaitis and E. Holvino, "Glossary of Group Relations Terms," 2004, available online: www.chaosmanagement.com, access date: January 2, 2007.

34. Smith, "Race, Gender, and Authority in the Workplace," 509–542.
35. P. Glick and S. Fisk, "An Ambivalent Alliance: Hostile and Benevolent Sexism as Complementary Justifications for Gender Inequality," *American Psychologist*, 56, no. 2 (2001): 109–118.
36. Martin and Meyerson, "Women and Power"; D. Merrill-Sands, J. Fletcher, and A. Acosta, "Engendering Organizational Change: A Case Study of Strengthening Gender-Equity and Organizational Effectiveness in an International Agricultural Research Institute," in A. Rao, R. Stuart, and D. Kelleher, eds., *Gender at Work: Organizational Change for Equality* (West Hartford, CT: Kumarian Press, 1999), 77–128.
37. S. M. Collins, B. Bosworth, and M. A. Soto-Class, eds., *The Economy of Puerto Rico: Restoring Growth* (Washington, DC: Brookings Institution Press and the Center for the New Economy, 2006); J. Duany, *Puerto Rican Nation on the Move: Identities on the Island and in the United States* (Chapel Hill: University of North Carolina Press, 2002).
38. H. A. Shepard, "Rules of Thumb for Change Agents," *OD Practitioner* 7, no. 3 (1975): 1–5.

14

WOMEN IN CORPORATE LEADERSHIP

Status and Prospects

Katherine Giscombe

While women in the United States have not historically occupied positions of power in private sector organizations, they have made gains in achieving positions of corporate leadership in the last several years. Many business organizations have recognized the need to diversify their employee base and leadership and have made efforts by hiring chief diversity officers and implementing detailed diversity and inclusion strategies. Nevertheless, a study by Catalyst, the nonprofit organization devoted to advancing women in the workplace, shows that in the last three years, growth in the percentage of women in corporations' most senior positions (called "corporate officer" and "top earner") slowed dramatically. In 2005, women held 16.4 percent of corporate officer positions, only 0.7 percentage points more than they did in 2002. Furthermore, the percentage of corporate officer positions held by women of color held level at a low 1.7 percent.[1]

What is the experience of being in corporate leadership like for women? Why should private sector organizations be concerned about diversifying their leadership? In this chapter I review Catalyst

Most of the research cited in this chapter was conducted at the Catalyst organization. The author gratefully acknowledges the Catalyst principal investigators, project managers, and key reviewers of those research projects, in particular Jeanine Prime, Nancy Carter, Paulette Gerkovich, Lois Joy, Meesha Rosa, Kate Egan, Margaret Yap, and Susan Black.

studies that examine the links between women in corporate leadership and profitability, the experiences and perceptions of women in corporate leadership, as compared with men, and the reasons for women's lack of progress into top-tier positions, focusing on the major barrier of gender stereotyping.

The Bottom-Line Study:
Gender Diversity and Profitability

Given companies' focus on profitability, it is not surprising that business leaders would like to understand whether there is a business case for gender diversity; that is, whether there is a profitability-linked reason for having more women in leadership positions or providing the means for women to get to these positions. And those companies that have already invested time, money, and other resources in programs designed to recruit, retain, and promote women now want to know whether their efforts and resources in diversity efforts have paid off.

For these reasons Catalyst undertook a research project titled "The Bottom Line: Connecting Corporate Performance and Gender Diversity" to see whether the concentration of women in corporate leadership positions was linked to the organizations' profitability.[2] For the study, we used a variety of data sources. First, we gathered the names and financial information of all the companies that appeared on the Fortune 500 list between 1996 and 2000. We chose this time period because it is one of considerable economic growth. After accounting for name changes and mergers and acquisitions, more than 660 companies remained.

We obtained gender diversity data from the Catalyst Census of Corporate Officers and Top Earners—the accuracy of which is verified with each company. Finally, we narrowed the list down to those companies for which at least four out of five years of data were available. The final sample consisted of 353 companies. We then divided those 353 companies into quartiles based on the percentage of women on their top management team—in other words, those roles that report to the CEO. The average percentage of women corporate officers in bottom-quartile companies, those with the lowest representation of women in these senior jobs, was 1.9 percent. By contrast, the average percentage of women corporate officers in top-quartile companies, those with the highest representation of women in these roles, was 20.3 percent.

The specific financial measures that we considered were return on equity and total return to shareholders. These two financial measures are meaningful to the business community and reflect critical elements of returns to shareholders. More specifically, return on equity is an accounting-based measure that reflects corporate financial performance; total return to shareholders is a value-based measure that reflects changes in stock price.

We compared the financial performance of the two quartiles, the top quartile (those companies with the highest representation of women in senior positions) and the bottom quartile (those companies with the lowest representation of women in senior roles). The group of companies with the highest representation of women on their top management teams had a return on equity that was 35 percent higher than that of companies with the lowest representation of women at the top. We also looked at total return to shareholders. Again, top-quartile companies outperformed bottom-quartile companies. Specifically, top-quartile companies had a total return to shareholders that was 34 percent higher than that of bottom-quartile companies. In sum, companies with the highest average representation of women on their top management teams financially outperformed companies with the lowest average representation of women on their top management teams.

The Catalyst study established a link between representation of women on top management teams and financial performance. While this study did not look at causation, a possible explanation is that the diversity of thought contributed by women on top management teams had a positive impact on the business. Another related hypothesis is that having a higher-than-average number of women on top management teams reflects superior talent management and human resources policies and practices, which in turn are part of an overall business strategy that is more sophisticated (and effective) for current conditions.

Women and Men in U.S. Corporate Leadership: Commonalities and Divergence

When Catalyst speakers present results of the Bottom-Line Study, with its clear link between women at the top and financial success for the business organization, audiences sometimes ask why there are not more women at the top. Insight on the relative lack of women in corporate leadership can be found in Catalyst's 2004 study titled "Women and Men in U.S. Corporate Leadership."[3] In this study, we selected respondents who were senior managers, specifically, those who held positions at the vice-president level and above, most within two reporting levels of the CEO.

This study found many parallels between men and women senior managers. They were similar in terms of the size of the companies in which they worked, almost identical in tenure at their companies and their current positions, how long they anticipated spending in their current positions, when they expected to retire, and how many hours per week they worked. There were also many attitudinal similarities between men and women in the study. The majority of women and men were satisfied according to many traditional measures of work satisfaction, including their view of their jobs and employers in general, and, to a somewhat lesser extent, their career advancement opportunities, financial compensation, and opportunities for development.

The media have recently been inclined to report on corporate women who opt out of business positions to return home to take care of their children. However, in spite of this media attention, according to the "Women and Men in Corporate Leadership" study, women's and men's aspirations to become CEO do not differ significantly. Majorities of both women and men in the study wanted to be CEO of an organization.

The following statement by a white woman exemplifies women's aspirations to the CEO role: "[I want to be CEO] because I think I can make a difference for this company. . . . I see a lot of phenomenal prowess that this company is trying to unleash. And I'm having an impact on that in specific areas that I'm working with. I think I can have a broader impact on that, to help the company grow, and be eminently more successful in the future."[4]

Men and women senior managers in the study were also similar in that they did not rule out the possibility of becoming a CEO: almost one in five women (19 percent) and 14 percent of men were not yet sure whether they wanted to be in the most senior role. Similarly, over one-quarter of each group (26 percent of women and 29 percent of men) said they did not want to be CEO. In addition, there was no significant difference between women who did and did not have children and their intention to pursue the top job. Aspirations differed among study participants based on whether they had line or staff responsibilities. More respondents in line positions than those in staff positions wanted to be CEO. This finding is not surprising given that line experience is typically required to become a CEO.

Strategies for Success

Executive women and men who participated in the "Women and Men in U.S. Corporate Leadership" study cited similar strategies as most important for their success: hard work, managerial skill, performance in high-visibility assignments, and demonstrated expertise. Despite these similarities in the most frequently used strategies for advancement, differences between women and men began to emerge when we looked at all strategies cited, not just the top strategies. For example, women were more likely than men to report seeking high-visibility assignments and networking within the organization, while men were more likely to report gaining line management and international experience. In other words, women were more likely to use strategies related to relationship building while men were more likely to gain particular types of experience.

This difference may reflect the fact that men are freer to use their abilities to succeed; it appears that opportunities are more easily given to men than to women, coming from their senior male counterparts. Conversely, women may not be given such opportunities because of stereotypical beliefs about women's abilities and interests, such as the assumption that women may not want a high-profile job or work requiring significant time away from family.

Women may be more likely than men to use strategies that highlight visibility and relationships because they need to advocate for their own opportunities to a greater extent. As women often occupy an outsider status in the corporate world, building relationships and gaining visibility are critical. It is also possible that men already have firmly established those relationships—through informal networks, for example—that are important to gaining career-building opportunities.

Barriers to Advancement

According to the "Women and Men in Corporate Leadership" study, as women advanced to senior levels they confronted the same barriers as men. These barriers included a difference in behavioral style from the organization's norm, lack of significant general management or line experience, and lack of awareness of organizational politics.

However, men's and women's views diverged when they considered opportunities for advancement and barriers specific to the work environment. Men expressed a more positive outlook than women about women's opportunities to advance to senior levels within their current companies. While 41 percent of men believe that opportunities have improved greatly over the last five years, only 30 percent of women believed so.

In general, women were much more likely than men to agree that they had challenges in getting to their current positions. Women also confronted an additional and pervasive set of culturally related barriers, including exclusion from informal networks, stereotyping, lack of role models, and an inhospitable corporate culture. For example, while almost half of women cited exclusion from informal networks of communication, only about one in five men cited such exclusion. The following statements by two senior white women give examples of exclusion from informal networks:

> And there would be other stuff, like playing poker or basketball on weekends . . . one time when we had a senior management meeting, afterwards, they went to a cigar bar. Finally, I told our CEO, "I find this offensive. Women don't want to go in there."[5]
>
> I have the old problem of all the men going into the bathroom, and coming out having made a decision! And I'm going, well, I wasn't there. . . . And then they go play golf. Again, I'm not there. You're treated differently. And it's subtle. I don't think I was always meant to be excluded, but at the time, I didn't play golf. And I wasn't about to go into the men's room![6]

These episodes cited by women can also be interpreted as expressions of male dominance. Certain conversations significantly control women by excluding them from the informal bonding men experience with talk about sex and sports. And while certain men's actions can be interpreted as expressions of their power and male identity, men typically do not recognize these actions as such. That is, where men may see humor, camaraderie, and strength, women may perceive crude, specifically masculine aggression, competition, intimidation, and misogyny.[7] This difference in perception can contribute to women's feelings that they are in an inhospitable corporate culture.

Gender Stereotyping: A Major Barrier to Advancement for Women

Almost half (46 percent) of women cited gender-based stereotypes as a barrier to their advancement in the "Women and Men in Corporate Leadership" study; perhaps not surprisingly, only 5 percent

of men cited this as a reason. Women clearly saw themselves disadvantaged by gender stereotypes.

Gender inequity in organizations is a reflection of societal relations between men and women. The lack of women in senior leadership positions mirrors the imbalance of power in the social
relations between men and women. Stereotyping supports this
underlying power imbalance by providing the means to limit
women's power and potential in organizations.

Stereotypes about race combine with gender stereotypes to present even greater challenges for women of color in business settings
than those faced by white women. This is a reflection of the double
outsider status of women of color in corporations, which is a theme
consistent with Catalyst research on women of color. The following quotations by women of color from varied backgrounds illustrate the additional effects of race on these women's experiences in
corporate settings.

> Staff are used to interacting with white women. They have their
> mothers, sisters, wives and daughters, so they can have a level of
> comfort around them that they can't necessarily have with us. They
> tell us all the time they are uncomfortable with black women. It
> becomes our job to make them comfortable.[8]

> I think, being Hispanic, sometimes the challenge is that most
> people will equate passion with anger. And passion is not anger, pas-
> sion is just passion. But, when most people are not passionate about
> what they do . . . and most people in a work environment are not . . .
> you just have to counter that by constantly telling people, "By the
> way, I'm not upset."[9]

> One of the problems with being an Asian woman is that there
> are certain stereotypes associated with being Asian and being a
> woman . . . the "China-doll syndrome." I don't fit into that image
> but that's a problem because people have an expectation [of who I
> am]. Then I'm so aggressive or have such a big mouth that it's like
> shattering an image even though [the] image is wrong. I think peo-

ple are taken aback when you shatter their illusion of what you should be. That in itself causes problems.[10]

"Taking Care" Versus "Taking Charge" Leadership Behaviors

Management literature implicitly links men and masculinity with management and authority. For example, typical leader character-istics cited in management literature are stereotypically male traits such as autocratic behavior and directiveness. Gender stereotyping assigns attributes to men that are consistent with those of success-ful managers and nonleader attributes to women. Common stereo-typical traits for women include sensitivity and emotionality, while stereotypical traits for men include aggressiveness and rationality. In other words, women are described as taking care of others while men are depicted as taking charge. In fact, a meta-analysis of more than forty studies has shown that men and women managers display few differences on people-oriented and task-oriented leader behav-iors.[11] However, gender stereotyping in business contexts still exist; women are depicted as better at people-orientation and men as more hard-driving and task-oriented. In spite of recent theories of leadership that have stressed interpersonal qualities commonly attributed to women (for example, collaboration and cooperation), as Rhode and Kellerman point out in the Introduction to this vol-ume, research continues to show that individuals displaying stereo-typically masculine styles are more likely to become leaders than those who display stereotypically feminine styles.

Stereotypical assumptions and thinking often form the rationale for decisions to withhold opportunities from women.[12] For example, a woman may not be offered a position because of beliefs that she will not want to travel or work in certain kinds of roles because of her obligations to family. Conversely, men have an advantage in attaining senior leadership positions because of the fit between how they are perceived and the attributes of senior leadership.

To understand the phenomenon of gender stereotyping better, in 2005 Catalyst surveyed a panel of senior business leaders, a third of whom were CEOs.[13] These business leaders rated how effective men and women are at ten essential leadership behaviors required of corporate leaders. The leadership behaviors consisted of the stereotypically feminine take-care behaviors of supporting, rewarding, mentoring, networking, consulting, team-building, and inspiring, and the stereotypically masculine take-charge behaviors of delegating, influencing upward, and problem solving. Consistent with gender stereotyping, both men and women in this senior-level sample judged men as superior on the take-charge behaviors of delegating and influencing upward. Both men and women judged women leaders as better at the take-care behaviors of supporting and rewarding.

A major finding from this study is that senior leaders engage in stereotyping. Senior executives, who are positioned to promote women into powerful roles, themselves hold gender stereotypes. And further, as will be discussed later in the chapter, male senior leaders tended to judge women leaders more harshly than they did male leaders.

Position Power Versus Interpersonal Power

Leaders use two primary sources of power. One is "position power," which refers to the way leaders use their positions in organizations, reflected by their specific titles such as "senior brand manager of new products marketing," to motivate others. Behaviors such as supporting, rewarding, and mentoring are associated with this kind of power because each requires some position of authority or control over important resources such as staffing and budgets. Alternatively, the leader behaviors of problem solving, inspiring, and team building rely on less formal interpersonal power. This sort of power does not rely on the leader's control of rewards or resources but on the leader's perceived expertise and charisma. Leaders can use respect for their expertise to inspire individuals and motivate teams to achieve organizational goals.[14]

Many businesspeople seem to assume that women have an edge on "interpersonal" power, given that women are judged as better than men at interpersonal relationships, because of women's supposedly greater emotive style. However, the panel of business leaders surveyed in Catalyst's stereotyping study did not perceive women as stronger than men in interpersonal power. Analyses showed that interpersonal power derives from perceived skill in team building, inspiring, and problem solving. Men in the study considered male leaders significantly better than women at this last important task.

Because men in the study saw women as less effective at problem solving, they were likely to also see them as less capable at inspiring and team building. More specifically, if men lack confidence in women's problem-solving competence, they may then be less open or even resistant to the inspirational appeals and team-building attempts of women leaders.

Being respected for one's problem-solving expertise is a source of interpersonal power or influence. Leaders who can command respect for their problem-solving expertise can use this respect to influence their followers, both individuals and teams. Stereotyping women as relatively ineffective problem solvers, therefore, undermines their interpersonal power.

In fact, interpersonal sources of power may be more important to effective leadership than position power. In the absence of interpersonal power, women leaders are left to rely on position-based forms of power; however, they often do not have senior-level positions that would provide a strong basis for this type of power.

Feminine Versus Masculine Occupations

Stereotypes often include the idea that women and men are good at different kinds of work. Consequently, type of occupation is a source of bias in individuals' perceptions. For example, when people think about an ideal nurse or social worker, they are likely to think of a woman. Similarly, when people envision an accomplished lawyer or medical doctor, they probably think of a man.

In the business world, stereotypically feminine and masculine occupations tend to be clustered in staff and line functions, respectively. People expect to find women doing well as human resources and public relations professionals while they expect to find men performing well as sales and general management professionals.

These occupational stereotypes, combined with occupational segregation, result in women leaders' being regarded more positively in feminine occupations than in masculine occupations. As noted in the Introduction to this volume, regardless of their true competencies, when women leaders work in occupations that are traditionally thought of as men's jobs, they are rated as less effective than when they work in women's jobs. This finding is consistent with other research that shows that women tend to be rated lower when they are enacting roles typically filled by men.

Women who manage large health care systems or cosmetic companies may be seen as more effective than women who manage steel mills or construction companies. Specifically, this study found that women and men who worked in stereotypically feminine occupations, such as human resources, rated women leaders' problem solving higher than that of men, whereas those who worked in occupations perceived to be masculine, such as general management, rated women leaders lower on their problem-solving abilities.

Male Versus Female Subordinates of Women Leaders

Another major finding from Catalyst's stereotyping study is that subordinates of women tended to judge women leaders more harshly on problem solving than those who were not subordinates of women. Some may think that because subordinates of women bosses judged women more negatively on problem solving, the subordinates were simply reflecting what they observed. However, perceptions are often filtered through stereotypical thinking. It is likely that these subordinates may have witnessed identical behavior between men and women leaders, but perceived the woman leader as less competent.

As mentioned in the Introduction to this volume, cognitive biases tend to exacerbate stereotyping. People are more likely to recall information that confirms their prior assumptions or to filter information in such a way that it confirms a stereotype. For example, if a subordinate observed a female boss taking time to ponder a decision, he may have judged her as indecisive and a poor problem solver and generalized this perception to women leaders. However, if he observed the identical behavior in a male leader, he might have judged the behavior as thoughtful.

The implication of this finding for women leaders is that if a leader's team and direct reports do not believe in her ability to solve problems, they will not be motivated to follow her direction. When women could be spending time focusing on implementing solutions, they may have to spend considerably more time than their male counterparts at getting buy-in from their team members. Besides suggesting the entrenched nature of stereotypes in business settings, this finding also suggests that simply hiring more women into management positions will not eliminate stereotypes; exposure to women leaders is not enough.

Counteracting Stereotyping

People stereotype without intending to, which makes the use of stereotypes difficult to address. To overcome this reflexive tendency, organizations need to create rigorous systems both to prevent stereotyping and to counteract the effects of existing stereotyping. For countering stereotypical perceptions of women, organizations should develop objective performance evaluation and succession-planning processes, educate managers about stereotyping, and showcase the successes of women leaders, especially in stereotypically masculine fields.

Develop Objective Performance Evaluation and Succession Planning Processes

To ensure that women's problem-solving expertise is not undermined by stereotypes, organizations need to ensure that performance management processes are structured to prevent it by defining and communicating performance evaluation criteria, creating explicit decision rules about how evaluation criteria are weighted, and implementing a system of checks and balances to safeguard against stereotypic bias.

Clearly define and communicate performance evaluation criteria. Common to many performance appraisals are evaluation criteria such as "innovation in approaching problems" or "demonstrated ability to execute." Given the stereotypically low perceptions of women's problem-solving ability, these are specific criteria where women may be especially susceptible to biased judgments. One way to reduce this disadvantage is to be very clear and specific about what behaviors or outcomes demonstrate problem-solving competence. The more organizations make their appraisal processes objective, with specific outcomes, the more likely they are to reduce bias in judgments.

Create explicit decision rules about how evaluation criteria are weighted. Gender stereotypes may cause people to attend to different kinds of information depending on whether they are evaluating a woman or a man, and as a result, different performance standards may unintentionally be applied to women and men. Using specified criterion weightings can help to ensure that women and men are judged by the same standards. For example, women are often penalized for lack of good citizenship (an expected attribute of women given their stereotype as more people-oriented than men) while men are not. At the same time, men often receive credit for exhibiting traits of good citizenship, while women do not.

Implement a system of checks and balances to safeguard against stereotypic bias. People may automatically use stereotypes to arrive at judgments. Organizations may not be able to consistently overcome this individual tendency, for example, during manager evaluation of staff members. Therefore, decision-making processes should be structured to ensure checks on the soundness of individual judgments on the back end, that is, after managers turn in performance evaluations or make recommendations about promotions or assignments. For example, in the case of women's being penalized for lack of good citizenship, Human Resources personnel could review all performance evaluations and ask the managers who do the rating if the same behavior is acceptable from men. Then Human Resources personnel could challenge those managers and ask them to cite gender-neutral facts to support their claims, such as evidence that the criteria are being applied equally to male and female evaluatees. Further, decisions about who is promoted or assigned to fast-track projects should not rest with single individuals or even with a single business or functional unit (for example, with Human Resources only). Multiple stakeholders should have a chance to weigh in on these important personnel decisions.

Educate Managers About Stereotyping

Individuals need to be educated about stereotyping processes and equipped with skills to self-monitor their perceptions. If this step is taken, organizations will be better able to limit bias at its source. For example, there is emerging evidence that people can break the habit of stereotyping if they

- Learn techniques to override automatic tendencies to use stereotypes.
- Learn to recognize the conditions that place them at risk for stereotyping.
- Have opportunities to practice interacting with people who are different from them (for example, in terms of gender or ethnic identity).[15]

Typical diversity training programs do not often achieve these learning objectives. By designing diversity programs that build on principles of bias reduction, organizations can better prepare themselves to address this very subtle but significant barrier to inclusion. Further, senior leaders can better support women in their organizations if those leaders examine their own stereotypes and resulting behavior. Leaders should not insist that women spend their valuable energies disproving stereotypes, nor should they penalize women whose behaviors do not fit stereotypes.

Stress Counter-Stereotypic Images of Women Leaders

People may be less likely to stereotype if they are continually exposed to information that disconfirms their stereotypes. To discourage stereotypes of women as poor problem solvers, organizations can highlight women's achievements in this area of performance. Such tactics may be particularly important in male-dominated settings where women are more susceptible to stereotyping.

Making Change in Business Organizations

To support the attitudinal changes discussed in this chapter, Catalyst recommends several programmatic components for achieving work environments more inclusive of women, typically required for making any level of change in organizations. These include having a strong business rationale, senior leadership commitment, strong accountability and measurement frameworks, and an effective communication strategy.

A Strong Business Rationale

In the United States, demographics in the marketplace and employee base are changing dramatically. To be successful, companies need to be an employer of choice. Companies that can attract, retain, and promote diverse employees will expand the talent pool available to them at all levels. A larger talent pool will mean a greater likelihood of success in the marketplace. At the same time, new customers, employees, and suppliers now come from all parts of the world, and it is important that leadership at companies having global presence reflects this reality. Breaking into new markets, understanding different employee cultures, and negotiating with non-U.S. suppliers often require a deep knowledge of country-specific work styles, expectations, and practices. A diverse leadership team is more likely to have this knowledge—and therefore more likely to succeed than a homogeneous team.

Senior Leadership Commitment

To counteract the effects of stereotyping, CEOs need to act in ways that demonstrate the business importance of women in leadership positions. One recommendation is for CEOs to demand and support gender-diverse candidate slates, selection teams, and outcomes when executive positions are filled. Although corporate boards of directors must approve all corporate officers, they generally support the candidates that CEOs recommend. CEOs who recommend women candidates to their boards demonstrate their commitment to diverse leadership teams and serve as powerful role models for managers throughout the organization.

Institute Accountability Mechanisms

Everyone from the CEO to senior leadership to local managers must be responsible for creating a diverse and inclusive culture at work. CEOs must insist on accountability mechanisms that will support change. What can be measured in an accountability framework includes the categories of talent management (for example, keeping track of the gender of all those promoted), inclusiveness of the work environment (often measured with employee surveys), and engagement with diversity and inclusion measures (for example, how many and what types of employees participate in training programs). Specific goals or targets need to be set: for example, specific numbers of women desired in certain positions, an increase over the past year in number of women promoted, or a lowering of the turnover rate among women in certain functions.

Real consequences, both positive and negative, and real attention or pressure from bosses, customers, and regulatory agencies are the drivers of accountability. Success or failure to achieve goals needs to be tied to at least one of these drivers. Negative consequences should be tangible, such as adverse impact on career movement or compensation (for example, an executive's bonus pay).

A principle for organizations to keep in mind in weighing the use of positive and negative incentives is to praise profusely and embarrass carefully. For example, a CEO at a major Fortune 500 company would require division heads to report their diversity results at yearly meetings. He would then identify the best-performing division and the worst-performing division. Because of the CEO's strategic (and infrequent) use of this embarrassment tactic, no division was labeled the worst for two years in a row.

Communicate

Any diversity strategy, including facilitating the advancement of women into leadership positions, will succeed only if it is communicated clearly and at all levels throughout an organization. CEOs and other senior managers should

- Explain the business case for gender diversity.
- Talk about stereotyping and its effects.
- Challenge code-speak and performance reviews reflecting double standards that hold women and men to different assumptions, behaviors, or metrics.
- Motivate managers to judge results and merits, not gender.

- Make the recruitment and promotion processes transparent so that everyone is held to the same standards, and every qualified employee has an equal chance at open jobs.

- State expectations explicitly and hold managers accountable for fulfilling them.

- Consistently apply diversity scorecards that can precisely measure change over time and highlight progress and setbacks.

- Publicly celebrate successes.

Summary

In spite of the demonstrated improvement in financial standing for companies with women in senior-level positions, women are still greatly underrepresented at that level. Catalyst research shows that stereotyping of women is a significant barrier to women's advancement. In particular, men managers perceive themselves as much better problem solvers than women managers. However, meta-analysis of more than forty studies on leadership shows few differences between women and men in workplace behavior and style. Clearly, actions, results, and merit—rather than stereotypic perceptions—should determine advancement in the workplace.

Because leadership consists of a set of separate but related behaviors, it was possible in the Catalyst stereotyping study to pinpoint where women leaders are vulnerable to stereotyping and to show how the negative effects of stereotyping on any one behavior can spill over to perceptions of other leader behaviors. For example, since inspiring, team building, and problem solving are related leader behaviors, a woman may suffer in interpersonal power because she is not seen as strong on problem solving. And, indeed, that result was true for women overall.

It is extremely challenging to create organizational change, particularly change that challenges deeply held beliefs and assumptions and is reflected and reinforced by the larger society. However, business organizations as role models for other institutions, and also as environments in which people spend much of their time, have a role to play in helping change stereotypical attitudes about women. While the mainly programmatic recommendations for change that Catalyst suggests tend to result in behavioral change, Catalyst also recommends that people look at deeper attitudinal change with our stereotyping work. The hope is that the combination of behavioral and attitudinal recommendations will lead to enduring change, overcoming gender stereotyping and other barriers to women's advancement into leadership positions in business organizations.

Endnotes

1. Lois Joy, *2005 Catalyst Census of Women Corporate Officers and Top Earners of the Fortune 500* (New York: Catalyst, 2006).
2. Margaret Yap, *The Bottom Line: Connecting Corporate Performance and Gender Diversity* (New York: Catalyst, 2004).
3. Paulette Gerkovich, *Women and Men in U.S. Corporate Leadership: Same Workplace, Different Realities?* (New York: Catalyst, 2004).
4. Gerkovich, *Women and Men in U.S. Corporate Leadership*, 14.
5. Gerkovich, *Women and Men in U.S. Corporate Leadership*, 20.
6. Gerkovich, *Women and Men in U.S. Corporate Leadership*, 20.
7. Joan Acker, "Hierarchies, Jobs and Bodies," *Gender & Society* 4 (1990), 139–158.
8. Katherine Giscombe, *Advancing African-American Women in the Workplace: What Managers Need to Know* (New York: Catalyst, 2004), 16.
9. Gerkovich, *Women and Men in U.S. Corporate Leadership*, 21.
10. Katherine Giscombe, *Women of Color Executives: Their Voices, Their Journeys* (New York: Catalyst, 2001), 36.
11. Alice H. Eagly and Mary C. Johannessen-Schmidt, "The Leadership Styles of Women and Men," *Journal of Social Issues* 57 (2001): 781–797.

12. Madeline E. Heilman, "Description and Prescription: How Gender Stereotypes Prevent Women's Ascent Up the Organizational Ladder," *Journal of Social Issues 4* (2001): 657–674.
13. Jeanine Prime, *Women "Take Care," Men "Take Charge": Stereotyping of U.S. Business Leaders Exposed* (New York: Catalyst, 2005).
14. Belle Rose Ragins and Eric Sundstrom, "Gender and Power in Organizations: A Longitudinal Perspective," *Psychological Bulletin 105*, no. 1 (1989): 51–88.
15. Stuart Oskamp, *Reducing Prejudice and Discrimination* (Mahwah, NJ: Erlbaum, 2000).

Part Four

Redefining the Problem, Recasting the Solutions

15

OFF-RAMPS AND ON-RAMPS

Women's Nonlinear Career Paths

Sylvia Ann Hewlett

For seventeen years, Nadja Fidelia successfully juggled the responsibilities of a high-profile career on Wall Street and life as a single
mother. Despite her sixty-hour workweeks she was a devoted mom.
Indeed, some of the strategies she developed to care for her son Jason
bordered on the heroic. When Nadja went on business trips, she left
a "treasure trail" of fun notes and jokey gifts around the house so that
her son could feel her presence every day. She also invited various
members of her extended family to live with her for stints of time so
that Jason would grow up with a sense of family.

But his childhood was ending. In 2003 Jason turned seventeen,
and as he started to talk about college, Nadja found herself feeling
heartsick. As she put it, "Despite my pride in the rich life opening
up in front of this fine young man, I also had a sense of impending
loss. It was beginning to realize that once Jason left for college I
would lose the dailiness of our life together—and miss it dreadfully.
As a single mother and an only child, we had been so close, so
reliant on one another."

So Nadja resolved to savor the remaining months she had with
Jason. She decided to turn the college application process into an
excuse to spend extended time with her son. "I developed this
vision. We would take some road trips across the country and look

---

Portions of this chapter appear in Sylvia Ann Hewlett, *Off-Ramps and On-Ramps: Keeping Talented Women on the Road to Success* (Boston: Harvard Business School Press, 2007).

at a whole bunch of campuses. And in between trips I would just be much more available—to listen and rub his back, to rustle up the odd impromptu meal and just plain "hang."

Nadja's plan needed her full-time energies for the better part of a year. So, one Monday morning, Nadja walked into her boss's office to resign from her job. At the time she did not think to ask for leave or for a flexible work arrangement. Although Nadja had co-chaired the diversity initiative at her firm and had been instrumental in making sure other people had access to such policies, it did not occur to her to ask for herself. The fact that Jason was an on-track seventeen-year-old was part of the problem. This was not a baby needing child care or a teenager strung out on drugs. Had he been going into rehab rather than to college it might have been easier to ask for help. As Nadja put it, "My issue seemed so entirely discretionary. The fact that my son was going to college and I felt bereft did not seem to be enough of a reason to get the firm involved."

In the end, Nadja was fortunate. She shared her decision to resign (and the reasons behind it) with a trusted mentor—someone who also happened to be a senior manager at the firm. He was horrified at the notion of losing such a valued employee and urged her to take a leave of absence rather than quit—to take whatever time she needed to be with Jason, but then to plan on coming back—he even offered her a reduced hour load when she returned.

Nadja was shocked—and tremendously relieved. Knowing that she had the option of coming back made a huge difference to her frame of mind. Although she had been prepared to quit and depend on savings for a while, she loved her job, and was thrilled at the prospect of being able to hang onto it.

She did take time out. For eight months she focused exclusively on her son—zigzagging the country taking long road trips, working on college essays, and simply hanging out with him. It was an amazing experience. For starters, her son was accepted at the college of his choice. In Nadja's words, "He was so happy and thrilled, and so was I. It felt like a team effort. . . . We got to do it together. Most importantly, we had a wonderful time. Just before I went back to work Jason went out of his way to thank me. He said that he would always remember this time as a gift."

Nadja went back to her job after those eight months out with a new sense of loyalty to her employer. It was one of those win-win situations. The firm not only held on to a high-performing, experienced female executive, the likes of which many Wall Street firms are scrambling to attract and retain, it won her renewed dedication. Nadja's appreciation is loud and clear. "I had a magical year and my company made it possible," she says.

Not everyone is as lucky as Nadja. The tugs and pulls of family (whether we're talking toddlers, teenagers, or elderly parents) continue to interrupt women's work lives. But the employment outcome is much less familiar. Few bosses reach out with this kind of caring attention. All too often a woman in Nadja's situation would have been forced to quit.

And many—way too many—do quit. That's why, about three years ago, a noisy debate erupted on both sides of the Atlantic over what Lisa Belkin of the *New York Times* called "the opt-out revolution."[1] For a number of months it was hard to turn on the television without encountering various talking heads scaremongering about a disturbing trend: large numbers of highly qualified women were dropping out of mainstream careers. Even the wild success of *Desperate Housewives* was attributed to a supposed glut of drop-out women—bored silly and looking for trouble on Wisteria Lane.

In the mainstream press there was a great deal of speculation on what might be behind this trend. Left-wing commentators tended to blame public policy (shortfalls in child care and flexible work options), while more conservative commentators simply blamed the victims. Women, it turned out, had a lot of problems that ranged from a failure of ambition to an unwillingness to work long hours. Larry Summers, a former president of Harvard, in an eye-catching speech, went so far as to accuse women of genetic inferiority.

Despite its heat, this debate has yielded little in the way of new insights or solutions, at least in part because of the absence of hard data. No one seems to know the basic facts: How many talented women are opting out? How many years do they stay out? How many want to get back in? And what policies and practices might help them get back onto that career highway?

In 2004 the Hidden Brain Drain Task Force targeted this subject area as a prime area for its research energies and set out to create a rich data set. In the summer of that year, three member companies (Ernst & Young, Goldman Sachs, and Lehman Brothers) sponsored a national survey designed to map the trajectory of women's work lives. The survey, which was fielded by Harris Interactive, comprised a nationally representative sample of highly qualified women and men, defined as those with a graduate or professional degree or a high honors undergraduate degree.[2] The survey research was supplemented by focus groups conducted within task force companies and companies on the outside (mostly "sister" companies in similar sectors). These focus groups serve to illuminate a much more intimate reality—the feelings and frustrations of the women on the front lines. The resulting study (published in March 2005 by the *Harvard Business Review*) paints a much more comprehensive and nuanced portrait of women's careers than has been available to date.[3] Here are some highlights.

Are Women Opting Out?

The answer is a resounding no. Sure, a sizable number take some time out. The survey data show that 37 percent of highly qualified women "off-ramp" (voluntarily leave their careers for a period of time). (See Figure 15.1.) But the amount of time spent outside the workforce is surprisingly short, on average 2.2 years. Across sector and occupation, the length of time spent off-ramped varies, ranging from 1.5 years in the banking and finance sector to 3 years in the legal profession. A little way down the road the vast majority of off-rampers (93 percent) are trying to get back onto the career highway. Media hype and overblown rhetoric notwithstanding, contemporary women are deeply committed to their careers.

Figure 15.1   How Many Women Off-Ramp?

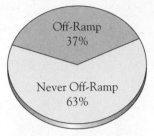

Source: Reprinted from Sylvia Hewlett, *Off-Ramps and On-Ramps: Keeping Talented Women on the Road to Success,* copyright 2007, by permission of Harvard Business School Publishing Corporation.

For instance, when we spoke with Janice, she was fighting a frustrating battle to get back on her career path.[4] An executive with twelve years of international experience in the reinsurance industry, an entrepreneur fluent in French, and the holder of a recent MBA degree from Duke University's Fuqua School, Janice thought that finding a new job would be a piece of cake, a thought that buoyed her considerable eagerness to resume her career. Indeed, Janice was welcomed by Human Resources staffers at the financial services firms she targeted when she tried to re-enter the workforce after having two children. But somehow hiring managers found it easy to turn her away. "They'd say, 'Yes, great résumé, but she's taken time off. I have an equal number of great managers who haven't taken time off,'" Janice says. Janice sees herself as a highly qualified executive, not as a person who has opted out or ditched her career.

Off-ramps are conspicuous and tend to create waves—we are, after all, talking about women quitting, and every empty desk tugs at a company's bottom line. But women can veer off the professional fast track in other ways. Some women choose what I call a scenic route. (See Figure 15.2.) They don't step out, rather they step back: taking a part-time job, a flexible work arrangement, a telecommuting option, or they turn down a promotion. For a period of time these women deliberately choose a less ambitious career path. This way they are able to look at the scenery, smell the roses, and fulfill serious responsibilities in the rest of their lives.

Figure 15.2   How Many Women Take a Scenic Route?

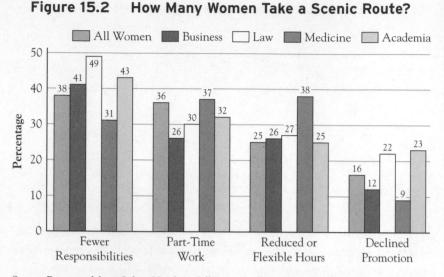

Source: Reprinted from Sylvia Hewlett, *Off-Ramps and On-Ramps: Keeping Talented Women on the Road to Success,* copyright 2007, by permission of Harvard Business School Publishing Corporation.

Rebecca, a public relations executive at a small but high-profile public affairs firm, is a perfect example of someone currently traveling a scenic route. Nearly three years ago, when Rebecca became pregnant, she approached her boss about putting a maternity plan in action. The firm was too small to fall under FMLA regulations. And although the firm has always been on the correct side of political issues such as women's rights, no employee had ever requested a maternity leave, let alone a part-time return. Rebecca was the first pregnant employee in fifteen years. The CEO and COO worked out a plan where Rebecca would get twelve weeks at half-pay and could be away for another four at no pay. When she returned part time, she would work Tuesdays and Wednesdays in the office and Thursdays from home. Rebecca has worked this way for almost three years now, and although she feels the arrangement works for her and her firm, she sometimes feels like she's in a holding pattern.

Rebecca falls in the pool of 16 percent of highly qualified women who our survey shows currently work part time. Part-time employment is more prevalent in the legal and medical professions, where

23 percent and 20 percent of female professionals (respectively) work less than full time, than in the business sector, where only 8 percent of women work part time. Another common work-life strategy is telecommuting; 8 percent of highly qualified women work exclusively from home, and 25 percent work partly from home.

Scenic routes seem to be as prevalent as off-ramps. Looking back at their careers, fully 36 percent of highly qualified women say they have worked part time for a period as part of a strategy to balance work and personal life. In addition, 25 percent say that they have reduced the number of work hours within a full-time job, and 16 percent say they have declined a promotion. What's more, a significant proportion (38 percent) say they have deliberately chosen a position with fewer responsibilities and lower compensation than they were qualified for, in order to fulfill responsibilities at home.[5]

Judith's story is typical. A senior executive at a Texas-based telecommunications company, this highly accomplished African American woman had both carved out an impressive track record in corporate America and done a fine job on the family front. She was justifiably proud of her long-standing marriage and well-adjusted children.

But unbeknownst to colleagues, Judith's life had become unsustainable. She was about to off-ramp—pushed out by the rigidities of a corporate culture caught in a time warp.

"The face time requirements were real and rigid. Core hours were 7:30 AM to 7:30 PM. God help you if you weren't present and available between those times. It wasn't unusual for an e-mail to go out at 5:30 PM announcing a meeting at 7:00 PM—which could then drag on to 8:30 PM. I never fully believed that these evening meetings were necessary. Very little was covered that could not have been dealt by e-mail—or in person the next morning. I always thought of them as some kind of test—you needed to prove by your physical presence that you were single-mindedly devoted to your job. Women of course tend to fail this test. Not too many women with family responsibilities are able spend evenings at the office, day in and day out."

In June 2003 Judith's frustrations came to a head. The corporation was streamlining some of its operations and offering attractive severance packages to senior executives. Judith took one—with alacrity.

"I saw this as a rare opportunity to take a sabbatical. I was exhausted. Worn out from twenty years of juggling twelve-to-fourteen-hour workdays and three children. And burnt out from the cumulative strain of 'battling the corporate culture.' I was hungry to recoup and reconnect with the rest of my life, most particularly my children, who were entering the teenage years. From a purely personal vantage point, the fact that the company was downsizing was a godsend—it afforded me a life-saving break."

In focus groups women talked about learning how to "stay below the radar." They were intent on doing a great job in the positions they held, but did not want to ratchet up. One reason they wanted to remain inconspicuously below the radar is that they did not want to run the risk of being offered a promotion. They feared that if they were put in the position of declining a promotion, it would reflect badly on their level of commitment. In the words of one woman, "I just don't think my boss would understand that my saying no has nothing to do with commitment—I love this company—it's just that I can't ratchet up until my daughter hits first grade."

Why Do Women Leave?

There's no simple, one-dimensional explanation for why women take time out. For most, career interruptions are a result of a complex interaction between "pull factors" (centered in the family) and "push factors" (centered at work).[6]

Going into this research I thought that the tugs and pulls around children would dominate. And to an extent I was right. For 45 percent of the women in this survey, a child care challenge—specifically the need to devote more time to children—was the issue that triggered the off-ramping decision. But other powerful pull factors are active, too. For example, 24 percent of women in the survey reported that an elder care crisis was the trigger issue—the one that forced them out. The pull of elder care responsibilities is particularly strong for women in the forty-one to fifty-five age group—often called the "sandwich" generation, positioned as it is between growing children and aging parents. One in three women in that age bracket reported having left the workforce for a period of time to care for a family member who is not a child.

We shouldn't forget that lurking behind these pull factors—all of which revolve around family care—is a traditional division of labor between men and women that remains entrenched and pervasive. Even when women are highly qualified and highly paid, they routinely pick up the lion's share of domestic responsibilities—typically 75 percent of housework and child care.[7] Indeed, in a 2001 survey conducted by the Center for Work-Life Policy, fully 40 percent of highly qualified women with spouses felt that their husbands created more work around the house than they performed.[8] So much for our dream of a fifty-fifty split!

Alongside these pull factors are a series of push factors—by which I mean features of the job or workplace that make women head for the door. (See Figure 15.3.) Twenty-nine percent of women report taking an off-ramp primarily because their jobs are not satisfying or meaningful. The data show that feeling underutilized or underappreciated are more significant problems than overwork. Not being consulted or not getting a sought-after (and deserved) plum assignment is much harder than dealing with than an additional responsibility. Only 6 percent of women off-ramped because the work itself was too demanding. It's interesting to note that in the business sector a variety of push factors are more important than pull factors. Fifty-two percent of women in business off-ramped at least in part because their career was not satisfying (versus 29 percent of women overall), while time for children was less important (43 percent). The contrast is even more dramatic in law, where 59 percent said their career was not satisfying—compared to 26 percent who wanted time for children. These figures indicate that certain work cultures—specifically large corporations and law firms—have done a poor job of developing a supportive environment for talented women.

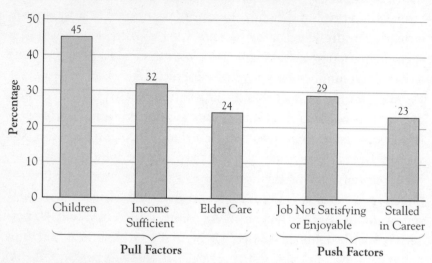

Figure 15.3   Reasons for Off-Ramping: Pull and Push Factors

Source: Reprinted from Sylvia Hewlett, *Off-Ramps and On-Ramps: Keeping Talented Women on the Road to Success,* copyright 2007, by permission of Harvard Business School Publishing Corporation.

Of course, neat distinctions between pull and push factors tend to break down in the hurly-burly of daily life. In the real world, most women deal with an interaction of pull and push factors—one often serving to intensify the other, creating a knock-on effect. For example, women are much more likely to respond to the pull of family when they feel hemmed in by a glass ceiling. In the words of one off-ramped television producer, "My two-year-old suddenly appeared needier—and yes, more appealing—the spring I was passed over for promotion. Objectively speaking, I don't think anything changed, but I was newly looking for a reason to take some time off and I wanted to believe that my child needed me at home full time."

In a strange way, this interactivity between pull and push is good news for companies. It means that nothing is written in concrete. A second child or a mother-in-law newly diagnosed with Alzheimer's does not necessarily mean that a woman will quit. Whether or not a woman off-ramps has a whole lot to do with

whether an employer can conjure up support—and opportunities—
in the workplace.

We also need to remember that, whether pulled or pushed, only
a relatively privileged group of women—those who are married to
high-earning men—have the option of not working. Indeed, for a
subset of women in the survey, the fact that they had a high-earning spouse was, in and of itself, an important trigger. Fully 32 percent of the women surveyed cite the fact that their spouse's earning
power "was sufficient for our family to live on one income" as a reason behind their decision to leave the workforce.[9]

As can be expected, the viewpoint of men as husbands and
fathers factor into a woman's decision to quit a job. Our survey
uncovers a wide range of opinion among men in terms of their attitude toward a wife's decision to off-ramp. More than half of all husbands (60 percent) claim they are enthusiastically supportive, but
55 percent also say they are either envious or angry. Money matters
loom large. Almost a quarter of the male respondents in the survey
(22 percent) say they are worried about the financial implications
of their wife's decision to quit. In one focus group I held, which
pulled together husbands of women who had quit, the conversation
centered on overload and burden. A surprisingly high percentage of
the men in the room felt resentful of the extra load dumped on
their shoulders and were concerned that they might not be able to
make up the shortfall in family income. Some saw their wife's quitting work as not being part of the original deal. One focus group
participant described his feelings this way: "I feel the rug has been
pulled. . . . I thought I was marrying a high-earning professional, not
a stay-at-home wife."

Why Do Women Want Back In?

Talented women who blithely throw their careers to the winds are
the exception rather than the rule. The survey data show that the
overwhelming majority of highly qualified women currently off-
ramped (93 percent) want to return to their careers.

Many of these women have financial reasons for wanting to get back to work. Nearly half (46 percent) cite "wanting to have their own independent source of income" as an important factor. (See Figure 15.4.) Women who participated in our focus groups talked about their discomfort with "dependence." However good their marriages, many disliked needing to ask for money. Not being able to splurge on some small extravagance or make their own philanthropic choices without clearing the decision with their husbands did not sit well with them. It's also true that a significant proportion of women seeking on-ramps are facing troubling shortfalls in family income: 38 percent cite "household income no longer sufficient for family needs" and 24 percent cite "partner's income no longer sufficient for family needs." Given what has happened to the cost of homes (up 55 percent over the past five years), the cost of college education (up 40 percent over the past decade), and the cost of

Figure 15.4   Major Factors for Reentry

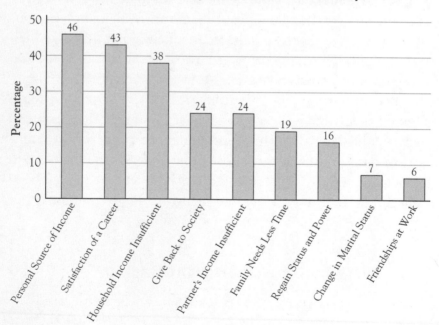

Note: Multiple responses allowed.
Source: Reprinted from Sylvia Hewlett, *Off-Ramps and On-Ramps: Keeping Talented Women on the Road to Success,* copyright 2007, by permission of Harvard Business School Publishing Corporation.

health insurance (up 87 percent since 2000), it's easy to see why many professional families find it hard to manage on one income.[10]

But financial pressures do not tell the whole story. Many of these women found deep pleasure in their chosen careers and want to reconnect with something they love. (See Figure 15.5.) Forty-three percent cite the "enjoyment and satisfaction" they derive from their careers as an important reason to return—among teachers this figure rises to 54 percent and among doctors it rises to 70 percent. A further 16 percent want to "regain power and status in their profession." In our focus groups, women talked eloquently about how work gives shape and structure to their lives, boosts confidence and self-esteem, and confers status and standing in their communities. As one former executive puts it, "Cocktail party chitchat is so much easier if you can claim to be a professional, even a lapsed professional. Besides which my children insist on it. My fifteen-year-old daughter doesn't want to be caught dead with a mom who is 'just' a housewife." For many off-rampers, their professional

Figure 15.5 Major Factors for Reentry (by Sector)

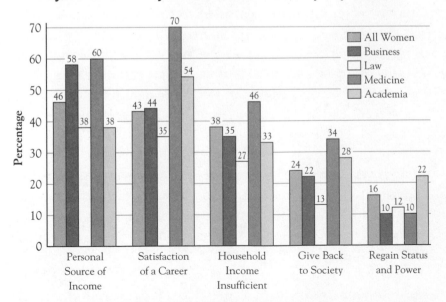

Source: Reprinted from Sylvia Hewlett, Off-Ramps and On-Ramps: Keeping Talented Women on the Road to Success, copyright 2007, by permission of Harvard Business School Publishing Corporation.

identity remains their primary identity, despite the fact they are currently taking time out. This makes a great deal of sense, given the length of women's working lives—which nowadays spans thirty-five to forty years. For most off-rampers, time out represents a mere blip on the radar screen.

Perhaps the most unexpected reason to return to work centers on altruism. Twenty-four percent of women currently looking for on-ramps are motivated by "a desire to give something back to society" and are seeking jobs that allow them to contribute in some way. In our focus groups, off-ramped women talked about how their time at home had changed their aspirations. Whether they'd gotten involved in protecting the wetlands, supporting the local library, rebuilding a playground, or being a Big Sister to a disadvantaged child, they felt newly connected to the importance of what one woman called "the work of care."

Lost on Reentry

If the overwhelming majority of off-ramped women have every intention of returning to the workforce, few understand how difficult this will be. The survey data show that while 93 percent of these women want to rejoin the ranks of the employed, only 74 percent manage to do so. And among these, only 40 percent return to full-time, mainstream jobs. (See Figure 15.6.) Twenty-four percent end up taking part-time jobs, and another 9 percent become self-employed.

The implications of these figures are clear: Off-ramps are around every curve in the road, but once a woman has taken one, opportunities to reenter a career are few and far between—and hard to find. Like Judith, a great many talented women find the on-ramping struggle a humiliating one: baffling, unfair, and replete with rejection.

When our "Off-Ramps and On-Ramps" article appeared in the *Harvard Business Review* in March 2005, it provoked a veritable flood of letters, e-mail, and phone calls. The response from the *HBR*

Figure 15.6   Employment Status
of Women Who Succeed in On-Ramping

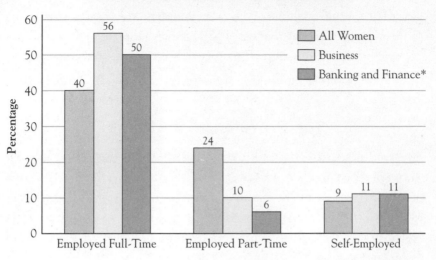

* Small sample
Source: Reprinted from Sylvia Hewlett, *Off-Ramps and On-Ramps: Keeping Talented Women on the Road to Success,* copyright 2007, by permission of Harvard Business School Publishing Corporation.

readership was up close and personal since so many women saw their life stories reflected in our data. Many were still smarting from having been cast aside in the wake of an off-ramp and their pain was sharp and raw. Judi Pitsiokos was one of many women who shared her story:

> I am a graduate of a top-ten law school who worked in the securities department of an AMLAW firm for six years before taking an off-ramp. After several years off raising my children I tried to gear up and reenter the workforce. Ten years later I am still trying to weasel my way back into a decent job. The best I have been able to come up with is working on my own, doing real estate closings, going to landlord-tenant court, etc. I am bored and angry—with myself and with the law firms who won't even look at my résumé. When I have had heart-to-heart talks with partners at major firms or legal recruiters, they say "why would we hire you when we can get a young kid right out of school" [I am looking for a job at the bottom rung].

"WHY?" I tell them, "because I am very smart, very well educated, have a track record, am done with child care responsibilities, and ready to work long hours." They laugh. Literally. I wonder what is wrong with a society that cuts smart women adrift when they take time off to raise children. The dollars lost to the economy must be astronomical.

The Prevalence of Stigma

Another powerful theme kicking around our focus group discussions was the pervasiveness of stigma. (Figure 15.7.) Across a range of sectors—in law firms, media companies, and investment banks—we found that women (and men) perceive many work-life policies (telecommuting, job-sharing, reduced-hour or part-time jobs, and so on) as essentially off-limits at their company. One new mother described Flexible Work Arrangements (FWAs) as "toxic." At her fast-paced tech company—which has an exemplary set of work-life policies—flexible work arrangements are so illegitimate, so poiso-

Figure 15.7   Stigma Attached to Using Work-Life Policies

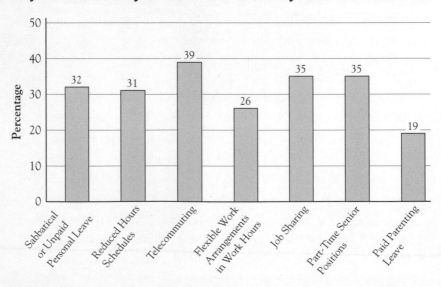

Source: Reprinted from Sylvia Hewlett, *Off-Ramps and On-Ramps: Keeping Talented Women on the Road to Success,* copyright 2007, by permission of Harvard Business School Publishing Corporation.

nous, that women routinely quit rather than take up policies that are on the books. Paid parenting leave seems to be a little less stigmatized than other work-life policies. Since the passage of the 1993 FMLA legislation, parenting leave has become established public policy, and this seems to have conferred a measure of legitimacy— at least for women. Still, a higher percentage of men perceive paid parenting leave as a stigmatizing policy.

The Penalties of Time Out

As we now know, women off-ramp for surprisingly short periods of time—on average, 2.2 years. However, even these relatively short career interruptions entail heavy financial penalties (Figure 15.8). Our data show that, on average, women lose 18 percent of their earning power when they take an off-ramp. In the business sector, penalties are particularly draconian: in this sector women's earning power dips 28 percent when they take time out. As one might expect, the longer you spend out, the more severe the penalty

Figure 15.8   Financial Penalties for Off-Rampers (Compared to Those with No Time Out)

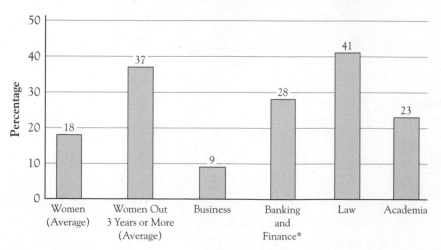

* Small sample

Source: Reprinted from Sylvia Hewlett, *Off-Ramps and On-Ramps: Keeping Talented Women on the Road to Success*, copyright 2007, by permission of Harvard Business School Publishing Corporation.

becomes. Women lose a staggering 37 percent of their earning power when they spend three or more years out of the workforce.

> For Rebecca, going part-time after her child's birth meant forsaking her yearly bonus. "At my company, bonuses are given out in January, when I was already back at work. When I went to my boss, he was like, 'Why does she think she's eligible for a bonus? She was on maternity leave the last three months of the year,' and I was like 'Of course I deserve a bonus. I was here nine months of the year.'" So far, during her nearly two years of part-time work, Rebecca has seen colleagues who had worked under her promoted, while she has financially languished. "I think probably I'll get a bonus with my next review; even though I'm working only part-time I'm bringing in a lot of business, and they recognize that. However, once I go back full time, it will take me years to get where I would have been if I had just gone back to work and not asked for a part-time arrangement."

Our findings in this area of financial penalties attached to time out jibe with the scholarly research. Columbia University economist Jane Waldfogel has analyzed the pattern of female earnings over the life span. When women enter the workforce in their early and middle twenties, they earn nearly as much as men do. And for a few years, they almost keep pace with men in terms of wages. For example, at ages twenty-five to twenty-nine, women earn 87 percent of the male wage. However, when women hit the prime child-raising years (ages thirty to forty), many off-ramp for a short period of time—with disastrous consequences on the financial front. Largely because of these career interruptions, by the time they reach the forty-to-forty-four age group women earn a mere 71 percent of the male wage.[11] All of which underscores the importance of sticking to the model. The male competitive model requires that careers take off in the decade after age thirty. In the words of MIT economist Lester Thurow, "The 30s are the prime years for establishing a successful career. These are the years when hard work has the maximum payoff. Women who leave the job market during those years may find that they never catch up."[12]

Downsizing Ambition

It turns out that earning power is not the only cost attached to taking time out. Women also downsize their ambitions, losing sight of their aspirations and losing faith in their dreams. One newly on-ramped woman described her changed attitude: "It took me three years to find this much-less-good job and during that time I had to accept that I had lost traction in my career. It was a bitter pill. I felt the unfairness of it—I had only been out for twenty months. But it was a fact nonetheless. So I've redefined what I can expect for myself." Another woman who participated in the same focus group described her old self—before an off-ramp—as this "soaring, thrusting person." That person doesn't exist anymore. In her words, "Reality bites."

Our survey data show that at young ages, men and women don't have much of a gap in terms of ambition. But there is a distinct drop-off in female ambition as women head through their thirties. In the business sector, for example, 53 percent of younger women describe themselves being very ambitious, while only 37 percent of older women are comfortable with this label.

In her 2004 book *Necessary Dreams*, psychiatrist Anna Fels argued convincingly that ambition stands on two legs—mastery and recognition.[13] To hold on to their dreams, women must attain the necessary credentials and experience, but they must also have their achievements and potential recognized in the larger world. The latter is often missing in female careers. Particularly in the wake of an off-ramp, employers and bosses tend to be skeptical about a woman's worth. A downsizing cycle emerges: a woman's confidence and ambition stalls; she is perceived as less committed; she no longer gets the good jobs or the plum assignments; this serves to lower her ambition further.

A final note on the penalties attached to time out. Penalties are not limited to individuals; companies also deal with significant costs when valued employees off-ramp. Our data reveals a salient and perhaps unexpected statistic: only 5 percent of highly qualified women attempting to on-ramp want to go back to the company they used to work for. Indeed, in business, banking, and finance, none of the women (0 percent) want to return to their previous employer. In retrospect, the vast majority of off-ramped women feel that they were not supported in those last months or weeks on the job—that their request for an FWA or a more meaty assignment was deflected or turned down. Some were made to feel that "they were letting the side down" when they struggled with the decision to quit.[14] The fact that these bad feelings linger are a wake-up call for companies. If employers expect to tap into this labor market—women returning after time out—they need to understand that the terms of disengagement matter.

What Do Women Want?

The survey data allow us to go beyond the facts around ambition to a complex vision of what women really want (Figure 15.9). At the top of the wish list in terms of career goals are a series of factors that go to the quality of the work experience itself. In terms of career goals, talented women very much want to associate with people they respect (82 percent); to "be themselves" at work (79 percent); to collaborate with others and work as part of a team (61 percent); and to "give back" to the community through the work they do (both inside their organization and outside in the larger world—56 percent). They also greatly value recognition from their company or organization (51 percent). Women tend to emphasize value sets rather than compensation or benefits. The only employment benefit to make it onto the wish list of the majority of the women in the survey is access to a flexible work schedule; this is a priority for 64 percent of the women in the survey. Only 42 percent cite a high salary, and only 15 percent cite a powerful position.[15]

Women's priorities thus constitute a sharp departure from the traditional male model and become yet another powerful reason why success within this model is so elusive for women.

In terms of the big picture, what is the significance of this data? Forty years after the women's revolution transformed female oppor-

Figure 15.9   What Women Want: Support, Flexibility, and Recognition More Important Than Money

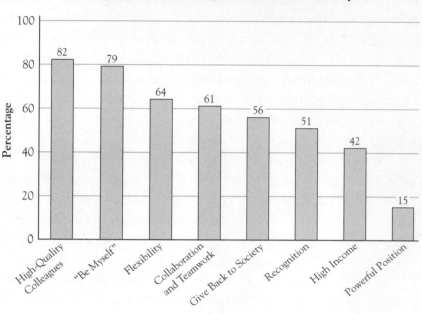

Source: Reprinted from Sylvia Hewlett, "The Hidden Brain Drain: Off-Ramps and On-Ramps in Women's Careers," *Harvard Business Review,* Research Report, copyright March 2005, by permission of Harvard Business School Publishing Corporation.

tunities, women's work lives remain very different from men's. Grouping together women who take off-ramps with those who take scenic routes, it seems that a majority have nonlinear careers. A great many women just need to step out or step to the side for a period of time. Looking back at their work lives, almost 60 percent of the highly qualified women in this survey describe their careers as nonlinear: they have not been able to follow the arc of a successful career in their sector.[16] An off-ramp or a scenic route has knocked them off course.

What this means is that large numbers of talented women fail to fit the traditional white-male model. They're unable to conjure up a continuous, lockstep career path, and they're badly positioned to "catch a wave" in their thirties. Besides which, their goals and values are profoundly out of sync with the typical career track.

Cloning the male competitive model is simply a huge stretch for a great many women. Now, obviously, some do manage to do it. Among them are women who sacrifice family life—and we should remember that childlessness is a huge issue among high-level corporate women, and at least some superwomen who somehow or other "do it all."[17] But these successful clones are in a minority and this chapter is not about them. It's about the other 60 percent: the ones who struggle with off-ramps and on-ramps and have a hard time claiming or sustaining ambition.

For three and a half decades policy wonks and business leaders have waited for women to get with the program. The challenge was thought to be about providing access and opportunity and then allowing enough time to go by so that the pipeline could fill. The reasoning was simple: if you created a truly level playing field so that men and women had equal access to employment opportunities, then, over time, as successive cohorts of well-qualified female professionals filled the pipeline, women would eventually be fairly represented at the top. This is not happening. Over the years there has been so much leakage from the pipeline that progress has effectively stalled. For example, the proportion women partners at law firms has climbed slightly over the last five years while the number of women CEOs at Fortune 500 companies has fallen slightly over the same period. If progress moves along at this pace, it will be a hundred years before we have a robust number of women in top jobs!

Reversing the Brain Drain

My advice—to policy wonks and business leaders alike—is to quit waiting. The pipeline won't work in a reasonable time frame because it relies on shoe-horning women into the male competitive model, and most of them don't fit. What we now need is the development of a second generation of policy that provides pathways to power for women with nonlinear work lives.

Endnotes

1. Lisa Belkin, "The Opt-Out Revolution," *New York Times Magazine*, October 26, 2003.

2. The survey targeted a nationally representative sample of 2,443 women and 653 men in the United States aged 28–55 who have a college degree with honors or a graduate degree. The survey was conducted online between June 23 and July 15, 2004, by Harris Interactive under the auspices of the Center for Work-Life Policy, a not-for-profit research organization.

3. Sylvia Ann Hewlett and Carolyn Buck Luce, "Off-Ramps and On Ramps: Keeping Talented Women on the Road to Success," *Harvard Business Review*, March 2005. See also Sylvia Ann Hewlett, Carolyn Buck Luce, Peggy Shiller, and Sandra Southwell, *The Hidden Brain Drain: Off-Ramps and On-Ramps in Women's Careers* (Boston: Harvard Business Review, 2005).

4. Research participants who requested privacy are referred to by first name only.

5. For this question, multiple responses were allowed.

6. Hewlett, Luce, Shiller, and Southwell, *The Hidden Brain Drain*, 16–21.

7. Scott Coltrane, "Research on Household Labor: Modeling and Measuring the Social Embeddedness of Routine Family Work," *Journal of Marriage and the Family 62* (November 2000): 1208–1233.

8. Sylvia Ann Hewlett and Norma Vite-Léon, *High-Achieving Women, 2001* (New York: Center for Work-Life Policy, 2002).

9. Hewlett and Vite-Léon, *High-Achieving Women*, 17.

10. Office of Federal Housing Price Oversight (OFHEO), "House Price Appreciation Slows from Record-Setting Pace, But Remains Strong," December 1, 2005, 15; State Farm citing data from the College Board, available online: http://partners .financenter.com/statefarm/learn/guides/collegesav/cspric.fcs, access date: January 17, 2007; Milt Freudenheim, "Health

Care Costs Rise Twice as Much as Inflation," *New York Times*, September 27, 2006.

11. Jane Waldfogel (Professor of Social Work and Public Affairs, Columbia University) in discussion with the author, July 17, 2001. See also Susan Harkness and Jane Waldfogel, *The Family Gap in Pay: Evidence from Seven Industrialised Countries* (London: London School of Economics, 1999), table 3.

12. Lester C. Thurow, "63 Cents to the Dollar: The Earnings Gap Doesn't Go Away," *Working Mother,* October 1984, 42.

13. Anna Fels, *Necessary Dreams: Ambition in Women's Changing Lives* (New York: Pantheon, 2004).

14. For a more detailed discussion, see Hewlett, Luce, Shiller, and Southwell, *The Hidden Brain Drain,* 29–36.

15. Hewlett, Luce, Shiller, and Southwell, *The Hidden Brain Drain,* 54.

16. Hewlett, Luce, Shiller, and Southwell, *The Hidden Brain Drain,* 28, exhibit 2.1.

17. Sylvia Ann Hewlett, "Executive Women and the Myth of Having It All," *Harvard Business Review,* April 2002.

16

ISN'T SHE DELIGHTFUL?

Creating Relationships That Get Women to the Top (and Keep Them There)

Karen L. Proudford

Much is written about leadership—including identifying the key traits of leaders, determining what behaviors effective leaders engage in, and determining conditions under which leaders can be effective. However, the social processes by which one becomes a leader are not often addressed. To do so here is beyond the aim of this chapter; however, I would simply note that an elemental process occurs when a leader is chosen or identified. One of the most fascinating, perplexing questions that both frustrates and challenges many of us interested in organizational life is: What does it take to enter the proverbial inner circle? Some process—which often seems akin to luck but may be a mix of luck and opportunity—allows individuals to pass through what often seems like an impenetrable boundary (for example, the glass ceiling). Even if one has only the opportunity to step just inside the circle, at the periphery, it nonetheless marks a significant passage into the realm where power and influence are granted.

For many women, the passage occurs by virtue of a relationship with someone on the inside, such as a husband or father. For others, there may be no clear mentor, no spouse or significant other in high position, no long-standing connection that would definitively signify to others what strategies to use in order to follow a similar, desirable path. In fact, that relationship may defy the easy explanations we typically rely on to explain a person's ascension into the leadership ranks. The relationship or set of relationships that ushered in the passage may be fleeting or even conflicted. It is, nonetheless, essential.

My purpose in this chapter is to consider the central role of relationships in creating opportunities for women. I discuss research that outlines key gender-based differences in relationship-building strategies, distinctions that might lead us to wonder how women and men (within and across race) have been able to work together toward women's advancement at all. The call to that work remains urgent, however, as the recent emphasis on mentoring and networking as effective methods for ushering women into top positions demonstrates. Those individuals engaged in such efforts are often faced with, and perhaps paralyzed by, the uncertain terrain that faces them as they attempt to navigate their way through gender differences. Here, I suggest that we "presume innocence" as a complementary (not exclusive) mode of interacting across gender (and race), and I end with several case illustrations that demonstrate the untidiness of attempting to do so.

Women Who Have Arrived—Or Have They?

For women in this country, the invitation to join the top ranks or inner circles of organizational life happens rarely—for women of color, virtually not at all. Catalyst reports no female CEOs of Fortune 100 companies and only eight in the Fortune 500. Catalyst further estimates that given current trends, it may take forty years before gender equity prevails at the highest levels of U.S. corporations.[1] Despite all the progress, the managerial ranks of many companies, and to a much larger degree their top executives and boards, remain the territory of white males.

Women who do manage to get to the top may find their stay untenable. The meteoric rise and equally stunning fall of several female CEOs have been viewed by some as the inevitable consequence of being at the top and by others as indicative of a worrisome trend for aspiring female executives. When Jill Barad was named CEO of Mattel in 1997, she was one of only three female chief executives of Fortune 500 companies. Barad's rise at Mattel was described as "storybook," due in large part to her role in growing Barbie line revenues from roughly $200 million to almost $2 billion annually.[2] By the late 1990s, the Barbie line accounted for almost 40 percent of Mattel's revenues, fueling Barad's ascension to CEO in 1997. *Business Week,* in a cover story, described Barad as "fierce [and] flamboyant" and as "breaking stereotypes about corporate success" by successfully balancing her roles as chief executive, wife, and mother.[3] The article heralded her competitive instincts and engaging, dynamic personality, and proclaimed her a role model for ambitious women in corporate America. Unfortunately, her tenure at the top was about to come to a premature end.[4] With Barbie sales at a plateau, Barad turned to acquisitions to fuel revenue growth. Mattel acquired The Learning Company, the largest and most costly of its purchases, in 1999. But Mattel's profits did not rebound; instead, the company continued to disappoint Wall Street with declining revenue and profits. Barad resigned in 2000 amid questions about her management style (now often described as abrasive), unfettered optimism despite huge losses, and inability to find and exploit growth opportunities at the company.

If Jill Barad was the first highly celebrated female CEO, Carly Fiorina of Hewlett-Packard is surely the most celebrated chief. The press again likened Fiorina's rise to a Hollywood story.[5] Fiorina was a star at Lucent Technologies, noted for her "silver tongue and iron will."[6] She was instrumental in handling AT&T's spin-off of Lucent, helped build a fresh brand for the new entity, and managed its $19 billion service unit. While Barad's early successes came at the company she eventually led, Fiorina's challenge was to transfer her winning ways to a new company. For a short time, it appeared that Fiorina would indeed meet that challenge by crafting a new vision for what many considered a lackluster, stodgy HP. But Fiorina's belief in the Compaq merger proved unwarranted. Insiders and outside critics noted the loss of jobs, the difficulty of merging two very different cultures, and the unwieldiness of managing a much larger company. The bitter battle between Fiorina and HP Board members over the merger also took its toll. In 2005, after just four and a half years at the helm, Fiorina was forced to resign.

Barad and Fiorina may have experienced what British researchers have called a "glass cliff," whereby the tenure of female executives is precarious and short-lived.[7] Interestingly, both Barad and Fiorina first made headlines by reviving declining products or companies. Barbie was a flat, if not dying, brand when Barad first took over. Similarly, Fiorina inherited HP at a point when the company's sagging fortunes and uncertain future were well known.[8] The small number of women in executive positions prohibits quantitative analysis that would confirm or deny a conclusion that women are likely to get their chance, if at all, in situations that more traditional prospects would find unattractive. In any case, that small number and the unrelenting attention given to their careers calls for an examination of the conditions under which women are invited into leadership ranks. It may be that women welcome the challenge of a turnaround; conversely, it may be that they are only offered such difficult challenges.

If there is indeed a glass cliff, a wide variety of factors seem likely to influence the development of this dynamic. My purpose here is to suggest, very tentatively, the role that relationships may play. Prevailing wisdom suggests that relationships are a significant component in determining the experiences of these women: how and when they are informed or put forward for opportunities, what advice they receive about whether or not to take them, what kind of management team they have in place, what should happen if there are difficulties, and so on. We know that perception may overrule facts in terms of reaching conclusions about one's performance—and allies are important to have if an executive is to survive downturns in organizational performance. Any executive, and perhaps especially any woman, who is placed into a top spot without a significant network of support relationships is likely to be at risk.

"Women's Ways" and Advancement

Few would argue with the assertion that climbing the organizational ladder necessarily involves finding a mentor or sponsor, so much so that young professionals fervently seek out mentors as if courting a spouse. Or, in fortunate cases, they enter into arranged relationships via formal mentoring programs. But other important relationships can support advancement as well, such as those established with subordinates, peers, and customers.[9] If indeed relationships are the key to career advancement, a lack of supportive relationships may provide a partial explanation for the small number of female CEOs. But is that a hasty conclusion? Are women not believed to be more adept at handling relationships and at understanding the need to attend to relationships? Much has been written about the different style of leadership that women bring—more collaborative, egalitarian, reciprocal—than their male counterparts. It has been argued that women's ways of interacting are poorly understood and discounted in the organizational environment.[10] If women do possess a particular skill in that arena, one would expect that they would benefit greatly from being in an environment where relationships are so vital to success. But it raises an interesting question: is women's facility with interpersonal interaction what has led some women to rise successfully to the tops of organizations? Or is it that women's way of interacting is ineffective, and that new, different patterns are needed in order to be successful?

Approaches to relationship building differ markedly for men and women in terms of three things that may impact attempts at advancement in an organization. First, the approaches differ in terms of the extent to which relationships reinforce or minimize status differences. Women have a tendency to downplay status differences, preferring instead to focus on equality and connectedness with their peers. Emphasizing status differences would make them appear arrogant and boastful, which would have a negative impact on their relationships.[11]

It is not that women are unaware of status differences or that they do not value them; they just do not call attention to them. Deborah Tannen has found, for example, that women tend to apologize as a ritualized way of maintaining balance in an interaction. For a woman to say "I'm sorry" may mean "I'm sorry that happened" rather than "I was responsible for what happened and apologize." Indicating sorrow is a way to make the other person feel as though their misfortune does not make them inferior. In fact, women may expect the other person to apologize in return, just to reinforce the equal and reciprocal nature of the relationship. Thus both persons are on equal footing. Moreover, lateral relationships tend to be quite important for women. Ella Bell has noted the importance of supportive relationships among black female peers.[12] Men, by contrast, tend to be quite comfortable highlighting status differences. They want the hierarchy to be clear and visible. They actively seek out individuals higher in the organization to help them and people below to buttress their efforts. An apology places them in a one-down position, so they offer or solicit apologies only in situations in which they think it is accurate or advantageous to have a verbal expression of their place in the line of command.

A second difference in the way men and women approach relationships centers on the extent to which relationships are viewed as developmental or instrumental. Women tend to be concerned about the other person, establishing and maintaining mutuality in the relationship and a commitment to the growth of the other person. They view relationships as desirable if they are contributing to someone's well-being and development. Men, however, tend to focus on the ways in which the relationship will allow them to be successful or advance in the organization, on how it will help them gain access to new or more resources, influence, and power. Joyce Fletcher, in her discussion of relational practice, makes distinctions in the use of the term "mutual empowering."[13] She notes that the traditional (male) definition of empowerment refers to a person "who has the information and authority to make decisions, to structure and prioritize tasks, or to improve process."[14] The relational practice described here, however, has little to do with authority and decision making. Instead, it refers to "the act of enabling, or contributing to, the development of another."[15] She cites instances in which female engineers actively use multiple strategies to reach peers they are instructing, to act in ways that help others preserve important relationships, and to protect people from their own lack of skill—all in an effort to construct a nonthreatening environment within which others can learn. One engineer explains: "Like, when Mark and Ed were working? They don't talk to each other—they just *do* it. Like, if they are showing you something, they don't talk while they are doing it, and if you don't know what is going on, then you are *lost*. But, like, when I was showing Cheryl, I talked the whole time so she would know what I was doing. I mean the whole thing is so that they'll be able to do it without you, right?"[16]

For the men, the interaction served its purpose—one knowledgeable person displaying his skill to another (or one lacking in knowledge trying to acquire that skill). For the women, it appears more important to share as much information as possible throughout the interaction, with the expectation that the person will then be able to proceed on her own. Moreover, having an ongoing dialogue might provide an opportunity for the engineer, as teacher, to learn from Cheryl.

The third distinction in male versus female approaches to relationships is the extent to which relationships are interpersonally focused or task focused. Women tend to emphasize connection, camaraderie, and intimacy when relating to others, while men prefer to focus on the task at hand. Tannen presents another clear example. When she asked students to submit audiotapes of cross-gender conversations, one woman's husband did so in these terms: "This is a good conversation . . . because it's not just him and me shooting the breeze, like 'Hi, how are you? I saw a good movie the other day,' and stuff. It's a problem-solving task. Each line is meaningful."[17] His wife disagreed, describing the conversation as "technical and impersonal."[18] Tannen also recounts the following: "A German student showed me a card she had received that her mother had covered with handwritten 'conversation' inquiring about her daughter's life and health and filling her in on family news. Folded into the card was a brief typewritten note from her father, telling her to go to the university registrar and obtain a form that he needed for tax purposes."[19]

For women, establishing rapport may take precedence over, though not subsume, attention to the task. In fact, women are likely to be more open about the task, to negotiate aspects of the work, and reformulate it based on their attempts at relationship building. By contrast, men may get together around the task, as defined— though connecting is unlikely to be viewed as a prerequisite for accomplishing the goal or objective.

Returning to our central question, one could imagine that women who focus on peers' developmental and interpersonal level would have difficulty navigating their way up the hierarchy in an organizational context dominated by status-oriented, instrumental, task-focused males. Whether these differences are genetic or rein-forced from early years by social learning processes, they represent very different ways of communicating and attempting to establish connection (or emphasize disconnection). All manner of opportunity arises for misinterpretation. For men, being seen as competent, influential, and powerful can be highly desirable, while for women, being seen as likable—nice and helpful—can be valued. Thus when a man in a work context approaches a woman and asks technical questions about a particular issue, it can be viewed as intrusive, rude, and demeaning. Or when men speak boastfully about some accomplishment, again in a well-understood (among the men) attempt to establish membership if not superiority in the group, they are exercising time-honored ways of interacting. For women, speaking about one's accomplishments might seem arrogant and offensive; they may expect that others, if they are so inclined, would compliment them on any noteworthy behavior. If that does not occur, they feel discounted, ignored, and as if their contributions are not valued. And for men—en masse—to validate what the other men have said or done has the potential to elevate a misunderstanding to a negative environment.

While these distinctions can be helpful in unpacking cross-gender interactions, they are not identity characteristics. In other words, all indications are that they are relative, context-bound patterns. For example, women are indeed interested in status differences; minimizing those differences in public settings is not an indication of a low value attached to them. Rather, it is an indication of the high value attached to connecting with others. Similarly, men often emphasize bonding with others as an important aspect of conducting work. However, their intention to connect is expressed very differently. Perhaps this is what makes building relationships across gender so complex in organizations: men and women share similar desired ends, but they have poorly understood, sometimes mismatched, ways of achieving them.

Presuming Innocence

Gender differences can make interacting quite difficult, that we know. People's biases and judgments about which way of interacting is better can influence their interactions. But what happens when we are wrong? What occurs when we think we know the other person's intentions, but we are simply incorrect? The question is not whether or not we were harmed by someone and did not know it (we want to be sure to ferret out those who would do us harm); the question is also about whether or not we have missed an opportunity by misreading intentions. It would be wise to exercise caution, but when have we just gotten it wrong? And what are the implications for the ability of women to build relationships that provide a foundation for our advancement in organizations? It is rare for a woman to have advanced without the assistance of a man, sometimes her husband, father, or other relative. In other cases, women have simply built the relationships that work; those relationships have at least involved crossing gender boundaries and, for women of color, they have probably involved crossing race boundaries as well.

Presuming Innocence in Action

Psychologist George Miller has said, "In order to understand what another person is saying, you must assume that it is true and try to imagine what it could be true of."[20] For the purposes of this discussion, I suspend the assumption that attempts to cross race or gender lines are motivated, in part or wholly, by some basic desire to injure, harm, discount, co-opt, or otherwise damage the other party. Suspending this assumption may seem unwarranted, given the sociohistorical context within which U.S. race and gender relations are embedded. After two decades either in corporate life or studying it—and studying the effects of race and gender directly—I am under no illusions about the perniciousness of racism and sexism. Nor do I excuse or condone acts of the "isms." Here, however, my assertion is that while sexism and racism are prevalent (and I would argue that they are), they aren't the only forces at play in the workplace. And while countersexist behavior may not dominate the workplace, it nevertheless exists and perhaps can be a source of positive change.

Case Illustration 1. Business schools are similar to corporate America in that they have relatively few females at the top, or as faculty members. At the university where I work, I am one of only two tenured female faculty members. At one particular meeting, I was the only female present. The purpose of the meeting was to review the slate of candidates for a vacant faculty position. The pool of applicants represented a mix, by gender. As this was my first such meeting, I was inclined not to take strong stands. Instead, I wanted to devote the bulk of my energy to observing and understanding how the group operated. As one female candidate's vita was discussed, one faculty member commented, "Well, she is just a delightful woman, but I don't think she is necessarily a good fit." I took note of the remark, which seemed innocuous, if general. A second female applicant's folder came up for review. The same faculty member—a white male—indicated that, "I think she's delightful, but I don't think she has the background we're looking for." I began to feel that sense of unease—that something was not quite right, but I did not have enough details to reach any conclusion. As discussion of the male candidates ensued, I noted (or it seemed to me) that each was discussed at length, with a serious consideration of his strengths and weaknesses. My unease began turning to frustration, suspicion, and mild irritation. Was this how meetings were to be conducted? Was I going to be a troublemaker by raising a concern? What impact would this have on my interactions with the other committee members? My negative response, however, was counterbalanced by my view of the faculty member. I knew him as a trusted colleague, one who consistently reached out to junior faculty (male and female) and offered advice and counsel. I knew that he often encouraged female students to pursue graduate studies. Still, I reasoned, maybe I did not know him as well as I thought. Perhaps now, as a member of this closed committee, I was seeing his true persona. As the third female candidate's name was raised, I felt myself stiffen. I hoped, above all, that she was not delightful. But, a moment later, as committee members said little, the faculty member said, "She seems like a delightful person, it's just that . . ." I could not let him finish that sentence. I had to interject, but did so as calmly as I could—and with some hesitation in my voice, "Now, are all of the women going to be delightful?" There was a brief pause, and then we all started laughing. With the ice broken, I explained that I really did not think we were giving serious consideration to the women. Even if we decided not to recommend hiring one of the female candidates, I believed we should engage in a reasoned discussion. We then returned to each female, reviewed her qualifications in depth, and completed our task. After the meeting, my colleague indicated that he really had no idea he had been using the same word repeatedly to describe the women. He said he was aware that he did not want to be perceived as "picking the women apart."

The question "Isn't she delightful?" is such a subtle, powerful way of affirming a woman's position outside the circle. It places woman at the outer edges, introducing just enough ambiguity and uncertainty to ensure that she will not be granted full membership in the sphere of influence. I would not suggest that this is a conscious or intentional process; it may in fact be a by-product of an attempt to articulate a nuanced opinion about a woman—or to avoid being labeled as a detractor. There is but one answer to the question; yet, if it is accepted, it places women in a kind of holding pattern on the perimeter of power, just inside the door, until some shock or force propels them inward toward full membership in the group.

Case Illustration 2. A serious consideration of building relationships must include an acknowledgment that awkwardness and clumsiness can often characterize the early stages of establishing a connection. In some cases, individuals simply cannot think of anything to say, particularly if they are interacting with a person of another race or gender, or both. If they have little data about the other person and group, they may well make a comment that seems inappropriate or offensive. Requiring people to be perfect (competent) is consistent with a short-term, rational-actor point of view.

In a diversity workshop I was co-facilitating, a white woman spoke of an instance in which she thought she was giving a compliment to a black coworker by indicating (after hearing the coworker give a presentation) that the person was very articulate. Many people are aware that this particular compliment can make many a black person bristle. After all, at one time, it was illegal for blacks to learn to read, and many developed speech patterns that deviated from formal English. A black person hearing such a compliment may take it as a put-down, an indication that the speaker regards it as unexpected or even unnatural for them to be so articulate, and react with hostility rather than pleasure. This reaction, by the way, is often cited by blacks regardless of educational level; in fact, highly educated blacks are often more incensed that someone should comment on their speaking abilities.[21] Ironically, this compliment may—

as discussed in the first case illustration—both affirm the person and underscore that person's perceived otherness. It may confirm his or her special status as an exception to the stereotypical view of most blacks. Isn't she (or he) articulate?!

During the workshop, the white woman wondered, "What did I say wrong?" Her focus was on whether or not the person was a good speaker. I have spoken with many whites who, having made comments that were not well received, have wondered if they were correct or incorrect in their assessment. In their view, whether or not they were correct was tied up with whether or not they were racist. They have, more often than not, been deeply disturbed by the prospect of making a remark that could be labeled as racist. I have asked them to consider that accuracy is not what is really at stake here. Moreover, additional data would be required before reaching a conclusion about whether or not they are racist. At a minimum, we would determine whether they only comment about speaking to blacks. One incident does not provide enough information to answer the question. If we presume their innocence, however, we may want to consider that the comment may simply be a compliment, a way to start conversation. Perhaps it was not the most artful way to begin a conversation, perhaps it was awkward; but it may, nonetheless, have been simply an invitation to talk.[22]

Getting Women In and To the Top

Our challenge, then, is to take on these characterizations, loaded as they are with sociohistorical cultural baggage, in a way that helps us move through them toward stronger relationships. This is no small challenge. Reading about and conducting research on such characterizations can test one's mettle, but living with these characterizations and calling attention to them as needed demands more than we sometimes feel equipped or willing to handle. The following case illustration is a vivid example of that challenge, replete with dynamics of race, gender, and status that often leave the parties involved reeling:

Case Illustration 3. Joleen (a black woman)[23] was a highly educated, accomplished attorney, interviewing for a position as partner at a prestigious law firm. Initially, she met with the two senior partners (both white men) over lunch to discuss the opportunity. Both expressed interest in her as a potential new partner in the office. She was invited to the firm headquarters for a day, during which she was interviewed by individual partners, taken on a tour of the facility, and introduced to the staff. She also gave a mock presentation to the entire group of partners who would vote on her candidacy. By the end of the day, Joleen felt certain that she would be extended an offer. Everyone had been polite and supportive, responding well to her presentation. She was presented with a portfolio and pen before she left, and the senior partners were already discussing the likely location of her office. Joleen was shocked when, the following day, one of the senior partners called to inform her that the partners had decided not to extend her an offer. His explanation for the decision was worse than the decision itself. They had all been impressed with her, he said. However, she had made two minor errors during her presentation, and the group was concerned about her ability to represent the firm effectively. He could not oppose a decision made by the partners. Joleen was stunned. Yes, she had remembered making one very minor error in citing a particular precedent, but she had immediately corrected herself. She noted the minor inconsistency in the phrasing used on one of her presentation slides, but wondered if this could possibly be a significant enough to warrant their decision. Suspicion and doubt began to enter her thoughts. Were these explanations actually convenient excuses for not issuing an offer? The firm, after all, had no black attorneys—male or female—at this location. Perhaps they were interested in interviewing her, but not hiring her, so that they could announce that they had considered a minority female candidate.

Fortunately, someone at Joleen's current law firm knew a senior partner (a black woman) in a separate location of the firm. Joleen's colleague urged her to call. The female partner was also surprised by Joleen's news. She had heard about Joleen's interview, reviewed her credentials, and been confident that she would make an outstanding partner. She promised to look into the matter. The next day, Joleen received a call from the managing partner (a white woman). The call began somewhat awkwardly, and the managing partner seemed surprised that the senior partner had notified Joleen of the decision. The managing partner indicated that one partner (a white woman) had expressed concerns during the partner meeting; the partner was known as someone who was highly critical. Moreover, the partner was the only attorney practicing in employment—Joleen's area. The managing partner reaffirmed that the firm was interested in Joleen and would like to extend her an offer, with one provision. Joleen was to work with the partner for the first six months of her tenure. The managing partner felt sure that the partner would change her opinion about Joleen during that time.

The offer did not sit well with Joleen. She was an experienced attorney, with the credentials and a track record that rivaled any other attorney at the firm. No other attorney had been required to fulfill such an arrangement. Why should she be required to work with this partner? How would this arrangement work? Would she be evaluated by the partner? Would the partner use this time to gather evidence against her? Was she about to join friends or allies? Everyone had seemed so friendly during the interview, but now she viewed them all with suspicion. Joleen contacted the black female partner, who assured her that the managing partner was held in high regard. The female partner who had blocked Joleen's appointment was not. Joleen felt paralyzed and contemplated joining a smaller, black-owned firm. The salary was lower, but she would not have the potential racial problems that she sensed were developing at this firm. She called the managing partner to decline the offer, but was pleasantly surprised when the managing partner indicated that "they," meaning the partners, had met during the morning and decided that the six-months' arrangement would not be necessary. Joleen accepted the offer, though she could not rid herself of a sense of dread. Hopefully, her time at the firm would not be as tumultuous as her entry.

Joleen's experience typifies many of the barriers and challenges facing women poised to enter largely unexplored territory. Race and gender are key elements of the case. First, a line is drawn that includes the newcomer; then it is redrawn (largely as a result of the influence of a woman) to exclude her; it is etched a third time to include her with conditions. One can almost hear the question, "Isn't she smart?" Finally—after it is clear that she will not accept the conditions—it is expanded to include her.

At each stage of the negotiation process, there is considerable ambiguity about who is an ally and who is not. The conversations with the male partners are straightforward and devoid of detail. The managing partner seems more willing to engage in a conversation about the opportunity—rather than simply a negotiation—but she, too, becomes the subject of suspicion, especially when suggesting that Joleen work with the partner who attempted to block her entry. Perhaps the managing partner was attempting to reach a compromise that would satisfy all parties, rather than simply stating that she had decided to overrule the partners' vote. However, Joleen does not view this unusual proposal as an opportunity for obtaining meaningful feedback at all. Moreover, she does not want her entry into the firm tainted by whispers about her lack of competence. Until she verifies with someone she trusts that the managing partner is a likely ally, her distrust and suspicion builds.

Stumbling Along

It may seem odd that I am arguing for the presumption of innocence and against the tacit acceptance of questions or statements that invite ambiguity. However, relationships are negotiated over time, including offers, rebukes, cues, and miscues. In over twenty years of working in and studying corporate life, I have seen no evidence of the perfect, error-free relationship. One of the most vexing challenges when interacting across race and gender is uncertainty. If we are certain about another's racism or sexism, that brings anger and frustration. But if we are uncertain but suspicious about it, that brings confusion, apprehension, and self-doubt. In some ways, it is easier to assume we know the other person's intentions, and we remain on guard against those intentions. If there is a mistake or inappropriate remark, we use it as confirmation of our initial suspicions. When there were few women in the management ranks, they gathered any information they could. Today, however, with more women reaching executive levels, they have more opportunities to ask questions and get clarification than ever before. We must be attuned to the perceptual errors that can plague any relationship, be willing to gather and critically examine data, and be committed to strengthening our relationship-building skills.

As researchers, our challenge is to look at relationships in a complex way so that we can generate the insights and evidence that inform practice. For example, much research continues to be founded on the underlying assumption that every person in an organization has, or should have, the same view. There is still a wish for unanimity and a longing for the data that would support it. However, research has shown conclusively that this is not the case. Individuals who are differently situated in the organization just do not see things the same way. Try as we might, we cannot always reconcile disparate views: there may be multiple stories to tell.[24]

There are also other instances in which presuming someone's innocence can help navigate through awkward, potentially divisive, moments. Though many people tend to focus on the interpersonal nature of interactions, there may be other, outside, influences that can cause a strong relationship to deteriorate. David Thomas discusses this situation in his article on the racial taboos that often hamper cross-race relationships.[25] He notes, for example, how black women who have white male supervisors or mentors may be labeled by their black peers as "the white man's slut." Consequently, black women may avoid interacting with white male mentors as a way to avoid being ostracized by their peers. Similarly, I have suggested that our way of looking at interpersonal interactions (and sometimes our insistence on looking at interactions as purely interpersonal) distorts our understanding of the behavior. I argue with race (and would suggest similar dynamics with gender) that we tend to underestimate the impact of outside relationships on our relationship with the other person.[26] Family and systems therapists, it seems to me, are far ahead of organizational scientists in terms of understanding that no interaction really involves only two people.[27] The person's peers, as an example, can have a significant impact on the relationship. This may not be desirable, but it exists.

One readily understandable example in an organizational context is the often-discussed role and influence of the wife or secretary to a male executive. An astute businessperson who is attempting to build a relationship with the executive would be wise to consider, to the extent possible, the dynamics of the couple, since the wife may exert a significant amount of influence over decisions, views, and preferences of the executive. Something similar could be said about secretaries. I would further suggest that similar dynamics may govern the relationships that men and women each have with their respective peers. This idea implies that we cannot take what the person is saying necessarily as a statement about private views; we must also consider how that individual might be influenced and— if we are interested in building a relationship—devise ways to help that person manage relationships with peers.

Researchers can also be more attentive to the variable nature of relationships over time. The presence of difficulties in a relationship does not necessarily portend failure. The encouraging news is that researchers now have access to increasing amounts of rich data, especially about difficult conversations involving race, gender, and other dimensions of difference. There is also a growing literature that examines positive relationships with an eye toward understanding the resilience of complex ones.

I attended a workshop recently during which women were able to talk candidly about the difficulties of building relationships across race, certainly a critical goal if all women are to rise in organizations. At one point, a black woman rose to express her frustration with white women. Why couldn't they see, she said, the injustice around them? How could they sit idly by, without trying to correct the problems? The whole group paused. Then, a white woman said quietly, "Some of us are—" It was a sobering invitation for others to consider that, as Miller suggests, we would be well served by imagining the truth of that statement.

Whatever the gains for women in corporate and other arenas, we must remember that some men are allies. For women of color, some whites—men and women—are allies as well. When the lines were drawn, these allies, often at their own risk, ensured that women were included in the circle. There are now more opportunities than ever to create the relationships that will propel women to the top and to the inner sanctum of organizations.

Endnotes

1. "2005 Census of Women Corporate Officers and Top Earners of the Fortune 500," (2005), available online: www.catalystwomen.org, access date: December 10, 2006.
2. See the teaching case "Learning from Mattel," Tuck School of Business at Dartmouth, 2000.
3. Kathleen Morris, "The Rise of Jill Barad," *Business Week*, May 25, 1998.
4. Average CEO tenure is seven years. Steven H. Kaplan and Bernadette A. Minton, "How Has CEO Turnover Changed? Increasingly Performance Sensitive Boards and Increasingly Uneasy CEOs," Working Paper, University of Chicago Graduate School of Business and the Ohio State University, July 2006.
5. "Profile: HP's Carly Fiorina," BBC News, September 4, 2001, available online: http://news.bbc.co.uk/1/hi/business/1524555.stm, access date: January 18, 2007.
6. Peter Burrows, "HP's Carly Fiorina: The Boss," *Business Week*, August 2, 1999.
7. Michelle K. Ryan and S. Alexander Haslam, "The Glass Cliff: Evidence That Women Are Over-Represented in Precarious Leadership Positions," *British Journal of Management* 16 (2005):

81–90. See also Barbara Brotman, "The Workplace: Under Fire," *Chicago Tribune*, January 9, 2002, available online: http://www.kellogg.northwestern.edu/news/hits/020109ct.htm, for commentary on Fiorina, Barad, Linda Wachner (former CEO of the Warnaco Group), Deborah Hopkins (former CFO at Lucent), and from the nonprofit arena Dr. Bernadine Healy (former head of the American Red Cross).

8. Colleagues Julie Elworth, Maureen Scully, and I have been interested in exploring the conditions under which women reach top positions. We wonder whether women are more likely to take the helm at organizations that are in decline.

9. Hence, for example, the 360-degree appraisal mechanisms.

10. Joyce K. Fletcher, *Disappearing Acts: Gender, Power, and Relational Practice at Work* (Cambridge, MA: MIT Press, 1999).

11. Deborah Tannen, *Talking from 9 to 5. Women and Men in the Workplace: Language, Sex and Power* (New York: Avon Books, 1994), 35–39.

12. Ella Louise Bell, "The Bicultural Life Experience of Career-Oriented Black Women," *Journal of Organizational Behavior 11* (1990): 459–477.

13. Fletcher, *Disappearing Acts*, 55, and at 48 (relational practice includes preserving, mutual empowering, self-achieving, and creating team).

14. Fletcher, *Disappearing Acts*, 55.

15. Fletcher, *Disappearing Acts*, 55.

16. Fletcher, *Disappearing Acts*, 58.

17. Deborah Tannen, *You Just Don't Understand: Women and Men in Conversation* (New York: Ballantine Books, 1990), 103.

18. Tannen, *You Just Don't Understand*, 103.

19. Tannen, *You Just Don't Understand*, 103–104.

20. Elizabeth Hall, "Giving Away Psychology in the 80's" (interview with George Miller), *Psychology Today*, January 1980, 38–50, 97–98.

21. Ellis Cose, *The Rage of a Privileged Class* (New York: Harper Perennial, 1995).

22. This raises the issue of *interpersonal competence*, a concept Chris Argyris posited years ago; however, he was thinking in terms of the multiple levels of conversation going on in any situation. His analysis did not incorporate differences of race or culture, though one would expect that race and culture distinctions would further complicate verbal interactions. Chris Argyris, *Interpersonal Competence and Organizational Effectiveness* (Homewood, IL: Irwin, 1962).

23. Pseudonym; some identifying information has also been changed.

24. Karen L. Proudford, "Viewing Dyads in Triadic Terms: Toward a Conceptualization of the In/visible Third in Relationships Across Difference," Working Paper No. 16 (Boston: Center for Gender in Organizations, Simmons School of Management, 2003).

25. David A. Thomas, "Mentoring and Irrationality: The Role of Racial Taboos," *Human Resource Management* 28 (1989): 279–290.

26. Karen L. Proudford, "Notes on the Intra-Group Origins of Inter-Group Conflict in Organizations: Black-White Relations as an Exemplar," *Journal of Labor and Employment Law 1* (1998): 615–637.

27. See, for example, Harriet E. Lerner, *The Dance of Anger* (New York: HarperCollins, 1985).

17

DISRUPTING GENDER, REVISING LEADERSHIP

Debra Meyerson, Robin Ely, Laura Wernick

Historically, much of the research on women and leadership has emphasized differences in men's and women's leadership styles and the structural and cognitive barriers in organizations that impair women's mobility and access to leadership opportunities.[1] As organizational theorists, we have focused our research on the social construction of gender and, in particular, on how organizational arrangements shape, and are shaped by, women's and men's actions, interactions, and identities at work.[2] Our insights about women and leadership have followed from our research on the organizational production of gender differences and gender inequality in the workplace and from our long-standing interest in developing change strategies to eradicate organizationally reproduced sources of inequality.

This chapter takes a different tack. The study we present contains a number of implications for women and leadership, but we did not begin our research with questions about women, gender differences, or gender inequality. Instead, we conducted an ethnographic study of men on two offshore oil platforms—a workplace that has traditionally rewarded men for masculine displays of bravado and for interactions centered on proving masculinity. In the organizations we studied, however, such displays and interactions were notably absent. We use this case to develop theory about how the operational and cultural conditions of an organization can disrupt conventional masculine interaction patterns and identity-construction processes by decoupling images of leadership and competence from idealized images of masculinity. Based on these observations, we speculate about how such disruptions may open leadership roles to women and to men who do not conform to traditional images of masculinity.

The organization we studied had undertaken a major culture change initiative that was designed to increase safety and effectiveness, but that had the unintended effect of profoundly changing how men enacted their masculinity on the job. The organization's self-conscious focus on increasing safety and effectiveness compelled workers to adopt a set of work practices that supported deep and ongoing learning; these practices had the secondary consequence of disrupting and revising the hyper-masculine codes of behavior that were normal in the oil industry. The organization's emphasis on learning affected how people did their work, how they interacted with one another, and, what may be most important, how they enacted leadership. Although the company did not set out to change the traditional gendered patterns of roles, relations, and leadership, its commitment to safety and effectiveness—which led it to instill in workers a commitment to learning—nonetheless accomplished such shifts in some striking ways. Thus our case reveals the tight connection between the way work is defined and executed, on one hand, and how organizations construct gender and leadership, on the other.

An Organizational Approach
to Gender and Leadership

A question addressed frequently in the literature on gender in organizations is this: Do women—whether due to socialization or biology—exercise leadership differently from men? Underlying much of the sex-difference research is a related question: If women execute their roles as leaders differently from men, do these differences explain (and excuse) the relative paucity of women in these roles? The research addressing these questions is adeptly reviewed in earlier chapters of this book; the answers it provides are far from definitive. To summarize, the results are mixed, but it seems that the differences between women and men in leadership style are small, consistent with gender stereotypes, context-specific, and arguably meaningful.[3] We suggest that the sex-difference approach to questions about women and leadership has outlived its usefulness, and we propose replacing it with an organizational approach.

The Miner's Canary

Rather than focusing on women's styles or leadership potential relative to men's, an organizational approach to gender sees women's experience as an opportunity for the organization to learn about itself—what it values and how it accomplishes its work—and to use these insights to inform cultural and structural changes. When any group, such as women, has trouble entering an organization or moving through its ranks, the organization has an opportunity to examine how its cultural and operational conditions, its basic assumptions, norms, and work practices, as well as its values and incentives, may be inhibiting more than simply the advancement of a particular group of people: they may also be inhibiting the organization's own effectiveness.

Lani Guinier and Gerald Torres use the metaphor of "the miner's canary" to describe this diagnostic approach.[4] Miners send a canary into the mine before they go in; if it dies in the mine, then it is a signal that something about the environment is toxic. Although Guinier and Torres applied the metaphor to the experiences of people of color in white institutions, any group—whether it be white women, people of color, or another group—that deviates from the organization's power-holders in some significant way can serve as the canary. A group's persistent trouble may signal something toxic in the environment more generally—toxic to people's well-being, to their relationships, and possibly to the organization's capacity to do its work. In short, the canary signals that the organization is probably not operating optimally.

The idea that an organization's standard practice is not always best practice, for women or for performance, is not new. Numerous scholars have documented how what initially appears to be a problem for women often points to a problem for the organization more generally.[5] For example, ubiquitous in corporations and law firms is the assumption that the amount of time a professional spends at work is a legitimate measure of commitment and contribution. Employees are measured against the ideal worker, who subordinates all other obligations to work and is thus available around the clock.[6] The practices that follow from this assumption penalize people— more often women than men—who have fixed schedules or responsibilities outside work, but who may nonetheless be committed and extraordinarily productive workers. Moreover, the practice of using time and singularity of focus as measures of employees' contributions may mask more accurate assessments of employee value, sometimes penalizing the most productive employees while rewarding less productive ones.

Employees who are not constrained by outside responsibilities may take these assumptions and practices for granted, as simply the way things are done, and adapt to them unquestioningly while overlooking the costs to themselves or to the organization. But change does happen. Case studies reveal how women's problematic encounters with these and other seemingly gender-neutral assumptions and practices have prompted some organizations to question and revise them, resulting in gains to both gender equity and organizational effectiveness.[7]

While our case study also illustrates the tight link between gender and traditional tenets of organizational life, we tell a slightly different story—one that doesn't start with gender but ends up there nonetheless. In this chapter, we describe the research site, our data collection method, and our results. We then explore our findings' implications for women and leadership.

Disrupting Masculinity: The Case of Two Offshore Oil Platforms

In contrast to their predecessors in the oil industry, the two offshore oil platforms we studied had been designed operationally and culturally to maximize safety and effectiveness. Because macho displays of bravado and invulnerability have been shown to undermine worker safety,[8] we were interested in how the new design and the culture that supported it might have altered traditional masculine interaction patterns, displays of masculinity, and images of leadership, despite the industry's traditionally hyper-masculine tradition.

Research Site

Both research sites were deep-water oil-drilling and production platforms located in the Gulf of Mexico.[9] Each platform is a self-contained community with space for outdoor work, production facilities, power generation, drilling operations, control rooms, living quarters, offices, library, gym, recreation area, and cafeteria.[10] The workforce on the platforms is predominantly male, and their work is hazardous. The hazards of the job come from working with volatile gases and liquids under high pressure and from moving heavy equipment, often in rough weather.

Regular workers, including company employees and contractors, live and work together offshore for two weeks (called a "hitch") at a time, followed by two weeks off duty. Most regular personnel work on one of four crews, and each crew works a hitch together on a rotating, staggered schedule. In addition to their crewmates, workers also have close contact with their counterparts in other crews and shifts because they share accountability for tasks that require intensive coordination. The facility is operational twenty-four hours a day, the standard workday is twelve hours, and everyone is on call twenty-four hours a day.

Data Collection

Our research team (three women and two men) gathered interview and observation data during five site visits to each platform over nineteen months. We traveled to the platforms by helicopter alongside employees making hitch changes. During each visit, we ate meals and shared living quarters with employees. We spent our first visit to each platform observing day-to-day work activities, inter-acting casually with workers, attending meetings, and informally interviewing more than twenty employees across a variety of func-tions. The next two site visits entailed semistructured interviews with a representative cross-section of employees and contractors. In total, we interviewed thirty-seven men across both facilities. Their tenure with the company ranged from six months to twenty-seven years, and on these particular platforms, from six months to six years. The final source of data came from participant observation and interviews conducted by a female member of the research team who worked a two-week hitch on each platform as a production opera-tor. Employees were aware of her identity as a researcher studying "diversity" in their work environment. In addition to participant observation, she conducted informal interviews with coworkers during lulls in the work and, because people live at the work site, after hours as well.

A Point of Contrast

Offshore oil platforms are dirty, dangerous, physically demanding, technically complex, and historically stereotypically masculine workplaces. The cultural norms, practices, and assumptions that typically govern worker behavior in male-dominated, dangerous workplaces such as these have been well documented. Numerous organizational ethnographies contain rich descriptions of how such organizations reinforce dominant societal norms of masculinity, encouraging workers to embrace and enact the belief that men should not appear weak, fearful, or vulnerable in any way.[11] Through early on-the-job socialization, day-to-day norms, and organization-ally sanctioned definitions of competence and leadership, members learn that the respect of their coworkers and the rewards of advancement require them to act and interact in accordance with these idealized images of traditional masculinity.[12]

The cost of deviating from prescribed images of masculinity in such contexts was illustrated in a Supreme Court case in which

Joseph Oncale, a 130-pound, twenty-one-year-old roustabout on an oil platform operated by Sundowner Offshore Services, violated the organization's norms by failing to act sufficiently manly. In the presence of the remaining crew, his supervisor and coworkers subjected him to sex-related humiliating acts to make clear to him and to all who witnessed his humiliation the cost of not conforming to organizationally sanctioned norms of masculinity.[13]

Ten years ago, the oil platforms owned and operated by the company in our study were like the masculine workplaces described in the literature—where masculine identity centered on appearing physically tough, technically infallible, and emotionally detached. But the platforms we studied were different. These platforms, built in the mid-1990s, were designed from the start to reflect the company's heightened priority on safety and effectiveness. A senior manager described the company's initiative as follows: "We were more and more frustrated with the fact that people kept getting hurt. . . . In the early nineties we made the commitment [to reduce injuries] that became known as Safety 2000."[14]

The contrast between these platforms and those on which many employees had started their careers was stark. An offshore installation manager and twenty-seven-year veteran of the company described the difference as follows:

> [Then] the field foremen were kind of like a pack of lions. The guy that was in charge was the one who could basically outperform and out-shout and out-intimidate all the others. That's just how it worked out here on drilling rigs and in production. So those people went to the top, over other people's bodies in some cases. Intimidation was the name of the game. . . . They decided who the driller was by fighting. If the job came open, the one that was left standing was the driller. It was that rowdy. But it's not like that at all now. I mean we don't even horseplay like we used to. There's no physical practical jokes anymore. Most stuff now is just good-natured joking.

An electrician offered the following reflection:

Ten, twelve years ago I just couldn't imagine sitting down with somebody like you and talking about these kinds of things. It was way more macho then than it is now. It was like, "Hey, this is a man's world. If you can't cut it here, boy, you don't need to be here." Now there is a little bit more of, "Let's learn what people are about," a little bit more about the personal and interpersonal relationships and that kind of stuff.

Platform leaders understood clearly that norms encouraging masculine displays of prowess placed lives in jeopardy and caused costly operational errors, thus impairing the organization's safety and effectiveness. Driven by this understanding, the company's leadership deliberately developed norms and practices to counter the roughhousing, hard-driving machismo culture that held sway in the past and on other platforms.

Learning and the Reconstruction of Masculinity

In the service of safety and effectiveness, these platforms adopted a set of work practices and norms centered on learning that all workers self-consciously integrated into their daily interactions and routines. The logic underlying these interventions was clear to everyone we interviewed: in organizations where the reliability of one system depends on others, small errors can cascade into large accidents that place lives at risk. Thus if you can't expose errors and learn from them, then you can't be truly safe.

These workers came to see that learning was fundamentally about questioning their assumptions: they became open to reevaluating their beliefs in the face of new information that contradicted what they thought they knew to be true. This stance was not always easy to take, but they understood the cost of being wrong. Hence, these workers were motivated to question their assumptions in case they were faulty. And when they did, they often reached conclusions that suggested fixes to their system—

and to their relationships—that they would never have considered but for their ability to question themselves and what they were doing.

Definitions of Competence and Leadership. Workers' commitment to learning changed how they related to one another, which in turn shifted their views of what constitutes competence and leadership. They no longer interpreted the admission of error or doubt as a sign of weakness or incompetence, because they understood that without such admissions their safety and effectiveness were in jeopardy. For example, one team leader described how much he appreciated getting feedback from his counterpart on another crew: "I didn't realize I was doing it wrong until he explained it, and that allowed us to do our job better, so I encourage him to give me that type of feedback."

Likewise, valued workers were no longer "the biggest, baddest roughnecks," but "mission-driven" people who "care about their fellow workers," are "good listeners," and "thoughtful," as these were the qualities deemed necessary to perform their work safely and effectively. One production operator described the kind of person who is most respected as one who "knows what he's doing, or if he doesn't, he'll take the time to do the research to understand what he's doing. It doesn't necessarily have to do with knowledge. And they're not worried about how fast they can get something done. They take the time to learn."

Being open to learning also meant being willing to express vulnerability—a sure sign of weakness in conventional masculine workplaces. Rather than demonstrating how tough, proficient, and cool-headed they were, as is the norm in traditional masculine workplaces, the employees on these platforms readily acknowledged their doubts and physical limitations, asked for help, and openly attended to their own and others' feelings. These expressions of vulnerability and the kinds of relationships they fostered are inimical to masculine images of heroic individualism and invulnerability that underlie traditional portraits of leadership.

In addition, in contrast to conventional dangerous workplaces where an imposing physical presence would command respect and be seen as leader-like, on the platforms, a presence viewed by coworkers as intimidating was seen as a threat to workers' capacity to learn, and therefore a quality to guard against. For example, a young, relatively inexperienced worker had precipitated an accidental shutdown in production by turning a switch upon the advice of a coworker—a "well-intentioned" 6-foot-4, 300-pound retired Chicago police officer. In the investigation of the incident, the young worker admitted that he had done so against his better judgment because he had felt intimidated by his coworker's imposing presence, making him reluctant to question his instruction. This exchange led to a larger team discussion about the need to watch out for one's potential to intimidate—however unwittingly—or to be intimidated.

Thus men on the platform engaged in few displays of stereotypical masculinity because the organization posed a different definition of competence and leadership—one that was the antithesis of the traditional masculine ideal. Men's sense of themselves and the qualities they respected in their coworkers had enlarged to include traditionally "subordinated" forms of masculinity, qualities that when displayed by men in other dangerous workplaces are devalued and demeaned by virtue of their feminine associations.[15] A production operator, who described the platform environment of the past as "macho," noted that now "there's room for both the softer side and the other one. But the change was very hard," he explained:

> [We had to be taught] how to be more lovey-dovey and more friendly with each other and to get in touch with the more tender side of each other type of thing. And all of us just laughed at first. It was like, man, this is never going to work, you know? But now you can really tell the difference. Even though we kid around and joke around with each other, there's no malice in it. We are a very different group now than we were when we first got together—kinder, gentler people.

It's important to note that the men did not repudiate traditionally masculine characteristics—they still exerted their physical strength and expressed their technical expertise—but they were not focused on proving them. In other words, they exhibited and valued these qualities when the work required them. Likewise, these men did not abdicate power, but they expressed it with less bravado. A forty-year-old production operator observed this difference as follows:

> I started working offshore when I was seventeen. Back then, there was much more profanity, much more posturing. If you didn't posture yourself in a position of power, then you set yourself up for ridicule. But over the years, with company training in the personal and interpersonal areas, people have learned that you don't have to present yourself in that fashion to gain power. You don't have to use profanity to make a statement that carries power.

Organizational Practices. A variety of organizational practices and norms supported men's learning behaviors, thus reinforcing revised images of competence and leadership. For example, "root cause analysis," a formal procedure designed to surface the underlying cause of particularly costly mistakes, such as "shut-ins"—accidents that halt the production of gas and oil—systematized the learning approach to mistakes and minimized the impulse to blame or cover up an error. As a production operator explained, when a shut-in occurs:

> There's a form or "go-by" of certain things that have to be asked. And let's say I did it. They're not trying to blame me or point fingers at me. Our intent is to get down to the root cause to prevent this from happening again. Was it a lack of knowledge, a lack of skill, or improper equipment? Was it an engineering issue where engineering needs to come in and take a look at this? We go through the whole thing. We have the mechanics in. We have the operators in. Very seldom do we have leadership in.

Other practices legitimated human fallibility as a fact of life. For example, one of the platforms established the "Millionaire Club" to "honor" workers whose mistakes had cost the company a million dollars. This ritual and other informal and formal practices made it acceptable and safe to admit and learn from mistakes—and unacceptable to hide from or blame coworkers for them.

Another organizational practice that helped institutionalize learning was the procedure called "observations," whereby a person monitors and documents on a standardized form a coworker's compliance with safety regulations. Forms were then collected, and the results aggregated and discussed at weekly team meetings. As one driller explained: "You ask the person, 'Do you mind if I do an observation on you while you're doing this job?' Then you do the observation and fill out the observation card and give the person some feedback on what he did right or what he can improve on or what he should have done." While it is possible that such practices could be seen as a form of surveillance and control, we saw no evidence of this attitude and no sign of people withholding information about coworkers. Workers frequently mentioned this practice as keeping them attentive to safety and as a source of learning and improvement.

The platforms also developed rituals that reinforced inclusivity, respect, and acceptance, and thereby supported learning. People are more likely to speak up, share concerns, and admit errors when they feel respected and valued by their coworkers.[16] The "recognition" ritual, a practice in which employees publicly declare their appreciation for a coworker's contributions, promoted these feelings by recognizing those whose actions might otherwise have gone unnoticed.[17] Every meeting began with this ritual. People were recognized for many things: getting up in the middle of the night to help solve a problem, going out of one's way to help a coworker, making a wonderful dessert the night before.

Most important, leaders on the platform modeled learning behaviors and openly revealed their own vulnerability while doing so, thus further reinforcing alternative images of competence and leadership. Workers regularly pointed these leaders out to us. One leader who personified these qualities was known for his bi-weekly "fireside chats"—on-site meetings in which he fielded questions from workers and listened to their concerns. Many spoke admiringly of his openness to feedback and willingness to hear people out: "People talk about how brave he is to do this," one worker noted, "because people criticize and gripe, and it rolls off him. He listens to everyone." A mechanic attributed the care with which coworkers treated each other to the leader's "focus on the humanity side" and to his having "raise[d] our consciousness to a person's feelings." Others noted that most of the leaders on the platform "walked the talk" by embodying the cultural values and qualities the company espoused.

Implications for Women and Leadership

Many mainstream organizations—not just traditional, dangerous, male-dominated ones—conflate stereotypical masculine traits with images of competence and leadership, and women pay a price.[18] This conflation places women seeking leadership roles in a classic double bind: those who enact idealized masculine images of leadership, by definition, violate idealized feminine images of womanhood, and vice versa.[19] The result is that women who are tough, confident, and decisive are demonized as bitchy, strident, and insensitive. By the same token, women who are sensitive, relational, and warm are discounted as weak, passive, and too nice. Either way, women are seen as unfit for leadership roles.[20]

Although few women worked on the platforms we studied (probably deterred by the two-week rotations offshore and the wider culture's continued association of men with these jobs), we believe this case offers important insights into how organizations can change these dynamics. Specifically, our findings suggest an interesting thought experiment: if other organizations were to adopt similar cultural and operational changes—instilling in their workforce a deep and abiding commitment to learning, for example— how might women's prospects for leadership change? Of course, we can only speculate, but we believe that such efforts would similarly revise definitions of competence and leadership, releasing aspiring women leaders from the damned-if-you-do, damned-if-you-don't dynamic that has traditionally blocked them from taking on leadership roles.

More generally, an organization's commitment to a set of work practices rooted in the real requirements of its work, rather than in stereotypical images of masculinity, should encourage both men and women to enact leadership behaviors that are responsive to the dictates of the particular situations they face rather than to the dictates of conventional masculinity. Under these conditions, people would be judged—and promoted—according to their contributions to the organization's mission. Leadership roles would be available to a wider range of people, not only to more women, but also to men who do not fit the conventional masculine image. In short, organizations, as well as people traditionally excluded from leadership roles, might benefit from such changes.

Despite the dearth of women on the platforms, some evidence supports these speculations. Where once women were all but banned in these off-shore environments, women are now making inroads, joining the workforce at a slow but advancing rate and moving into leadership positions as foremen, team leaders, asset managers, and directors. As mentioned earlier, the persistent underrepresentation of women is apt to be due to the idiosyncratic features of this type of work: it requires workers to be away from home for fourteen days at a time, the work is still physically demanding, and female companionship is limited. Nonetheless, the fact that women are moving into these traditionally masculine workplaces— and into leadership positions—bodes well for the possibility that other organizations, unencumbered by these idiosyncrasies, could make even greater strides.

Our research highlights the futility of debates over whose leadership style—women's or men's—is most effective. Such questions become moot when the criteria for effective leadership flow from the real requirements of work. What matters, therefore, is not which stereotyped style is more effective, but rather what behavior will be most effective in a given situation. This insight is lost on those whose primary goal is to live up to one stereotyped image or the other, or to find just the right blend of the two. Platform workers did not simply replace the content of one idealized image with another one and then set out to prove their fidelity to the new ideal. Rather, they replaced efforts to prove their masculinity with efforts to work together more effectively. Driven by these concerns, questions about the relative merits of "masculine" or "feminine" leadership styles are irrelevant because people are no longer beholden to gendered standards.

Conclusion

Our study of two offshore oil platforms illustrates the inextricable connections between the cultural and operational conditions of work, on one hand, and the workplace dynamics of gender and leadership on the other. One of the more intriguing aspects of this research is that, despite its impact on gender, the company's change initiative had nothing to do with women. Women were not the targets of change. Rather, the targets were the organization's culture and operations, and as a result, the men changed. Released from the requirement of performing masculinity traditionally associated with dangerous work, men expressed a broader repertoire of personal qualities, including qualities that their conventionally masculine scripts had precluded men acting on in the past. We argue that these changes in turn created a work environment that may be a model for other organizations seeking ways to support women's success.

Two questions arise, however, concerning the generalizability of our findings. First, is it always effective for an organization to do away with conventional images of masculinity in its definitions of competence and leadership? On the platforms, conventional displays of masculinity clearly undermined learning, thus jeopardizing workers' safety and effectiveness. But do some types of work necessitate expressions of conventional masculinity? Our answer to this question is that it depends on whether such actions are anchored in efforts to prove masculinity or in efforts to respond to the real requirements of work.

We argue that problems associated with masculinity lie not in masculine attributes in themselves—many tasks require aggressiveness, strength, or emotional detachment—but rather, in men's efforts to prove themselves on these dimensions, whether in the dirty, dangerous setting of an offshore oil platform or in the posh, protected surroundings of the executive suite. When a job on the platforms called for physical strength or a show of courage, workers rose to the occasion and bore no costs for doing so, because they were not driven by a desire to prove their masculinity. Such demonstrations were unnecessary because these workers were not evaluated against gendered metrics. Similarly, in other workplaces—such as the trading floor of Wall Street, where value is created by people taking calculated risks—workers must often be competitive and aggressive to do their jobs well. Problems arise, however, when workers enact these behaviors to prove their masculinity, preventing them from inquiring into the actual requirements of their work. In sum, while proving one's masculine credentials can have certain benefits—indeed, many successful careers have been built on such strivings—we argue that the accompanying, often hidden, costs to relationships, others, and the organization can be high. Organizations can help mitigate these costs by critically examining their assumptions about what makes for competent and effective workers, and in so doing awaken to the leadership potential of women.

The second question concerning the generalizability of our findings is this: If workers are not faced with the possibility of blowing themselves up, will they be willing to trade in their traditional conceptions of masculinity, competence, and leadership for alternative ones? Workers on the platform saw clearly how pursuing masculinity put lives at risk; they were therefore highly motivated to jettison their old ways and embrace new ones.

When the stakes are not so high, what will motivate workers to make these shifts? As our case demonstrates, people need a compelling motive to revise basic assumptions, modes of behavior, and definitions of self,[21] and being invested in a meaningful purpose that demands making such revisions may provide such a motive.[22] For platform workers, that purpose was safety. More broadly, research suggests that people regard as meaningful purposes that connect them to others, such those that advance social ideals, enhance relationships, or make contributions to others' well-being.[23] When people perceive that old assumptions and behaviors may contradict or compromise the pursuit of those purposes, they may be motivated to abandon their old patterns.[24] On the platforms, organizational practices that endorsed safety as the company's highest priority were a primary way of inspiring in workers a sense that they were responsible for others and that the company was taking responsibility for them.

Identifying purposes that both inspire employees and further the organization's mission is no easy feat. We believe, however, that the goal of making organizations more equitable, humane, and effective depends on meeting this challenge.

Endnotes

1. Judith Kolb, "Are We Still Stereotyping Leadership? A Look at Gender and Other Predictors of Leader Emergence," *Small Group Research 28* (1977): 370; Gary N. Powell, *Women and Men in Management* (New York: Sage, 1988), 45–49; Alice Eagly and Blair Johnson, "Gender and Leadership Style: A Meta-Analysis," *Psychological Bulletin 108* (1990): 233–256.

2. Robin Ely and Debra Meyerson, "Theories of Gender in Organizations: A New Approach to Organizational Analysis and Change," in B. Staw and R. Sutton, eds., *Research in Organizational Behavior 22* (Greenwich, CT: JAI Press, 2000), 103–152; Robin Ely and Debra Meyerson, "Unmasking Manly Men: The Organizational Reconstruction of Men's Identity," Working Paper #07-054, Harvard Business School,

2007; Robin Ely and Irene Padavic, "A Feminist Analysis of Organizational Research on Sex Differences," *Academy of Management Review*, forthcoming.

3. Alice Eagly, "The Science and Politics of Comparing Women and Men," *American Psychologist 50*, no. 3 (1995): 145–158; see also Alice Eagly, "Should Psychologists Study Sex Differences: On Comparing Women and Men," in D. Anselmi and L. Law, eds., *Questions of Gender: Perspectives and Paradoxes* (New York: McGraw-Hill, 1998), 93–98.

4. Lani Guinier and Gerald Torres, *The Miner's Canary: Enlisting Race, Resisting Power, Transforming Democracy* (Cambridge, MA: Harvard University Press, 2003).

5. Work based at the Center for Gender in Organizations at Simmons Graduate School of Management has referred to this analytic approach to organizations as the "gender lens," and researchers have used this approach to identify organizational interventions that simultaneously increase an organization's effectiveness and eradicate a persistent source of gender inequity. This "dual agenda" approach has been described in Deborah Kolb, Joyce K. Fletcher, Debra Meyerson, Deborah Merrill-Sands, and Robin Ely, *CGO Insights No. 1: Making Change: A Framework for Promoting Gender Equity in Organizations* (Boston: Center for Gender in Organizations, Simmons College, October 1998), and in Lotte Bailyn and Joyce K. Fletcher, *CGO Insights No. 18: The Equity Imperative: Reaching Effectiveness Through the Dual Agenda* (Boston: The Center for Gender in Organizations, Simmons College, July 2003). See also Ely and Meyerson, "Theories of Gender"; Rhona Rapoport, Lotte Bailyn, Joyce Fletcher, and Bettye Pruitt, *Beyond Work-Family Balance: Advancing Gender Equity and Workplace Performance* (San Francisco: Jossey-Bass, 2001).

6. Lotte Bailyn, *Breaking the Mold: Women, Men, and Time in the New Corporate World* (Ithaca, NY: Cornell University Press, 1993); Joan Williams, *Unbending Gender: Why Family and*

Work Conflict and What to Do About It (New York: Oxford University Press, 2001).

7. Bailyn and Fletcher, *The Equity Imperative*.

8. Carol Chetkovich, *Real Heat: Gender and Race in the Urban Fire Service* (New Brunswick, NJ: Rutgers University Press, 1997); Frank Barrett, "The Organizational Construction of Hegemonic Masculinity: The Case of the US Navy," *Gender, Work, and Organization 3* (1996): 129–142; Karl Weick and Kathleen Sutcliffe, *Managing the Unexpected: Assuring High Performance in an Age of Complexity* (San Francisco: Jossey-Bass, 2001).

9. We have described this case more completely in Robin Ely and Debra Meyerson, "Unmasking Manly Men: The Organizational Reconstruction of Men's Identity," Working Paper #07-054, Harvard Business School (2007).

10. While the platforms had many similarities to Erving Goffman's "total institutions," the fluid participation, the coming and going of members, and the nearly constant communication with the outside world via telephone and e-mail differentiate these organizations from the bounded units Goffman described. See Erving Goffman, *Asylums: Essays on the Social Situations of Mental Patients and Other Inmates* (New York: Anchor Books, 1961).

11. Features of dangerous workplaces and in particular the norms of masculinity that characterize these organizations have been documented in a number of ethnographies, including Chetkovich, *Real Heat;* Barrett, "The Organizational Construction of Hegemonic Masculinity"; S. Bird, "Welcome to the Men's Club: Homosociality and the Maintenance of Hegemonic Masculinity," *Gender and Society 10* (1996): 120–132; Irene Padavic, "The Re-Creation of Gender in the Male Workplace," *Symbolic Interaction 14* (1991): 279–294.

12. Ely and Padavic, "A Feminist Analysis."

13. Ely and Meyerson, "Unmasking Manly Men."

14. Note that these and other changes resulted in a decline in the company's accident rate by 84 percent. In the same period, the company's level of productivity (number of barrels), efficiency (cost per barrel), and reliability (production up time) came to exceed the industry's previous benchmark.

15. Robert Connell, *Masculinities* (Boston: Polity Press, 1995).

16. See, for example, Amy Edmondson, "Psychological Safety and Learning Behavior in Work Teams," *Administrative Science Quarterly 44* (1999): 350–383. Edmondson shows that leveling power through practices that encourage inclusion contribute to workers' sense of psychological safety, an important antecedent of team learning.

17. Joyce Fletcher, *Disappearing Acts: Gender, Power, and Relational Practice at Work* (Cambridge, MA: MIT Press, 2001). Fletcher details the processes by which these relational forms of work are systematically feminized and made invisible in traditional workplaces, which devalues people, particularly women, who perform these tasks.

18. Debra Meyerson and Deborah Kolb, "Moving Out of the 'Armchair': Developing a Framework to Bridge the Gap Between Feminist Theory and Practice," *Organization 7* (2001): 553–608; Jennifer Pierce, *Gender Trials: Emotional Lives in Contemporary Law Firms* (Berkeley: University of California Press, 1995).

19. Kathleen Jamieson, *Beyond the Double Bind: Women and Leadership* (New York: Oxford University Press, 1995); Deborah Rhode (ed.), *The Difference "Difference" Makes: Women and Leadership* (Stanford, CA: Stanford University Press, 2003).

20. Madeline Heilman, Aaron S. Wallen, Damiella Fuchs, and Melinda M. Tamkins, "Penalties for Success: Reactions to Women Who Succeed at Male Gender-Typed Tasks," *Journal of Applied Psychology* 89 (2004): 416.

21. The present chapter has not focused on identity concerns, but we view the shift in constructions of masculinity as a funda-

mental shift in how men define themselves as men. We focus on the identity implications in Ely and Meyerson, "Unmasking Manly Men."

22. J. Crocker, N. Nuer, M. A. Olivier, and S. Cohen, "Egosystem and Ecosystem: Two Motivational Orientations for the Self," working paper, University of Michigan, 2006.

23. For review, see J. M. Podolny, R. Khurana, and M. Hill-Popper, "Revisiting the Meaning of Leadership," in B. Staw and R. M. Kramer, eds., *Research in Organizational Behavior* (Greenwich, CT: JAI Press, 2005).

24. Crocker, Nuer, Olivier, and Cohen, "Egosystem and Ecosystem."

Acknowledgments

This volume grew out of two companion conferences sponsored by the Center on Ethics at Stanford University and the Center for Public Leadership at the John F. Kennedy School of Government, Harvard University. The Stanford conference was made possible by the cosponsorship of the Center for Leadership Development and Research at the Stanford Graduate School of Business, The Stanford Faculty Women's Forum, and the Clayman Institute for Research on Women and Gender. The invaluable assistance of Stanford Center Associate Director Lawrence Quill and Program Coordinator Bisera Rakicevic-More is also gratefully acknowledged. The Harvard Conference was made possible by the cosponsorship of the Women and Public Policy Program and especially by the Women's Leadership Board. Additionally, the staff of the Center for Public Leadership provided its usual gracious and impeccable administrative support.

The authors are also grateful for the assistance of Samir Randolph and Clia Goodwin in preparing the manuscript for publication.

The book is dedicated to Ellen Kellerman and Elizabeth Cavanagh, whose guidance and support have meant more than we can ever adequately express.

Contributors

Barbara Kellerman is James MacGregor Burns lecturer in public leadership at Harvard University's Kennedy School of Government. She served as executive director of the Kennedy School's Center for Public Leadership from 2000 to 2003, and as research director from 2003 to 2006. Kellerman has held professorships at Fordham, Tufts, Fairleigh Dickinson, George Washington, and Uppsala universities. She also served as director of the Center for the Advanced Study of Leadership at the Academy of Leadership at the University of Maryland. Kellerman is author and editor of many books, including *Leadership: Multidisciplinary Perspectives* and *The Political Presidency: Practice of Leadership*. She appears often on media outlets such as CBS, NBC, PBS, CNN, NPR, and BBC Radio, and she has contributed articles and reviews to, among others, the *New York Times*, the *Washington Post*, the *Boston Globe*, the *Los Angeles Times*, and the *Harvard Business Review*. Her most recent book is *Bad Leadership: What It Is, How It Happens, Why It Matters*. Her next book, on followership, will appear in 2008.

Deborah L. Rhode is the Ernest W. McFarland professor of law and director of the Stanford Center on Ethics at Stanford University School of Law. She is the former chair of the American Bar Association's Commission on Women in the Profession, former president of the Association of American Law Schools, and former director of Stanford's Institute on Women and Gender. She is the author or coauthor of nineteen books and more than two hundred articles in the areas of gender and professional ethics. Her recent publications include *Gender and Law* (with Katherine Bartlett), *Moral Leadership*, *In Pursuit of Knowledge*, and *The Difference "Difference" Makes: Women and Leadership*.

Laura M. Bacon is a research fellow at the Center for Public Leadership (CPL) at Harvard University. Working with Professor Todd L. Pittinsky, she studies intergroup liking (allophilia), collective narcissism, and leadership. She recently coauthored a national study on Americans' confidence in their leadership (http://www.ksg.harvard.edu/leadership/nli/2006/). She also helped to convene an international conference on Intergroup Leadership, and is involved in CPL's leadership development initiative, managing their cocurricular workshops. Prior to joining the Center, she served as a Peace Corps volunteer in Niger, West Africa, for over two and a half years. She is currently a cellist in the Boston Philharmonic Orchestra. Bacon graduated from Harvard College, Phi Beta Kappa with honors, with a B.A. in psychology.

Rosalind Chait Barnett is a senior scientist and director of the Community, Families, and Work Program at Brandeis University's Women's Studies Research Center. Her research focuses primarily on the relationship between workplace conditions and the well-being of working families as well as the effects of gender on those relationships. Her research has been supported by the Alfred P. Sloan Foundation, the National Institute of Mental Health, the National Institute for Occupational Safety and Health, and the National Science Foundation. Alone and with others, she has written seven books, thirty chapters, and more than a hundred peer-reviewed academic articles. She is also a frequent national and international lecturer and op-ed contributor to such newspapers as the *Washington Post*, the *Boston Globe*, and the *Los Angeles Times*. Her most recent book, with Caryl Rivers, is *Same Difference: How Gender Myths Are Hurting Our Relationships, Our Children, and Our Jobs*.

Linda L. Carli, an associate professor in the department of psychology at Wellesley College, received her Ph.D. in social psychology from the University of Massachusetts at Amherst. She has published and presented important research on the effects of gender on group interaction, communication, and influence; women's leadership; and reactions to adversity and victimization. Currently, her research focuses on gender discrimination and the challenges faced by professional women, and she teaches courses in organizational and applied psychology. She is active in professional organizations in psychology and management and serves on the Executive Board of the Association of Women in Psychology. In addition to her teaching and research, Carli has developed and conducted diversity training workshops and negotiation and conflict resolution workshops for women leaders and has lectured on gender and diversity for business, academic, and other organizations.

Drude Dahlerup graduated from Aarhus University in Denmark, and has since 1998 been professor of political science at Stockholm University, Sweden. She was a visiting scholar at Radcliffe College, Harvard University, 1981–82, and a visiting professor at Birkbeck College, University of London, 2003–04. She has published extensively on women in politics, social movements, and feminist theory, for example, *The Redstockings: The Development, New Thinking and Impact of the Danish Redstocking Movement 1970–1985*, volumes 1 and 2 (in Danish). She is editor of *The New Women's Movement: Feminism and Political Power in Europe and the USA*. Her latest edited collection, *Women, Quotas and Politics*, is the first global study of the use of electoral gender quotas. See the Web sites www.quotaproject.org (with International Idea) and www.statsvet. su.se/quotas.

Alice H. Eagly is professor and department chair of psychology, James Padilla chair of arts and sciences, and faculty fellow in the Institute for Policy Research, all at Northwestern University. Her interests include the study of gender, attitudes, prejudice, and stereotypes. She has a special interest in the relation of gender to leadership. She has written or edited several books and numerous journal articles and book chapters. She conducts research using a wide range of methods, including meta-analysis. Her awards include the Distinguished Scientist Award of the Society for Experimental Social Psychology, the Donald Campbell Award for Distinguished Contribution to Social Psychology, and the Carolyn Wood Sherif Award of the Society for the Psychology of Women for contributions as a scholar, teacher, mentor, and leader.

Robin Ely is an associate professor of organizational behavior at Harvard Business School. She investigates how organizations can better manage their race and gender relations while at the same time increasing their effectiveness. Her research in this area focuses on organizational change, group dynamics, learning, conflict, power, and identity. Ely has published numerous articles on these topics in books and journals and lectures both in the United States and abroad to academics and practitioners alike. For the past several years, she has maintained an active faculty affiliation at the Center for Gender in Organizations, Simmons Graduate School of Management, in Boston. Prior to joining the faculty at Harvard Business School, she was at the School of International and Public Affairs, Columbia University, and at Harvard's John F. Kennedy School of Government. She received her Ph.D. in organizational behavior from Yale University and her bachelor's degree from Smith College.

Richard L. Fox is associate professor of political science at Loyola Marymount University, Los Angeles. He has also taught or held academic positions at Union College, Rutgers University, University of California-Santa Barbara, College Year in Athens, California State University-Fullerton, and the University of Wyoming. He is the author of *Gender and Dynamics in Congressional Elections*. He is also coauthor of *It Takes a Candidate: Why Women Don't Run for Office* and coeditor of *Gender and Elections: Change and Continuity Through 2004*. He has authored or coauthored numerous articles and book chapters; his work has appeared in the *Journal of Politics*, *American Journal of Political Science*, *Social Problems*, *Political Psychology*, *PS*, *Political Research Quarterly*, *Politics and Gender*, and *Public Administration Review*. He has also written op-ed articles, some of which have appeared in the *New York Times* and the *Wall Street Journal*.

Katherine Giscombe is senior director in research and head of the Women of Color Practice Area at Catalyst. Previously, she supported marketing and new product development in a variety of Fortune 500 companies. She is a member of the Academy of Management and has published on career development, mentoring, the business case for diversity, and glass and concrete ceiling issues. Other research interests include economic mobility issues among middle-class African Americans. As a Catalyst media spokesperson she has been interviewed by National Public Radio, CNN-FN, CBS Radio, the *Boston Globe*, the *San Francisco Chronicle*, and *Essence*, among others. Honors include the 2007 "Legacy of Leadership" award from Spelman College and selection in 2005 by the *Network Journal* as one of "25 Influential Black Women in Business." She is on advisory boards for Black Enterprise Women of Power Summit, Working Mother Media Best Companies for Women of Color, Women's Inter-Cultural Exchange, and Girl Scouts Girls and Leadership Study. She received her B.A. in psychology and her Ph.D. in organizational psychology from the University of Michigan.

Ronald A. Heifetz is the King Hussein bin Talal lecturer in public leadership and founding director of the Center for Public Leadership at the John F. Kennedy School of Government, Harvard University. Known for his seminal work during the last two decades on the practice and teaching of leadership, his research focuses on how to build adaptive capacity in societies, businesses, and nonprofits. His book *Leadership Without Easy Answers*, currently in its thirteenth printing, has been translated into many languages. He coauthored the best-selling book *Leadership on the Line: Staying Alive Through the Dangers of Leading* with Marty Linsky. His teaching is studied in *Leadership Can Be Taught* by Sharon Daloz Parks. Heifetz is a principal in Cambridge Leadership Associates and consults extensively in the United States and abroad. He is a graduate of Columbia University, Harvard Medical School, and the Kennedy School, and a physician and cellist who studied with the Russian virtuoso Gregor Piatigorsky.

Sylvia Ann Hewlett is an economist and the founding president of the Center for Work-Life Policy, a nonprofit think tank seeking to fully realize female and minority talent over the life span. She is also the director of the Gender and Policy Program at the School of International and Public Affairs, Columbia University. In the 1980s Hewlett became the first woman to head up the Economic Policy Council—a think tank composed of 125 business and labor leaders. Hewlett is well known for her expertise on gender and workplace issues. She is the author of five critically acclaimed nonfiction books, including *When the Bough Breaks*, *Creating a Life*, and *The War Against Parents* (co-authored with Cornel West). Her latest book is *Off-Ramps and On-Ramps: Keeping Talented Women on the Road to Success* (Harvard Business School Press, 2007). She is also the co-author most recently of *Harvard Business Review* articles "Off-Ramps and On-Ramps: Keeping Talented Women on the Road to Success," "Leadership in Your Midst: Tapping the Hidden Strengths of Minority Executives," and "Extreme Jobs: The Dangerous Allure of the 70-Hour Workweek." Her articles have also appeared in the *New York Times*, the *Financial Times*, and the *International Herald Tribune*. She has taught at Cambridge, Columbia, and Princeton Universities and held fellowships at the Institute for Public Policy Research in London and the Center for the Study of Values in Public Life at Harvard. She has appeared on *60 Minutes*, *The Today Show*, *Good Morning America*, *Newshour with Jim Lehrer*, *Charlie Rose*, *Newsnight with Aaron Brown*, *NBC Nightly News*, *The Oprah Winfrey Show*, *The View*, *All Things Considered*, and *Talk of the Nation*. A Kennedy Scholar and graduate of Cambridge University, Hewlett earned her Ph.D. degree in economics at London University.

Anita F. Hill was born on a small farm in rural Oklahoma, the youngest of thirteen children, and attended Oklahoma State University and Yale Law School, where she earned her J.D. in 1980. She is currently on the faculty of the Heller Graduate School at Brandeis University in Waltham, Massachusetts, as a professor of social policy, law, and women's studies, and is a recipient of the Fletcher Fellowship for her work on race and education.

Hill is the author of numerous articles on international commercial law, bankruptcy, and civil rights. She has given numerous presentations, most notably on race and gender equality. In addition, she has appeared on several television programs, including *Face the Nation*, *Meet the Press*, *The Today Show*, and *Good Morning America*. Her commentary has been published by *Newsweek*, the *New York Times*, the *Boston Globe*, and *Ms.* magazine.

Evangelina Holvino is president of Chaos Management, Ltd., and senior research faculty at the Center for Gender in Organizations (CGO) at the Simmons College School of Management. Holvino has over twenty-five years of experience as an organizational consultant and educator both in the United States and internationally. Her consulting expertise lies in the areas of global diversity, organizational change, and leadership development, with a focus on Latinos. Her research, writing, and speaking focus on the intersections of race, gender, and class, and the opportunities and challenges these differences create in organizations. She is the founder and director of the Advancing Hispanics Leadership Workshop, a leadership development program for Latino mid-level managers, and is a recipient of the Anna Maria Arias Latina Entrepreneurship award for 2005. She is currently researching the career development of Latinas in U.S. corporations.

Nannerl O. Keohane is on the faculty of the Woodrow Wilson School and the Center for Human Values at Princeton University, and is also affiliated with the Program in the Study of Women and Gender. From 1981 until 2004, she served as president of Wellesley

College and then Duke University. Her publications include most recently *Higher Ground: Ethics and Leadership in the Modern University*, as well as *Philosophy and the State in France: The Renaissance to the Enlightenment*, and *Feminist Theory: A Critique of Ideology* (coedited with Barbara Gelpi).

Keohane has taught at Swarthmore College, the University of Pennsylvania, and Stanford University. She is a member of the Harvard Corporation. She received her B.A. from Wellesley College, M.A. from St. Anne's College, Oxford, and Ph.D. from Yale University. Her current research interests concern leadership and inequality, including gender issues.

Ruth B. Mandel is Board of Governors professor of politics at Rutgers University, where she directs the Eagleton Institute of Politics. From 1971 through 1994, she directed Eagleton's Center for American Women and Politics (CAWP). Mandel teaches and writes about women and leadership, focusing on U.S. women's political history and women in electoral politics. Author of numerous publications about women's changing political roles, she is currently thinking about women and the presidency. Mandel's public service includes an appointment on the governing board of the U.S. Holocaust Memorial Museum, where President Bill Clinton named her vice chairperson (1993 to 2005). She led the process to create the museum's Committee on Conscience, established in 1996 to alert the public to current genocides. Mandel's B.A. in English is from Brooklyn College; her M.A. and Ph.D. in American literature are from the University of Connecticut. She holds honorary doctorates in public service and public administration from Chatham College and Georgian Court University.

Debra Meyerson is associate professor of organizational behavior at Stanford University's School of Education and (by courtesy) Graduate School of Business and codirector of Stanford's Center on Philanthropy and Civil Society.

Meyerson's research has focused on conditions and change strategies that foster equitable gender and race relations in organizations. Her current projects investigate the gendered construction of leadership, the role of philanthropic institutions in diffusing social innovations, and the blurring of work-life boundaries through communication technologies. Meyerson is author of *Tempered Radicals: How Everyday Leaders Inspire Change at Work*. Her research has been featured in national media including the *Wall Street Journal, Inc., Business Week*, and others. She has repeatedly been named by the *San Francisco Business Journal* as one of the Bay Area's most influential women in business and was honored by the National Organization for Women as "Educator of the Year."

Pippa Norris is director of the Democratic Governance Group at the U.N. Development Program in New York. She is currently on leave from her position as the McGuire Lecturer in comparative politics at the John F. Kennedy School of Government, Harvard University.

Her work compares elections and public opinion, political communications, and gender politics in many countries worldwide. A well-known public speaker and prolific author, she has published almost three dozen books. Her work includes *A Virtuous Circle* (winner of the 2006 Doris A. Graber award), *Digital Divide, Democratic Phoenix, Rising Tide: Gender Equality and Cultural Change Around the Globe* (with Ronald Inglehart), *Electoral Engineering, Sacred and Secular* (with Ronald Inglehart; winner of the Virginia Hodgkinson prize), and *Radical Right*. Her most recent book is *Driving Democracy: Do Power-Sharing Institutions Work?*

Todd L. Pittinsky is an assistant professor of public policy at the John F. Kennedy School of Government and research director of Harvard's Center for Public Leadership. His research investigates positive intergroup attitudes: the conditions under which they develop and how they shape the ways people think, feel, and behave. To date, this work has involved the study of positive stereotypes, allophilia, and leadership effects on intergroup liking. Pittinsky earned his A.B. in psychology from Yale University with honors, his M.A. in psychology from Harvard, and his Ph.D. in organizational behavior from the Harvard Graduate School of Arts and Sciences and the Harvard Business School. He is editor of the forthcoming volume *Crossing the Divide: Intergroup Leadership in a World of Difference*.

Karen L. Proudford is associate professor of management at the Graves School of Business and Management, Morgan State University, and affiliated faculty at the Center for Gender in Organizations, Simmons School of Management. Her research, writing, and consulting interests include group and intergroup dynamics, leadership, diversity, and conflict. She received her B.S. degree in accounting *summa cum laude* from Florida A&M University and her M.A. and Ph.D. degrees in management from the Wharton School of the University of Pennsylvania. Prior to beginning her career in academia, she held positions at Honeywell and IBM. Her work has appeared in *Group and Organization Management*, the *Journal of Labor and Employment Law*, the *Journal of Career Development*, *The Diversity Factor*, and the *International Review of Women and Leadership*, the volume *Addressing Cultural Issues in Organizations: Beyond the Corporate Context*, and, most recently, *The Handbook of Workplace Diversity*.

Laura Morgan Roberts is an assistant professor of organizational behavior at the Harvard Business School. She received her Ph.D. in organizational psychology from the University of Michigan. Roberts examines the pathways by which individuals become extraordinary within culturally diverse work organizations. Her research identifies systems and practices that build competence, agency, and purposeful connection across dimensions of difference. She focuses on the self-presentation strategies that individuals employ to demonstrate their capability, establish credibility, and develop high-quality relationships with diverse constituents in a variety of professional settings, including medicine, academia, journalism, and financial services. Her work has been published in the *Academy of Management Review*, *Harvard Business Review*, and the *Journal of Organizational Behavior*.

Brian Welle is an organizational psychologist at the Internet company Google, where he develops new strategies for hiring a diverse workforce. Prior to joining Google, Welle conducted research at the intersection of diversity and organizational leadership as a postdoctoral fellow at Harvard University's Center for Public Leadership. Welle's former role as a director of research at Catalyst—a nonprofit organization committed to the advancement of women in business and the professions—gave him additional opportunities to research, provide consulting services on, and speak publicly about the career challenges faced by women and employees of color. Welle received his Ph.D. in industrial and organizational psychology from New York University in 2004.

Laura Wernick is a Ph.D. student in the joint doctoral program in social work and political science at the University of Michigan. She examines effective roles people with power and privilege can play in supporting movements that address the root causes of social and economic justice. Her research in this area looks at philanthropy, class, democracy, and power; cross-race, cross-class coalition building, and community organizing among people with power and privilege. She is also a research associate at the Harvard Business School, where she works with Robin Ely on research investigating diversity, power, and learning in organizations. She received her M.A. in social work and M.A. in public administration at Columbia University and her B.A. at the University of California-Berkeley.

Marie C. Wilson is president of the White House Project, co-creator of Take Our Daughters and Sons to Work Day and author of *Closing the Leadership Gap: Why Women Can and Must Help Run the World*.

In 1998, while president of the Ms. Foundation for Women, Wilson founded the White House Project in recognition of the need to build a truly representative democracy—one where women lead alongside men in politics, media, and business. She left the Ms. Foundation in 2004 after two decades, to devote her full energy to the project.

Over the past eight years, under Wilson's direction, the White House Project has led ground-breaking research and program initiatives like "Who's Talking?" in 2001, which highlighted the gender disparity on Sunday morning talk shows, where men outnumbered women 9 to 1 as guests; "Vote, Run, Lead," in 2000, to engage women in the political process as voters, as activists, and as candidates for political office; and most recently the "The Real Security Initiative" in 2005, to fundamentally change the landscape of national security debate by equipping women leaders with solid messages and training to speak authoritatively on these issues.

Born and raised in Georgia, Wilson has five children and five grandchildren. She resides in New York City.

Index

275–276; current efforts to increase leadership opportunities for, 280–281; diagnosing problem of underrepresentation of, 231–233; feminism's impact on, 279–280; ranking of countries with, 2–3, 228–229, 233–236, 245n5, 247nn22–23, 252, 273; underrepresentation of, 2–3, 163, 197, 227, 252, 253, 273, 274; U.S. media coverage of, 163–167, 251, 276. *See also* Elective office; Electoral gender quotas; Judges; Women as presidential candidates

Women of color: authentically engaged, 335, 340–344; authenticity denied by, 350–351; in corporate leadership positions, 383; in-group favoritism and, 11; "just world" bias and, 9; stereotyping of, in corporate leadership, 390–391; underrepresented in leadership positions, 2, 274. *See also* Race

Women, Quotas and Politics (Dahlerup), 228

Women's Armed Services Integration Act, 158

Women's Campaign Fund, 279, 280

Women's History Month, 169

Women's issues: gender differences in commitment to, 17–20, 51n104, 53nn111–112, 107, 121n46; women's leadership on, 26

Woodhull, V., 284, 289, 304n3

Woolf, V., 66, 75–86; *A Room of One's Own* (Woolf), 75–80, 90n16; *Three Guineas*, 75–76, 80–85, 90nn24–25, 91nn28, 32

Work hours: equating commitment and productivity to, 414, 456; inflexibility of, 13–14

Work-family conflicts: gender differences in family roles and, 11–13; need to address, 28–29; policy-practice gap in, 14–15; public policies to address, 32, 61n179. *See also* Opting out; Parental leave

Work-life balance: authentic engagement characterized by, 341–342; Woolf on, 86, 91n32

Work-life policies, 28–29, 422–423

Workplaces: benefits of authenticity in, 330; dangerous, masculine norms in, 458–460, 471n11, 472n14; gender similarity in values in, 154–155; psychological contract in, 331–332

Wylie, A., 75

Y

Yoder, J. D., 101

Z

Zimbabwe, 2, 201